How Much Does It Weigh?

Bingo Sun Noon

The Robobike Press

Published by Robobike Press
1104 SE Linn St.
Portland, OR 97202 USA

503-206-6352

www.Robobike.com

Bingo@Robobike.com

LC Control No.: *2007940776*
Noon, Bingo Sun
How much does it weigh? : design and build your next bicycle / Bingo Sun Noon.
p. cm.
ISBN: 9780979275401

Cover Design by Bonita Caliente and *Pretty Hot Designs*

In the Beginning, God created the Dandy-horse
And saw that it was good

Dedicated to Gene Berlatsky of the Arizona Bicycle Club
1919 - 2002

Table of Contents

Design and Materials

Projects

Workshop

Projects

SECTOR ZERO

When considering transportation options, nothing is more efficient than a man on a bicycle except, of course, a woman on a bicycle.

How much does it weigh? Funny you should ask. You can ride the world on a home built bicycle of your own design, climb the highest peaks, cross deserts and traverse continents. When you are finished, the question asked is "How much does it weigh? "

This attraction to gravity has somehow become the benchmark by which bicycles are judged. Cheaply built, cheaply sold bicycles, whose target audience is the unrefined cyclist, are heavy. These bicycles also return poor performance. This fact is not in dispute. For this reason, a heavy bicycle has come to mean bad bicycle. Only if you frequently carry your bicycle up a flight of steps should weight be the primary design goal. Sadly, that is not the case.

If factors other than attraction to gravity are used to judge bicycle performance, then it becomes clear why the freedom to target specific design goals is important to the builder/designer. For example, few things are more terrifying than a high speed descent on a lightweight tandem that is so flexible as to be out of control. It may be the lightest of the light, but it is still a nightmare. Keep this in mind when trying to decide whether or not to build. If you are convinced that a 24 pound bicycle is "better" than a 26 pound bicycle, then don't even think about starting a project. You will do something to save weight that is really dumb. It happens all the time to pros; amateurs too are not immune. Another important point to consider is that there is no shortage of good quality bicycles at reasonable prices in bicycle shops throughout the world. If you are contemplating building a high-performance mountain bike that duplicates current or mainstream designs then you are wasting your time. Good bikes are generally not cheap. Even so, not all expensive bikes are good. Even some really expensive bikes have chains that are too short, have aluminum fasteners on brake parts, have handlebars that are prone to breaking and have frames that crack at the usual predictable places. Are these good bikes?

The type of bike that lends itself to home built projects is the odd bicycle, the unusual bicycle, the type of bicycle not normally found in bike shops because they are not in great demand. Go to a shop and price a high performance tandem, a front wheel drive delivery bike (if you can find one), or a high performance folder. An exquisite tandem can be built for hundreds of dollars and your labor. That's a far cry from the thousands of dollars off the shelf tandems demand. Ditto for recumbents. A simple short wheel base recumbent can be built for less than a hundred dollars in one day, particularly if the builder knows how to recycle components. Not an easy task for a beginner, mind you, but hardly a challenge for the seasoned metal worker.

This book does not claim to be the final word in bike design. It is only a passable source of bikes not currently available but still in demand on the street. It is hardly mainstream. At the same time, it gives a good outline of how a lifelong professional metal worker would attack the problem of fixturing, jigging, fitting and fastening together a thoroughly acceptable bicycle. It offers advice on welding and machine shop equipment, some of which is surprisingly affordable. It warns against hazards that may kill a project. Every project in this book has been built at least once.

The projects are broken up into groups for different levels of metal working experience. The Robobike team has decided to adopt the rating system in use by the International Association of Machinists. Apprentice, Journeyman and Master are the categories. The IAM follows a rigid time requirement to jump from one category to another. Feel free, however, to factor in unusual experiences or talents that may place you higher than what is dictated by the metal working trade unions when determining what project is right for you. Talent is something not even the IAM can measure.

Finally, build a bike and ride it with pride. Never, under any circumstances, weigh your bicycle. Then you can answer truthfully, when asked "how much does it weigh?"

"I don't know." Good luck.

Bingo

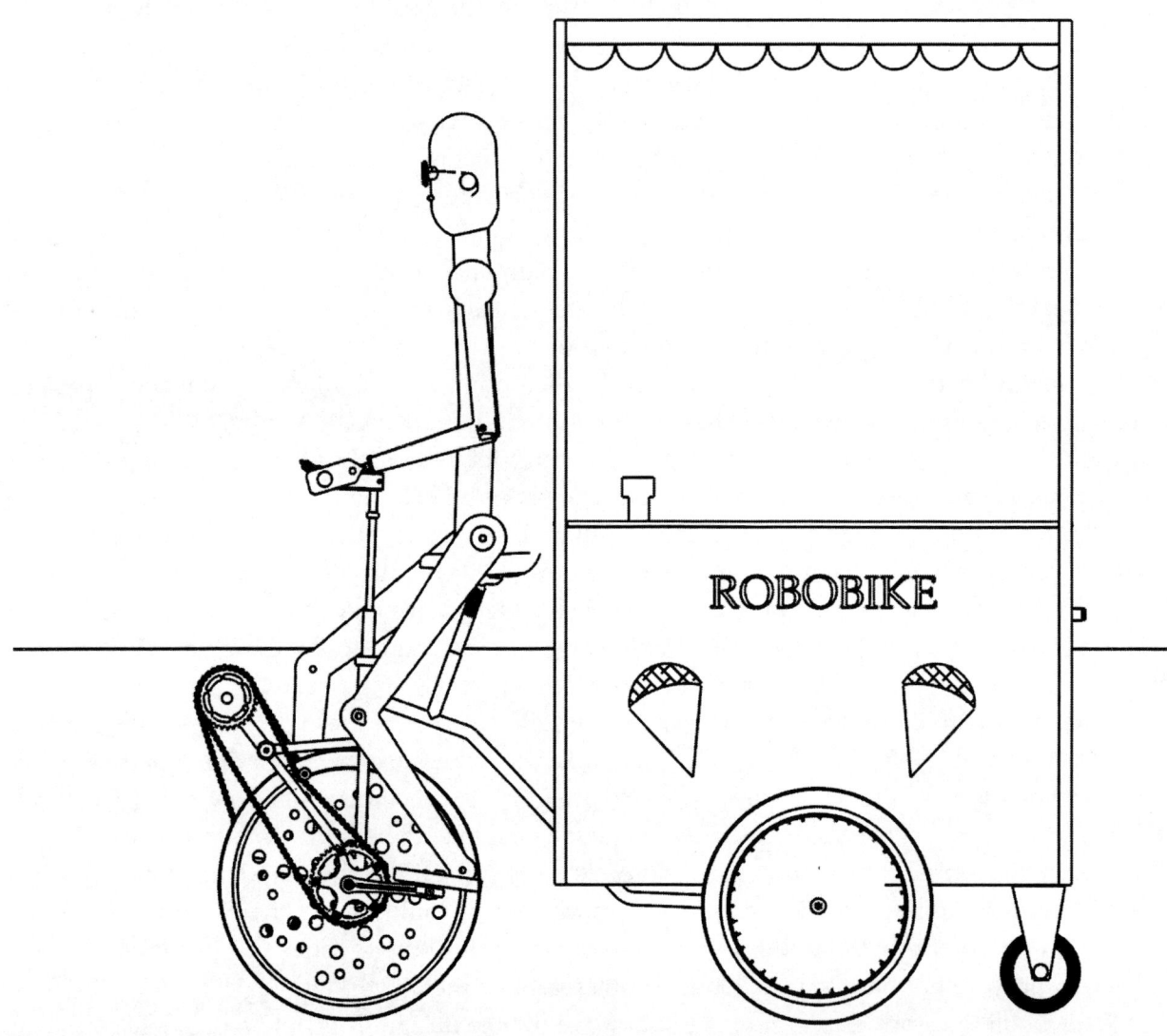

Robotrike

Original configuration shown here.
The Robotrike was used to haul shop equipment and bottles of welding gas. Like all tricycles, it is unstable and difficult to ride. The bearing added to the longitudinal axis on the Mark II model improves handling tremendously but complicates the building process. It is easy to see how this layout becomes a pedalcab or rickshaw.

Robobike Vietnam

Robobike swims in the primordial slime

The speedometer was red lined at 48 mph. At this speed, the engine of the 58 microbus is revving like it was going to blow up. Thirty six horsepower doesn't get you much, but today, running well past redline, it got the VW moving up I-270 in St. Louis at 54 miles per hour. No wonder the damn thing would eventually swallow a valve. The whole point of its effort is to deliver its driver to McDonnell-Douglas so he can build fighter bombers. Thousands of miles away, a young man is serving cold beer to soldiers. Nearby, another slightly older young man is beginning the slow process of killing himself chain smoking while he cleans his machine gun. So begins the partnership that today is Robobike.

The three men who began Robobike all have a Vietnam connection. As an aerospace worker, Krilson learned his craft repairing battle damage, building rapid firing cannon, tweaking hydraulic controls and doing metal work at a highly meticulous level. He also learned drafting, layout and NC control. On a typical work day, Krilson is surrounded by co-workers scared the war and the overtime will end. War is good business. Everyone makes a lot of money when the bullets fly. After four years of the American dream, Krilson chucks it all and goes to Canada. There he finds sanity.

Bingo Sun Noon, the bartender, is tired of explaining his name. He is 14 years old. Apparently, his mother saw a sign outside an American army church in Saigon and thought that she would name her son after the pastor. After all, the boy's father was an American so doesn't she have to give her son an American name?

AMERICAN SERVICES CHAPEL
PASTOR:
BINGO SUN NOON

John Shewmaker, USMC, doesn't give a rat's ass about nothing. He's got 3 squares, free smokes, all the beer he can stand and no reason to think things could get better. Another week or two and he's styling on the Santa Monica pier.

None of the three knows anything about bikes in 1975. Funny how things change.

The Robobike Way

Everyone at Robobike past and present embraces the automobile free lifestyle. Take a moment to reflect on this as it is the only way to understand what is important in what we are doing. Living auto free is liberating. Easily the biggest challenge to going car free is in the area of load carrying. Think about it. If you have to transport purchases home from market on a bicycle, wouldn't you want something more than a cheap wire basket from the discount store? Does your bike have the structural integrity to haul 300 pounds of potting soil or four bags of concrete pre-mix? Of course not. Nor does your store bought frame have the integrity and the extra room to carry a child safely in comfort. Load carrying is the number one issue in living automobile free.

Mission statements are a load of crap. However, Robobike is a modern, 21st century concern. We value our employees and endeavor that each and every one takes time from his duties to learn the Robobike way. Part of that is our mission statement which is; <u>Just do the best you can.</u>

Although it sounds easy it is often difficult to do the best you can. The corporate world stifles initiative. It smothers creativity. Your boss at work might feel threatened by someone who does a good job. Mixed messages, designs driven by marketing pressures, employees concerned with perpetuating their jobs above all else contribute to results that are not the best we can do. Sometimes just getting to the end of the day is the best you can do. We have found that unless you truly believe in what you are doing and are given the freedom to do it, you cannot do the best you can.

Though our mission statement is clear and concise with little room for misinterpretation, the Robobike way is really about examining life as lived by someone who is not interested in taking an automobile with him everywhere he goes. Every one of our projects is the result of a need, whether utilitarian or recreational, that cannot be met using a store bought bicycle. Delivery bikes are not readily available at a reasonable price nor are recumbents. You can't buy a high performance tandem for less than a ton of money but you can build one for next to nothing.

Only few bicycle shops have the cyclist's best interest at heart. They are a business and like any business, they have to cover expenses. Robobike came into being in part because of bike shops. There is no reason having a tire treated with self sealant compound should cost half a day's pay. One or two incidents like this are enough to motivate someone to take a stab at building. The ability to make a few simple measurements and drill/tap a hole goes a long way towards doing an end around the bike shops. Our apologies to bike shops everywhere but you can't deny the way things are.

You will find our projects rated by skills levels. These skills are adopted from the International Association of Machinists, the IAM. Apprentice, Journeyman, and Master are the classifications. The IAM is a wonderful organization. Too bad labor unions are in decline. They brought us out of the dark ages but they can't seem to prevent our slide backwards from whence we came.

Apprentice level usually describes someone with talent but no experience. Other important characteristics include the ability to learn both from books and from example. Most apprenticeship programs run for three years after which a journeyman's card is issued. A journeyman can perform most tasks asked of a metal working professional short of gear hobbing, ID grinding, or thread grinding. These tasks are usually given the specialist denomination but really do fall under journeyman skills. CNC machining is also included under journeyman. The master designation is given after 10 years. Today, the master level includes software, particular CNC programming utilities and CAD. Though some shops will advance a member by counting calendar months, the real world is a bit different. It is usually the case that some individuals have incredible skills after a few years while others never get the hang of it ever. For our purposes of project classification, we will use the textbook definition of all skill sets. When we say master level skills, for example, we mean that a mill setup does not have to be explained. Since journeyman skills are not the same for everyone, a sine plate or angle plate may be included in the graphics to help in deciphering the intent of the designer and to point the builder in the direction of an elegant solution.

Another important issue to keep in mind is the choice of processes. If you decide to weld an aluminum frame, for example, you should be the one to decide if you want to send it out to heat treat and what to specify. Robobike sends all the aluminum we weld to the furnace but you may choose not to. The choice is yours but be sure you understand the consequences of not doing so.

As the world continues to moan about the shortage of fossil fuels and the wars over oil continue and even increase, you can be one of those who blames someone else for your troubles or you can adopt the automobile free lifestyle like we have at Robobike. Who knows, you might even like it. Like I said before, it really is quite liberating. But whatever you do, just do the best you can.

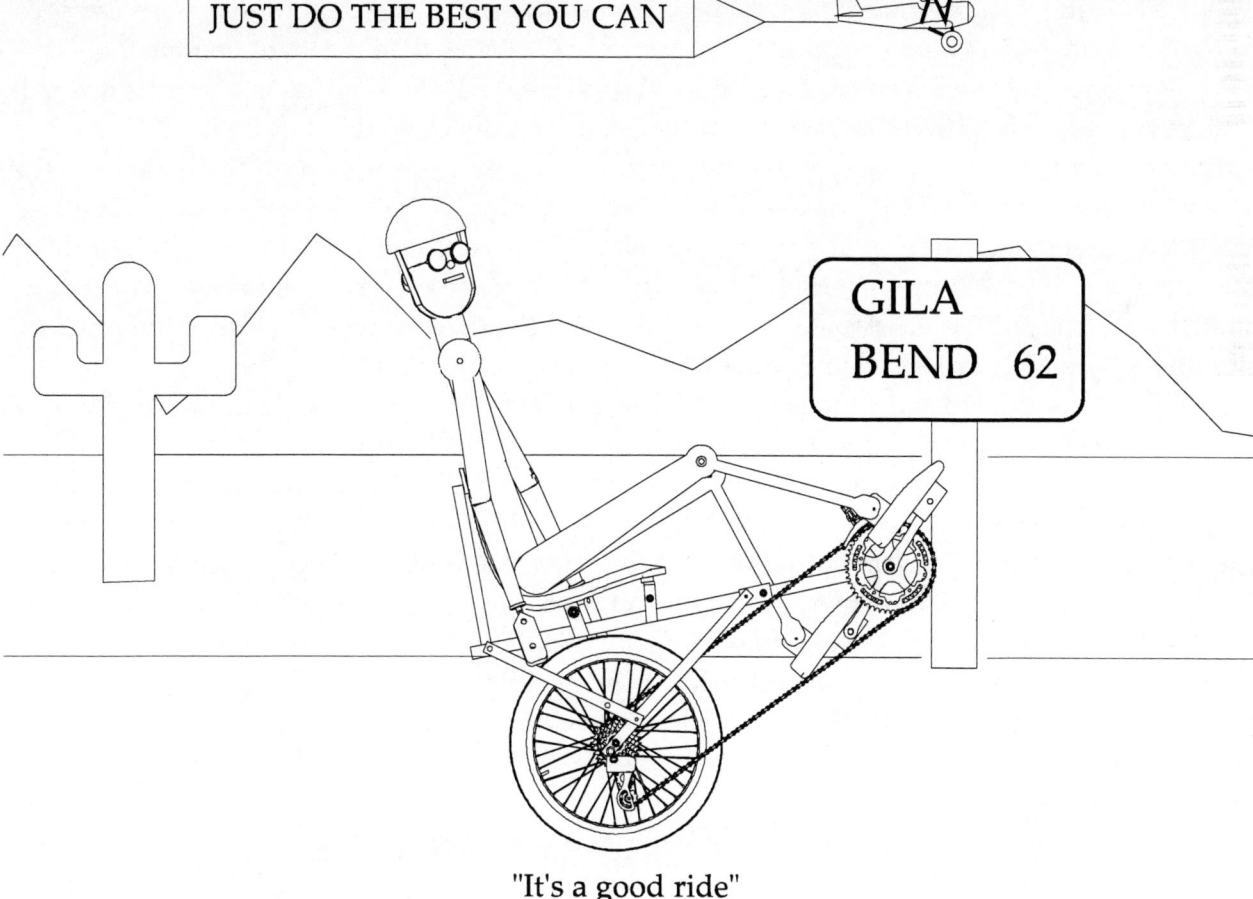

"It's a good ride"

The Process of Elimination

Or

Know what it is you do well?

Rightly so, the first time bicycle builder gives a great deal of thought on how to proceed before beginning a project. There is doubt, confusion and mystery surrounding a first time bike project. Doubt as to ability. Can I really build my own bike? Confusion from reading too many bicycle magazines, and finally, the mystery. Sweet, sweet mystery. There's no way to dispel the mystery of bike building other than building a bike. Until the first project is discussed in the past tense, the mystery remains. So, if the only way to get past the mystery of bicycle building is to build a bicycle, then how do I start? The short answer is skills.

Skills Assessment

Knowing your strengths and weaknesses is not only desirable, but an absolute requirement before deciding a course of action. Some mechanics are excellent machinists and fitters but lousy welders. Go with your strengths and don't be afraid to seek help honing your skills. Also, reject the notion that one medium is superior to another. A titanium frame welded by a technician without expertise is hardly "better" than a nicely brazed frame made from low carbon steel tubes salvaged from a demolition site. In this case, the steel frame has more value than the titanium frame.

Are your skills suitable for bike building? Possibly. I have seen frames built using stick welders but I shudder every time I do. Some look nice, most don't. If you use this type of equipment, or some other process not normally found in a bike shop, optimize the design to fit the process. Be aware that the designs intended for silver solder, GTAW, GMAW and stick will all have design details suited for that process. The silver soldered frame will have lightweight tubes assembled with doublers or lugs, the GTAW and GMAW frame may have either butted tubes or internal doublers and the stick welded frame will have a highly experience welder at the controls. Stick, though a simple process to understand, is one of the most difficult to master.

If you are absolutely determined to weld an aluminum frame but don't know how to weld aluminum, then the major hurdle is easy to spot. Help is available from every angle if you know how to ask for it. There is the community college or trade school option, always a good one to be sure, but make sure that classroom time is only part of the syllabus. It is important to know why you choose a rod with a certain chemical makeup and when to use backup. However, you can't learn welding from a book anymore than you can learn how to play a piano by reading about Liberace. Study and research are certainly valuable parts of the learning experience. Many frame building schools are available that offer hands-on welding instruction coupled with classes covering all aspects of the bike building process. Included may be tube selection, measuring, geometry, machine work, etc. But don't forget, the best way to learn to weld is practice, practice and more practice.

Jigging, clamping and fixturing are skills that need to be acknowledged before attempting a project. Do you know how to clamp two tubes in such a manner that their centerlines lie in the same plane? This is actually the essence of frame building. The same way a commercial airplane builder will fabricate airplanes using jigs and fixtures, so too will a bike builder. The jigging and clamping may be no more than a pair of locking pliers, but that counts. Along with that comes inspection. Inspection is often accomplished using the same piece of tooling used during the fusion process. This is the reason Robobike invests so much time building top quality jigs. Calibrated eyeballs are the number one piece of equipment in the inspection department. Knowing what and how to measure is probably the most difficult and least understood skill needed by the first time builder. People who do it everyday, all day (machinists) are the best. If you know one willing to help with some mentoring, then do not hesitate to ask. There is no substitute for coaching.

Can you miter a tube to fit another? A file is all you need but there are certainly other methods. Robobike uses a milling machine to miter tubes but not everyone has that option. We also, from time to time, use a file. Doesn't make a lot of difference to the tube.

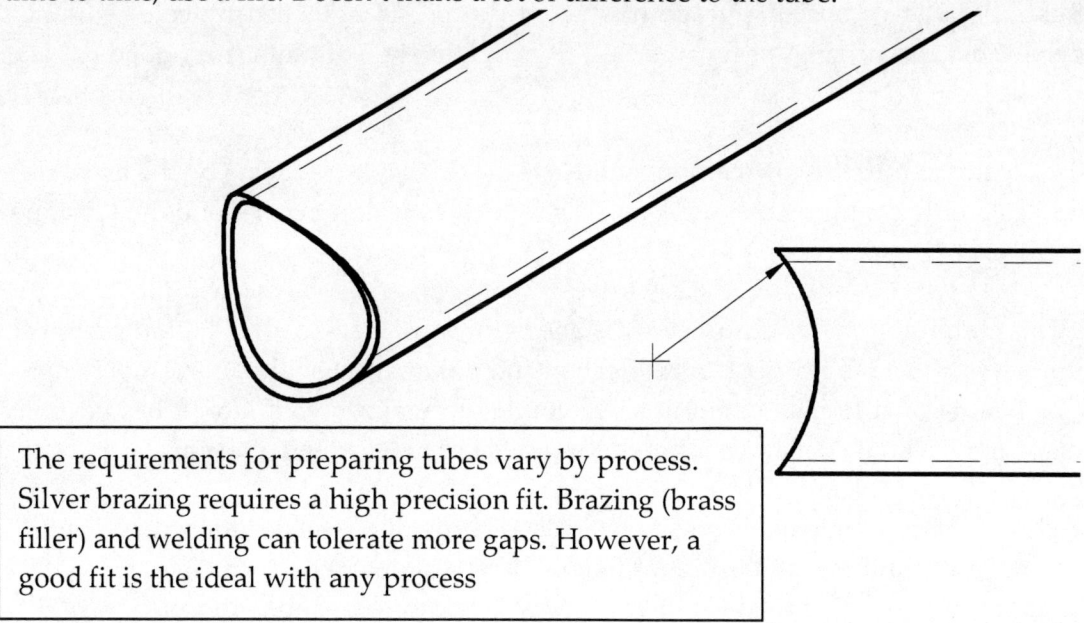

The requirements for preparing tubes vary by process. Silver brazing requires a high precision fit. Brazing (brass filler) and welding can tolerate more gaps. However, a good fit is the ideal with any process

Available shop equipment weighs in on the choice of which bike to build. It is possible to build a perfectly acceptable load carrying bike using square aluminum tubes, spacers and bolts, but for the same reason that supersonic airplanes are not built of wood, high performance machines are not bolted together. If your equipment consists of only a hand held drill and a hack saw, you can still build your own bicycle but will have to accept a different set of design constraints than those found on TIG welded steel bikes. Square tubes are easy to build straight and true. This is one of the strengths of the concept. We've already mentioned one of the weaknesses but you will soon learn another. As with all bicycles of your own manufacture, you will have to accept being scrutinized by other cyclists, particularly those who measure the value of a bicycle in kilograms. The guys who know the most are the ones who know the least. Get ready for it.

Finally, a tremendously large part of a project is translating what is shown on the page in both text and drawing to a working machine. Some builders use CAD, some use a pencil. In either case, a drawing is crucial unless you are working directly from a model. We at Robobike use CAD for all our projects and encourage its use. That isn't possible for all but it is certainly a valuable tool.

Choose your project based on your skills set. Add to your skills set if you need to, but never say "I can't build a bicycle". That's just plain silly. Approach every project as a collection of small tasks. Always use personal protective equipment such as dark goggles, gloves and ventilators where needed. Do not weld indoors without an assistant, fire extinguishers and a properly ventilated welding booth. Always use common sense. You can't lose if you do all that.

Steel

1010 This is one of the most widely used low carbon steels for low strength applications. It is best suited for parts whose fabrication involves moderate to severe forming and some machining. Its weld-ability is excellent and it can be case hardened for wear resistance by cyaniding.

1018 is a popular carburizing grade of steel. It can be strengthened by cold working or surface hardened by carburizing or cyaniding. It is relatively soft and has good weldability and formability.

1020 is a general-purpose low-carbon "mild" steel. It is easy to fabricate by the usual methods such as mild cold or hot forming and welding. It is weldable by all processes and the resulting welds are of extremely high quality.

4130 This chromium-molybdenum alloy is one of the most widely used aircraft steels because of its combination of weldability, ease of fabrication and mild hardenability. In relatively thin sections, it may be heat treated to high strength levels. In the normalized condition it has adequate strength for many applications. It may be nitrided for resistance to wear and abrasion.

4140 This chromium-molybdenum alloy is a deep hardening steel used where strength and impact toughness are required. It has high fatigue strength making it suitable for critical stressed applications. It may be nitrided for increased resistance to wear and abrasion.

4340 This chromium-nickel-molybdenum alloy is a widely used deep-hardening steel. It possesses remarkable ductility and toughness. With its high alloy content uniform hardness is developed by heat treatment in relatively heavy sections. Its high fatigue strength makes it ideal for highly stressed parts.

6150 This chromium-vanadium alloy steel is similar to 4340. It has good hardenability, good fatigue properties and excellent resistance to impact and abrasion.

8620 This is a "triple alloy" chromium-nickel-molybdenum steel. It is readily carburized. It may be heat treated to produce a strong, tough core and high case hardness. It has excellent machinability and responds well to polishing operations. It is easily welded by any of the common welding processes, although the section should be heated and stress relieved after welding.

9310 This chromium-nickel-molybdenum alloy is a carburizing steel capable of attaining high case hardness with high core strength. It has excellent toughness and ductility.

4620 This nickel-molybdenum alloy is a carburizing steel capable of developing high case hardness and core toughness. It can be forged similarly to the other carburizing grades. Because of its relatively high nickel content, it is not as readily cold-formed.

5160 This carbon-chromium grade of spring steel has a high yield/tensile strength ratio, excellent toughness and high ductility. It is very difficult to machine in the as-rolled condition and should be annealed prior to machining. It is not readily welded, but it can be welded by either the gas or arc welding processes if the section involved is preheated and stress relieved after welding.

52100 This high carbon-high chromium alloy is produced by the electric furnace process and then vacuum degassed to meet the rigid standards of the aircraft industry for bearing applications. It develops high hardness and has exceptional resistance to wear and abrasion.

The previous was used with permission, Aircraft Spruce and Specialty Company, Corona, California

Maraging Steel

Recently, the bicycling world has heard quite a lot about maraging steel, an alloy of iron and nickel (up to 18% Nickel) with a few other elements added to the mix. The name comes from its structure, which is the cubic form (body centered cubic) of steel known as martensitic or martensite combined with its tendency to age harden, subsequently maraging. Maraging steels test very high in tensile strength. Somewhat new to the bicycling world, it has been around the aerospace shops for a long time. It is quite tough. Although it excels with the highest values for ultimate tensile strength of all the commercially available steels, care should be used when selecting this material for your project. Since resistance to fatigue is more important than tensile strength for bicycle work it is difficult to understand why maraging steel is being used at all. Weldability is good and crack propagation properties are good but its less than stellar fatigue performance leaves some doubt as to its suitability. Not only that, maraging steel is difficult to drill, ream and turn much less tap. Some reference materials claim maraging steel is easy to machine. That simply is not true. It is nasty stuff. The chips are long and stringy. Use it at your own peril.

Drawn over mandrel

There is another issue involving steel tubes that is all together different from the chemical content. Tubes that have no seam are considered superior to tubes that have a weld seam as a consequence of the tube making process. Either variety of tube is suitable for bicycle building. A project that is more than just an amusing little diversion should be built using seamless or DOM (drawn over mandrel) steel. Most DOM is commonly produced from low and medium carbon steels such as 1020 and 1026, DOM tubing is also available in other standard steel grades such as 1008, 1010, 1015 and 1035; in special grades such as 1024, 1040, 1045 and 1050; 4130, 5130, 8617 and 8620; and in near-equivalent DIN grades.

The seamless or welded seam issue is meaningless. Don't be misled. The only issue involving selection of steel tubes is the AISI number. Carbon steel is 1008, 1018 or some other number beginning with 10. It can be recognized by its discoloration in the seam area that runs the length of the tube. Chrome-moly is AISI 4130. This latter steel is far superior in tensile strength and because of that, thinner walled tubes can be used to achieve the same result. The actual analysis is a bit more involved than that, but that is the heart of the matter. Keep in mind that the thicker wall is easier to join by welding by novice welders.

Aluminum

Aluminum is a silverish white metal that has a strong resistance to corrosion and like gold, is rather malleable. It is a relatively light metal compared to metals such as steel, nickel, brass, and copper with a specific gravity of 2.7. Aluminum is easily machinable and can have a wide variety of surface finishes. It also has high thermal conductance and is highly reflective to heat and light. It is used in its pure form or alloyed with other metals. The welding of aluminum requires huge amounts of hear due primarily to the high rate at which it conducts heat away from the weld zone.

1100 – Pure Aluminum (at least 99.0% pure) Easy to form, low strength and cannot be heat treated by any means.

2024- Aluminum Copper alloy, Used extensively for airplane skins and other structure. Cannot be welded, is heat treatable, and generally not used for bicycles except for small machined parts, etc.

3003 Aluminum-Manganese alloy, Good formability and easy to weld. Cannot be heat treated. Used extensively in tubing applications such as for moving fluids and gases.

5052 Aluminum-Magnesium alloy, Easy to weld, moderate strength, cannot be heat treated. Good all around choice for sheet metal work.

6061 Aluminum, Magnesium, Silicon, The best choice for the home bicycle builder who wants to build an aluminum frame. Easy to weld using 4043 filler rod, can be heat treated but has good as-welded characteristics if proper technique is used; tubes usually supplied in T6 condition. Also available as bars, square tubes, rounds, sheet and plate.

7005 Aluminum-Zinc alloy (Also 7075) Neither one of these is a good choice for the home shop except for small pieces requiring high strength such as doublers or machined brackets; difficult to form, 7005 is not so difficult to weld but is prone to fatigue cracking. Can be heat treated to high strength. 7075 cannot be welded.

Other nomenclature you will run into if you buy aluminum involves condition. Here are some examples:

T3 - solution heat treated, cold worked and naturally aged.

T4 - solution heat treated and naturally aged.

T6-solution heat treated and artificially aged. This is how you will buy 6061. T6 is the same as T651.

T7 - solution heat treated and overaged.

T8 - solution heat treated, cold worked and artificially aged.

O (pronounced OH) is the annealed condition.

Heat treatment after the welding process restores mechanical properties lost during welding. However, proper heat control and the use of heat sinks negate many of these detrimental effects.

You will have to choose your technique and processes carefully if you want to weld an aluminum frame. Robobike builds aluminum frames on a regular basis with good results. We never use aluminum thinner than .090″ (1.25mm) in our welded products but the bike factories do. Custom sizes are even thinner. If you don't want to heat treat, use thicker tubes.

Carbon fiber

Early Egyptians had straw mixed with clay. We have carbon fiber. The material that has become so prevalent lately in the bicycler's world needs just a few lines of discussion. If strength to weight is considered (though strength is not generally defined for this ratio), materials can be compared in a different manner than that already shown. The square root of the modulus of elasticity divided by density is a good way to compare strength to weight, ($\sqrt{E}/\varrho$). Using the same methods to evaluate carbon fiber and other composite materials that we use to measure metals often give some unbelievable results. If you are a true geekoid bike scientist, then do a web search for classical lamination theory to get a good idea of what is happening in your composite bicycle. Good tensile, poor compressive, lots of different failure modes exist in addition to those found in metals. It is completely reasonable to expect to see buildings, highway bridges, automobiles and furnishings made of carbon fiber and other composites some day soon. Unless, of course, the world melts first.

Form factor

Although most of your work on custom projects will no doubt involve straight gauge tubing, no discussion about bicycle materials would be complete without examining tubes of varying wall thickness. The staff at Robobike has over a century of combined experience working in airplane factories and none of us has ever seen a tube with varying wall thickness used in an aerospace application. We have decided to leave it to others to explain its use in the bicycling world. We never use it though it is easy to see why you would want to. The types of bikes built in our shop don't warrant the extra expense of these butted tubes.

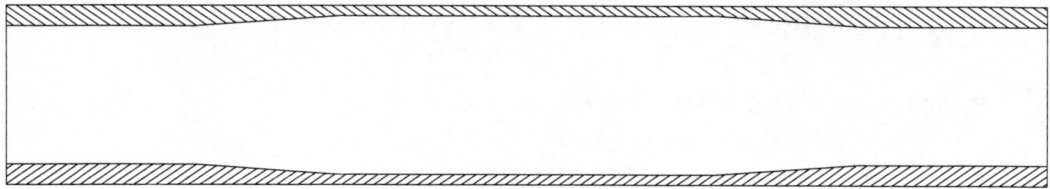

Cross section of butted tube
Scale is exaggerated

Butted tubes are formed by the upset method, which is the same way rivets are set. Bucking (or butting) improves the mechanical properties somewhat but a bigger plus is the increased wall in the vicinity of the weld. The downside can be found by asking a long time bicycle mechanic where seat tubes break. The type of fatigue failure common on lightweight bicycles ridden by big strong guys is shear where the extra thickness gives way to the thin section. Be sure to consider this before spending big bucks on very thin tubes. Also, if using butted tubes be aware of the manufacturer's recommended trim length. Don't cut away the thick section and try to join the thin section. That is a recipe for disaster.

We will examine the issue of wall thickness a bit later. It cannot be emphasized enough; the projects that you will be building in your home bicycle shop are not lightweight machines with short, fatigue-limited life spans. Subsequently, tubes chosen for your projects will not be in the sub-millimeter range in the wall thickness department. Leave that work to the pros.

Mechanical Properties

Why we build them stout

Fatigue, as we will see, is a big killer of bike frames. It and its effects are also known in the bicycle world as getting soft or losing stiffness. However, before examining the elements of bike design contributing to factors of safety, fatigue and projected lifespan, the terms need definition. The bicycling world often has its own terms for elements concerning strength. We have no choice but to use terms and definitions as they appear in reference materials not targeted to bicycling, so there might be some discrepancy. Also, since a round tube is the easiest shape to analyze, that is the shape we use here when comparing materials. The objective is to give the builder skills needed to examine a design with a critical eye and to balance the risks against the rewards of pursuing a course of action. The transmission of mechanical power is the biggest force acting on a bicycle, subsequently, we concentrate our analysis there.

Area for round tubes is defined as $[\pi (D^2 - d^2)]/4$. Example, a tube 1.125 inches in diameter with a .040 wall, has an area of .136 in². D is the outside diameter and d is the inside diameter of the tube.

Moment of inertia (denoted as I) is a means of comparing different shapes. This property is often manipulated by designers and why modern bicycles have larger, thinner tubes than bicycles made many years ago. The calculation of the actual value is complicated and won't be discussed here. For round tubes $I=.049(D^4-d^4)$.

Stress: load per unit area. A 2mm diameter spoke used to lift a hundred pounds is stressed at 20,000 psi. The spoke will increase in length while under load but will return to its former length when unloaded. This is because the spoke is stressed within its elastic limit.

Strain is the amount by which a body changes as the result of applied stress. The spoke in the above example will stretch .0006 inch per inch of length. Hooke's law applies.

Ultimate Tensile Strength is the stress at which a material breaks. A typical spoke is made from steel with a minimum tensile strength of 100,000 psi (100ksi). Subsequently, the spoke in the above example will lift 500 pounds easily before breaking. These values are approximate and may vary from one batch to another, but only slightly. Yield strength is the point where the test sample does not return to its original size. Values for tensile strength are well known for all materials.

Section Modulus, denoted Z, is the moment of inertia divided by the distance to the extreme fiber. In round tubes, it is I/r. This property is used in calculations to predict failure due to fatigue. For round tubes, $Z=.098(D^4-d^4)/D$.

Modulus of elasticity, or Young's modulus, is the ratio of unit stress to unit strain. It is written as pounds per square inch; very useful for comparing one material to another. One example is Steel, with its modulus of elasticity of 30,000,000 psi, is stiffer than Titanium with its modulus of elasticity of 16,000,000 psi. Stiffness of materials is often confused with rigidity of frames.

Stress and Relaxation

By Bingo Sun Noon

Robobike has built all types of bicycles using all types of materials. We take the position that the classic torch brazed frame is still about the best it gets for custom bike building at home.

Choosing a medium in which to work in order to render a custom machine normally takes little deliberative effort. Skills are a much bigger factor in choosing materials for your design than any results derived from a discussion about tubes. Even so, knowledge is power and the bicycle builder who shuns technical data is not doing the best he can. You must always do the best you can. Although tons of resource materials exist about choosing tubes for a custom bike, some are quite misleading and only perpetuate bias against some truly well designed and well built machines.

The frame is one of the first in the world to be made from XXX steel, and weighs only one kilogram. It has ultra thin wall thickness and is at least twice the strength of most standard steel tube sets currently available. This frame is due for production in early 2006.

Though paraphrased, this ridiculous claim is actual text culled from a popular bicycle magazine. Anyone not skeptical about this bit of information should take a pass on bicycle building and take up telescope making or some other intellectual stimulation to pass the idle hours. Only the truly ignorant are impressed with blather of this sort. If you want to become knowledgeable about metals and metal working as they apply to bicycle building, read the magazines but also dig in to some real engineering data. There is greater benefit in learning to do structural analysis of bridges and railroad cars than you'll get from reading magazines. Don't get me wrong. Bicycle magazines are great fun but they are a misleading source for insights into metalworking and frame material selection. They concentrate on frames built with weight as the primary design goal and largely ignore mainstream, classic designs and those machines built for specialty applications. Choosing a set of tubes because of something you read in a magazine is a recipe for disaster. Paper thin materials are only for the highly experienced metalworker. Robobike does not endorse bike building using potentially unsafe practices and materials.

Comparing materials Everyone wants a bike built to high efficiency, has a nice feel and can be shown off with pride. Knowledge of a few basic concepts will help you avoid potential threats and ensures a successful project. Let's look at some well known standard methods for evaluating strength of materials and see if we can manipulate a steel tube so that it becomes *"at least twice the strength of most standard steel tube sets currently available"*. Exposing the above quote is a good place to start on the road to understanding.

The following list shows the mechanical properties usually discussed in regards to tubes used in high and medium quality bicycle frames. The single most important design target is fatigue life which is calculated using these properties.

	Alloy Steel	Titanium	Aluminum
Elastic modulus	30,000,000 psi	16,000,000 psi	10,000,000 psi
Mass density	0.28 lb/in^3	.16 lb/in^3	.10 lb/in^3
Tensile strength	105000 psi	124000 psi	45000 psi
Yield strength	90000 psi	122000 psi	40000 psi

These are typical values. (90,000 psi is also written 90ksi)

The first property, elastic modulus, is also known as the modulus of elasticity or Young's modulus. It is simply strain/stress. You pull on a tube (load it in tension) and it stretches. The amount of stretch is different for all materials. Young's modulus is used in the following bit of comparison:

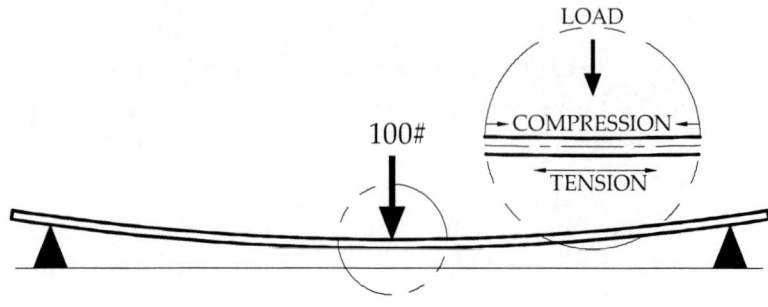

A length of 1.125 inch diameter tube with a .040 inch wall is supported in two places 24 inches apart and loaded with one hundred pounds dead center. Though the tube is being bent, the tensile load (the part of the tube being stretched) is what concerns us here. This tube profile has an area of .136 square inches and the moment of inertia is .0201. The deflection of this tube for various materials is:

Alloy steel	.048 inches
Titanium	.090 inches
Alum 6061 –T6	.144 inches

These values are derived using the well known and accepted formula for deflection:

Deflection in inches = $(WL^3)/48EI$ where
W is the load in pounds
L the length between supports
E is modulus of elasticity (inherent to the material)
I is moment of inertia (calculated from the tube profile)

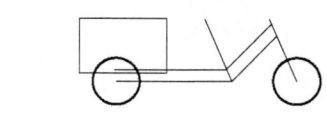

Do a deflection calculation when using a long wheel base!

By changing nothing but E (the modulus of elasticity) in the above formula, it is possible to compare one material against another. With this test and other tests of similar nature, steel is always the clear winner.

Comparing tube shapes and sizes

The moment of inertia, I , is how different shapes, or profiles, are evaluated. A thorough examination of the moment of inertia is too complex for this discussion so let it be said it is the accepted method used to compare two or more tubes of unequal size. It works. Since the factor I is in the denominator of our equation, increases in I result in reduced deflection. Like all elements of a design, there are drawbacks to manipulating the value of I. These drawbacks include such things as increasing the chances of dinging the tube and reduced weldability, both because of reduced wall thickness. A dent in a tube creates a stress raiser. Designers of aluminum frames manipulate the moment of inertia to compensate for the lower modulus of elasticity and tensile strength of aluminum over steel. These manipulations result in some very efficient and rigid frames. Here are some examples of different profiles of tubes and their moments of inertia. This property can explain why many frames have tubes with cross sections that are not round. It is possible to choose a section that contributes more effort in one axis and less in another.

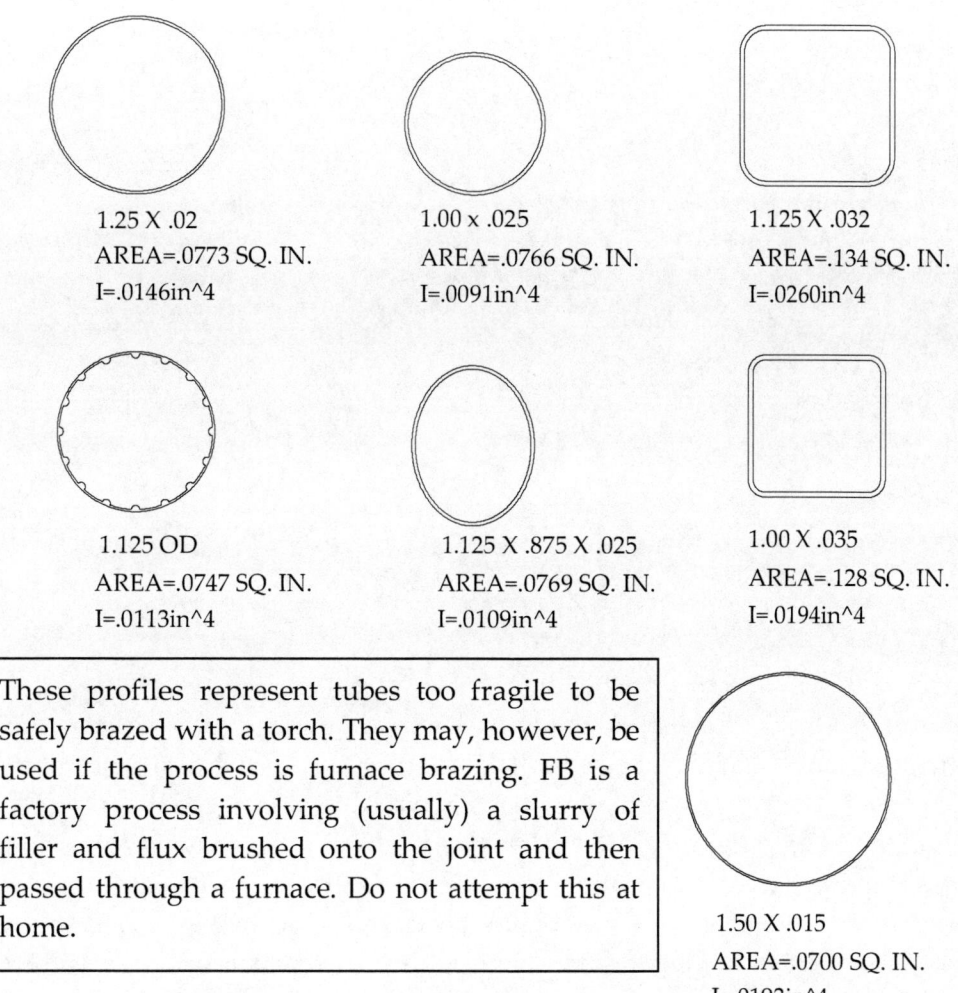

1.25 X .02
AREA=.0773 SQ. IN.
I=.0146in^4

1.00 x .025
AREA=.0766 SQ. IN.
I=.0091in^4

1.125 X .032
AREA=.134 SQ. IN.
I=.0260in^4

1.125 OD
AREA=.0747 SQ. IN.
I=.0113in^4

1.125 X .875 X .025
AREA=.0769 SQ. IN.
I=.0109in^4

1.00 X .035
AREA=.128 SQ. IN.
I=.0194in^4

These profiles represent tubes too fragile to be safely brazed with a torch. They may, however, be used if the process is furnace brazing. FB is a factory process involving (usually) a slurry of filler and flux brushed onto the joint and then passed through a furnace. Do not attempt this at home.

1.50 X .015
AREA=.0700 SQ. IN.
I=.0193in^4

Though very thin tubes are too fragile for torch brazing, a steady hand and meticulous preparation can produce good results using a heat sink, relatively low temperature silver solder and doublers. Compare these profiles to those shown on the next page which can all be torch brazed easily. So, have we found the secret of building a frame that *"is at least twice the strength of most standard steel tube sets currently available"*? Depends on whom you ask. The short answer is that while frames are comprised of tubes that are easy to evaluate separately, dedicated test equipment is needed to properly test a complete frame. We will continue to emphasize this point. It is the difference between stiffness and rigidity.

A one inch diameter tube with a .025 wall is considered quite thin. Nobody would use this stuff and expect a long fatigue life unless they were building picture frames or something equally innocuous. Despite that, the shops that advertise very light frames do indeed use tubes of this size. The moment of inertia for this profile is .0091 inch^4. The area of this profile is .077 square inches. The deflection for a 24 inch length of 4130 steel, 1.00 x .025, loaded with 100 pounds is .105 inches. Increase the wall thickness to .050 and the deflection is reduced to .056 inch. Area and the mass are both increased substantially as is the projected lifetime of the frame. A one inch tube with a .050 wall is a good choice for the top tube on a bicycle project. A one inch tube with a .025 wall is not. This conclusion, once again, has more to do with the brazing or silver solder process than anything else inherent in the tube's mechanical properties.

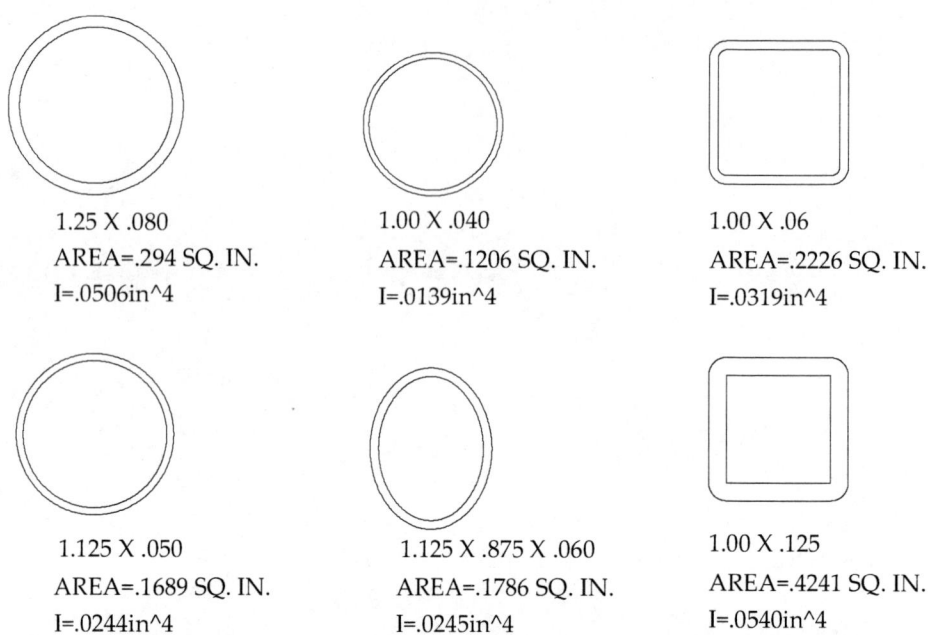

1.25 X .080	1.00 X .040	1.00 X .06
AREA=.294 SQ. IN.	AREA=.1206 SQ. IN.	AREA=.2226 SQ. IN.
I=.0506in^4	I=.0139in^4	I=.0319in^4

1.125 X .050	1.125 X .875 X .060	1.00 X .125
AREA=.1689 SQ. IN.	AREA=.1786 SQ. IN.	AREA=.4241 SQ. IN.
I=.0244in^4	I=.0245in^4	I=.0540in^4

THESE PROFILES CAN BE TORCH BRAZED EASILY

The other properties in our list are easily understood but need to be clearly defined. Mass density is pounds per cubic inch. Clear enough. The other two properties, tensile strength and yield strength, need a few more descriptive words to avoid confusion as to which is which. Tensile stress is a load applied along the longitudinal axis of a tube. Hooke's law requires that the tube (spring) stretches at a linear rate. Stop pulling and the tube returns to its former length. Springs are used to represent tubes in tension when modeling structures. You have reached the yield point when the tube no longer returns to its original shape. Ultimate, or tensile strength, is the max value reached for stress on the stress/strain plot. At some point, the tube will no longer be able to resist stress. It grows and grows as you pull it. These values are derived from tests and are well known. It is not uncommon for an engineer to specify a tensile test on each batch of material to ensure toughness and ultimate strength. Usually, both values (ultimate and yield) are given when comparing or specifying materials.

Examining tubes is only a small portion of a complete analysis. Volumes have been written about mechanical properties of materials so it is naive to think a few paragraphs can cover all the important aspects relevant to the frame builder.

Brazed versus Welded

Since bikes are a collection of frame elements and looking at the properties of each individual element doesn't paint an accurate picture of the entire package, then what does? An examination of the way the tubes or frame elements are joined is a good place to start.

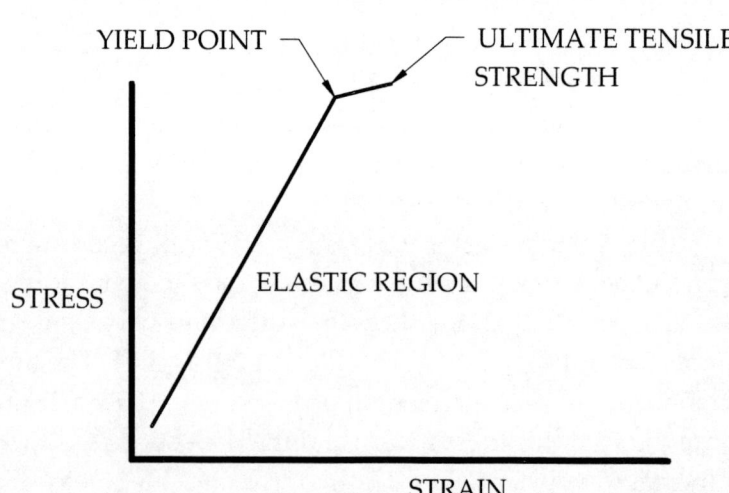

A brazed joint relies on intergranular migration of the filler metal into the base metal for perfect adhesion and maximum strength. This migration is a time-temperature thing. You must hold the joint at a specific temperature for a period of time before adhesion is all it can be. It is not enough to simply melt filler metal around two tubes. Really thin tubes require a furnace to hold them at a stable temperature for the migration to happen properly. Also, the tensile strength of both the base metal and the filler metal factors into rigidity of frames. Filler metals used in brazing have lower tensile strength than frame materials.

A welded joint, however, is created by fusion and not adhesion. The tensile strength of the weld fillet is nearly as strong as the base metal. Since the filler metals of brazed joints all have lower tensile strength than the base metal, it is safe to assume that the failure of a joint will most likely be the result of the filler giving up the ghost (fatigue) and not the tube itself. This is why welded joints are approved by the Federal Aviation Administration for aircraft structures and brazed joints are not. Poorly designed brazed joints fail catastrophically with little warning. For that reason, brazed joints built without doublers should have massive fillets to increase the safety factor. Doing so will greatly reduce the chance of failure. This is also the reason that light tube sets are built with lugs. Lugs increase the surface area of the joint and thus the adhesion. There are other reasons too but this is number one. To avoid confusion, the staff at Robobike refers to lugs and all other similar features as doublers. We have found a number of definitions and descriptions of cast and stamped bottom brackets, sockets, frame gussets etc. We apologize to all you people who know all about these things and don't agree.

The frame builders at Robobike use both brazing and welding. Neither is better.

Comparing frames and tube selection

We have touched on another property, not of materials, but of frames. That property is resistance to fatigue. Fatigue is usually the root cause of frames that lose their enthusiasm after many miles. The harder these frames are ridden, the quicker the frames "get soft".

Ask a long time bicycle mechanic about broken frames and where it is they break. Usually, the seat tube breaks near the bottom bracket and the stays break where they join the drop outs. Sometimes the drop outs themselves break at their thinnest section. They don't break when they are new but after many miles. The failure mode is fatigue.

High cycle fatigue is a relatively low stress repeated many many times. Low cycle fatigue is high stress repeated only a few times. The distinction between low cycle and high cycle is generally given as 50,000 cycles. When a seat tube shears just above the bottom bracket casting or when the rear triangle breaks at the drop out, it is because of high cycle fatigue. The root cause is poor choice of a bicycle. A big guy riding a lightweight bike is the classic scenario for high cycle fatigue.

The pedaling action itself is an example of fatigue in action. An impulse generated by the left pedal is following immediately by thrust generated by the right pedal. The stress reversal causes deflection in the bottom bracket. First it deflects down on the left side and then it deflects down on the right. Such a reversal is counted as one cycle. Likewise, the rear dropout experiences similar reversals. The greater the stress, or pull of the chain, the greater the magnitude of the impulses. It should be remembered that the stress need not be in the opposite direction to be considered a cycle but merely a change in direction or magnitude.

Fatigue, Cycles to Failure; the S-N plot

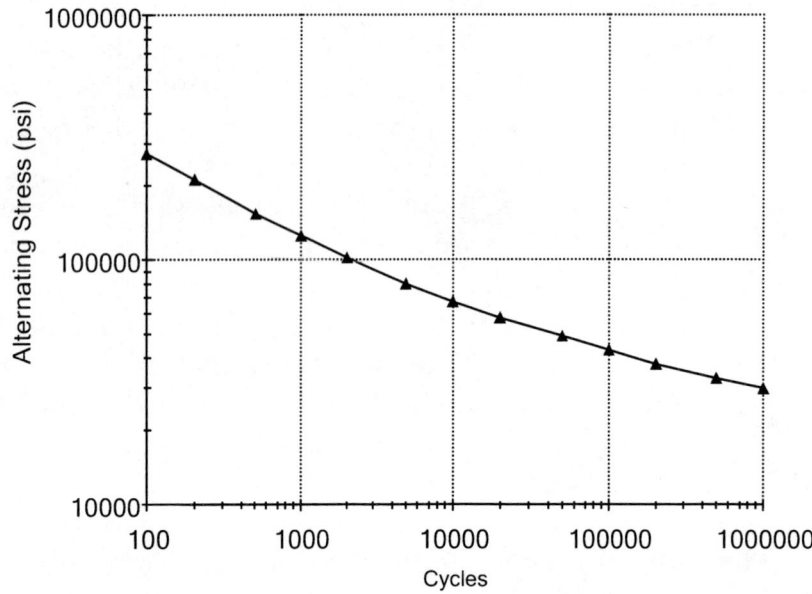

This plot is known as a S-N curve. The scales are log-log. The S is stress and the N is the number of cycles or stress reversals. As you can see, reducing the stress increases the lifetime of a frame element. Each dot on this graph represents a point at which a steel tube can be expected to fail. A tube with 90 ksi ultimate tensile strength subjected to 90,000 psi stress will fail at one stress reversal cycle. The same tube stressed at 5,000 psi will last forever. Stress is defined by force per unit area and is given as psi (pounds per square inch). The fatigue life of a bike may be increased several ways. They include:

1. Reducing the stress by pedaling with less effort
2. Increasing the modulus of elasticity of the frame material; e.g., changing from aluminum to steel
3. Increasing the diameter of the tube
4. Increasing the wall thickness of the tube

Robobike does indeed examine structures using analysis programs but even so, the weakness of a design may be easy to overlook unless you have an idea of where to look. The obvious points of interest include changes in section (thick to thin like in butted tubes) or stress raisers created by couples. Let's look at an example of fatigue failure that showed up in a Robobike design. The bike is the Clipper, a descendent of the Nile Crocodile. Terms used for this exercise include:

Z = Bending Modulus, from tables or CAD model
M = Bending moments, or the load applied to a tube
f = Resulting stress in pounds per square inch

Z can be found using tables for round tubes or calculated using $Z = .098[(D^4 - d^4) / D]$. D is outside diameter and d is inside diameter of the tube.

The reason you want to know any of this stuff is to determine *the fatigue limit*. This is the point where the structure is able to withstand an infinite number of stress reversals without breaking.

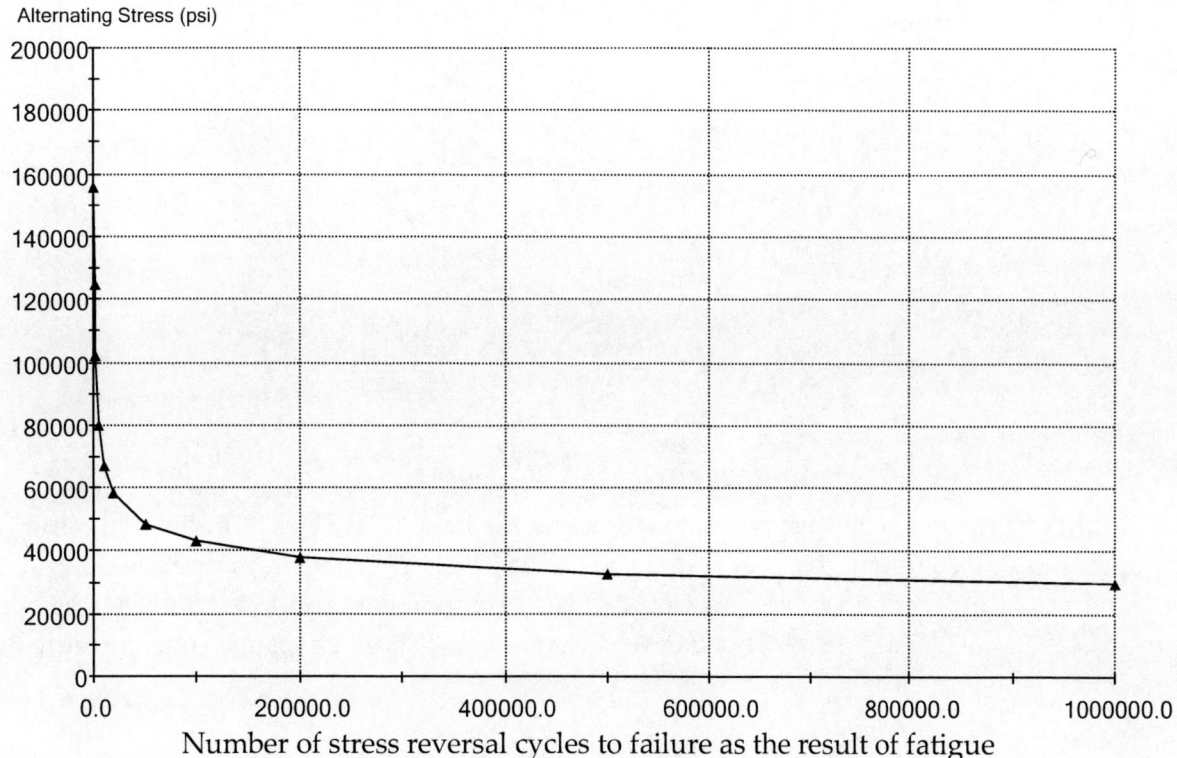

Alternating Stress (psi)

Number of stress reversal cycles to failure as the result of fatigue

This is a linear plot of the same data as shown in the previous logarithmic plot. It is for AISI 4130, chrome-moly steel, normalized. It is easy to see where on this plot the fatigue limit can be found. Stressed to 30,000 psi, the tube will fail at one million cycles. The number of cycles to failure increases as the stress is reduced. Limit the stress to 20ksi and the fatigue life approaches infinity. The next step is to determine how much stress our bike is absorbing. Looking aft at a bottom bracket attached to the end of a seat tube cantilevered out from a frame such as was the case with the Clipper; we see that in this view, normal to the seat tube, the stress is about 17ksi.

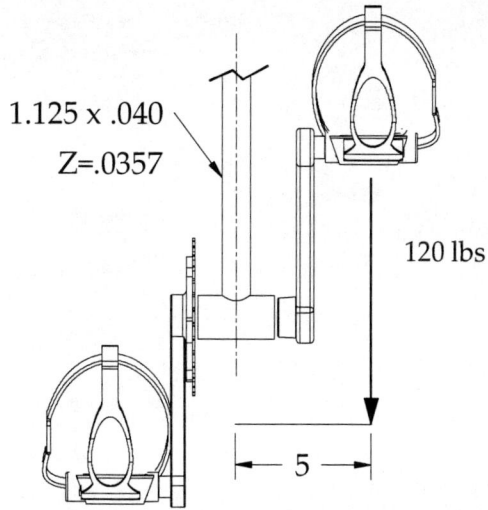

1.125 x .040
Z=.0357

120 lbs

5

BENDING MOMENT = 5" X 120# = 600 IN-LBS
SEAT TUBE STRESS M = Zf   600# = .0357f

Or: $f = M/Z$ Seat tube stress is 16,800 psi. Use this to predict fatigue life.

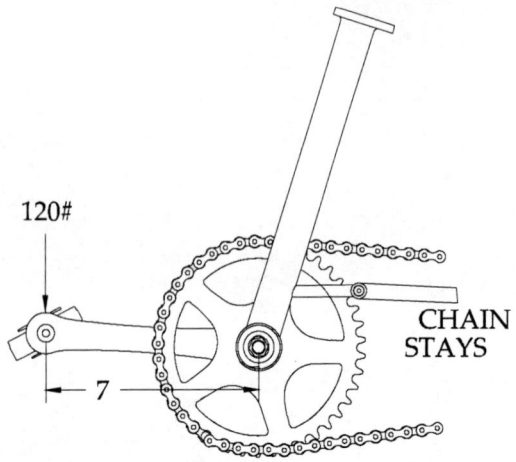

120#

CHAIN
STAYS

7

In this view, it is seen that the bending moments are 120# x 7"= 840 in-lbs. Plugging this new value into our equation gives us a stress value of 24ksi. This is uncomfortably close to the limit of failure at one million cycles. As you can see, the moments resulting from the pedaling action are constantly changing in direction and magnitude. These snapshots only capture two instants in the power cycle.

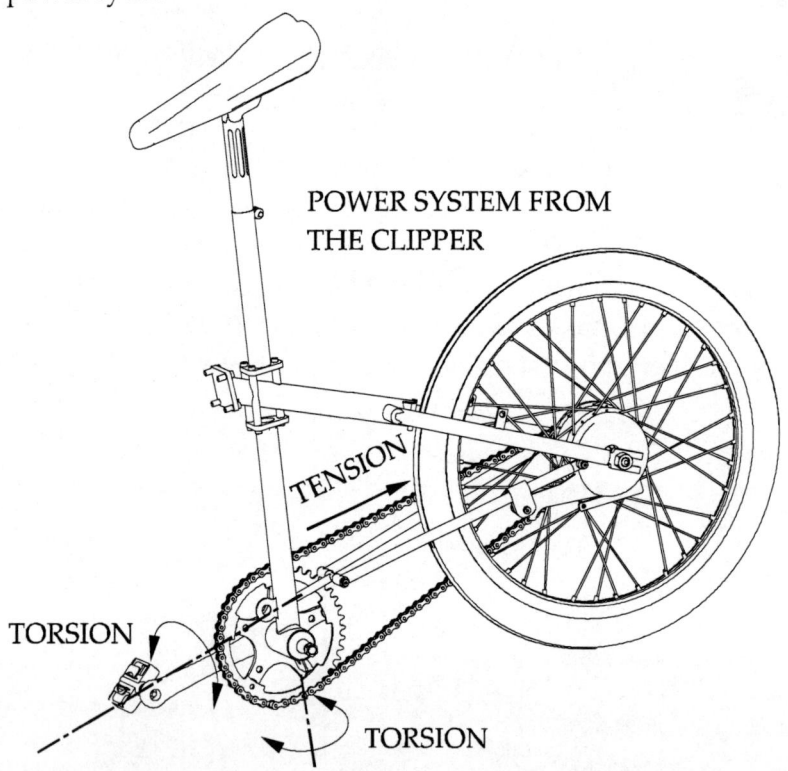

POWER SYSTEM FROM
THE CLIPPER

TENSION

TORSION

TORSION

Stress is not in one direction nor is it constant. This view of the power system of the Clipper, shown with the near side crank arm removed, shows the resultants of some of the force vectors generated as a result of the pedaling effort. Tension on the chain results in torsion about the seat tube axis. The downward force on the pedal creates torsion about the longitudinal axis. A two piece doubler added to the lower portion of the seat tube where it joins the bottom bracket corrected this obvious design flaw. This work was done after the bottom bracket broke off the seat tube while riding leisurely down a flat and level road.

The Clipper, an ancestor of our current travel bike, is built using this size seat tube, 1.125 x .040. The bottom bracket is a stay braced cantilever, sticking out unsupported from the frame. There is no downtube on the Clipper. Using the stress-number plot, it is expected that the seat tube will break due to high cycle fatigue after fewer than 2 million stress reversal cycles. This is 6000 miles assuming a sixty inch gear (60*π*2,000,000/ (5,280*12). The seat tube broke at approximately 1500 miles where the chain stays join the seat tube and was repaired using a two piece doubler around the break. The fact that it broke before it was expected to tells us that the 120 pound force was exceeded, probably during hill climbing, and the stress was higher than the tube could handle. It now has over 750 miles on the repaired tube. If it had broken half way between Abu Simbel and Luxor, out in the desert, that would have been really something to write home about. It is clear that our original tube selection for this piece was insufficient in either diameter or wall thickness or both. As you can see, predicting fatigue is not an exact science, especially when faced with a lack of empirical data.

Using a 1.250 diameter tube with a .040 wall (Z= .0446) drops the stress from 24ksi to 18ksi resulting in a big improvement in fatigue life.

These calculations may be all well and good for predicting fatigue failure, but working backwards, it is clear to see how tube selection benefits from the process. Many modern CAD programs can also calculate the effects of stress raisers and other stress related details that tend to concentrate stress and localize strain. Robobike uses these tools routinely and would not think of building a new design without a thorough examination of stresses and fatigue. Finite Element Analysis is the discipline used to describe these studies.

This succinct exercise in fatigue and high cycle failure goes a long way towards explaining the current trends in bicycle design. Larger diameter tubes, even if they are thinner, result in better performance than smaller diameter, thicker walled tubes. However, these thinner tubes present a bigger challenge for the frame builder. Aluminum bikes require heat sinks during the welding operation and steel tubes require lugs. That is why we at Robobike do not advocate venturing into the realm of very light materials. The quote we used at the beginning of this discussion has not been proved by our calculations nor has it been disproved. The reason is that the claim of being stronger than other tubes is not defined as to strength. There is no mention of fatigue in these claims, and for good reason.

Some values of Z; Tube diameter and wall thickness

1.00 x .032 = .0228	1.00 x .040 = .0279	1.00 x .048 = .0326	1.00 x .064 = .0414
1.125 x .032 = .0292	1.125 x .040 = .0357	1.125 x .048 = .0419	1.125 x .064 = .0535
1.25 x .032 = .0364	1.25 x .040 = .0446	1.25 x .048 = .0525	1.25 x .064 = .0673

The stress-number curves shown up to now are for steel. Each material will have its own distinct stress-number curves that show the characteristics for that material. For example, a steel tube will fail after one million cycles when stressed at 29000 psi. In order for an aluminum tube to survive for one million cycles, the stress must be reduced to 9,000 psi and for titanium, the stress must be reduced to 16,000 psi. That is why aluminum bikes are not built with the same size tubes that are common for steel bikes. Titanium, in spite of all that has been written about its incredible mechanical properties, pales in performance when compared side by side with alloy steel. Or does it? When comparing materials, are you comparing similar sized tubes or tubes that weigh the same? Big difference. Aluminum and titanium compare favorably with steel when the tubes have the same mass but steel is the clear winner when the tubes are the same size.

Comparing fatigue resistance between materials

For the sake of comparison, we will not change the example already described. One hundred twenty pounds of force applied to a crank arm seven inches in length and spun at 90 rpm results in a torque of 70 ft-lbs. (54.5 kg, 175mm and, 95 N-m) resulting in, with a cadence of 90 rpm, a power output of 1.2 horsepower. (We use the value of 550 ft-lbs / sec for one horsepower or Torque x RPM / 5252 = hp to arrive at this figure. No cyclist, living or dead, can produce this much power except in very short bursts. However, for design purposes, it gives us a comfortable safety factor and gives some protection in the low cycle fatigue mode. In fact, when standing on the pedals at a slow cadence, the 120 pound figure is exceeded regularly by many cyclists. The fact that this impulse is not continuous throughout the pedaling cycle and the cadence is reduced when this much effort is applied, brings the calculated horsepower down to the more believable ¼ to ½ hp range. A professional cyclist, riding up an eight percent grade at ten miles per hour, produces a half horsepower. Anyone who has seen the Tour de France can appreciate that figure.

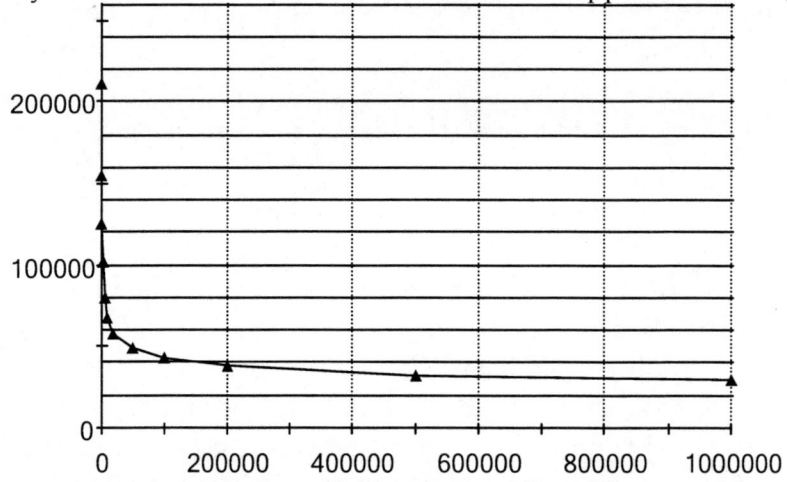

Steel, 4130, One million cycles to failure when stress is 29,000 psi

With the S-N curves, we find that the equivalent Aluminum tube, 1.125 inches in outside diameter will have a wall thickness of 3/16 inch.

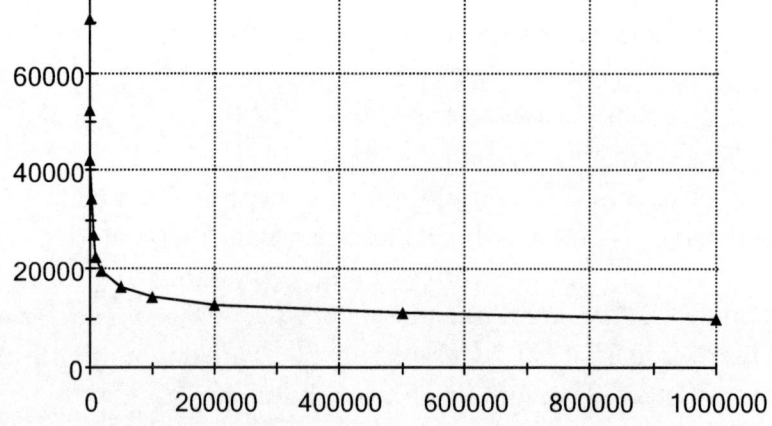

Aluminum, 6061-T6, One million cycles to failure when stress is 9,000 psi

28

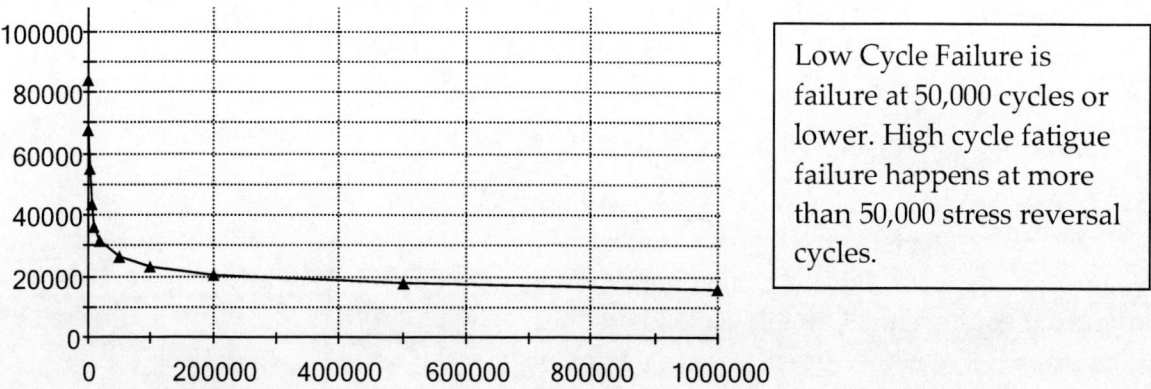

Titanium, 5Al,2.5Sn One million cycles to failure when stress is 16,000 psi

The equivalent titanium tube, 1.125" outside diameter, will have a wall thickness of .080".

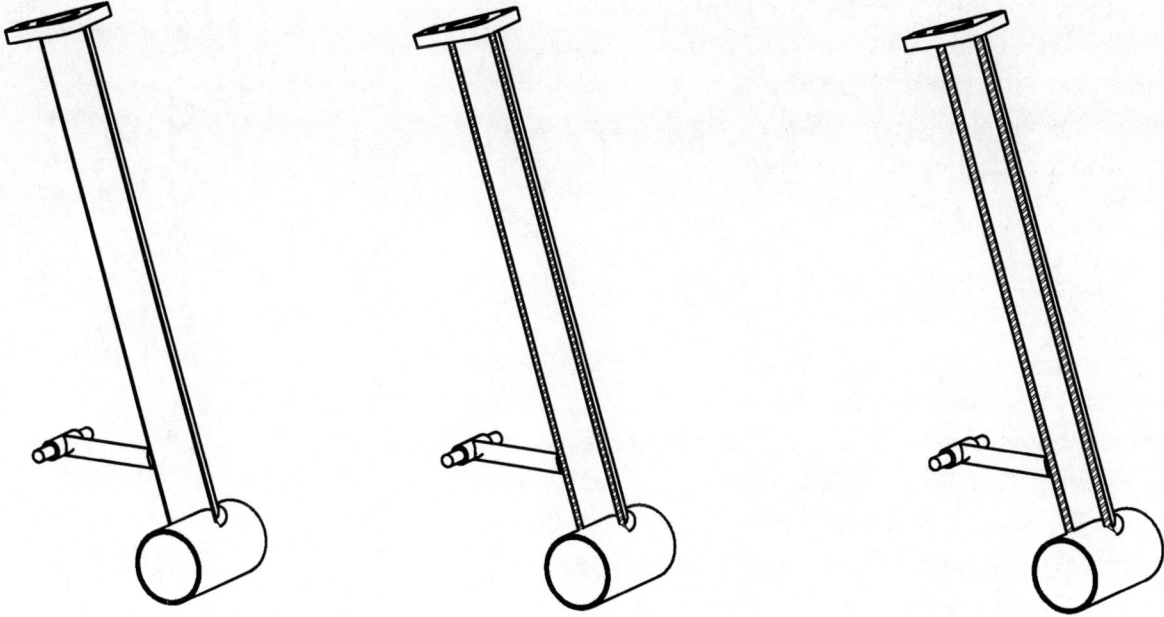

A steel tube, left, titanium tube, center, and aluminum tube, right, all
sized to meet the same fatigue design goal. 1.125" OD tubes shown in cross section

There are other ways to obtain the required equivalency. By increasing the outside diameter of the tube to 1.25 inches, we find that an aluminum tube with a wall of .125 and a titanium tube with a .06 wall match the fatigue resistance of the 1.125 x .040 steel tube. Increasing the outside diameter to 1.375 reduces the required wall thicknesses to .094 and .048 respectively. In this last example, the aluminum tube has the same mass as the smaller diameter steel tube, the titanium tube has only 85%. From this point on, increasing the outside diameter while reducing the wall thickness of both the aluminum and titanium tubes results in tubes with better fatigue characteristics than our steel tube. A 2 inch diameter aluminum tube with a .040 wall has slightly better fatigue characteristics but only 63% the mass of a Ø1.125 x .040 steel tube. However, these thin aluminum tubes are quite difficult to join by the fusion process without specialized, dedicated tooling and equipment and often require post weld processing such as heat treatment.

All Loads Great and Small

By Bingo Sun Noon

Living the bicycle lifestyle is impossible without the ability to carry loads safely and comfortably. Children, adult passengers, building materials, guitar amps and touring equipment all qualify as loads as they apply to this exercise. Whether great or small, light or heavy, mastering load carrying is essential and not all that difficult. Mostly it's about controlling your center of gravity, avoiding phugoids and ensuring adequate braking power.

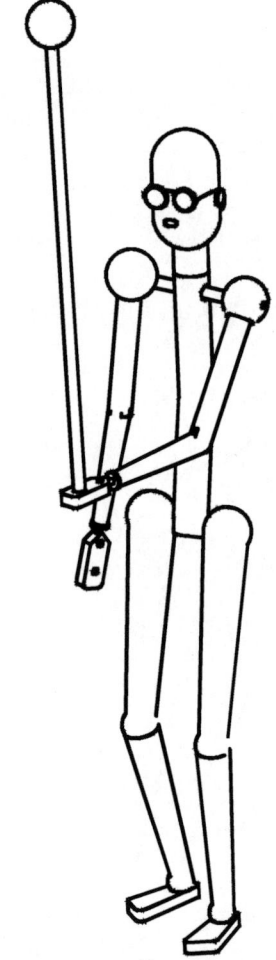

There are three design criteria to consider when building or modifying a bike for load carrying. Numbers one and two are crucial. The third is illustrated by the fellow shown at the right. Imagine a coconut impaled on a stick. The longer the stick, the easier it is to balance the coconut.

Keep your coconut as high as possible.

The other two design elements are not quite so simple. They involve keeping the centers of mass as close together as possible. This is very important. Also, be aware of where the center of gravity is found along the longitudinal axis. If given the freedom to do so, bikes would always translate about the center of gravity. They do not have that freedom (only airplanes and submarines do) but the concept is a valuable tool all the same. High rigidity is required for load carrying. So is balance. A properly designed front loader is tail heavy when ridden empty; a rear loaded bike is heavy on the front end when ridden empty. Anyone who has ridden a tandem solo knows this. These effects can be reduced a bit but will always be there. That's just the way it is. And what is it about those phugoids anyway that makes them so important?

Power?

.88 x percent grade x V x W = ft-lbs/min.   V is mph, W is weight in pounds 1hp = 33000 ft-lbs/min

Designing a load carrying bike always means increased structure. This is true for two reasons. The first of these is easy to comprehend. A large mass being moved down the road follows all the laws of motion as far as wanting to continue going straight. Attaching a lever in the form of a bike frame to that mass and moving it around disturbs its steady state equilibrium. The second reason is not so obvious. If you are creating more power to move the load, then more structure is needed to resist the reactions to that power. Do you know how much power you produce? Most riders think they do but usually overestimate the amount.

Example of estimated power: a 250 pound load traveling at 10 mph up a four percent grade requires 8800 ft-lbs/min. just to overcome gravity. (.88 x 4 x 10 x 250 = 8800). This is .27 horsepower or about two hundred watts. All losses due to friction and air resistance are ignored in this example. Generating this amount of power for any length of time is not possible for most recreational cyclists. Even so, you should design for twice this amount. As described in earlier portion of this book, metal fatigue is more of a bicycle slayer than the magnitude of the load. The number one source of metal fatigue is a slightly flexible structure subjected to a high number of stress cycles such as individual pedaling impulses. More load requires more power and more structure. Straightforward as can be.

So how much power do you produce? Using the formula shown above, it is possible to estimate the amount of power produced using a hill and a bike computer with an altitude function. For best results, the hill should be a steady rise and continue for some length. Dividing the altitude gained by the distance traveled will give you the grade in percent. The rest is substitution. There are errors in this trigonometric approach but they are insignificant. Friction must be added but that is quite difficult to estimate. We use ten percent but it is actually higher. Using a hill for the tests eliminates the need to determine and add air resistance as the uphill grade slows down the bike to a point that air resistance is negligible.

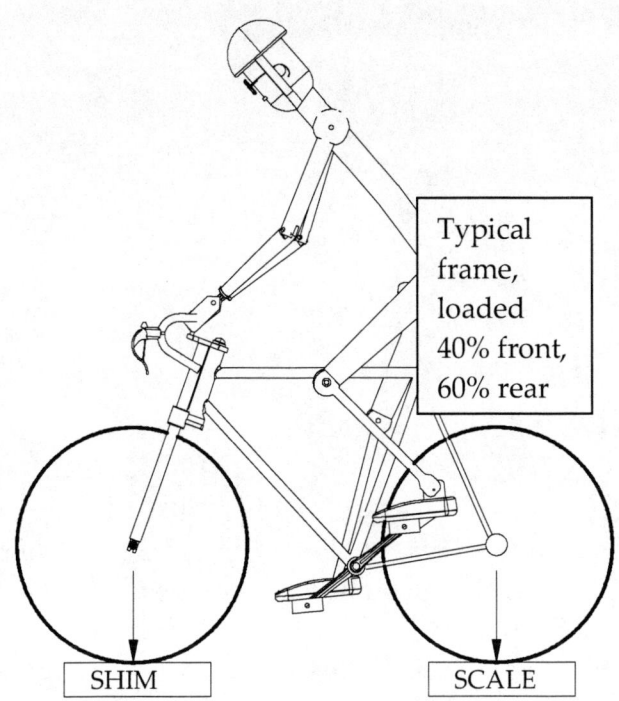

Typical frame, loaded 40% front, 60% rear

SHIM   SCALE

Weight and Balance, an often overlooked but very important characteristic

The thousand words shown here illustrate the principle involved in determining the balance point. Designing a bike for load carrying, if done properly, means knowing (and controlling) the balance point. Moving the rear wheel aft places more weight on the front wheel. Moving it forward has the opposite effect.

To find the balance point (arm) of a rider seated on a frame, use the method shown on the left. Although you are actually finding the center of gravity for the rider/bike combination, for all practical purposes, the result is the center of gravity of the rider in this riding position. The distance aft of datum is the arm of the rider. Datum is the front axle. Arm is distance from datum. The weight shown on the scale is 120 pounds. Total weight of bike and rider is 200 pounds.

Arm x Weight = Moments   Arm = Moments / Weight

With a 40 inch wheel base, 120 pounds on the scale equates to 4800 in-lbs of moment.

Therefore, Arm, or balance point, is 4800 / 200 or 24 inches. Twenty four inches is 60% of the wheel base, 60% of the weight of the entire package is carried on the rear wheel. If the scale and the shim are reversed, it is found that weight on the front wheel is 80 pounds. Since the arm of the front wheel is 0, the complete equation is: Total moments = {(0 * 80) + (120 * 40)} = 4800. Arm = total moments / total weight = 4800 / 200 = 24. This is inches aft of datum.

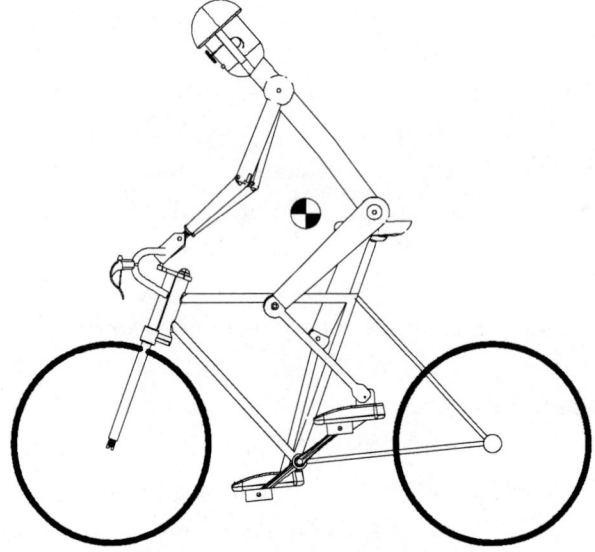

The typical frame, stretched from 40 to 50 inch wheelbase, changes the balance point to midway between the wheels. Since the weight of the bike is known at 30 pounds, and the weight and arm of the rider are known as 170 pounds at 24 inches, a scale is no longer needed. The equation becomes: [(0 x 15) + (24 x 170) + (50 x 15)/ 202 = 24. Weight distribution is 26/50 front 24/50 rear or 52% front, 48% rear. Now, add fifty pounds 45 inches aft of datum.

Store bought bikes have a wheelbase of one meter. This is a general rule and is a design element as old as bicycling itself. It is a good place to start, especially when starting a new design.

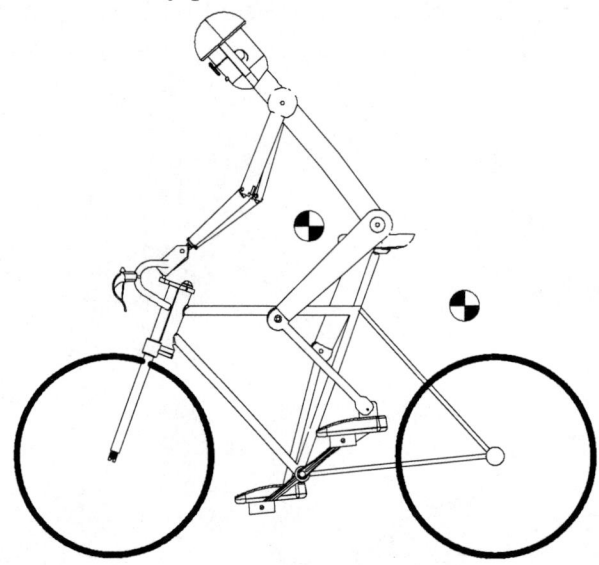

The balance point moves aft to: [0 x 15) + (24 x 170) + (45 x 50) + (50 x 15)] / 250 =28.3
A 50" bike with a 170 pound rider at 24 inches aft of datum, a 50 pound load 45 inches aft of datum and a 30 pound frame balances at 28.3 inches aft of datum. This amounts to 56% of the total weight on the rear wheel. Such a bike is easy to ride when loaded. It is nose heavy when not loaded. Not terribly so, but nose heavy none the less. Using the technique shown here, it is easy to design a well balanced bike for load carrying. However, that's not the whole story.

More than one clever design from the workshop at Robobike has wound up in the recycling pile even though its designer built a perfectly balanced and thoughtful solution to carrying a load down the road. Our front wheel drive recumbent is a perfect example.

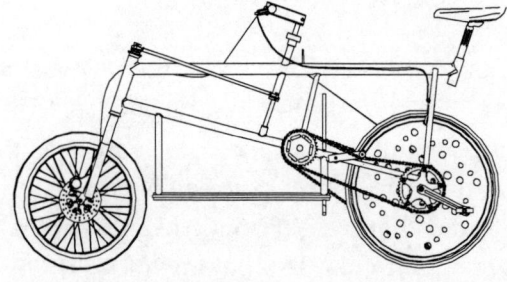

Delivery Boy

Herein lies the challenge of load carrying. Two separate mass centers must be connected to one another and connected to the roadway via two wheels. Doing the Hokey Pokey, the wiggles, shakes or whatever you want to call them, show up when control inputs are out of phase with the reactions to those inputs. Known as porpoising (phugoid oscillations) in airplanes, they are annoying and potentially deadly. Adequate structure and center of gravity control tame these types of events. Two large masses on a bike frame (or any moving structure for that matter) contribute to their propagation. A bike with the CG too far aft is potentially dangerous in this regard.

The bicycle designer must also give some thought to how the bike rides without the extra load. Trailers are the obvious solution to carrying a load some of the time.

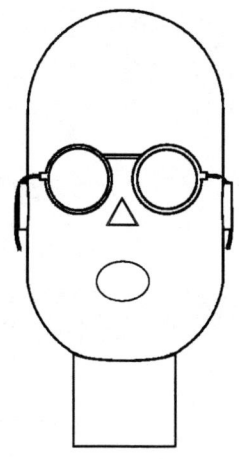

All design work involves compromise. Excellent load carrying ability often means sacrificing other qualities such as comfort and performance. A bike suited for high speed performance is not suitable as a load carrier. Conversely, don't expect to build a load carrier that can stay with the big boys.

The Pickup

Apprentice skills required to build a load carrying bike with improvements in load control

The scope of work for the Pickup Conversion comprises:

1. Preparing a donorcycle in such a way as to make it ready for the weld shop, that is, thorough cleaning of the frame, removing the bottom bracket axle, and removing the paint from the work area. All cables to the rear of the frame are removed. All grease from the bb shell is cleaned with solvent followed by soap and water.
2. Building a simple jig for measuring and for holding the frame during the cutting and welding operations.
3. Prepare a piece of threaded rod to use as a rear dropout spreader.
4. Cutting the seat stays where they join the top tube
5. Cutting the chain stays near the bottom bracket
6. Bending the chain stays
7. Cutting the seat stays near the brake mounting bridge
8. Bending the seat stays
9. Fabricating and fitting a tee
10. Adding a patch at the chain stays
11. First pass brazing
12. Fitting an uptube from half inch square steel tube
13. Finish brazing
14. Adding a rear rack from quarter inch round.

> Creating a task list is one way to plan your project, particularly for those with little experience. This chronological plan emphasizes fitting all components before brazing.

The finished project

This is the perfect choice for a first project. It is a useful bike to have around. It is easy to build. The recommended process is torch brazing.

The Pickup Conversion

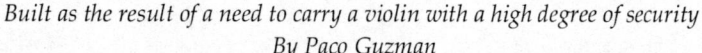

Built as the result of a need to carry a violin with a high degree of security
By Paco Guzman

Funny bikes with different size wheels are a hallmark at Robobike. The Pickup is one funny bike. It is an eye catcher. The concept of using a donorcycle began with the Pickup conversion. The ride becomes somewhat harsher than the original bike but it is not a problem except on day long cruises. Increased frame rigidity has that effect. Unless you take a peek behind you, there is little to indicate that the frame has changed. As the above illustration suggests, the rear wheel is BMX size 20″ diameter. The gearing is reduced by 20 per cent but that's a useful change. The following is written by Paco Guzman, the head mechanic at Superior Bicycles, Superior, AZ.

Superior Bicycles Are Above Average

Sorry, had to get in a good word about Superior bikes. This project has some serious load carrying capability. I don't mean big heavy loads, but medium sized loads held securely and always under control. The Pickup gains most of its increased rigidity from the fact that more steel is added to the frame. Also, the stays are shortened up. The result is an increase in the natural frequency (in Hz) of the rear structure. The perfect analogy for this type of modification is the tuning fork. Shorten the legs and the frequency increases (higher pitch) but the displacement (amplitude) is reduced. From a structural point of view, this is a good thing, usually. As most designers know, increasing the rigidity in one region of a structure tends to change the point of failure, not eliminate it. The way to do that is to increase the rigidity of the entire structure. The builders at Robobike don't spend a lot of time examining the natural frequency of structures but they do spend a lot of time with modern CAD and modeling programs. A function of many of these programs is frequency mode analysis. A frame like this is, when examined with such a program, may uncover weaknesses and design flaws not readily apparent. We have found that increasing the resonant frequency of a structure improves its performance. This is a particularly useful method for increasing the fatigue life of a bike frame, especially load carrying bike frames.

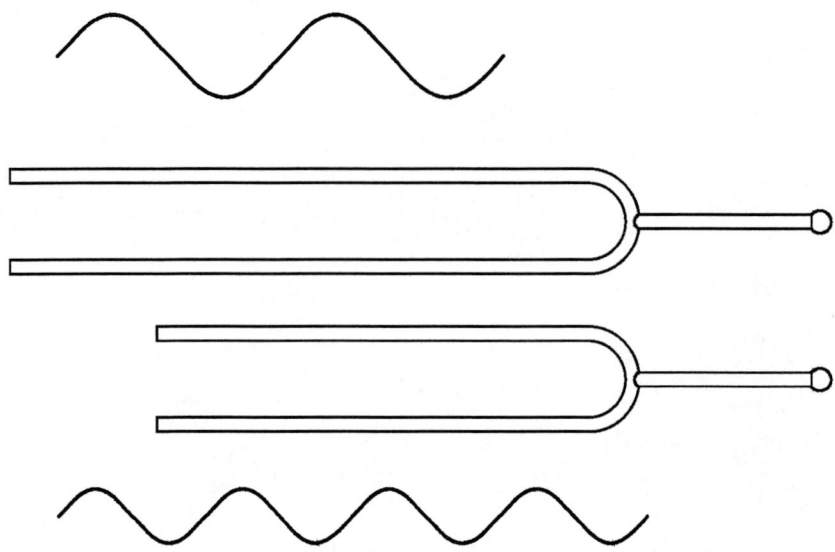

Shortening the legs of the tuning fork increases its resonant frequency
Resulting in vibrations of lesser displacement (magnitude)

This type of load carrying machine has limits in placing the centers of mass along the longitudinal axis. As discussed later in the chapter about building the Loveboat, having a mass aft of the rear wheel contact patch leads to instability. Some bodacious loads can be carried as long as they are placed forward of the rear axle. Overhanging the rear wheel is OK as long as the load is not a substantial mass. A guitar and case can be bungeed to the rear rack without any problems. You'll have to build Delivery Boy if you want to carry bags of concrete.

Begin construction by selecting a donor bike that is a product of good workmanship and built with industry standard materials. The prototype Pickup was built using a Schwinn LeTour from the mid 1980's. Built in Taiwan and furnace or induction brazed, it is a lugged frame using DOM tubes. It is exactly what you want. These are excellent bikes that sold for less than they are worth mostly because mountain bikes were selling like hotcakes about that time. Remove the wheels, rear brake, rear derailleur and disassemble the bottom bracket. This last bit is to ensure new grease is added after the brazing operation. The frame being stripped and cleaned, there is nothing to do but cut right to the building phase and tackle this project by the numbers. Begin by taking a measurement.

Step one; measuring the bike using a jig.

The chain stays will be cut and bent by the difference in the wheel radii of the old and new wheels or about three and a half inches. We need some way to determine when the stays have been bent the proper amount.

A length of aluminum square tube, a piece 5/16 threaded rod for the front axle and a piece of 3/8 threaded rod for the rear spreader are needed for this step. You will need six nuts and six washers for each piece of threaded rod. For all practical purposes, any material will work for the main body of the jig. A good, clean, straight piece of construction lumber or hardwood will be OK if you do not have any square tube. Center the fork on the jig. Record the beginning measurement as shown in the figure and remove the bike from the jig.

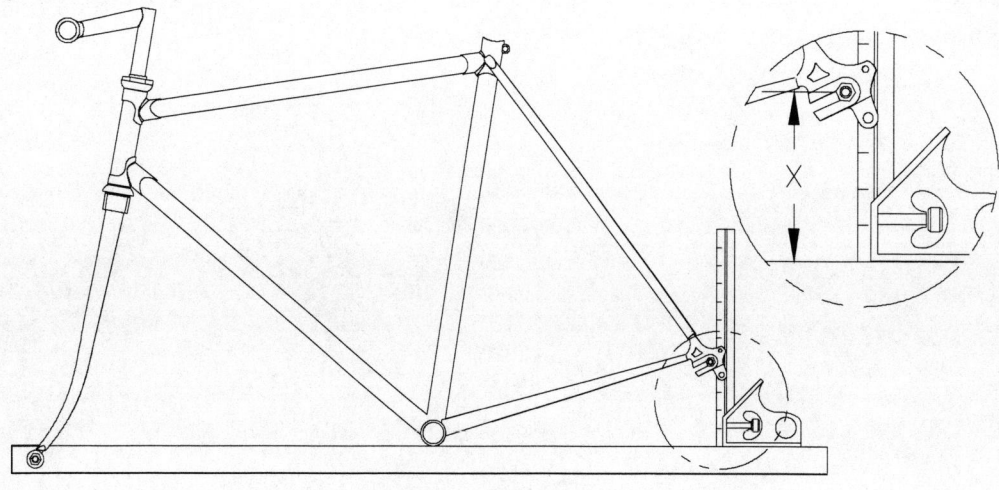

Measuring the frame

Step two; cut the seat stays.

The next step is to cut the seat stays where they join the cluster at the top tube. You want to cut it as clean as you can and try to leave as little as possible of the stay. Resist the temptation of removing the stays with a torch as doing so reworks the filler material in the cluster. Keep in mind that ours is a furnace brazed frame and torching it certainly screws up the joint. When it's time to add the uptube, we'll come back to this issue.

Step three; the chain stays are cut most the way through at a spot far enough away from the bottom bracket so that brazing around the cut will not affect the bracket. Four inches is a good minimum value as to where to cut.

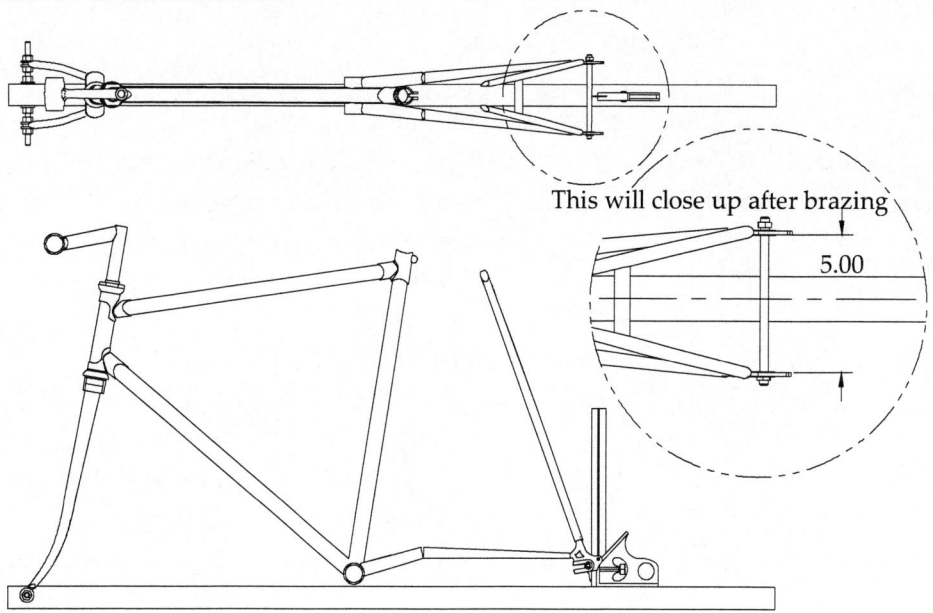

Step four; bend the chain stays down by your previously calculated amount. There is a cosine error introduced with our method because you are not measuring normal to the line connecting the wheel centers. You can calculate the amount of bend yourself or use our number, which is 3.25". Notice the spreader installed between the drop outs. Spread the drop outs to five inches. Another piece of tooling is needed to align everything before brazing. The following illustration shows how it is installed.

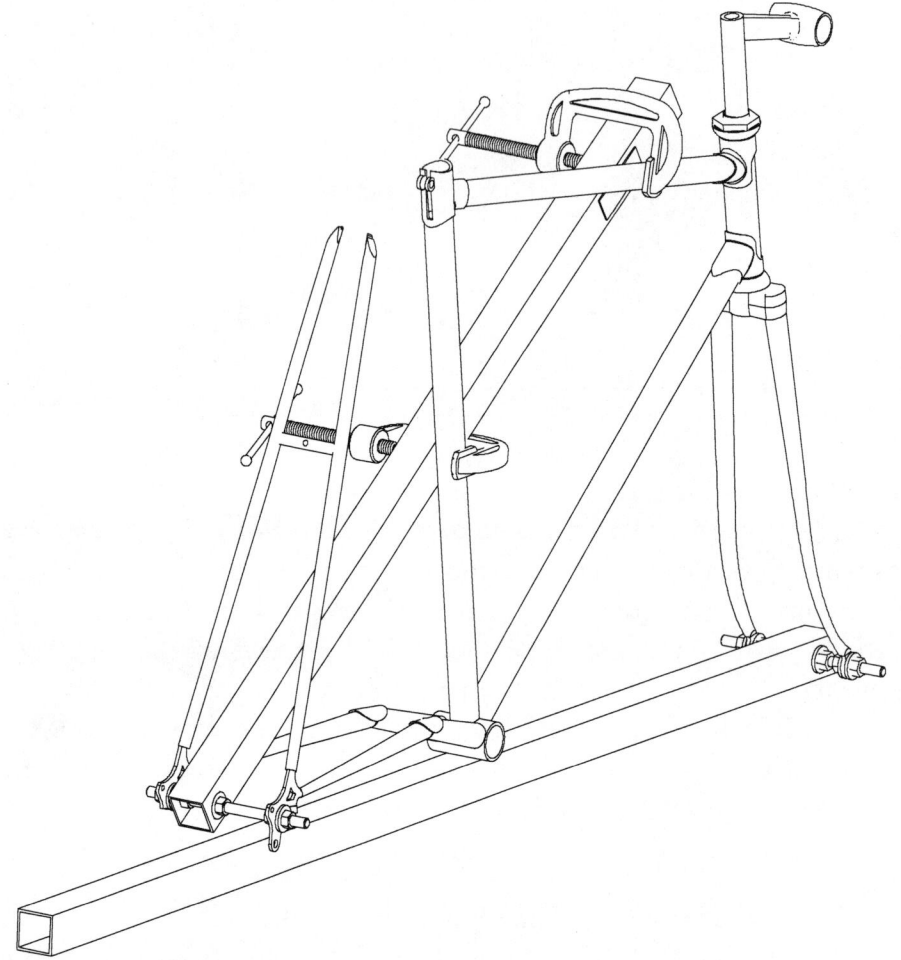

Notice also that the top tube is 1″ diameter and the seat tube is 1.125″. That is why a 1/16″ thick shim is shown between the top tube and the jig where the upper C clamp is installed. Also notice the patches laid over the gash in the chain stays where they were cut and bent. Any piece of scrap steel, about .040″to .070″ thick, bent over a bolt with a hammer or squeezed in a vise will work.

This type of workmanship is what we call *Intelligent Design* at Robobike. A good choice for the chain stay patch detail is a piece of chain stay or seat stay cut from a junk bicycle. The stays on

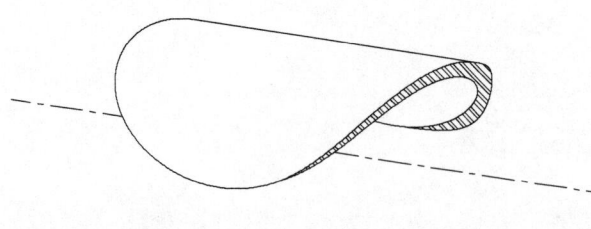

your bicycle are not round. They approximate an ellipse. You want to bend the patches so they lie in close proximity to the gash being patched. A gap cannot be avoided, but try to keep it as small as possible. The sources for this kind of material are many and varied. Remember, there is no undo button on your brazing torch so make sure the chain stays are spread evenly. Clean everything until you get tired and then tack the patches in place.

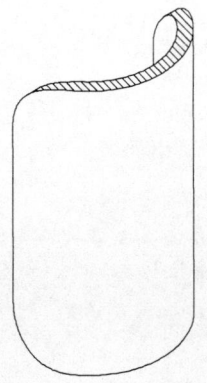

The seat tube doubler is required to prevent fatigue failure. Stresses are concentrated whenever one tube joins another. A doubler will distribute these stresses over a wider area and, by definition, reduce stress.

Load per unit area (stress) is what it is all about.

The purpose of the seat tube doubler is to distribute stresses directed at the main triangle over a wider area. Carrying a load will no doubt cause the bike to fishtail. Controlling that is done by making the connection between the rear and main triangles as rigid as possible. The doubler contributes greatly to this rigidity. The doubler can be cut from an old piece of seat tube or down tube, split with a hack saw and opened up a bit by massaging with a hammer. Tack it in place 11.5 inches up from the bottom bracket measured center to center. This number guarantees shoe clearance. While you're at it, cut a couple more pieces from the same seat tube or down tube you used for the doubler. These pieces will be used for the TEE.

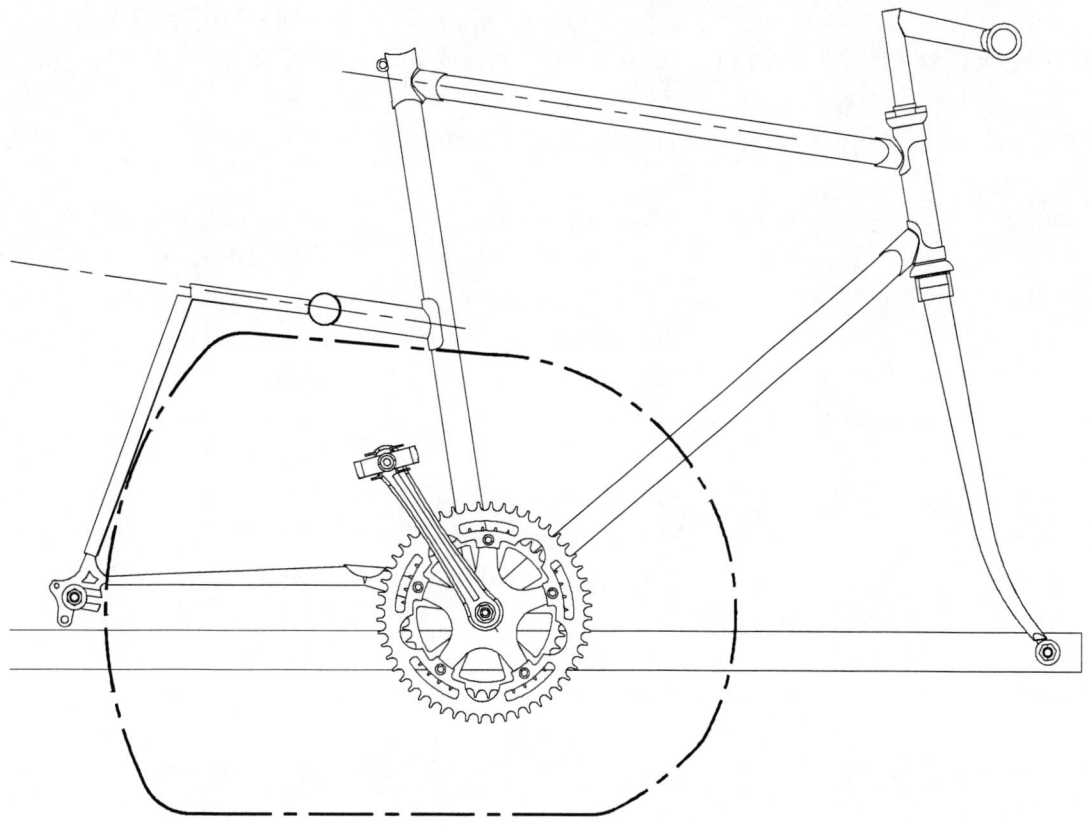

Shoe and ankle clearance

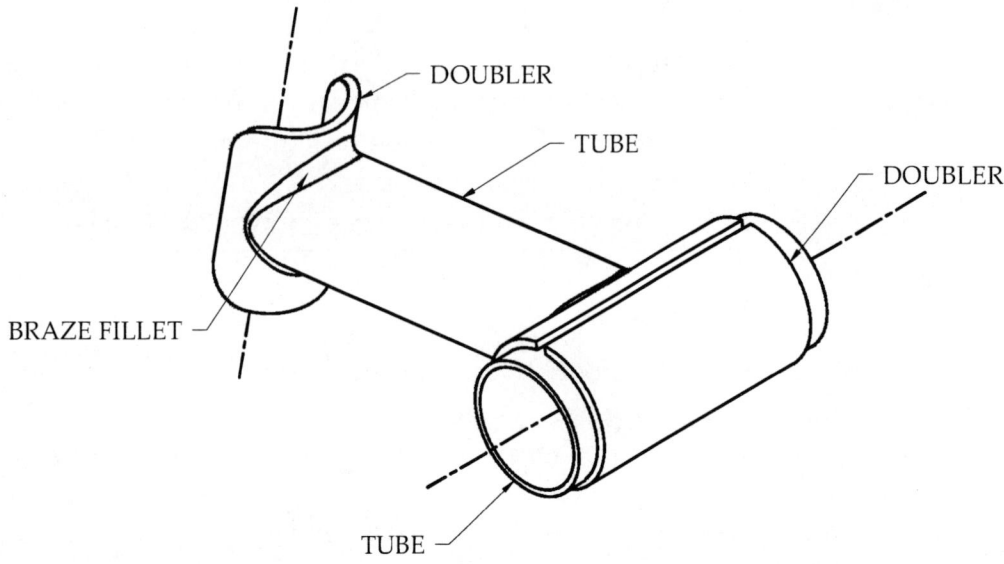

DOUBLER

TUBE

DOUBLER

BRAZE FILLET

TUBE

The TEE

The tee can be built off the bike as a unique sub-assembly and added at a single step or it can be built up a piece at a time. The latter method is a bit easier but only if the whole thing is built straight and true. If you have a tendency to hold things together by squeezing them between your knees while you weld, then build it a piece at a time. Nobody likes building a crooked ass bicycle so making it straight at this level of completion is a good idea. The tee is made up of four pieces, one of which is split to act as a doubler. This last bit makes the whole thing more reliable and less prone to breaking.

Add an uptube of half inch square tube of carbon steel. It is installed from the area of the bottom bracket to the cross piece where the brakes are to be mounted. Since you don't want to drill through the uptube to mount the brakes, give some thought to how the cluster comes together. On our versions of the Pickup, we braze in a flat piece that hangs down towards the wheel for the purpose of attaching a caliper brake. Using a disk brake is the best solution to all braking requirements. Adding the uptube changes the rear parallelogram to a triangle. A keen observer may notice that without the uptube, the structure is a four bar linkage. If you have never experienced the four bar linkage, do a web search and you will find lots of interactive 4 bar sites. It is great fun to design your own and a good insight on why parallelograms are to be avoided. Gussets in the corners will control the tendency to rack if you don't like the idea of adding the uptube. In four bar language, you are grounding or fixing another bar by adding a gusset. The cross piece where the seat stays are bent is likewise made from half inch square tube.

Clean everything. Remove every molecule of paint and sand to bare metal everywhere you will be brazing. Tack everything then do a root pass and a finish pass using a generic, inexpensive flux coated brass rod. Most welders refer to this type of rod as bronze but it is really copper and zinc, which is brass. Braze everything all at once. If you want to clean between passes, it certainly won't hurt anything. Clean by chipping, soap and water, or by filing and sanding. Sandblasting is by far the easiest but we all don't have access to this process.

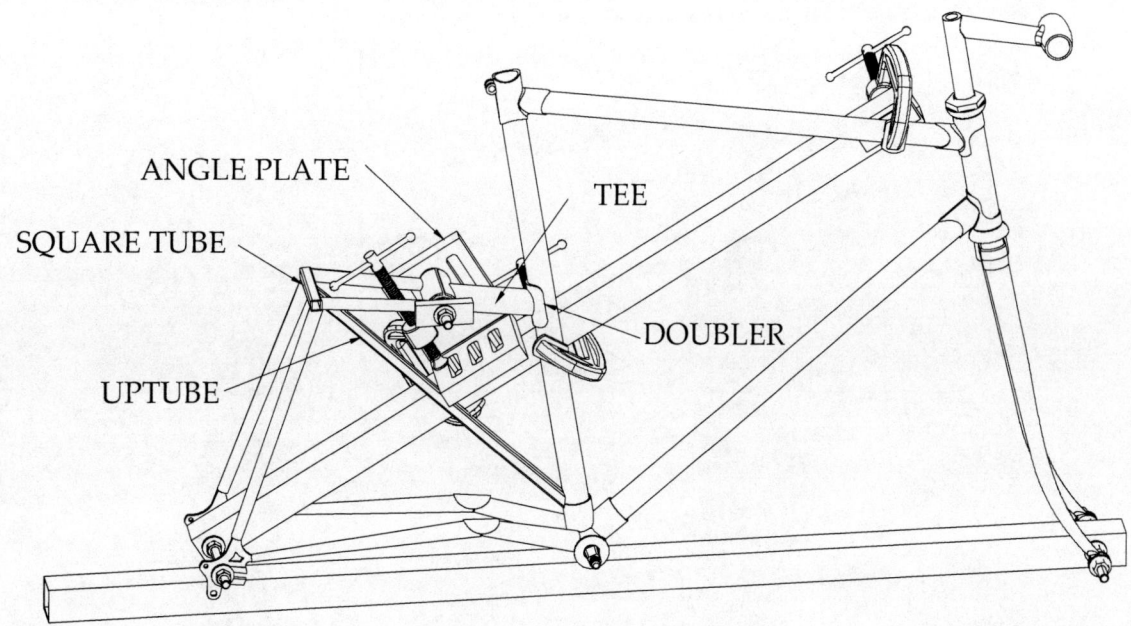

ANGLE PLATE

SQUARE TUBE

TEE

DOUBLER

UPTUBE

Illustration showing set up for brazing operation. The tee is held perpendicular to the frame by the use of an angle plate and a through bolt.

The optional rear rack is bent from a quarter inch rod and brazed on. Its addition makes the Pickup a more useful tool for transporting moderately sized loads. If you are thinking about carrying a child with this bike, then put those thoughts out of your mind. This bike is not intended for such service. There are better ways to carry a child. Take a look at the Aluminum Limo.

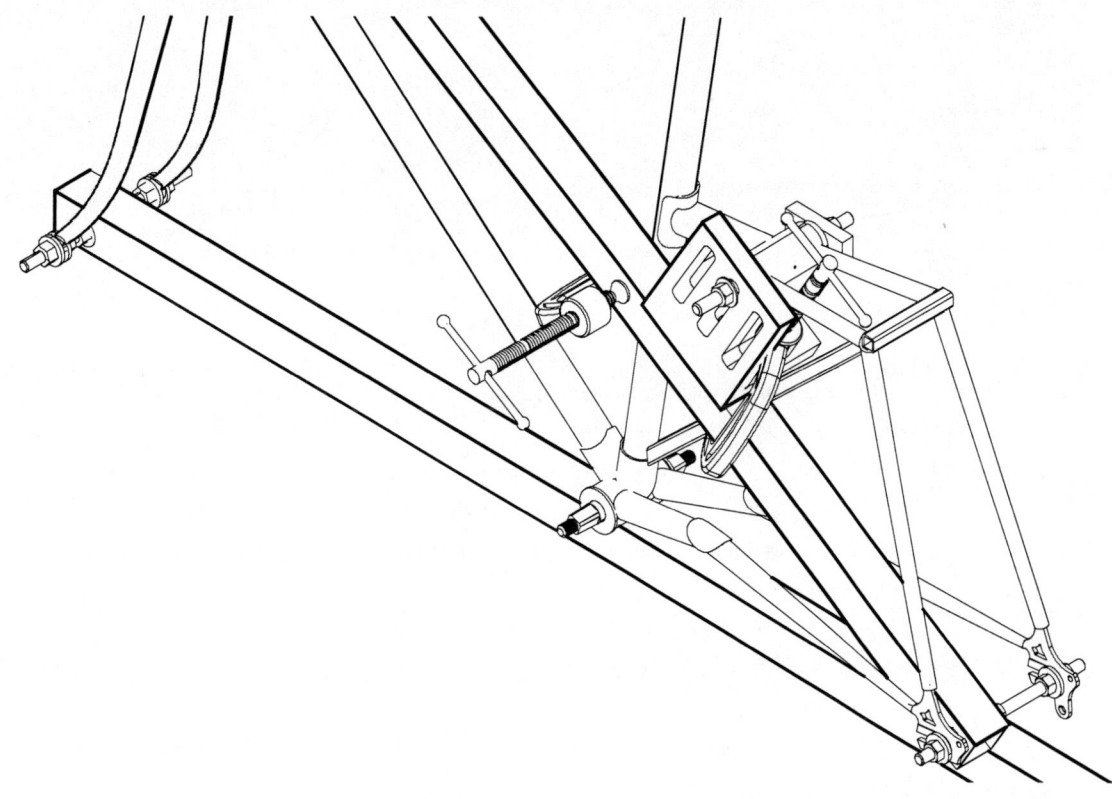

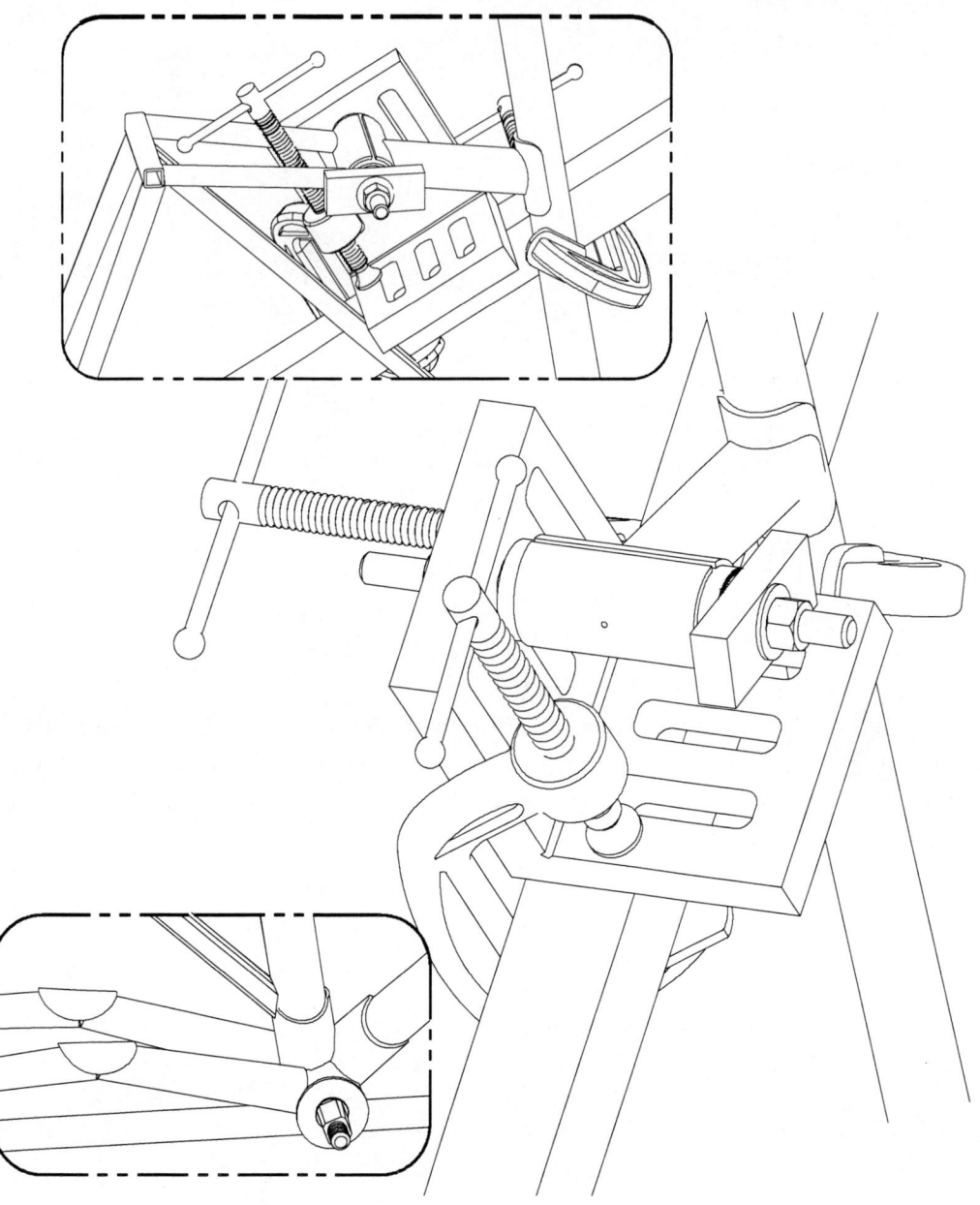

Method of clamping Tee to seat tube

The chances that your copy of the Pickup conversion will be a source of pride are increased tremendously if the structure added during the upgrade is square and symmetrical. The piece of square tube used to hold the rear axle in alignment during the building process is shown here supporting an angle plate. The angle plate is clamped to the square tube and supports the cross piece portion of the TEE. This strategy allows the TEE to be added one piece at a time or added as an assembly. The welders at Robobike prefer building the TEE one piece at a time with cleaning and inspection done between each step.

Once the TEE is tacked in place, the angle plate can be moved to support the stays and the half inch square cross piece added where the seat stays are bent.

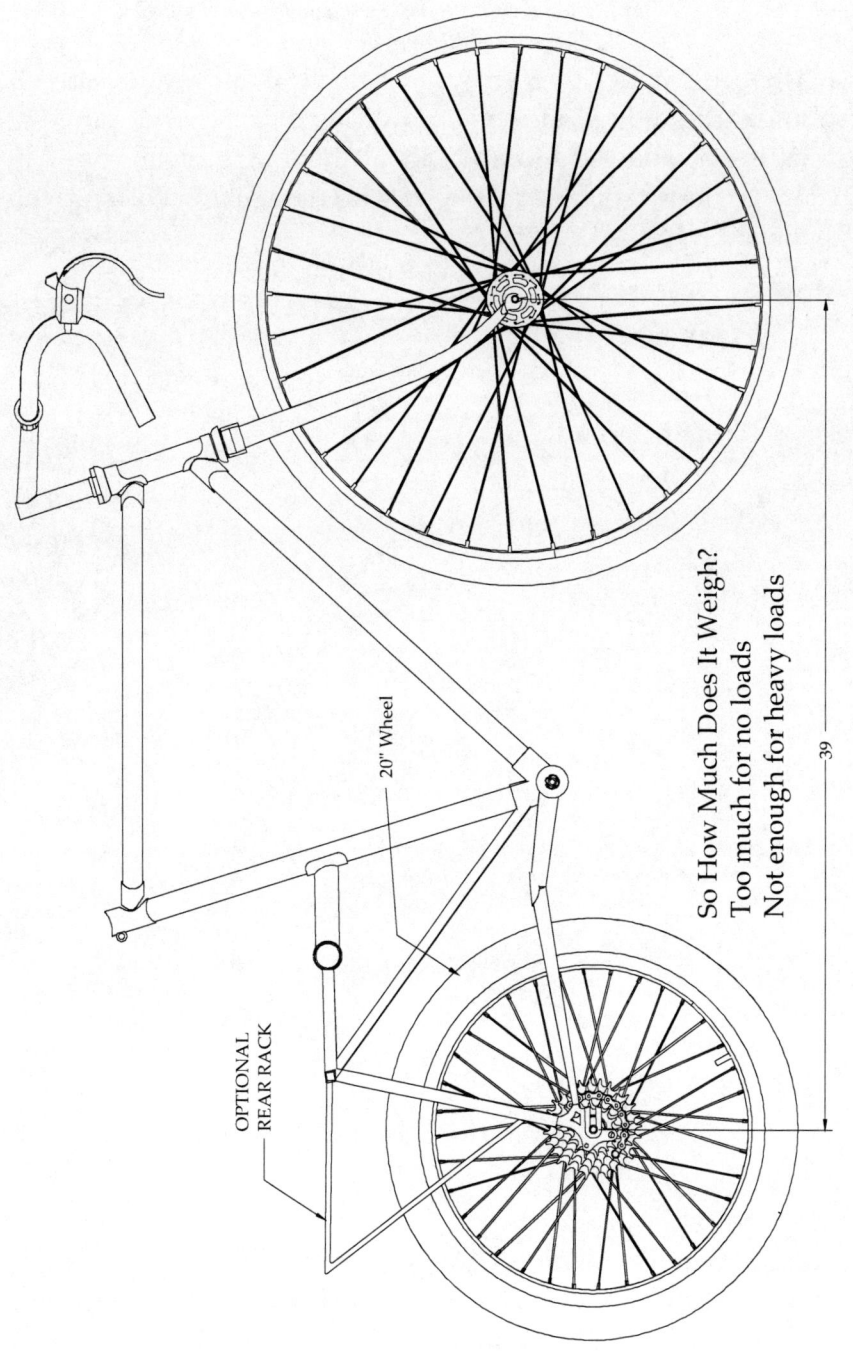

20" Wheel

OPTIONAL REAR RACK

So How Much Does It Weigh?
Too much for no loads
Not enough for heavy loads

39

Single Wheel Bike Trailer

An all purpose attachment to make your life easier. For apprentice level skills.
By Dom Caliente with a little help from all

Hauling spuds is what this trailer does. It was originally built to prove a concept. That concept was not proved to be true though in the world of logic, it does not prove it false. The prototype was built so that it was allowed to swing about the longitudinal axis. Why this was important escapes me but the trailer was all over the road with the trailer hooked up this way. The current hitch fixed the handling problems.

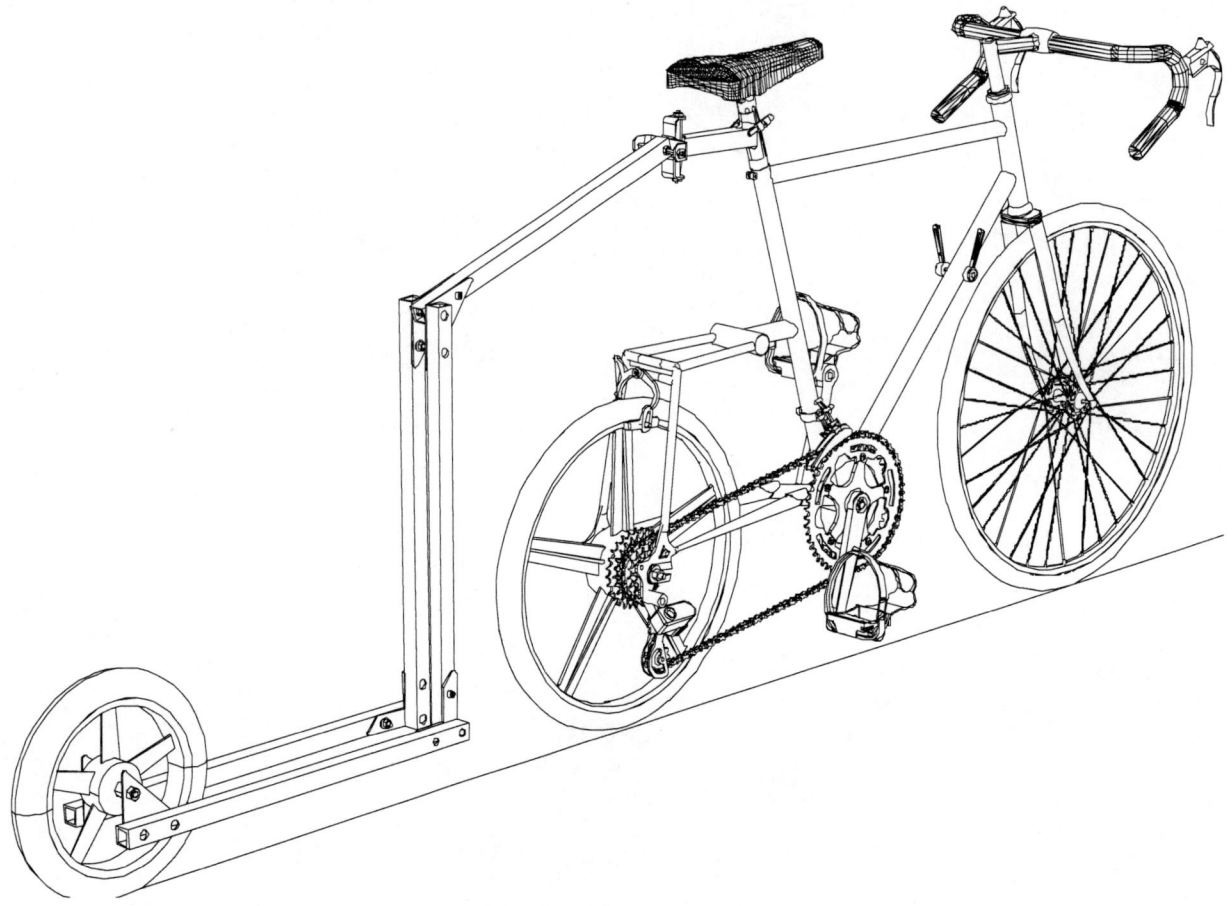

Building the trailer itself requires no special skills other than using a hack saw and drilling holes. It is easy to build and is a good project for the beginner. The hitch is not an easy bit of work but we'll cover that in a bit. The hitch is included in the kit finished and ready to use. To build the trailer you will need some square tubing and a small bit of aluminum flat stock an eighth inch thick. Rather than describe every step, have a look at the drawings. They certainly are easy enough to understand.

The top view includes a detail close up of the arrangement of the fasteners in the frame. Large clearance holes are drilled to allow the installation of the hardware. The 3.50 dimension is the sum of 3 one inch square tubes and four 1/8" flat gussets.

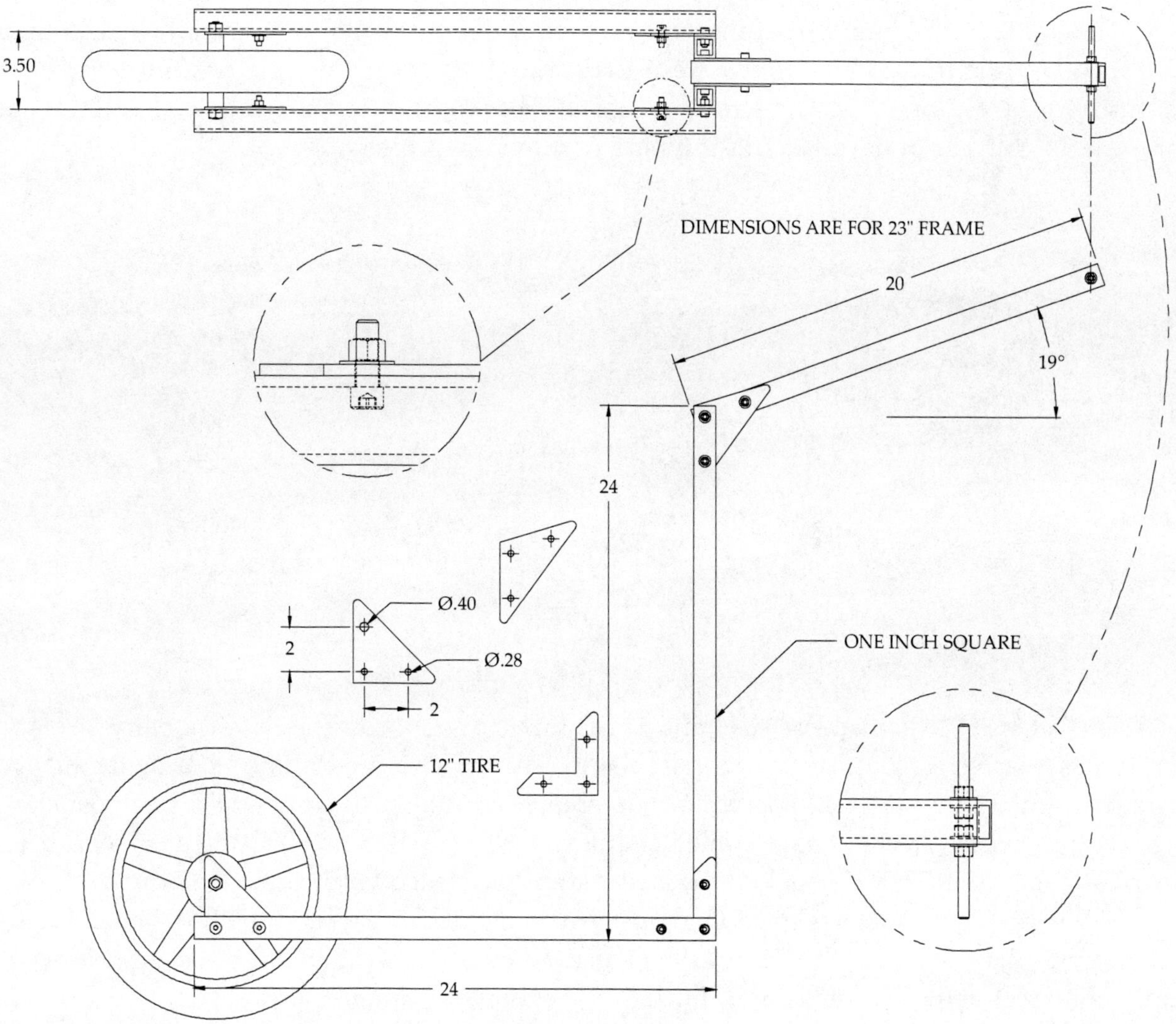

3.50

DIMENSIONS ARE FOR 23" FRAME

20

19°

24

ONE INCH SQUARE

Ø.40

2

Ø.28

2

12" TIRE

24

Side and Top Views

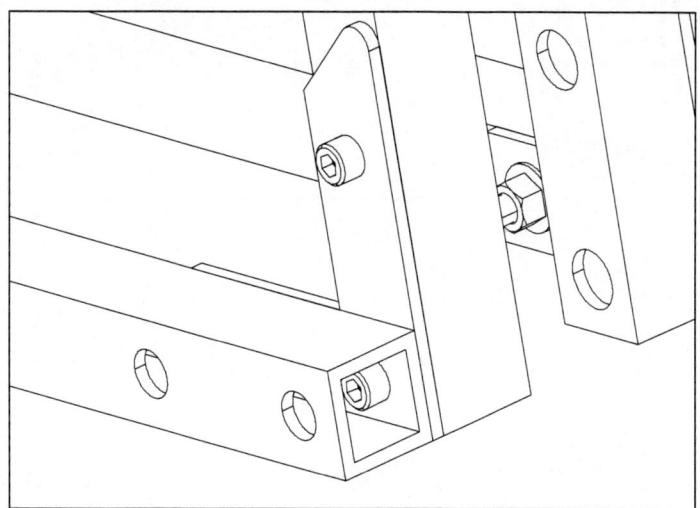

Bolts should not be installed so that they collapse the tubes. The use of socket head cap screws requires drilling a 9/32" hole through both sides of the square tube and a 3/8" or larger through one wall for screw access. Tighten securely after checking alignment.

Close up of assembly detail. Notice brackets between frame tubes.

The frame can be built from 1 inch square tube with either a .06 or .12 wall thickness. Either one works. Use the thicker tube if you want to do heavy hauling. Note the configuration of the screws shown in the top view. The screws are installed so they only clamp one wall and not both to prevent the collapse of the tube. This is typical of the entire project.

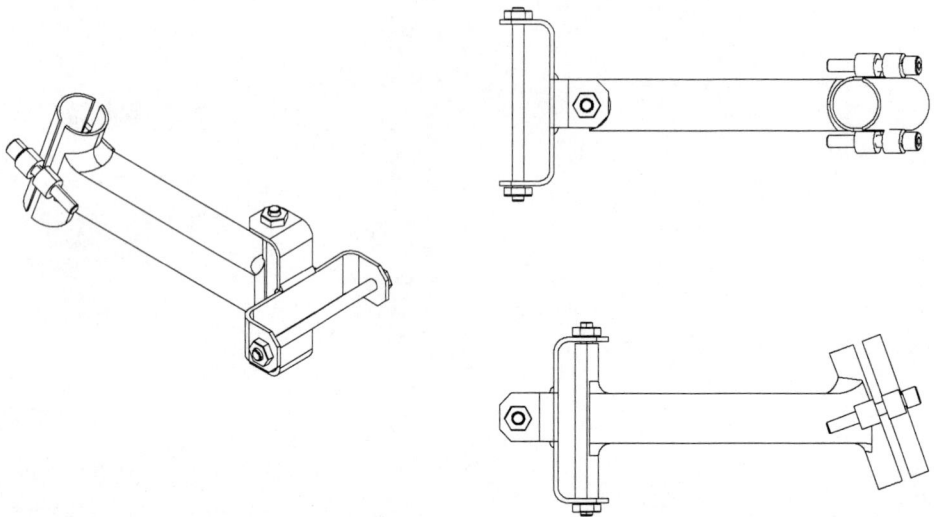

The hitch itself is made of steel and it is brazed or welded. This hitch is very strong. It incorporates a universal joint and a seat post clamp. The trailer is load limited not by the hitch or the trailer frame but by the seat post itself. You should not pull a trailer using a seat post clamp unless the seat post is steel or heavy walled aluminum. Never pull a trailer using a carbon fiber or other plastic seat post. They do not have the shear strength needed for the job.

The vertical screw allows freedom of movement about that axis and the horizontal screw is fitted through the tongue of the trailer allowing movement about that axis. Use thread locking compound to secure the fasteners on the hitch.

You will find that the trailer pulls easily and tracks perfectly. It is an easy to build project and is a must have for Robobikers everywhere.

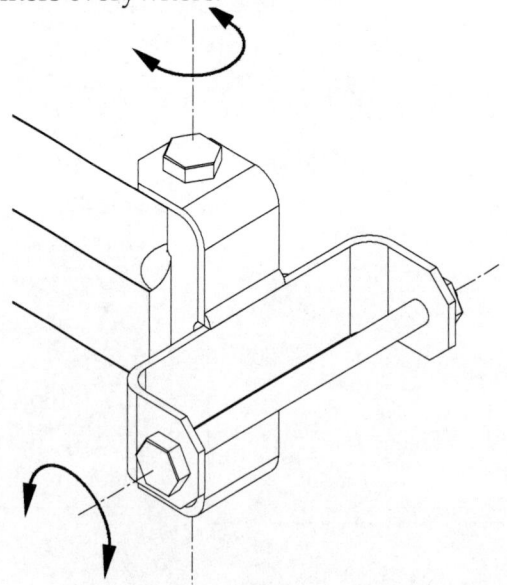

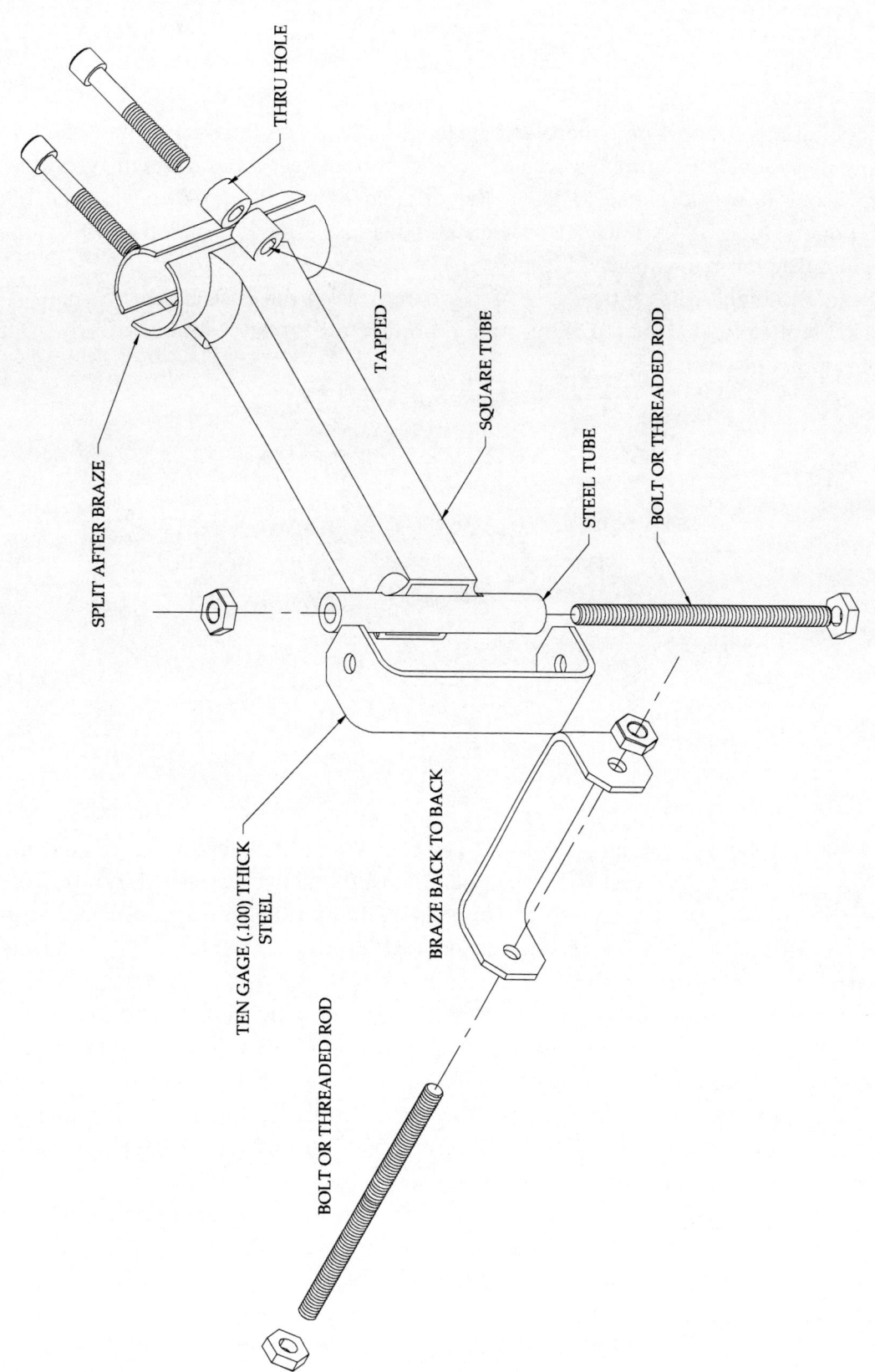

THRU HOLE

TAPPED

SQUARE TUBE

STEEL TUBE

BOLT OR THREADED ROD

SPLIT AFTER BRAZE

TEN GAGE (.100) THICK STEEL

BRAZE BACK TO BACK

BOLT OR THREADED ROD

Semper Quadratus

Robobike has been using square and rectangular cross sections since day one for tooling and welding jigs. Our first recumbent was made with round steel tubes, but when it came time to make a revision, it was decided to leave the original alone and to duplicate the bike with aluminum square tubes. It performed so well and was so easy to build that we adopted this method of building for mainstream designs.

By far, the biggest advantage to using square tube is the ease in which changes can be incorporated. Not only that, but drilling and clamping are greatly simplified when large flat surfaces present themselves as they do.

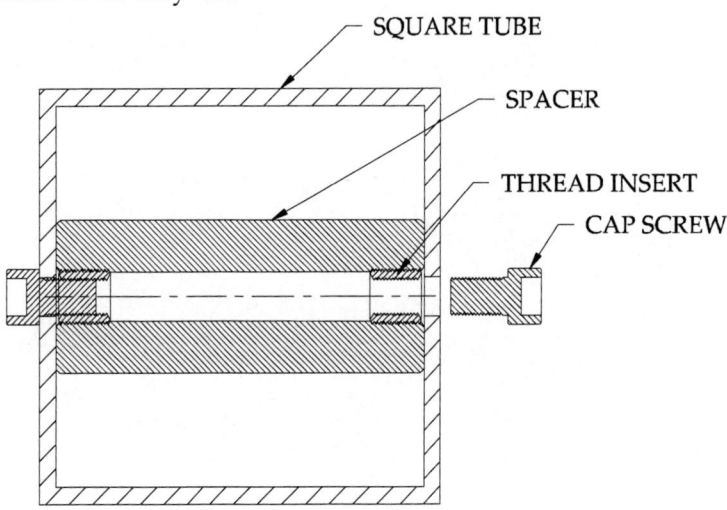

This section view shows an advanced technique where the telescoping frame member has thread inserts installed in each end. The use of the inserts allows disassembly numerous times without worrying about the integrity of the threads. Although the thread inserts are desirable, a bolt all the way through with the requisite washers and nut works well too. If this latter method is used, a piece of aluminum tube may be cut to length and used as a spacer.

One issue that needs to be considered with this construction method and that is the quality of hardware. Poor quality bolts and nuts are often indistinguishable from the good stuff. That is why we use nothing but Grade 5 or Grade 8 hardware bought online from an industrial supplier. We always use coarse threads unless there is a real need for fine threads. We use US standard nuts and bolts but ISO metric hardware is perfectly acceptable. In fact, if the finished bike is used as a travel bike, give some thought to what is available on the shelves of hardware stores at your destination. Having a source of spares available locally cuts down on the spare parts you need to carry in a tool kit. Anyone who has traveled with a bike in developing countries knows that simply finding a screw to fit your application involves some effort.

The following projects illustrate how we Robobikers have used square sections for both bikes and shop tooling. By the way, square tubing compares favorably to round tubes in mass, moment of inertia and section modulus. Download the strength of material calculator at Robobike.com to see the proof.

Building bikes with square tubes is an easy way to get started as a framebuilder.

Giving Direction

By Krilson

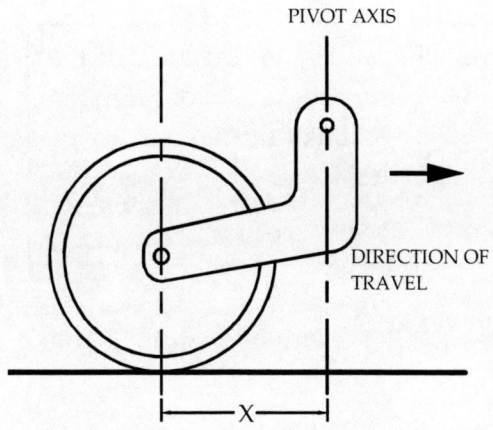

PIVOT AXIS

DIRECTION OF TRAVEL

X

Caster; stability to pivoted wheels while in motion

Stability and control is what steering is all about. Though some bikes, such as long wheel base recumbents, have special needs and ergo, special solutions, most bikes have tried and true steering arrangements. Your home built bike will too.

This first drawing illustrates a fundamental concept for all steered vehicles. The wheel contact patch is behind the point where the steering axis meets the road. The wheel is self centering and seeks its trail position. Dimension X is known as *trail* in all texts describing any steered, wheeled vehicle. It is where good bike designers begin.

The vertical axis was used in the early days of cycling but soon fell out of favor. Though stable, the entire weight of the front end must be shifted in the direction of the turn and once accomplished, a push on the handle bars in the direction of the turn is required to maintain the turn. Such a force is known as understeer.

The second illustration shows a vertical axis such as found on airplanes, shopping carts, and other types of trolleys. Notice the trail has been reduced substantially. Understeer is greatly reduced but still present. The entire weight of the front end must be shifted to execute a turn but this force is less

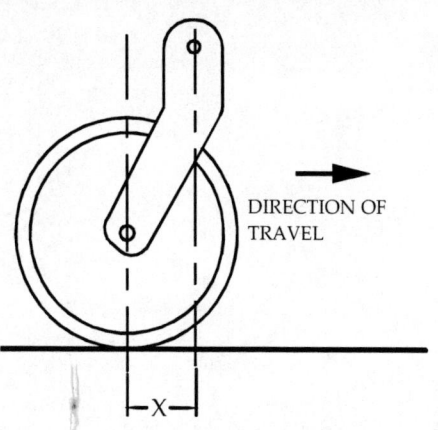

DIRECTION OF TRAVEL

X

than the first example. Some ordinary bicycles used this type of arrangement though X was reduced to almost nothing. Most ordinary bikes, however, used a form of modern steering geometry that features oversteer. This is best described as a push on the bars in the direction opposite the direction of turn to prevent the rate of turn from increasing. Oversteer in modern road bikes is so slight that most riders don't notice it. It is directly related to and a function of trail.

The **short wheel base recumbent** discussed later in this book gives a good explanation of trail as it relates to modern steering geometry. It is an easy concept to understand. The chosen head angle of your home built project drives another control input, especially if allowed to get too radical. That force is that of having to lift the front end as it pivots around an inclined axis, shown here in this third illustration. That force can be overwhelming if the head angle gets too crazy.

Never build a bike with understeering tendencies and keep head angles to well established norms and you won't have any trouble with control. Control is paramount. The Robobike staff push the limits all the time. Too weird, though, and it's a do over.

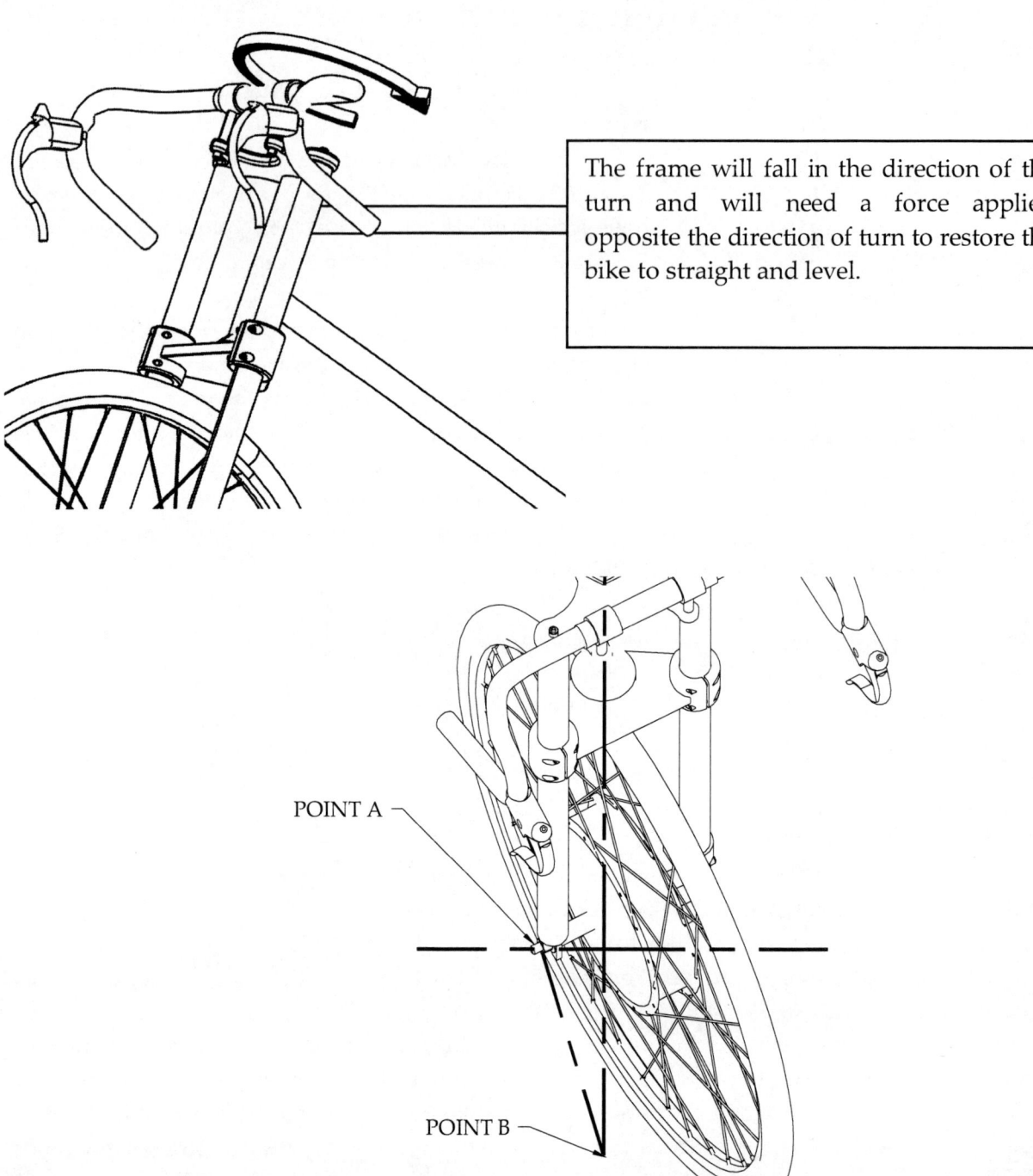

The frame will fall in the direction of the turn and will need a force applied opposite the direction of turn to restore the bike to straight and level.

POINT A

POINT B

Point A is the wheel contact point; Point B is the intersection of the steering axis with the road surface. The greater the distance from point A to point B, the greater the oversteer. Increasing the head angle as measured from the vertical axis increases this tendency. Increasing the wheel diameter increases oversteer. It must be remembered that oversteer is a good thing in bicycle stability unless there is too much. It is directly associated with trail. Designing a stable bike means trail is at least 2 inches but less than four. There are, of course, exceptions to this rule, but it is something that should be checked.

The next chapter is the first project where head angle and trail are set by the builder. Build straight. Build true. Build straight and true.

The Aluminum Limo

Bonita Caliente   Journeyman skills

This is the bike that started our fascination with long wheel bases and dissimilar wheel sizes. It was built by one of our staff who did not have welding skills and during a time when the rest of the crew was busy with streamliner tandem recumbents, motorized unicycles and other useless projects.

History

The original Limo was introduced in 1985 as a child carrier right from the start. The Limo was ridden regularly with the Arizona Bicycle Club based in Phoenix and was retired when the next generation child carrier was ready. This bike was the subject for laughter and derision when first introduced. It must be remembered that the early 1980's was just the beginning of the mountain bike craze and cyclists were even less inclined than they are now to accept anything that didn't fit the mold. Times have changed. The Limo, though still an eye catcher, is less of a sensation today.

The Steel Limo   photo by John Whitford

The bike was introduced with a 27 inch wheel front and a 24 inch wheel aft. It had drop bars, Downtube shifters and a five speed cluster driven by a double chainwheel for a ten speed arrangement covering 36 to 96 gear inches. The bike originally did not have the reclining seat and it became apparent very soon that there was a need for such a feature.

Anyone wanting to play around with building a bicycle rickshaw might want to think about building the prototype using this building technique. The Limo is easy to build and easy to revise. It is also quite a good platform to haul batteries and motors. The building technique, that of using square tubes and assembled with fasteners, was driven by the fact that the builder had access to machine tools but only limited access to a torch. After a year of service, the Limo was converted first into a beer truck by the addition of a keg in place of the baby seat and later chopped up and converted into a short wheel base recumbent. The child carrying duties then fell to the Steel Limo. The Steel Limo did service as a high speed, long range battery powered bike with the addition of a 750 watt series wound motor driving the rear wheel. The rear area was large enough and rigid enough to carry 50kg of sealed lead-acid batteries. This is 110 pounds of batteries. There will be more discussion later about this remarkable bicycle in the electric bike section.

The name, Aluminum Limo, is quite descriptive. However, as an amusing twist of coincidence, the builder of this bike, while working in a shop in northern Mexico, was introduced to a co-worker named Alfredo Limo. Consequently, the bike then became known as Al Limo, although it loses its effect when translated into Spanish.

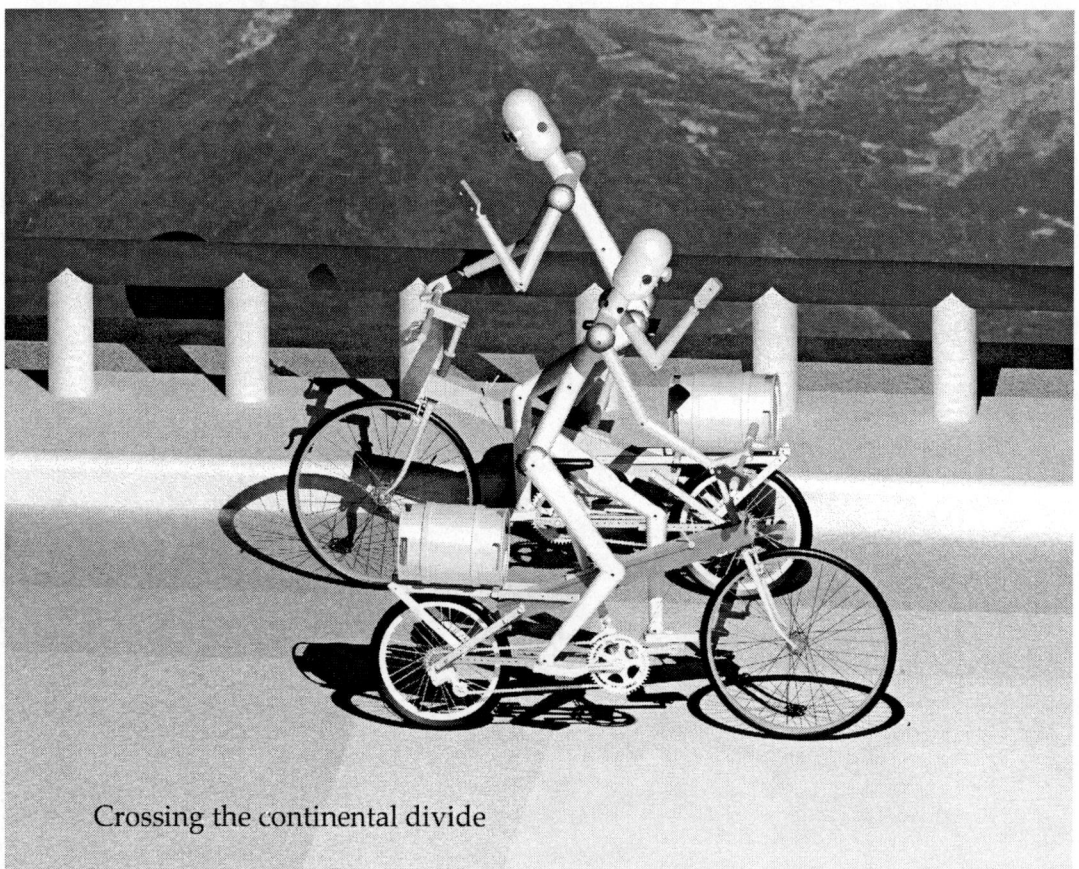

Crossing the continental divide

The Kegger, as it is known, also transports building materials, musical instruments, purchases from the market and numerous other hard-to-transport-by-bicycle items.

Although a twenty inch wheel is shown in the drawings and in this picture, the only copy of the square tube version of this bike used the already mentioned 24 inch wheel. Any diameter wheel will be acceptable though the working drawings show a BMX wheel. The Steel Limo was built with the smaller wheel.

A tremendous amount was learned about heavy hauling from the Limo series of bikes. The biggest being just how awful these bikes are when ridden solo. The required structure makes for a rigid frame and the unloaded condition moves the center of gravity forward several inches. The sensation is a bike that is hard nosed and not light and nimble like most bikes. Short of carrying ballast to move the CG aft, there is nothing that can be done about this.

Design

Load carrying is the assigned task for this bicycle. Like all good designers, we looked around for something to copy that carries a load and can be made to have two wheels, one of which driven by a chain. The categories of load carrying machines we examined were wheelbarrows, golf carts, shopping carts, dollies, and trailers. Since positioning the load is a big part of designing a bike that is a pleasure to ride, weight and balance techniques were applied to find the general layout. We at Robobike place a great emphasis on weight and balance. Even more important than weight and balance is control of the bike and its load, especially with a child aboard. These are fundamental concepts that drive the design.

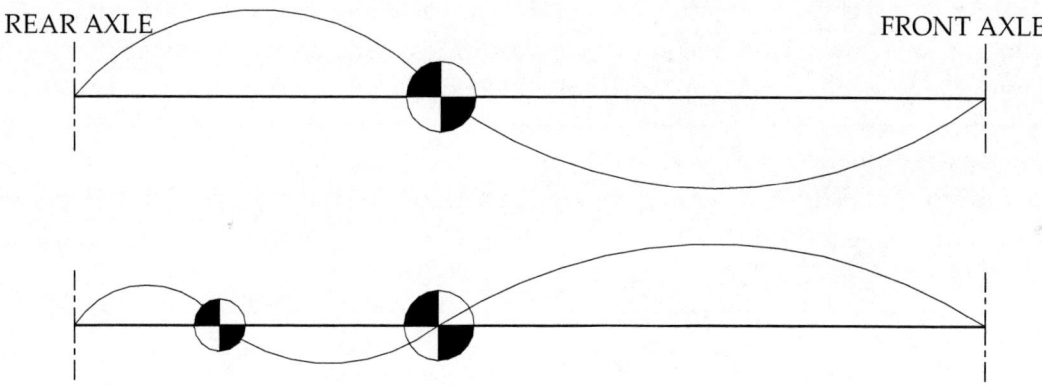

Top View Looking down, front wheel to the right

Control inputs act directly on the mass centers of the loads via the structure of the frame. The rider, by far the bigger load, must be connected rigidly to the rear wheel and to the mass center that is the rear passenger. This prevents the control inputs becoming out of phase to the reactions to those inputs. If that were allowed to happen, the bike becomes uncontrollable, entering into a series of oscillations from which recovery is uncertain. These phenomena meant the death of many an airplane when powered flight left the era of open cockpit fabric covered biplanes and entered the era of modern, high speed all metal airplanes. The prototype of the Japanese Zero crashed during its development because of flutter, a type of oscillation similar to what we have here. The corrective action for this condition is to increase rigidity. That usually means a more massive structure or a change to a stiffer material.

Loads are rarely, if ever, static while under way. Structural members are subjected to cyclic compression, tension, bending and torsion. Not only should a frame be rigid, but it must be stiff. It is important for the frame designer to know the difference between these two requirements. A frame built using bamboo can be made to be rigid but it cannot be made to have much stiffness.

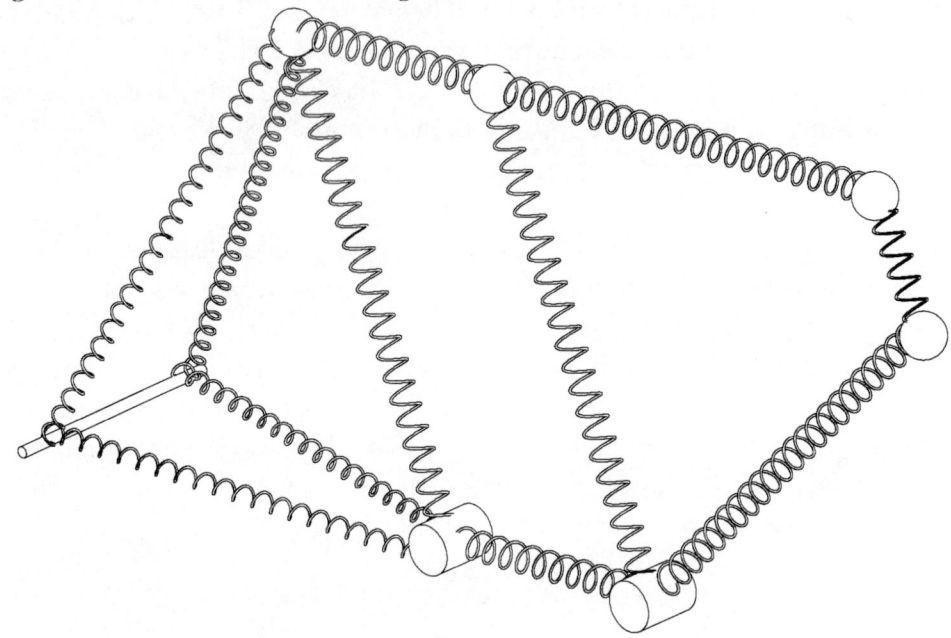

It is common practice to describe a structure such as a bike frame as a system of springs in accordance to Hooke's law. Individual springs have stiffness. The complete system is said to have rigidity. Manipulating stiffness and rigidity is what bike designers do.

> Any object that is initially displaced slightly from a stable equilibrium point will oscillate about its equilibrium position. It will, in general, experience a restoring force that depends on the displacement from equilibrium.
>
> Hooke's law

Our bike was meant to be built from square section aluminum right from the beginning. That being said, a massive cantilevered aluminum frame was taking shape on the drawing board of the chief designer at Robobike, Bonita Caliente.

Balance

A conventional road bike, built to the usual proportions, balances with roughly 60 per cent of the total vehicle weight on the rear wheel. Using 40" as a standard wheelbase, the balance point, with rider, is 24" aft of the front axle. For all practical purposes, the weight of the bike can be ignored and this balance point can be assumed to be that of the rider in a normal riding position. This constraint, the center of gravity of the rider, is the starting point for a design whose goals are excellent child carrying characteristics, plenty of room for the passenger, a 40/60 front/rear weight distribution, and a stout frame. The terms weight, arm and moments will be used for the following bit of calculation.

Wt. lbs		Arm Inches	Moments lb-in
Weight of rider	170	24	4080
Weight of passenger	40	46	1840
Wight of frame front	20	0	0
Weight of frame rear	20	48	960
Totals	250	NA	6880

Total moments/total weight = 27.5 inches Weight distribution per cent front/rear 43/57

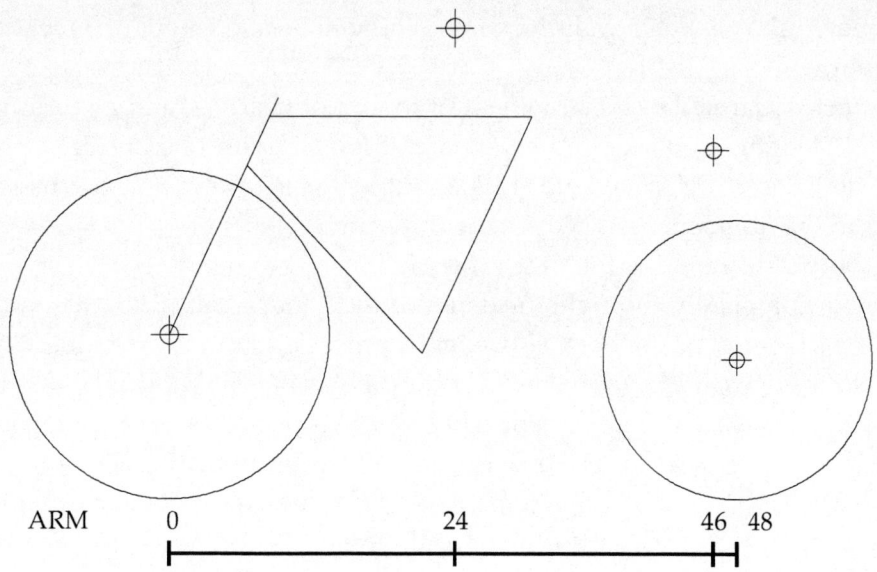

A bike with a 48" wheel base, a 170 pound rider at 24" aft of datum and a 40 pound child 46" aft of datum balances 27.5" aft of datum. Datum is the front axle. This is our design.

Concept

The Limo began as a non traditional bike right from the start. All parts of the bike were to be built without the benefit of any welding technology. The skills were not to be artificially constrained as the builder was in possession of many years experience in the machine trades. Even so, needless complexity is usually an indication of a poor design so complicated mechanisms were avoided. What appears to be hard to build bottom brackets and head tubes are actually quite easy for an experienced machinist. There is no need for CNC equipment anywhere in this design though it is always nice to be able to use these machines.

The small wheel was chosen for several reasons. A small wheel is easier to move forward than a larger wheel, creating extra room for the passenger. Bringing the wheel forward moves the center of gravity aft relative to the axles. Center of gravity placement is always a concern with a long wheel base bike. These bikes tend to be nose heavy unless remote steering permits placing the operator somewhere other than within reach of the front end. There is no inherent performance advantage with the smaller wheel and only a slight disadvantage in the form of increased rolling resistance. Notice that our bike has lots of room in the passenger compartment and changes to the passenger area can be made without having to work around a bigger wheel. In response to the fact that children enter sleep mode when transported by bike, the rear seat reclines thirty degrees. The recliner controls a sleeping child much better than the upright position. Square section aluminum was chosen as the medium. This selection was made to reduce the work needed to incorporate revisions expected with a growing child. The same bike built in steel using brazed tubes is faster, more efficient and less tiring over the same distance. These attributes, however, are the result of the increased stiffness of steel over aluminum and the reduced flexure in the joints. Despite that, this is a very rigid bike.

Building the Limo

You will need a milling machine capable of boring a 1.375″ diameter hole and a lathe with the capacity to thread both right hand and left hand 24 TPI. It is possible to use the lathe to do the boring work if you know how to fixture the square tube on the cross slide but we won't cover that here. Every piece of this bike is aluminum except the fasteners. Let's start with the main tube, a piece of 3 inch square tube with .125 wall thickness. You will need a length of 3 feet.

The main tube

The three inch square tube has a moment of inertia of nearly 2, and a modulus of elasticity of 10 million. A 24″ length supported on the ends and loaded with one hundred pounds right in the middle has a deflection of close to zero. Talk about factor of safety! You can use a smaller tube if you want, but run the numbers first. We use the three inch tube.

Drill and bore a 1″ hole for the seat tube (more on that later). The head tube requires a 1.375″ diameter hole completely through on center an inch and a half from one end. Don't worry too much about the precision of the hole. However, it must be square to the tube. Get a nice clean hole and break all the edges. You can make the head tube to fit. The head tube is pushed through the hole and held in place with epoxy cement. The cement is to prevent the front end of your bike from dropping out of the frame when the bike is lifted off the ground. There are other ways to affix the two, such as a split clamp, but the cement is quick and easy. Besides, it gives everyone something to talk about. Don't apply the cement until you are absolutely sure it is together forever because it is quite a task to get them apart.

Drill one of the holes for the chain stays. You will drill the second hole later at assembly. All the attachments, such as water bottle cages and down tube shifters, are added later.

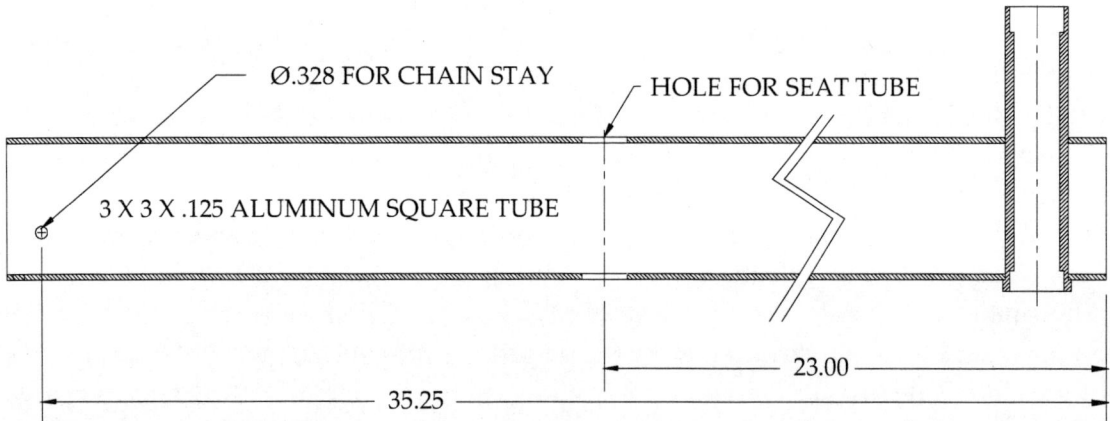

Main tube showing location of head tube, seat tube and hole for chain stays. Make the head tube with an over all length to match your fork. The addition of a second passenger adds very little that can be construed as extra loads to the steering axis outside the usual forces that occur during heavy braking. Bore the head tube for the head set and don't forget a generous chamfer to ease assembly of the bearing cups/cones. The prototype used all road bike stuff and a fork with a 1″-24 threaded steering tube. The inch and three eighths diameter can be adjusted to match the hole bored in the square tube. The 30.2 mm, the headset cup body diameter, is approximately equal to 1 3/16 inches. *(Remember, nothing beats a measurement!)* The staff at Robobike always installs the lower cup and checks it for runout in the lathe using a dial indicator. It is not likely you'll find a problem but it has happened. We paid big money for a fancy head set a few years back and found that the concentricity was not very good. Since then, we always use the cheap stuff as it is often as good and easier to discard. Use the tailstock to drive the cup home.

Head Tube

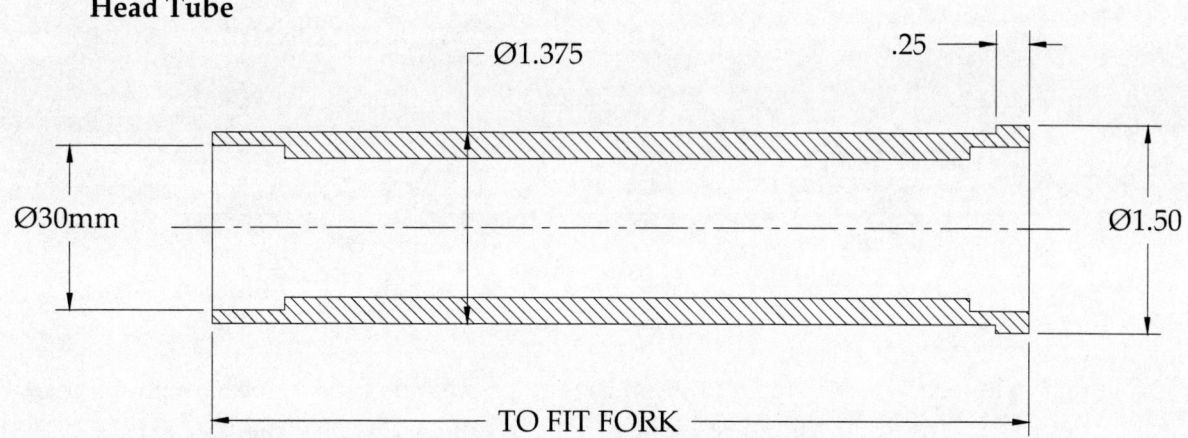

The head tube is made from steel or aluminum.

Measure your bearing cup before boring the head tube for a light press fit. The 30mm shown here is approximate.

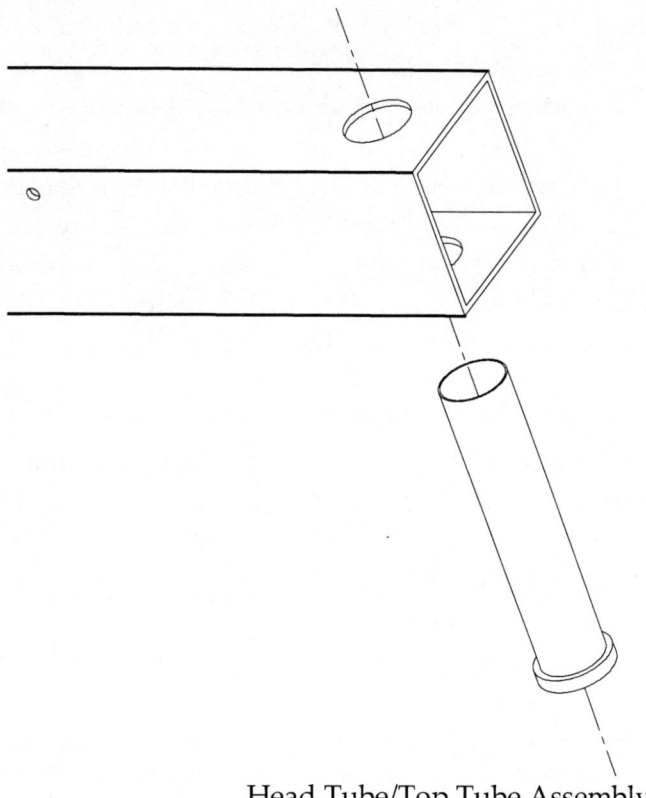

Head Tube/Top Tube Assembly

Upper chain stays

The upper chain stays are ½ x 1 rectangular section 6061 T-6 aluminum. They need to be clamped together when drilled to ensure alignment. This pair of stays gets clearance holes everywhere except for the tapped hole for the rear changer.

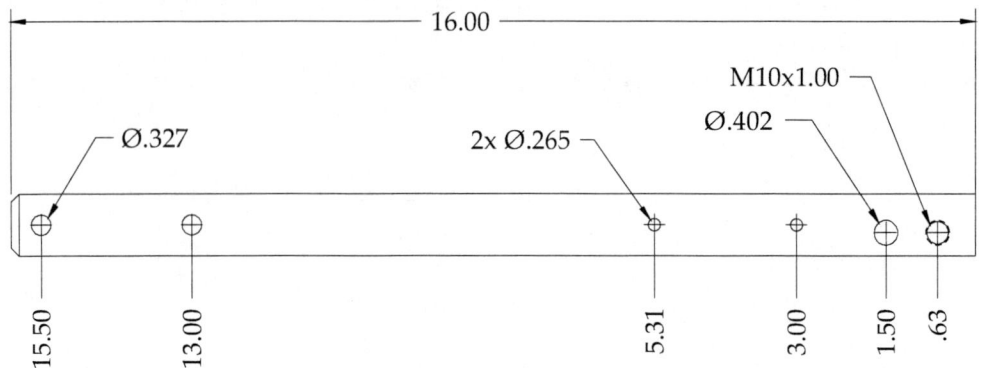

Most rear axles are 10mm diameter but on the minus side. Be sure to measure the diameter of your axle before drilling the axle holes. Notice that the hole drilled for the rear axle is biased towards one edge to give some extra wall thickness on one side. Do not slot the axle hole. Wheel removal on this bike requires that a stay be removed first. A M10x1 tap will be needed if the rear changer is to be mounted in the normal fashion. Your favorite industrial supply web site will gladly send you a tap if you can't find one locally. Many of these ecompanies make more emoney on eshipping and ehandling than they do on their emerchandise so be sure to get assurances from a customer service representative that they will not send you six trivial items in six separate shipping containers. The ways of the eworld are startling indeed so take care. Likewise, when buying aluminum online for this project, buy all you need at one time from the same source.

Some low end bicycles have a stamped steel bracket for mounting the rear changer. These work well and incorporate a means of adjusting the angle of the dangle, but there are so many of them that it is difficult to come up with a blanket statement that covers their use. You can use one if you want. We like them. Bicycle manufacturers use them, among other reasons, to reduce assembly rejects at the factory.

Prepare the spacers needed to buttress the inside of the 3" square main tube and the spacers between the chain stays and main tube. Assemble everything you have so far for an alignment check. Afterward, drill the second chain stay mounting hole in the main tube.

We've changed the arrangement of the spacers since this bike was new. Originally, the spacers were one inch rounds. The inner nuts used in conjunction with tubular spacers allow the removal of a single stay. Servicing the rear wheel requires removal of a stay. With the old arrangement, the entire rear triangle lost its alignment when the wheel was removed. Even using air free tires, the wheel must be removed from time to time. The current arrangement works much better. Alignment is maintained if a single stay is removed. The threaded rod may be increased to 3/8 diameter but that is only necessary for big loads or severe service such as the electric motor option. The biggest risk to breaking the bolts is over tightening. We buy alloy steel (4340) threaded rod instead of cheap hardware store rod. Some of this inexpensive thread stock is lacking in quality and may contain weaknesses in the form of poorly rolled threads. Always use a torque wrench.

58

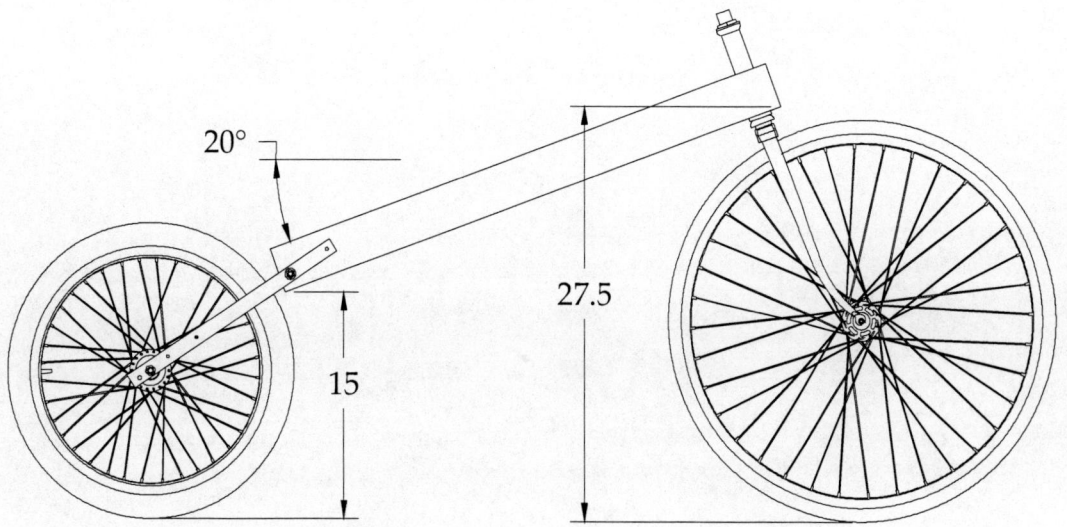

20°

27.5

15

Alignment check and drilling the second hole for chain stays

Clamp the main tube to an upright and adjust until you reach the head tube angle you want to use. The angle shown here results in nearly 3 inches of trail when used with a fork with 2 inches of recurve. Use 15 degrees with straight forks.
Hint: Prepare the lower chain stays, seat tube, bottom bracket and include them in the mockup

This building technique does not require a jig for assembly but care must be taken that everything is straight when the bolts are brought up to specified torque. Alignment is checked with straightedges, squares and a calibrated eyeball. There is a substantial margin of safety in the design but that margin erodes quickly if poor quality hardware is subjected to extreme amounts of torque during the tightening process.

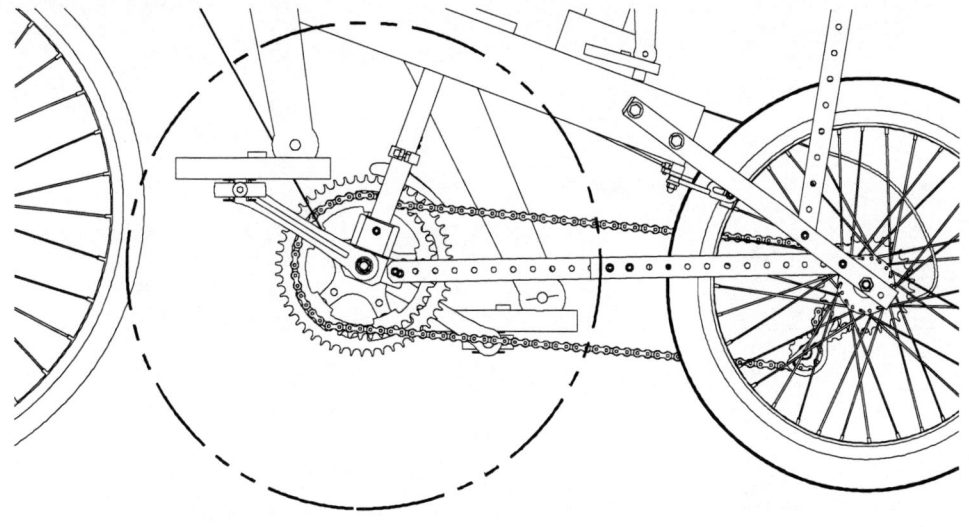

Shoe Clearance

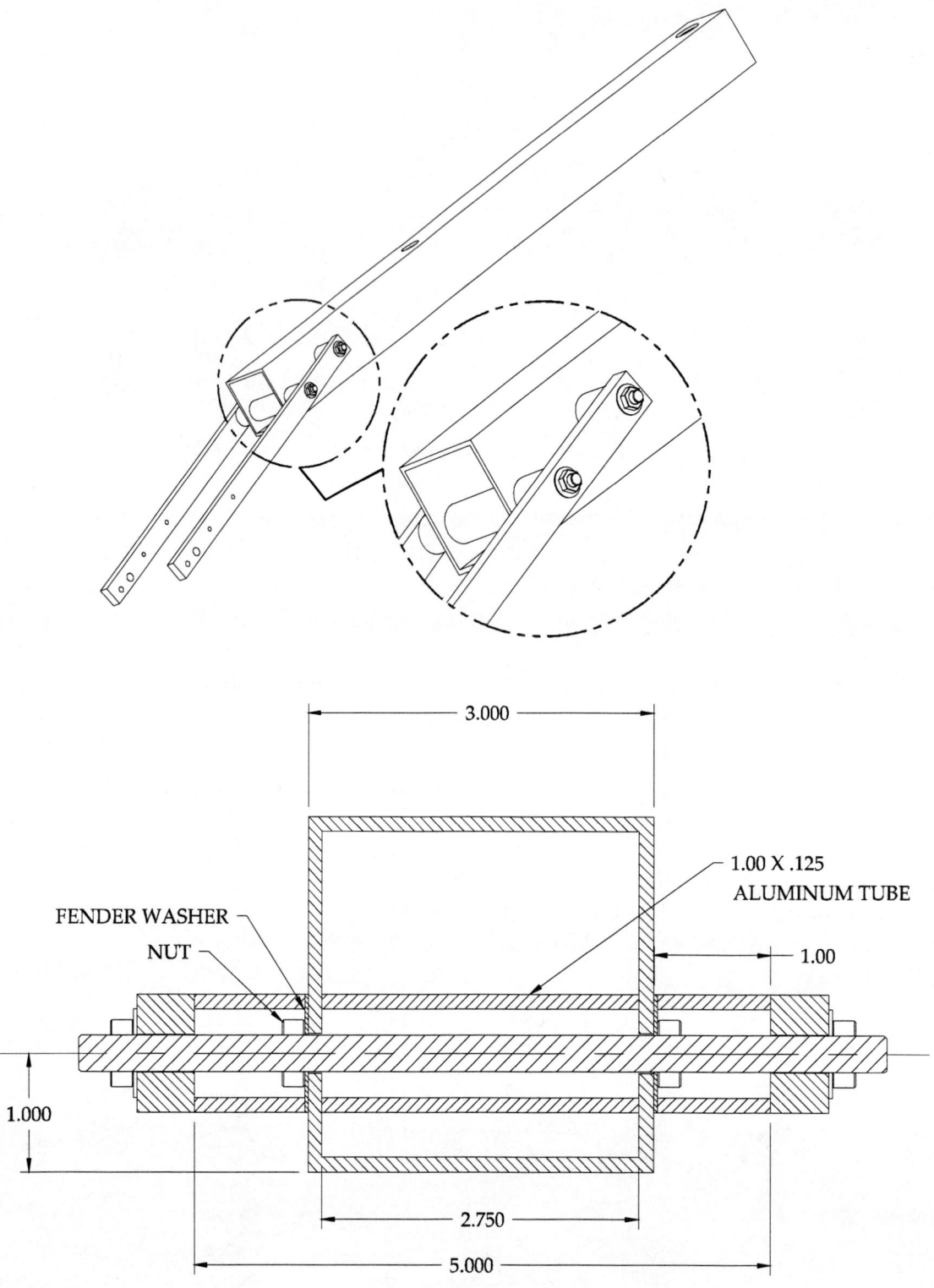

Looking forward normal to the main tube; the spacers are one inch aluminum tubes with a .125 wall. (Ø8.5mm), the bolts are 5/16 or M8. Use Grade 5 or grade 8 and not any of the lesser grades.

Rear Triangle

The stays in place at this point define the look of the bike and, to a certain extent, are all that is needed to make a bicycle. However, this not being a static world, things are not that simple. Each pedal impulse causes the wheel to move forward as a result of the tension on the chain. Coupled with the increase in the wheel base when the weight of the rider is applied to the frame, some additional structure is in order. That is certainly obvious to all but the most casual observer but this being a different kind of bike, the obvious needs to be stated. We at Robobike find that it is much better to include the obvious in the description of a project than to leave it out. Confusion is avoided. The structure that completes the triangulation of the rear triangle comprises the lower chain stays, the bottom bracket and the seat tube.

The Power System

The bottom bracket, lower chain stays, seat tube and seat tube clamp make up the power system.

The bottom bracket is truly an odd bit of design work. There is much that can be done to reduce the blockiness of the thing but why bother? Robobike has a pair of threaded spuds (lathe tooling that fits the headstock taper) that accept bottom brackets so the square ends can be turned but that operation is not shown here. The guys around the shop began referring to this as the industrial strength bottom bracket but as sure as morning follows night, the design began showing up on other bikes around the shop. Funny thing, it was first sketched by the mother of the child for whom this bike was originally made.

The lug for mounting the lower chain stays will be tapped ¼-20 from each side. The left hand thread for the fixed cup is on the chainwheel side just like on a real bicycle. Nothing else is really important so have a bit of fun designing the look of this Robobracket. Don't make the mistake of trying to lighten it up too much. Leave it stout. There's a lot of stress on this piece. Lots.

The seat tube clamp, a split affair of the easiest construction, is used to set the bottom bracket ground clearance height, the next step in the assembly process. Drill a one inch hole, make a saw cut(s), drill 5 clearance holes and that is just about all there is to it. This can be made out of any scrap piece of ½"aluminum. Its primary duty is to take the axial load on the seat tube in the form of the rider's weight.

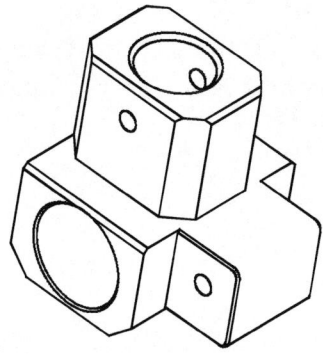

Robobracket

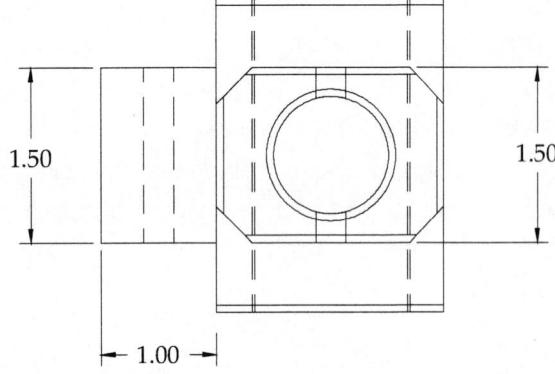

1.50   1.50

1.00

The bottom bracket incorporates
a socket for the seat tube and
two tapped holes for the chain
stays. It is an aluminum hogout.

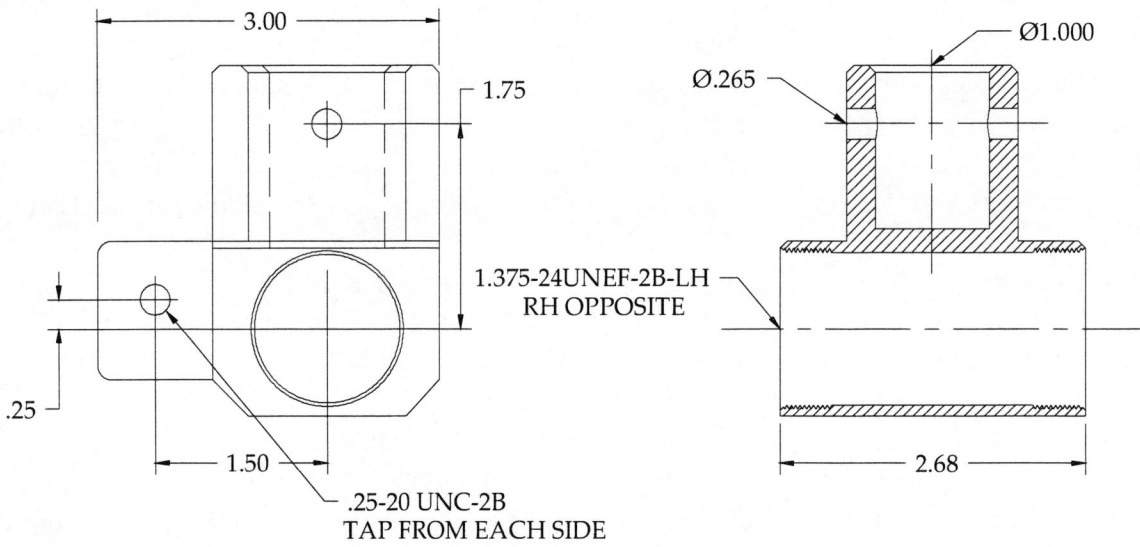

3.00

1.75

Ø.265   Ø1.000

1.375-24UNEF-2B-LH
RH OPPOSITE

.25

1.50

2.68

.25-20 UNC-2B
TAP FROM EACH SIDE

This hog out should be made from 6061-T6. The one inch diameter is meant to fit the one inch seat tube, whether a solid round of aluminum or a steel tube. Those of you with bike building experience will cringe at the thought of using a solid piece of aluminum for the seat tube. While certainly not the first choice for this application, it must be remembered that the prototype used this arrangement mostly because we had a piece laying around. It worked fine.

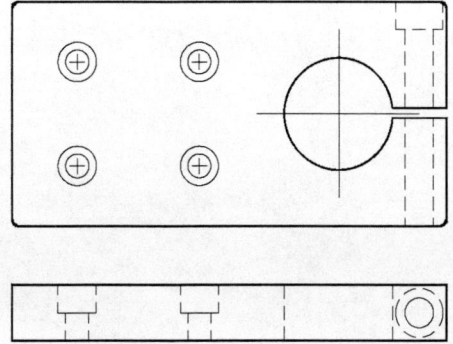

The seat tube clamp sets the bottom bracket height and transfers the axial load on the seat tube to the main tube.

The seat tube clamp must fix the seat tube to the main tube. The four cap screws securing the clamp to the main tube require nuts. The best way to accomplish that is to drill a clearance hole through the wall opposite on the main tube allowing socket access. One screw is sufficient but four is better. You are clamping a piece of half inch thick material to a piece of 1/8" material so fatigue cracking around the hole is a distinct possibility especially with heavy riders. A second clamp placed on the bottom of the main tube should be considered if you plan on riding hills or if you are a heavy rider. The concern is not failure but squeaks. This is not a trivial piece so take some care. The saw cut to allow collapse of the clamp must be wide enough to do the job so two cuts is the recommended procedure. Use a 1/16" feeler gage to judge the minimum gap. Also, the hole for the ¼" clamp bolt should be drilled 9/32 through and the bolt installed with washers and a nut. No tapped holes in bare aluminum here, please. Put a piece of 1 inch round aluminum (6061 T6) through the main tube, install the bottom bracket and set the ground clearance with the clamp. You will have to work on the seat tube later to affix the saddle so be sure to mark the location of the seat tube in the main tube. Drill the seat tube for a bolt on the bottom bracket end. The lower chain stays complete the power system.

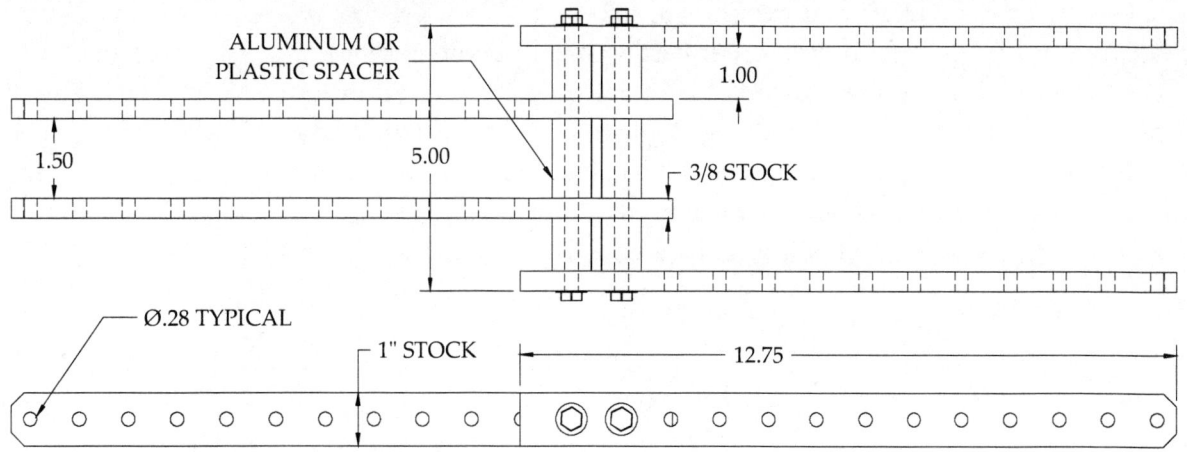

Lower Chain Stays Assembly

There is not much to explain here. You will have to prepare four pieces of 3/8 x 1.0 stock 12.75 inches in length. Decide where the holes are drilled as each bike will be slightly different. There is enough overlap to compensate for errors so don't worry too much about getting these exactly right. Through bolts with nuts are shown in this view but a much cleaner assembly results from using ¼-20 socket head cap screws five inches long. You need tapped holes and thread inserts to use the five inch bolts. The one area of this design where shoe clearance is a problem is right here. There's not much clearance side to side. With an average shoe size (45) clicked in an SPD, there is an inch clearance from the heel of the shoe on the head side of the bolt and ¾ " on the nut side. This is using a six inch long bolt trimmed just a bit after the nut is installed. The five inch cap screws offer a bit more clearance for each shoe.

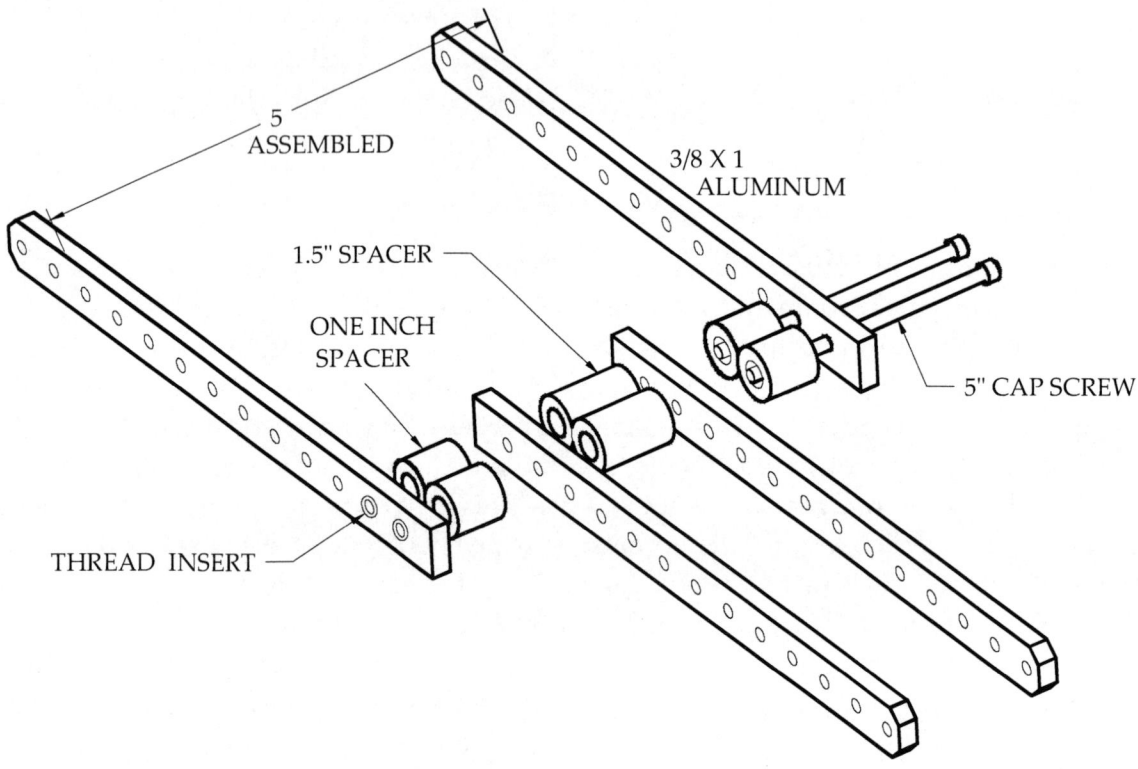

The lower chain stays perform several functions. They prevent the rear wheel and bottom bracket from moving closer to each other during each power impulse and they keep the bottom bracket aligned with the axis of the bike. They increase the overall rigidity of the frame. The first item is not insignificant. When an impulse of 100 pounds force is applied to a crank arm of 7 inches length, 700 inch-lbs of torque is generated. Translate this torque through a chain wheel with a 3 inch radius and you put the chain in tension to the tune of 233 pounds. Tension = 7/3 x 100lb. A big guy standing on the pedals and working through a tiny chain wheel can do way more than that, so do good work.

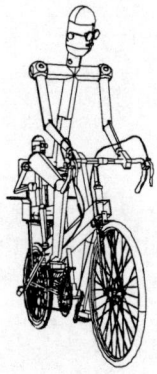

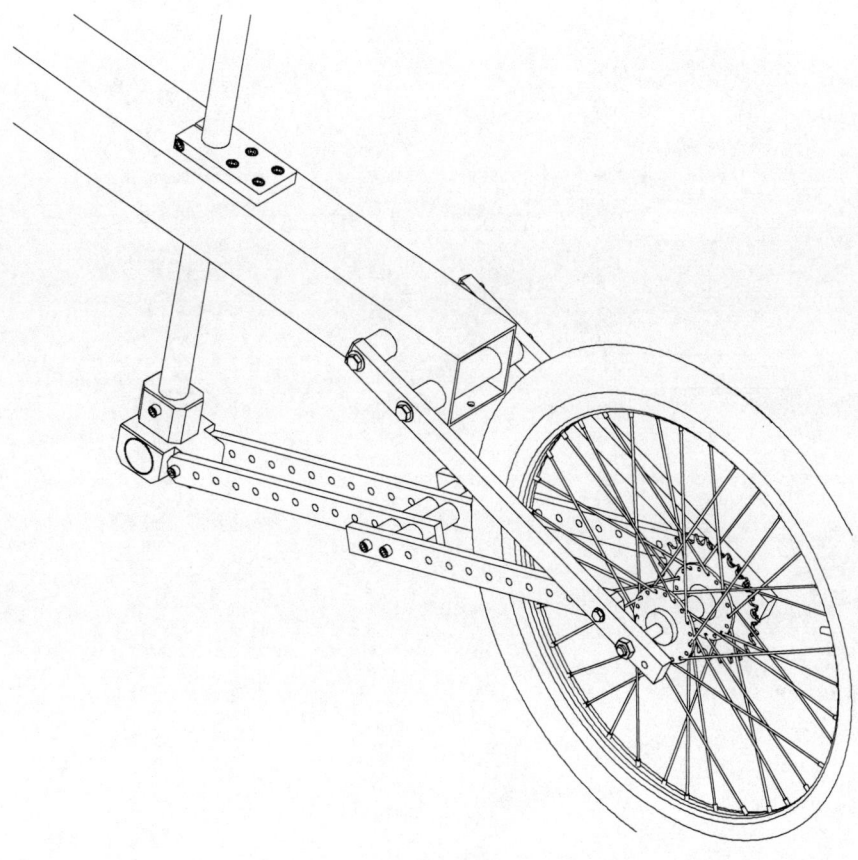

Install the bottom bracket cups, bearings and axle, the crankset, chain and rear changer and get ready for the fitting up. To get to the point shown here in this drawing, the seat tube and seat tube clamp must be ready to go. Because we made the prototype with a piece of one inch round aluminum for the seat tube (not a tube), that is how it is presented here. The reason we used the round instead of a tube is because we had one in the shop and we didn't have a tube. If you don't like this idea, then back up to square one and have a look at all the details that cross paths with the seat tube. The hole in the main tube, the seat tube clamp and the bottom bracket will have to be modified to use a tube. We stick with the original design because it works and the cantilever has not been tested with other size tubes. The round is more expensive that a tube and that could be reason enough to change. A one inch round this length weighs less than 2 lbs (.9kg). We have included drawings showing a 1.25 x .125 steel tube substituted for the round. This is overkill for a seat tube unless you are building with low carbon steel. Remember, the one inch round was used because it was laying around the shop. No other reason.

For those of you who have an interest in comparing the two pieces:
The one inch round suspended on supports 24" apart and loaded with 100 pounds dead center, the deflection is .06 inches. This is same amount as a 1.125 x .09 tube.
The 1.25 x .125 tube deflects .04".
The inch and a quarter tube weighs only 57% as much as the round and is stronger. If this is important to you, then make the substitution. Either one is sufficient. The important part is that the saddle is supported by a frame element cantilevered out from the main tube. The cantilever makes for a much cleaner frame and works with multiple configurations.

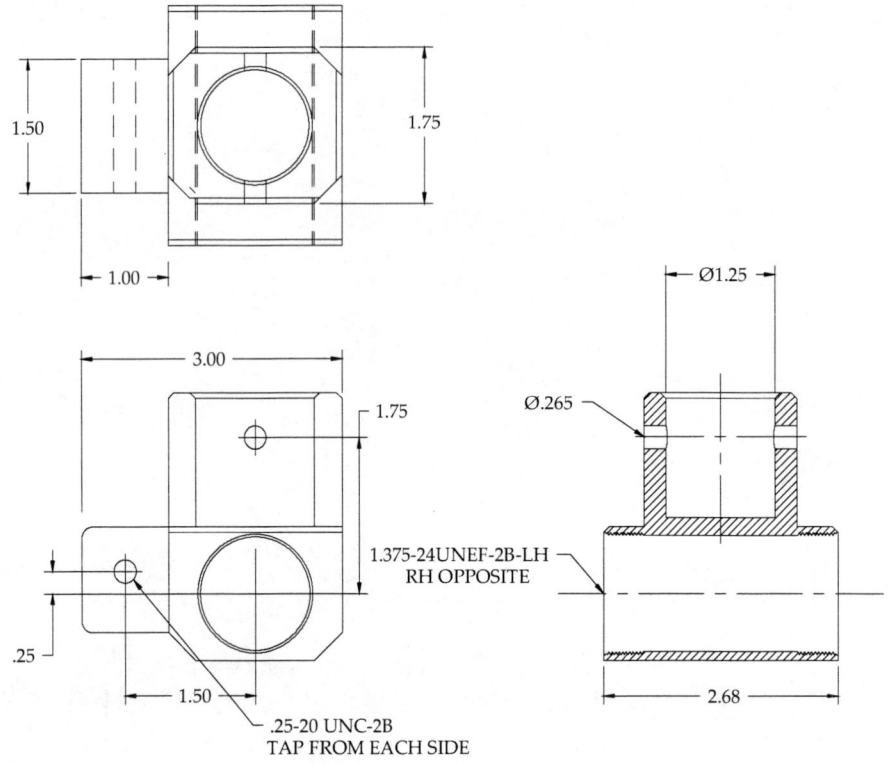

The bottom bracket that fits the 1.250 diameter seat tube

The Passenger Seat

The whole purpose of building this project is the transport of a child. Although we've used this bike to haul concrete, guitar amps, batteries and motors, child carrying is its reason for being. Consequently, we will show that aspect of the bike.

There are some "one size fits all" child seats around that clamp onto standard issue bicycles. Though hardly the best solution for child carrying, valuable insight can be gained by close scrutiny of these accessories. By all means, take a look at these seats. Notice particularly the seat belt and any other restraint system. Your seat will incorporate a restraint system. One feature these seats lack is provision for a sleeping child. Young children especially will spend a substantial portion of ride time asleep. The child seat on the Limo reclines up to 30 degrees.

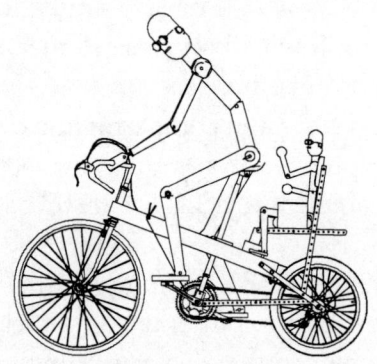

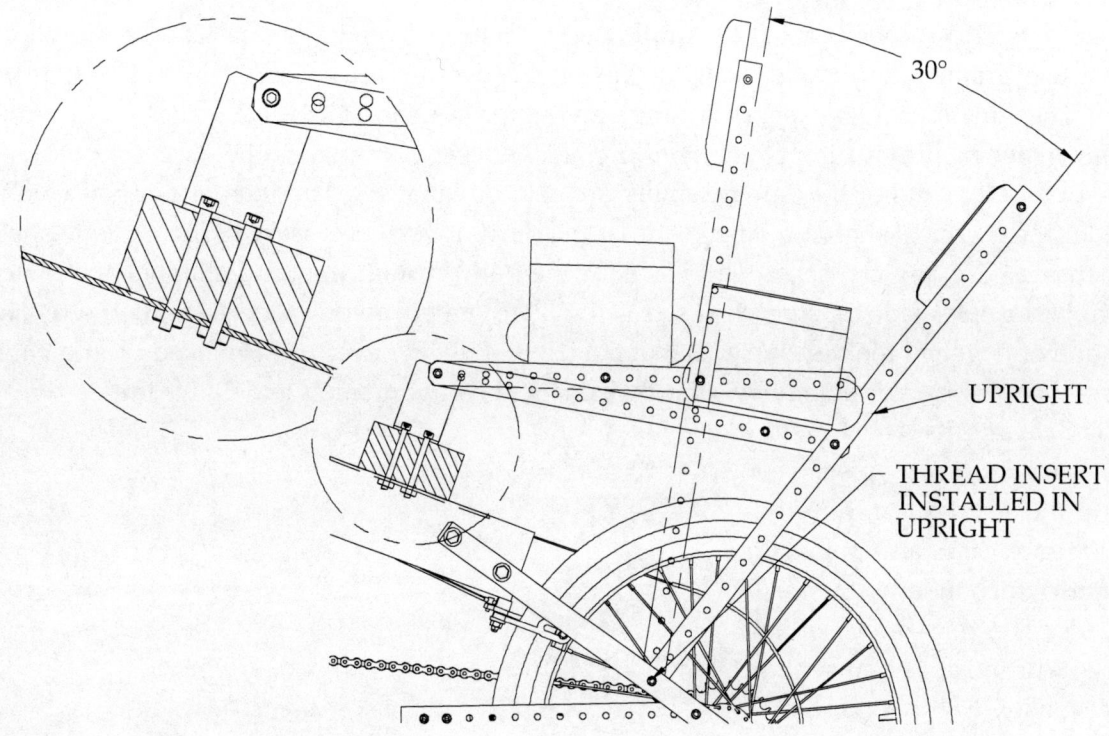

30°

UPRIGHT

THREAD INSERT
INSTALLED IN
UPRIGHT

To make a thorough examination of this bike seat, it is best to look at four separate subassemblies. Those are; the nose pivot, the seat and its attachment, the uprights and head rest and finally, the restraint system.

Note the section view above showing the cap screws inserted through the channel, the plastic spacer and the main tube. These screws anchor the entire seat assembly. Do not cut corners, these two bolts need to be properly torqued and safetied, preferably by use of a nylon lock nut designed for this purpose. Or, if you would rather, this is certainly an appropriate application for thread locking compound.

The Nose Pivot

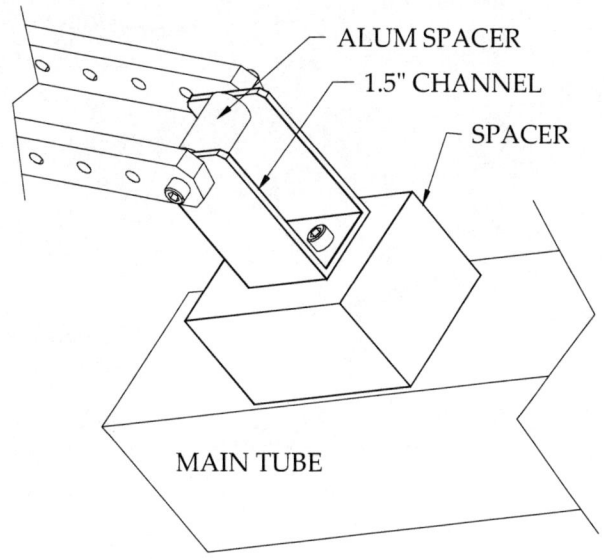

ALUM SPACER

1.5" CHANNEL

SPACER

MAIN TUBE

Please refer to the nose pivot illustration . The piece marked "spacer" can be aluminum, plastic or close grained hardwood. This is one of those rare cases when a wooden spacer is acceptable. The function of the spacer is to raise your passenger an extra 2 inches off the road. Raising the center of gravity improves handling. The spacer also makes the assembly easier to build. The other elements of this sub-assembly are self explanatory. The inch and a half channel can be wider than what is shown but be aware of the design work necessary to incorporate such a change. You may use any cap screw you want for the bolt through the rails, channel and spacer. Our design philosophy is to use the same size screw everywhere so only one size Allen wrench is carried in the emergency tool kit. We at Robobike use ¼-20 whenever we are faced with a choice like this. As you can see, this assembly is hardly a challenge but attention to detail is imperative.

The Seat and its Attachment

Another simple piece of work. Bend the seat bottom out of a piece of .06 thick 6061 aluminum. It is secured to the channel with small button heads. The rails and channel are also 6061-T6 mostly because that is the easiest alloy to buy online. All the holes in the ⅜ x 1 aluminum rails are tapped except for the two for the

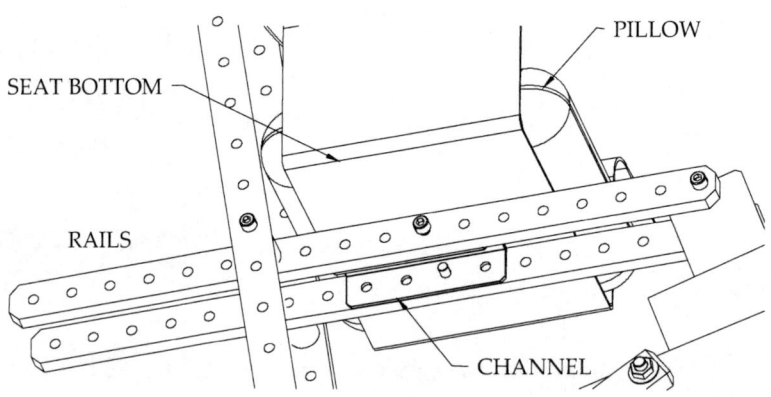

nose pivot. Moving the seat fore and aft requires that the cap screws be removed. The channel has clearance holes in the side and the cap screws pin the channel in position. There is no need to clamp it further, but use wing nuts as a safety feature. The weight of the passenger will hold it down in position. The channel is 1.5 wide with a 1/8 wall. With that said let's look at the...

Uprights and Head Rest

Tap the holes and install thread inserts on the bottom end of the uprights. You want to avoid using nuts on these pivot screws because of the possible interference with the chain. When going from upright to recliner, these screws need to be loosened and then

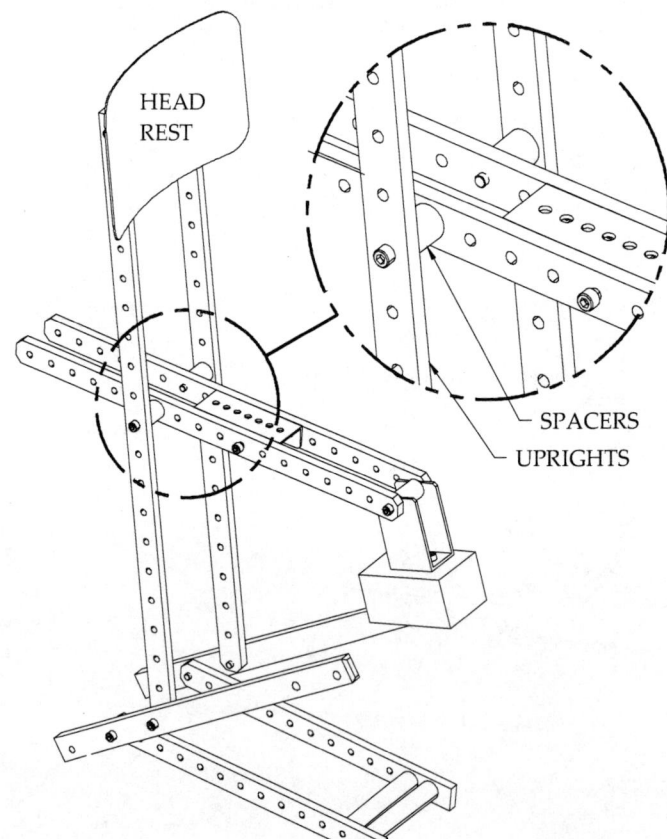

retightened. That's the easiest

solution to making a convertible seat. The head rest is 1100 aluminum or plastic. Your passenger will be wearing a helmet so be sure the head rest actually supports the head. Head support is most important when the child is asleep.

The spacers have through holes and the seat rails have tapped holes. Use a screw that is long enough so there are visible threads when tightened. That is a good fail safe way of knowing everything is drawn up tight. When going from recliner to upright or vice versa, remember to tighten and loosen the screws in the same order and use a checklist even if it is only memorized. A sample check list is:

Nose Pivot Screws	check	Seat Rail Screws	check
Lower Pivot Screws	check	Dog Defense System	check

The restraint system must have at a minimum a lap belt, a multi-point shoulder harness and a foot rest. Be sure to use a clasp or means of attachment that cannot be manipulated by the child. Handlebars are an option but get in the way when loading and unloading the seat.

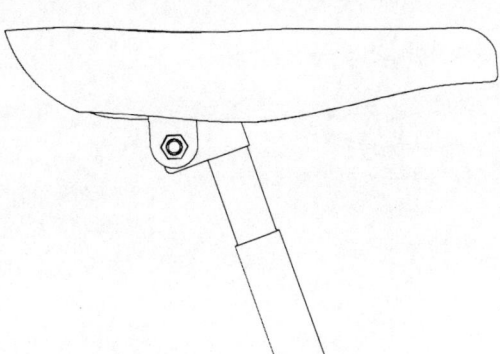

Saddle Adjustment

The Limo is not an easily adjusted piece of equipment. Everything is fixed, including the saddle height. The saddle clamp is one of those steel clamps made up of a bunch of stamped pieces. To make it work, the seat tube is turned on one end to 7/8" diameter and trimmed to length with a hack saw. That's right; saddle height adjustment is done with a hack saw so if you cut off too much, it is too short. How's that for low tech? It's really not as bad as it sounds though sharing the bike between two or more riders is almost impossible. Remember, this is a custom bike built for one rider. This detail, coupled with the need of a split bushing on the front changer to make the clamp secure, might be reason enough to use a larger tube than the one inch round used in the drawings. It's your bike so you can do anything you want. The original worked perfectly with the configuration shown and was ridden regularly for years. This is the simplest, most elegant solution for mounting a saddle on the end of a round. Besides, it is easy to measure a bike that fits you and transfer that measurement to your project.

Other issues for fitting up the Limo are shifters and brakes. Stem shifters are the easiest. We used our own modified down tube shifters. Use caliper brakes to save work. If you want brakes suitable for mountain riding, use disks front and rear. Avoid the brakes that advertise as being the lightest in the field, you'll pay more and won't be happy with the performance. Carrying a child around town on level ground is what this bike is designed for so don't lose track of that. Uphill is a lot of work with a child aboard. Downhill is too.

The number one risk to a child is an unleashed dog. If you live in an area with free range dogs, you want to carry water bottles for self defense, air horns, or ride with a companion who runs interference and supplies support services. A child strapped into a seat like this experiences sheer terror when dogs take an interest.

Finally, by the time your child grows up to be a teenager, she will remember your days on the Limousine. Make those memories happy ones.

Robobike.com offers detailed construction plans for this project that show cut sizes and construction details.

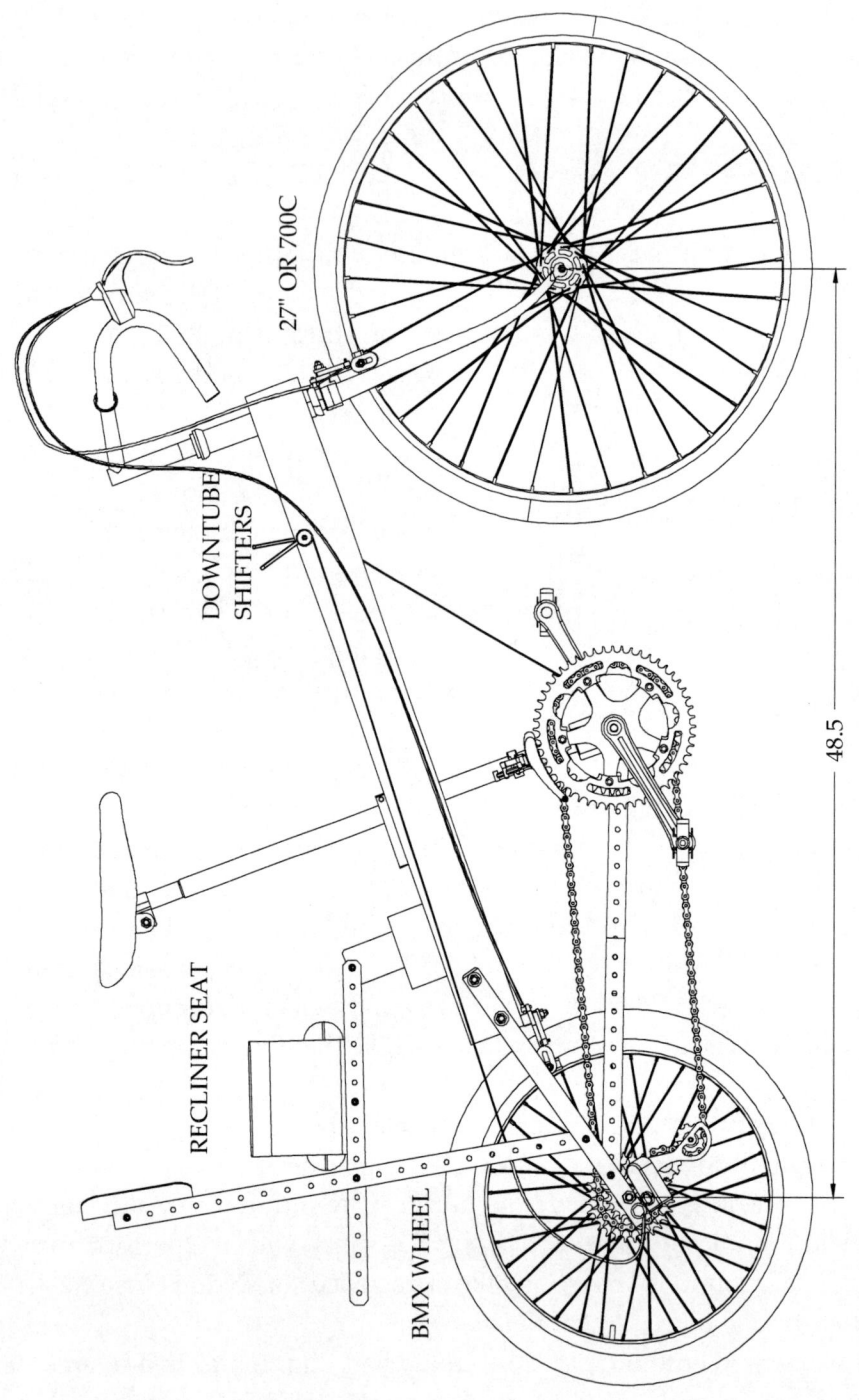

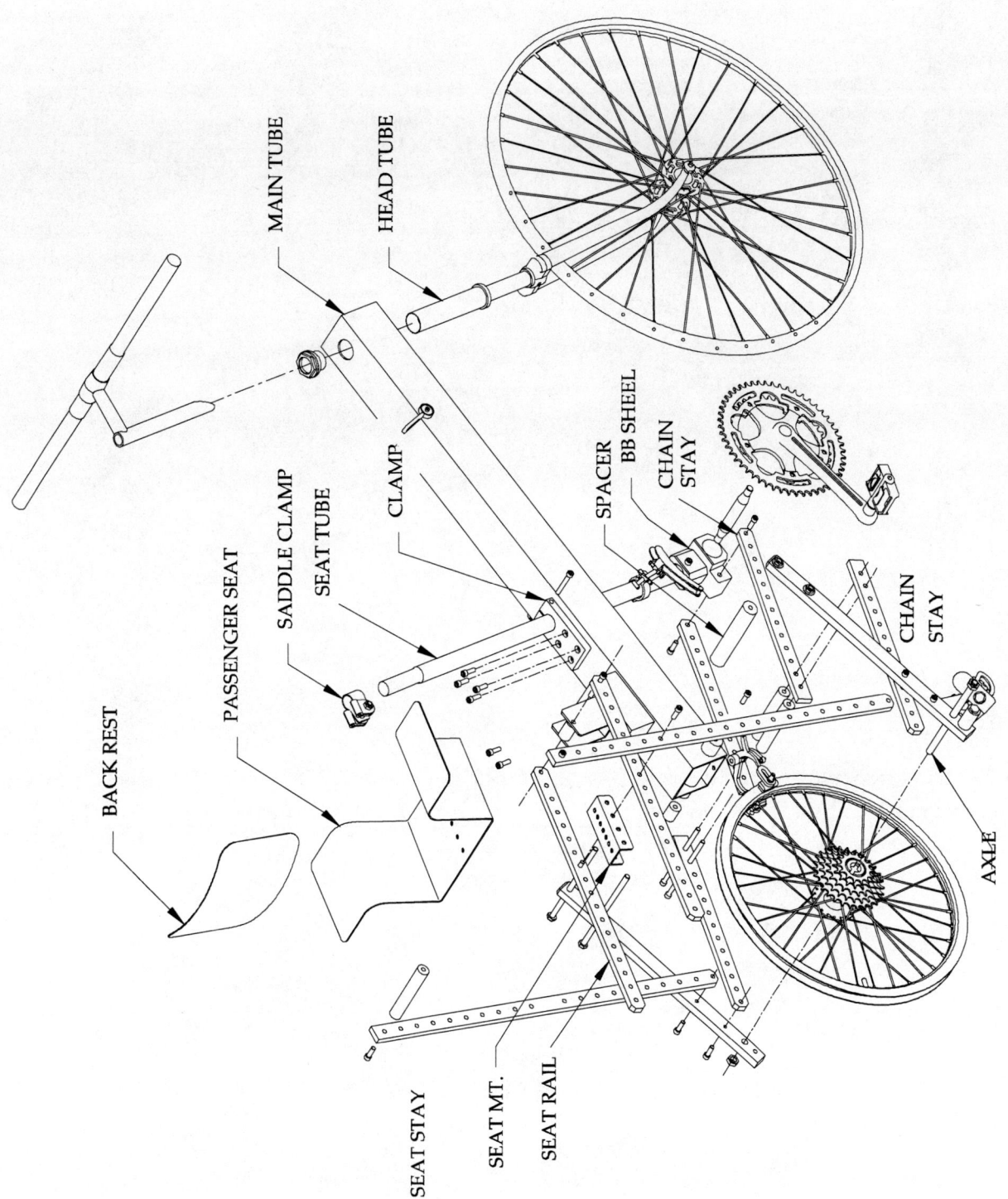

MAIN TUBE

HEAD TUBE

SADDLE CLAMP

SEAT TUBE

CLAMP

SPACER

BB SHEEL

CHAIN STAY

CHAIN STAY

AXLE

PASSENGER SEAT

BACK REST

SEAT STAY

SEAT MT.

SEAT RAIL

71

The Limo makes a plenty rigid platform for heavy hauling. Hauling batteries is all the rage with amateur bike builders so no doubt you will consider this frame for that purpose.

This view of the Limo shows off its chain line and modular construction. The Limo has been used as a platform for testing new designs, heavy hauling, battery power and a number of other tasks. The battery powered version has reached 80kph.

Bonita Caliente showing off the Limo

The latest rendition of the Limo.
Notice the absence of stays, both seat stays and chain stays. The bike as shown is ready for a battery pack and an electric motor; a large capacity luggage basket; a child seat or a seat for an adult. The Aluminum Limo is truly an all purpose load carrying machine.

The Short Wheel Base Bent

By Carla Jones

A simple project for the beginner with apprentice level skills

It is best that we not have a discussion as to the merits of recumbent bicycles. Those who like them really like them a lot and those who don't will always outnumber those who do. Instead, we shall present a simple straight-forward design that can be built with entry level metal working skills. No welding or brazing is required for this project.

To appreciate the design fully it is best to examine the steps that lead to the final geometry. They are denominated as follows.

Design constraints

One: The bike does not require any welding or machine shop skills. Easy to build.

Two: No hazards such as front wheel/shoe interference.

Three: A comfortable sitting position allowing a foot to be placed firmly on the ground from a seated position.

Constraint number one tells us a donor bicycle will supply the bottom bracket and head tube assembly. This building technique, using a donor cycle, has been used on other projects at Robobike and used successfully. It is the only design solution that satisfies the first constraint.

Constraint two is easy enough, the crank axle is to be placed above, behind or forward of the front wheel to prevent interference and potential loss of control.

Finally, an upright, comfortable sitting position within easy reach of the ground is easy to visualize. Additionally, those with recumbent experience can appreciate how important it is to prevent the knee joint extending to its maximum. After some miles of locking and unlocking the knee joint, it becomes a comfort issue. Therefore, some provision must be made for fore and aft adjustment of the saddle position. Also, the feet will not be higher than any other part of the body to prevent blood starvation of the lowest extremities. This final bit is also the result of previous recumbent experience.

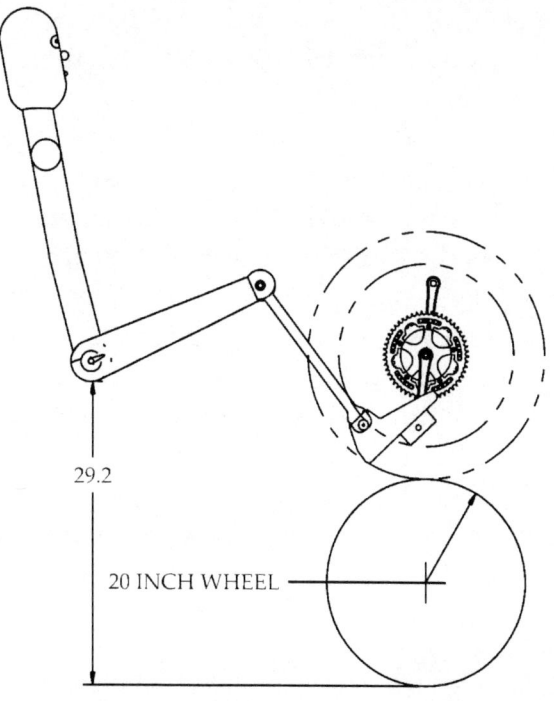

29.2

20 INCH WHEEL

Long or short?

Main stream recumbent bicycles fall into two general classes. Short wheel base bikes have the crankset forward of the front wheel and long wheel base bikes have the crankset behind the front wheel. Both designs are popular and both have their good points. How to choose between these two most popular classes? With what we have to guide us at this point, a definitive choice is not possible. Since there is nothing in our design criteria to eliminate one or the other, let's examine both.

Before doing that, however, let's try placing the crankset directly above the front axle so that the heel of the shoe does not interfere with the tire in any way.

With the rider's feet directly over the front wheel, we see that the rider is too high to place both feet on the ground. By switching to a 16 inch wheel, the riding position is lowered by the difference in the radii of the two wheels, lowering the rider to 27 inches. Using a logical query requiring a yes/no response, we ask if this is acceptable. The answer is no. We must eliminate this configuration. The riding position needs to be lowered. By how much? Measure the height of your knee above the ground while standing and add five inches. That is as good a place to start as any. This measurement is not a constraint or a rule, but should be considered a tool to help us arrive at the proper seating position.

Long wheel base (LWB)

Since we've eliminated the option of placing the crankset above the wheel, that leaves placing the crank axle either in front of (SWB) or in back of (LWB) the front wheel. The most popular long wheel base design exists in one fundamental configuration. In order to avoid an extremely long wheel base, it uses a small front wheel and places the crankset as close as possible to the front axle. Some designs place the cranks too close to the wheel and suffer from the too common ailment that plagues the recumbent community, front wheel interference. We can use a smaller wheel, however, and for the purpose of this analysis have chosen the 16" wheel common to children's bicycles. Though good quality rims and tires are not as hard to find in this wheel size as they once were, they are not common. With the rider placed well behind the front wheel and lowered to an acceptable height, it is clear that this solution is not in violation of our design constraints, at least not yet. However, in order to make everything work, some bodacious tricks have to be pulled off by the builder.

First, let's examine the minuses. Look at the following illustration and mentally pencil in some method of bringing the handlebar or steering linkage to a point where the rider can put his hands on it. A shallow angle is needed to generate enough trail and to move the handlebars closer to the rider. The latter is not quite the issue with under the seat remote steering but remote steering is not something a novice builder should attempt. Other elements in the steering geometry also contribute to the difficulty of this design making it a poor choice for a builder with apprentice or beginner level skills. Most professionally built long wheel base recumbents use rock solid steering geometry assembled with custom components. That is not something that can be put together by the amateur first time bike builder. That reason, the issue of (constraint one) manufacturability, will go a long way towards disqualifying the long wheel base design. Solutions do exist but nothing like sticking a stem in a fork and riding away. Another minus is the length of the bike. Bringing the rear wheel forward to the 60 inch station changes the weight distribution to 25/75 front/rear. This is OK but it would be good to have more weight on the front wheel for braking efficiency and to prevent snow plowing.

On the plus side, the chain run is straight with no requirement to lift the return side over the fork like on a short wheel base bike. The seating position is comfortable and safe.

Be mindful that we have ignored the weight of the bike itself for our weight and balance estimates. The balance point moves forward to a more acceptable value if we include the weight of the frame and all components and accessories.

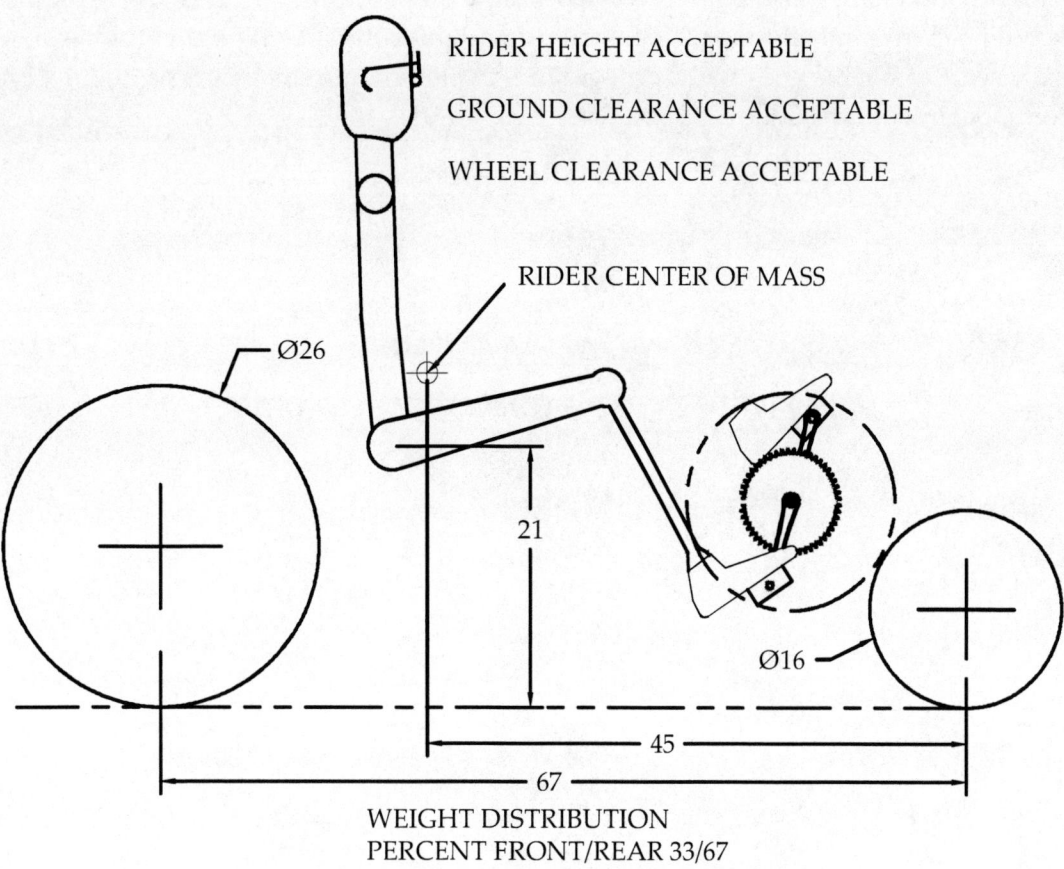

WEIGHT DISTRIBUTION
PERCENT FRONT/REAR 33/67

A typical long wheel base recumbent design

The short wheel base (SWB)

The classic short wheel base design can be sketched with good weight and balance characteristics, an easily built steering mechanism and reasonable seating position.

First, the minuses. Without a doubt, the need to raise the return side of the chain around the fork is a minus. The seating position is not quite as good as the long wheel base bike but those with recumbent experience have differing opinions about this. Many like the higher seating position for reasons of increased stability and greater visibility.

The pluses: Easy to build with no special or hard to build features.

Our design comes to us via the process of elimination. The crankset directly over the front wheel violates our rule that the rider be able to put his feet on the ground comfortably from a seated riding position. The long wheel base bike is not a project for a beginner because of the steering system. All that remains is a bike with conventional steering angles using easy to find off the shelf components having reasonable weight and balance characteristics, aluminum rims for good braking and is easy to build. The bike has its crankset placed forward and above a BMX 20″ diameter wheel.

It is one thing to sit at a computer and generate the world's best overall recumbent design. It is quite another to move out to the work area, pick up a hacksaw and start hacking. I am assuming that the builder has limited experience with metal working so the following descriptions will be highly detailed. Those with metal working experience may find these work instructions tedious, but keep in mind all those things you do without conscious thought. The need to clamp a tube in a vise or to a table goes without saying to a veteran but remember; we were all rookies at some point. Begin with the donor.

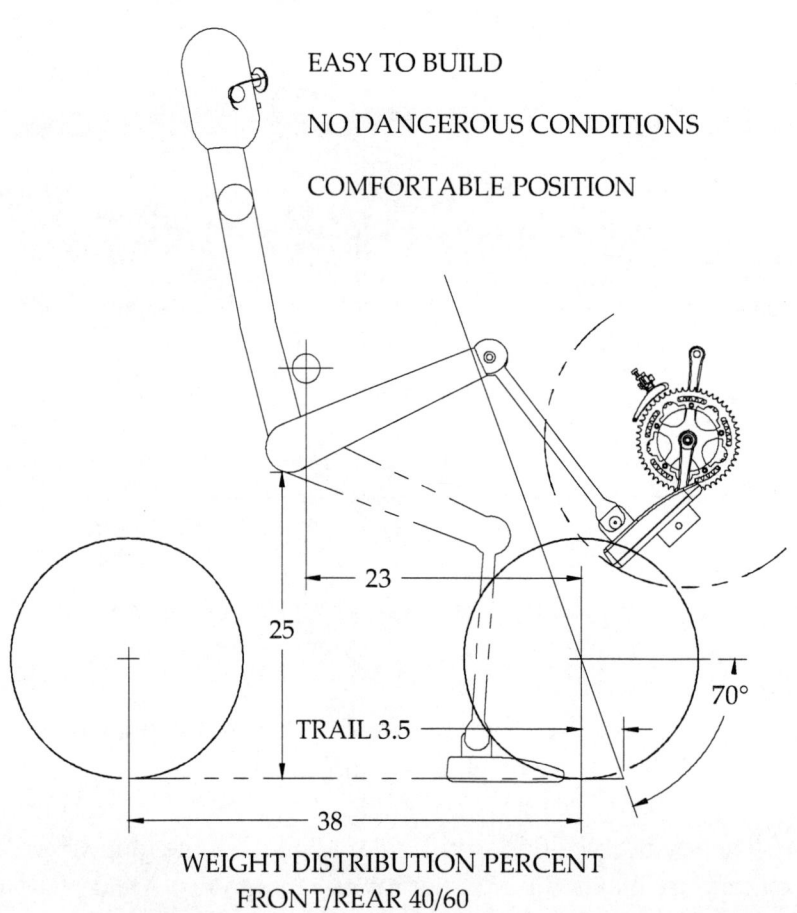

EASY TO BUILD

NO DANGEROUS CONDITIONS

COMFORTABLE POSITION

23

25

70°

TRAIL 3.5

38

WEIGHT DISTRIBUTION PERCENT
FRONT/REAR 40/60

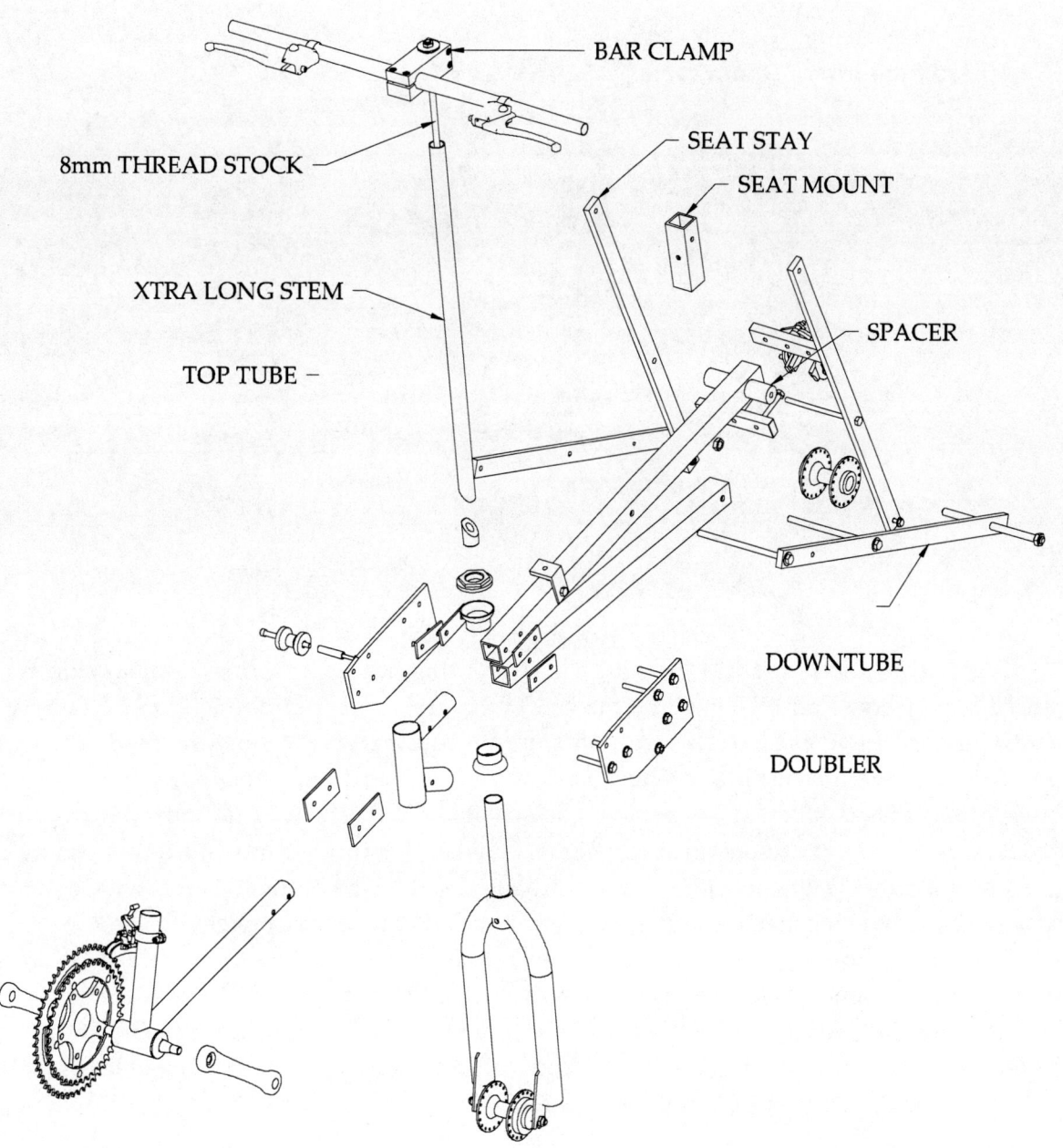

BAR CLAMP

SEAT STAY

SEAT MOUNT

8mm THREAD STOCK

XTRA LONG STEM

SPACER

TOP TUBE –

DOWNTUBE

DOUBLER

The Head Tube Assembly
The Heart of the Bicycle

A head tube from a Donor cycle

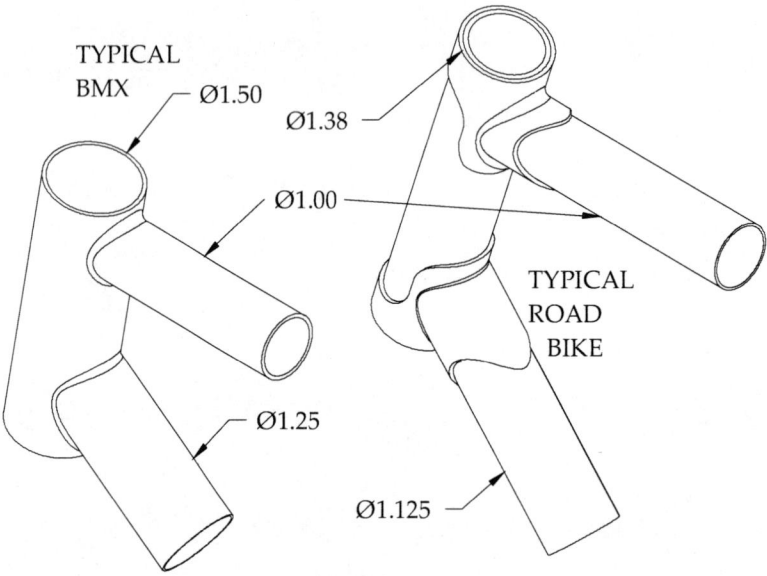

TYPICAL
BMX — Ø1.50

Ø1.38

Ø1.00

TYPICAL
ROAD
BIKE

Ø1.25

Ø1.125

This part of the recumbent bicycle requires finding a head tube/fork combination from a discarded bike. Choose a BMX bike like the head tube drawn here on the left not because of the outside diameter of the tube, which is superfluous, but because you will be using a BMX fork and wheel. The bearings are not interchangeable between different styles of bikes, so a BMX fork requires a BMX head tube cut from, you guessed it, a BMX frame. The only dimension that absolutely needs to be is the one inch (25.4mm) diameter top tube. It must fit into a square tube with a one inch inside dimension, or more properly, a 1.25 inch square tube with a ⅛" wall thickness. This is how the material is specified when ordering from a supplier.

When removing this piece from the donor frame, the work piece (frame) must be securely clamped to a work bench, held in a vise or otherwise firmly attached to the world. A hacksaw can be used to make the two cuts. Use a blade marked bi-metal and use a fine pitch blade. Twenty-four teeth per inch is acceptable but 32 is better. You will need the finer (32 tpi) blade later so it is a good idea to get one of these. Do not use a carbon steel blade to cut steel. Bi-metal is what you want.

You will be drilling the head tube for bolts later and you might think about drilling the holes for those now while you have it ready. Don't do it. You will never get the head tube to line up with the holes in the top tube so for now; simply cut the head tube and liberate it from the frame. Clean up the cut with a file or sandpaper so there are no sharp edges. Remove the fine pitch blade from your hack saw and put in a blade with 18 teeth per inch. Once again, only use bi-metal blades because they cut easier, straighter and last longer. This is the blade you will use for cutting aluminum and plastic. Do not use it for steel. It cuts steel OK but you want a good sharp blade for working on your aluminum and cutting steel dulls it a bit.

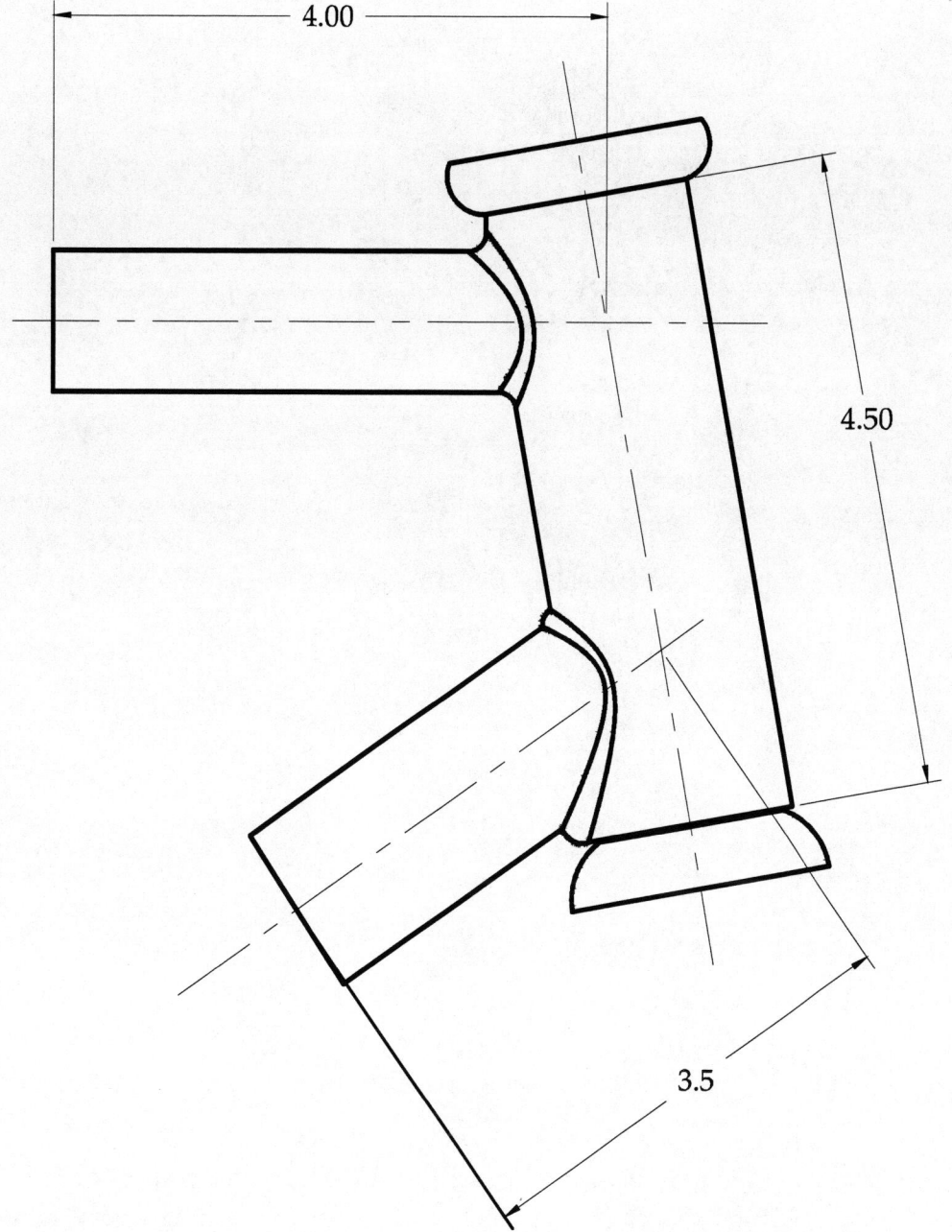

The BMX head as it appears after being removed from a frame. The 4.50 length (11.5 cm) can be longer but not much shorter as it may interfere with the doublers added later. Notice that the dimensions are drawn from the intersection of the centerlines. Using a straightedge and marking pen, draw them on your head tube. You will use them later.

Take a hammer, an aluminum or wooden punch and remove the bearing cups from the head tube.

The Top Tube
All dimensions in inches with millimeters shown in brackets

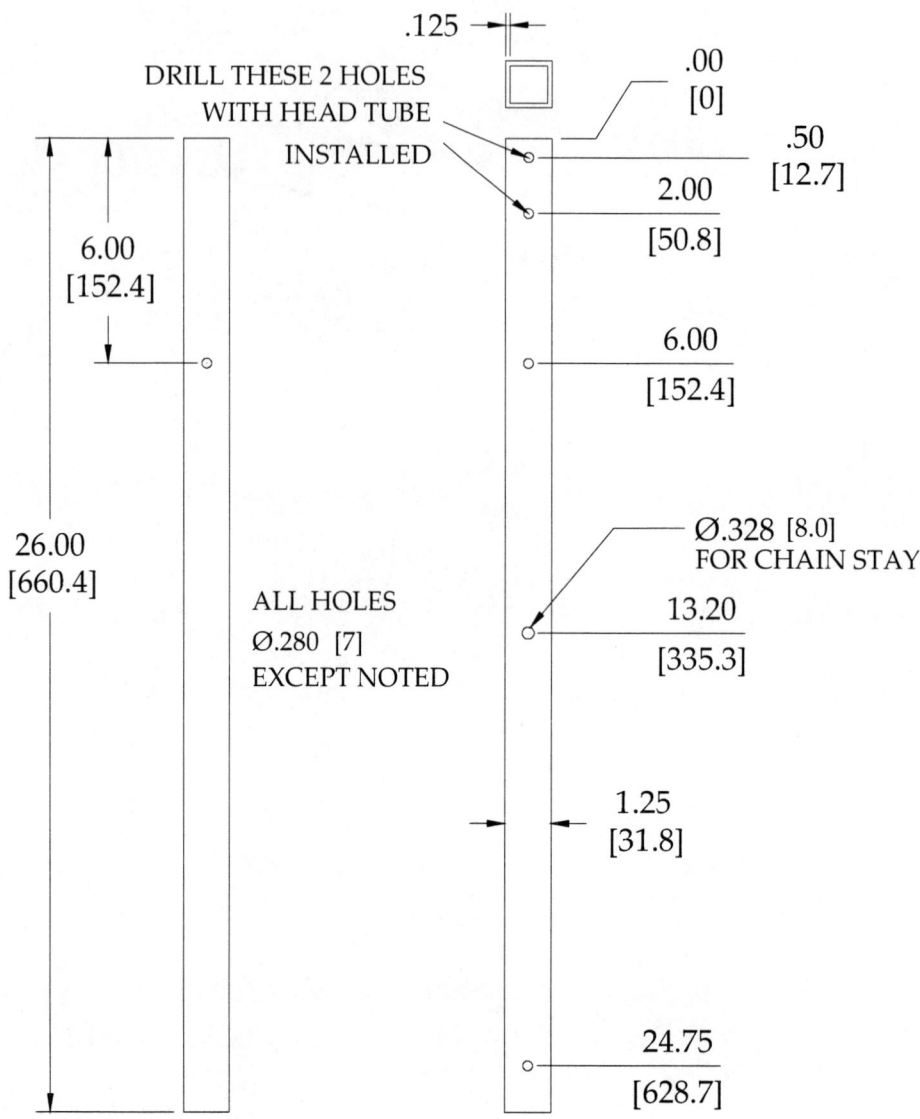

.125

DRILL THESE 2 HOLES
WITH HEAD TUBE
INSTALLED

.00
[0]

.50
[12.7]

2.00
[50.8]

6.00
[152.4]

6.00
[152.4]

Ø.328 [8.0]
FOR CHAIN STAY

13.20
[335.3]

26.00
[660.4]

ALL HOLES
Ø.280 [7]
EXCEPT NOTED

1.25
[31.8]

24.75
[628.7]

Cut a piece of 1.25 square tube 26 inches long and drill all the holes you see here except the two for the head tube. The tube should be clamped securely for the drilling operation and you should always wear safety glasses when using any cutting tools, including hack saws, punches and hammers.

If you are taller than 6', add two inches to the top tube length in case you need extra for mounting the saddle.

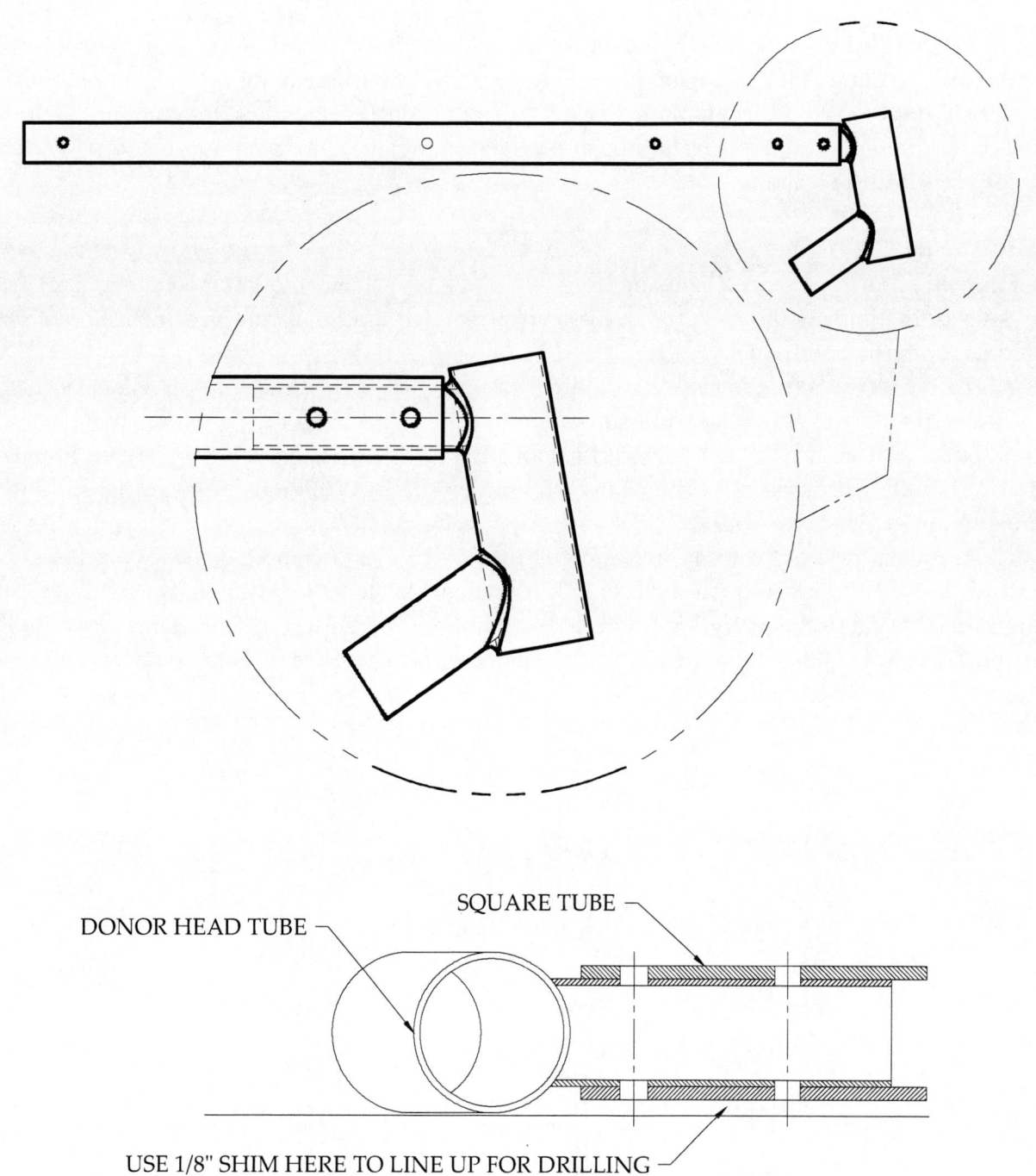

DONOR HEAD TUBE

SQUARE TUBE

USE 1/8" SHIM HERE TO LINE UP FOR DRILLING

Install the head tube into the top tube and drill two holes through. If your head tube is an inch and a half diameter, then a ⅛" shim between the work table and the top tube aligns everything nicely. If the head tube is something other than 1.5", then the shim can be calculated quite easily by taking; (head tube diameter − 1.25) / 2. Do not hammer the head tube into the top tube. If the paint is removed and the donor is prepared properly by sanding and cleaning, a little grease or soapy water used with a twisting motion will do the trick. Be sure to chamfer the end of the square aluminum top tube with a file before attempting assembly.

Once the head tube is installed in the top tube, reinstall the bearing cups and fork. If you have never installed bearing cups, one trick we use at Robobike is to put them in the freezer for an hour before installing. They shrink up just enough to make the whole thing go together with just a tap from a piece of wood or aluminum. Never hammer on bearings with anything other than wood or aluminum. Putting the head tube in the sun for an hour helps even more. Use new, clean grease on the headset bearings.

The Jig

The following drawings show a jig made from two pieces of inch and a quarter square tubing. This size is used to eliminate the need for shims and offsets that are the result of using different size materials for the jig and frame.

The jig is merely a means of holding the bike in such a way as to allow accurate measurement and assembly. You will want to remove the frame from the jig to do any drilling or cutting but always return to the jig for verification. The fork is clamped using a piece of threaded rod and six nuts with washers. Center the fork but don't tighten the nuts until the jig upright is clamped in place. That way, you won't capture any misalignment.

The beginnings of the frame are clamped into your jig. Shown here is the fork centered on the threaded rod with the square tube exactly centered. Alignment on the jig in the transverse plane is easy to do, but equally important is the point where the top tube is clamped to the jig upright. This controls the angle the head tube makes with the vertical axis and subsequently the handling qualities of your bike.

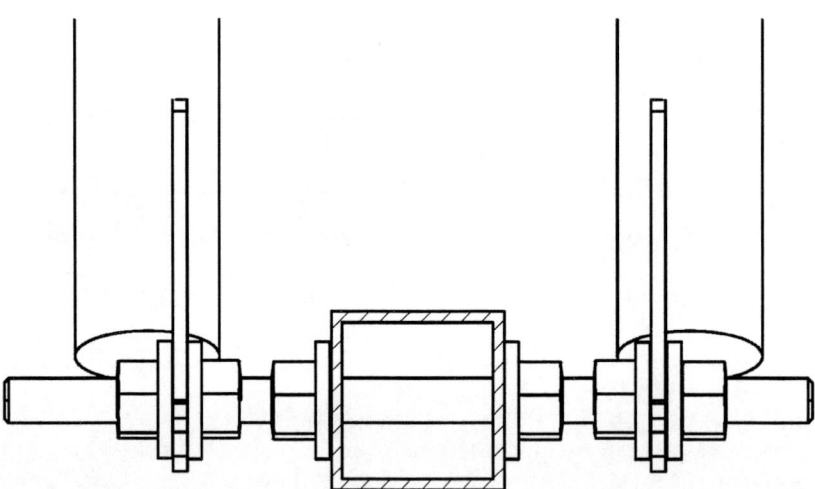

The threaded rod is 5/16-18 (M8). You will also need six washers and six nuts. Center the fork as shown in this view. A ruler is all that is needed to measure the spacing. While you are here, measure the drop out spacing and record that figure somewhere. You will need to know that if you upgrade your wheel or make any other changes such as adding a disk brake.

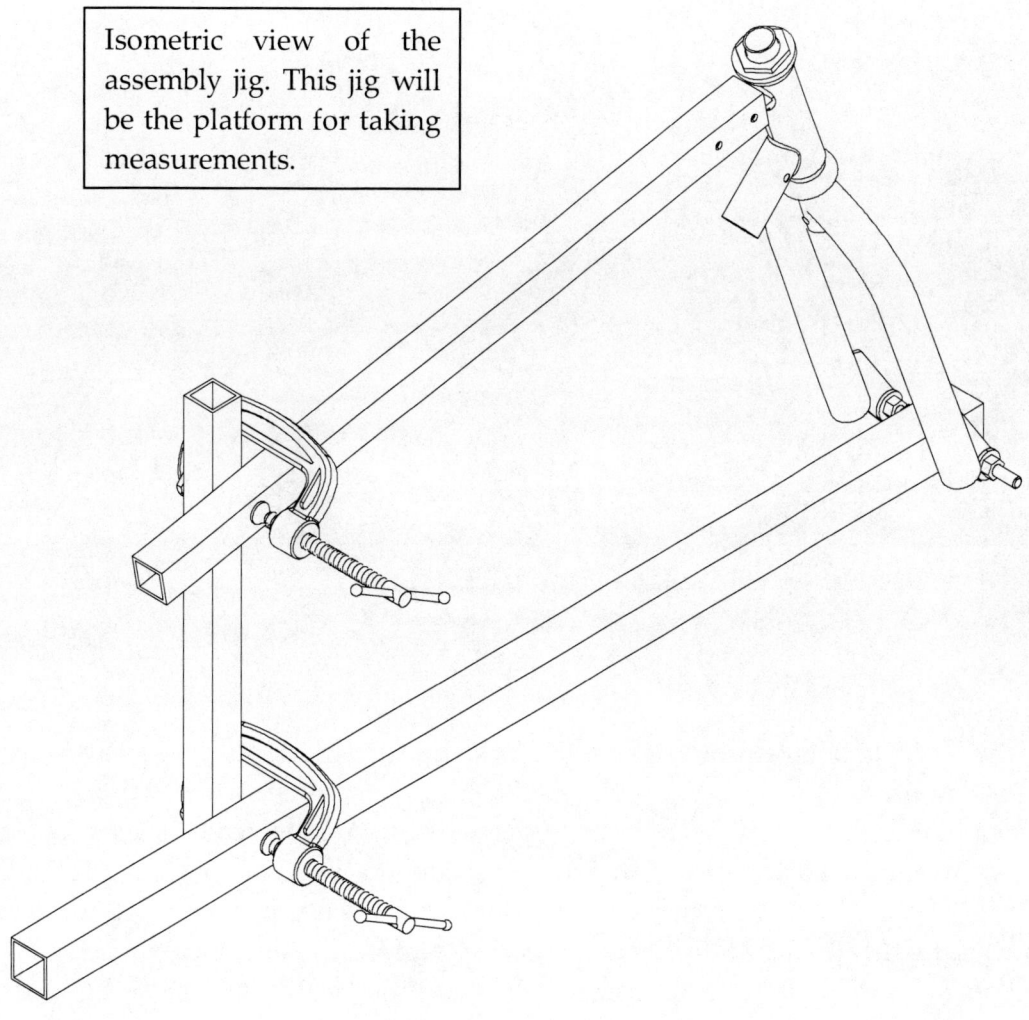

Isometric view of the assembly jig. This jig will be the platform for taking measurements.

Setting the Steering Angle

When clamping the top tube to the jig upright, how do you know when you've reached the proper angle? What is the proper angle? Why is any angle better than any other? Good questions all.

The steering axis is 20°± 3° measured off the vertical. This is generally known as a 70° head angle in the bicycle world. It does not matter if you measure using the horizontal or the vertical as your reference point.

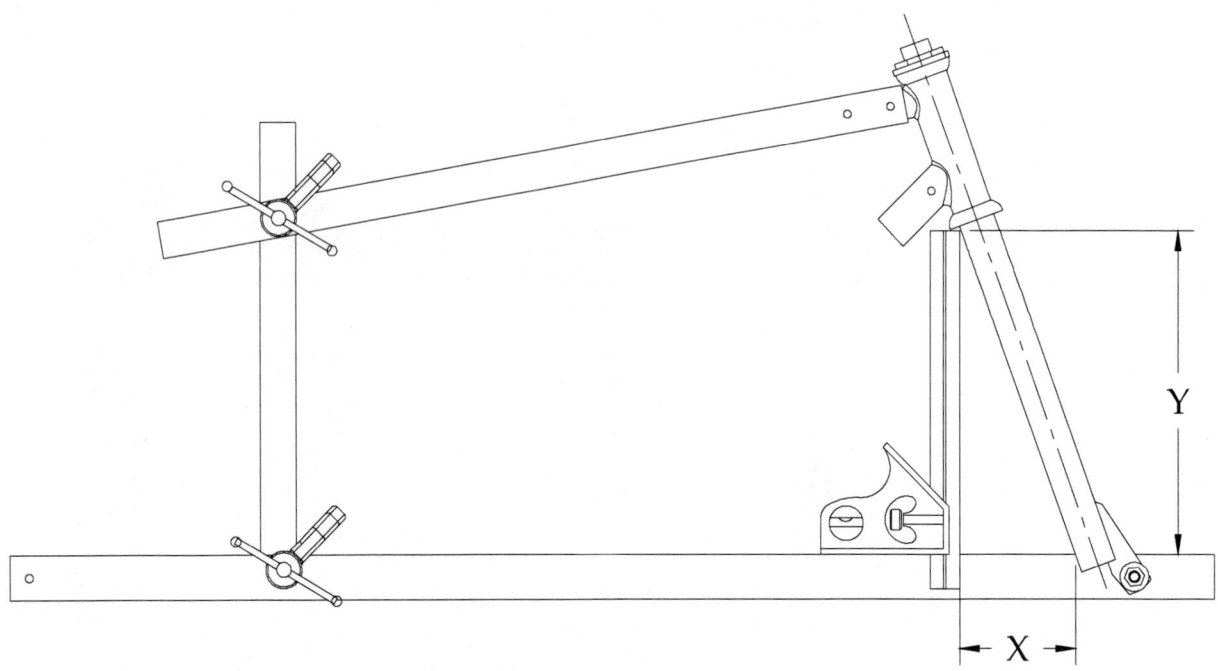

You can always lay a bubble protractor on the fork. That is a perfectly good way to measure the head angle if accuracy is not important to you. An easier and better way is shown in the drawing above. Lay a ruler vertically on the jig so that you get the two measurements shown here as X and Y. Divide X by Y then hit the inverse function and tangent buttons on your calculator. Twenty degrees is the target. This recumbent bicycle requires a twenty degree angle for a number of reasons including the placing of the handlebar, rider comfort and the much written about steering attribute known as trail. There is no reason to be concerned with trail as you build this bike. A twenty degree angle is adequate. If you have been looking at other recumbents as preparation to building this project, you have seen some really odd combinations of wheel size and head angle. Take a few minutes to do a web search to learn about trail if you have an interest. From a practical point, though, it is much ado about nothing until you get into the region where oversteering tendencies get very high.

Oversteering can best be described as a push forward on the left side of the handlebar while in a left turn. The bike wants to increase the rate of turn and the operator is there to prevent it. The greater the force required to prevent an increase in the turn rate, the greater the oversteering. A certain amount of oversteer is required for control. Highly maneuverable bikes such as those ridden at the velodrome have little trail and little oversteering tendencies and are not able to be ridden hands off easily. Touring bikes, on the other hand, have more trail and higher oversteering tendencies.

Notice that the jig has a hole drilled for the rear axle or in this case, the piece of threaded rod used to simulate the rear axle. You will use a piece of 3/8-16 threaded rod with six nuts and six washers just like on the front. The wheelbase is 36 inches.

The Chain Stays

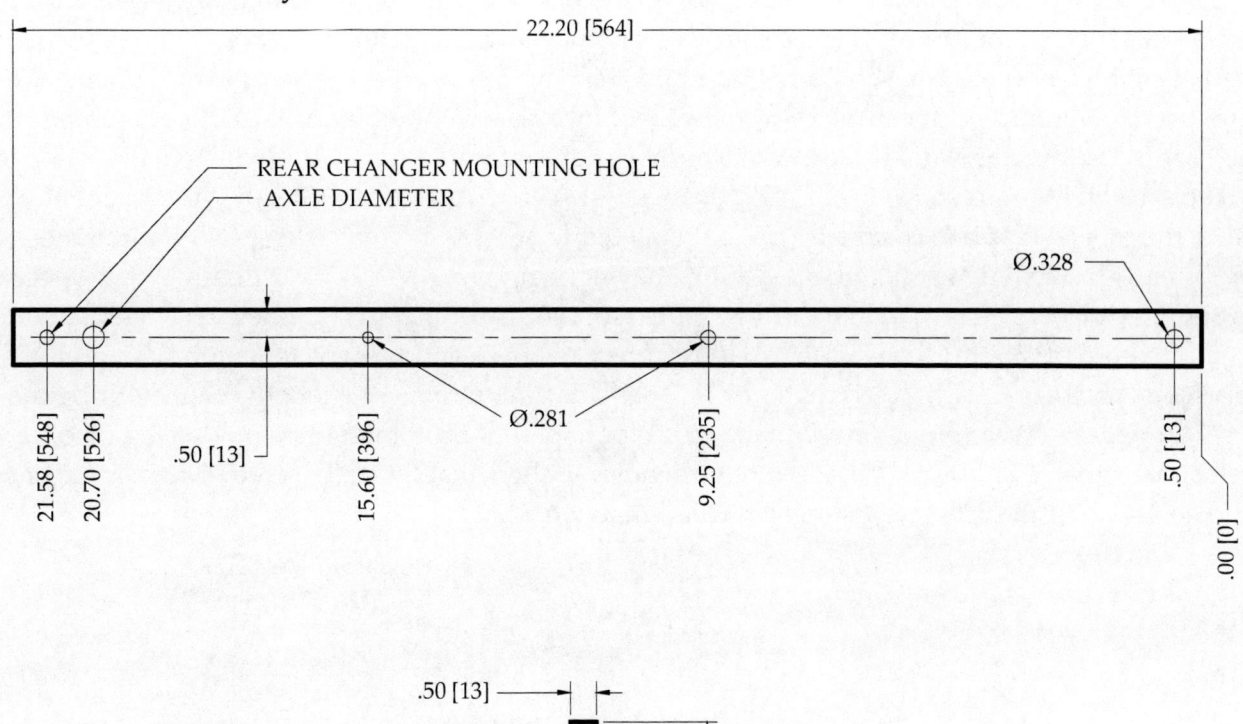

Clamp two pieces of ½ x 1 aluminum together. They are drilled at the same time to ensure that they come out identical to each other. Do not drill the holes for the seat stay at this time. That gets done later. The rear changer mounting hole is tapped ¼-20. Drill with a 13/64 or number 7 drill and then tap. You will mount a changer that has been modified by removing the swivel feature found in the 10mm mounting screw. The added width of the stays prohibits mounting the changer with a steel bracket or claw as it is known to some. If you plan on using a geared hub, you don't need this hole unless you want to maintain the multiple freewheels up front and want to use the tensioning feature of the changer to keep the chain tight.

Measure the rear axle diameter to select a drill bit for this hole. Servicing the rear wheel requires the removal of one or both stays. Do not slot the hole for the axle. We usually remove the stay opposite the chain side for service. We'll cover how to do that next.

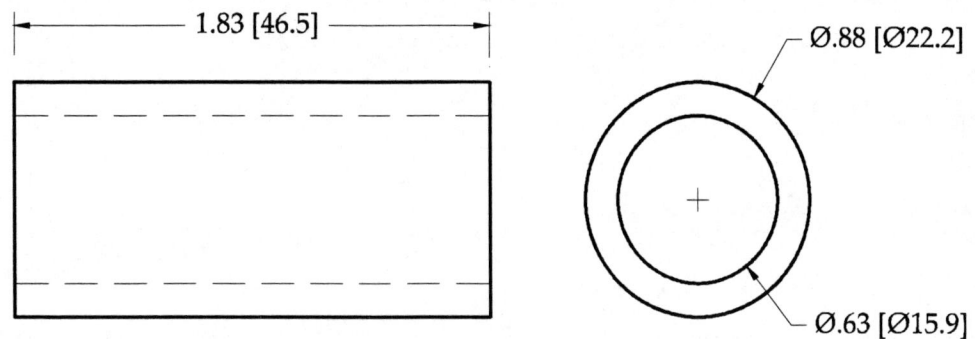

Four required at this length, two required at a length of one inch

When we began building this bike, we used a one inch cube of nylon to buttress the square tubes. This buttressing prevents the collapse of the tube and allows the assembly to be tightened against solid resistance. You should not build this bike with supporting the inside of the tube. We now use an aluminum tube in place of the cube. Since you will be buying a piece of aluminum tube for the extra long stem, we use whatever material is required for that. It will be either ⅞ or 1 inch diameter. We are showing the .875 diameter spacer with a .125 wall. An added benefit of using the tube is that one chain stay can be removed to service the rear wheel without removing the other. This maintains alignment during the servicing so that the bike doesn't have to go through the process again. Begin by cutting a piece of the spacer material to one inch length. If you do not the use of a lathe, then cut the spacer slightly oversize and bring it to length with a file. It helps to mark the cut with a piece of tape on either side and to rotate the length of tube during the cut. You will need two pieces one inch long and four spacers 1.830 to1.840 long. This is 1/32 of an inch shorter than 1⅞. You will also need four fender washers that fit a 5/16 screw. Often, a washer marked ¼ will fit the 5/16 screw snug, which is what you want.

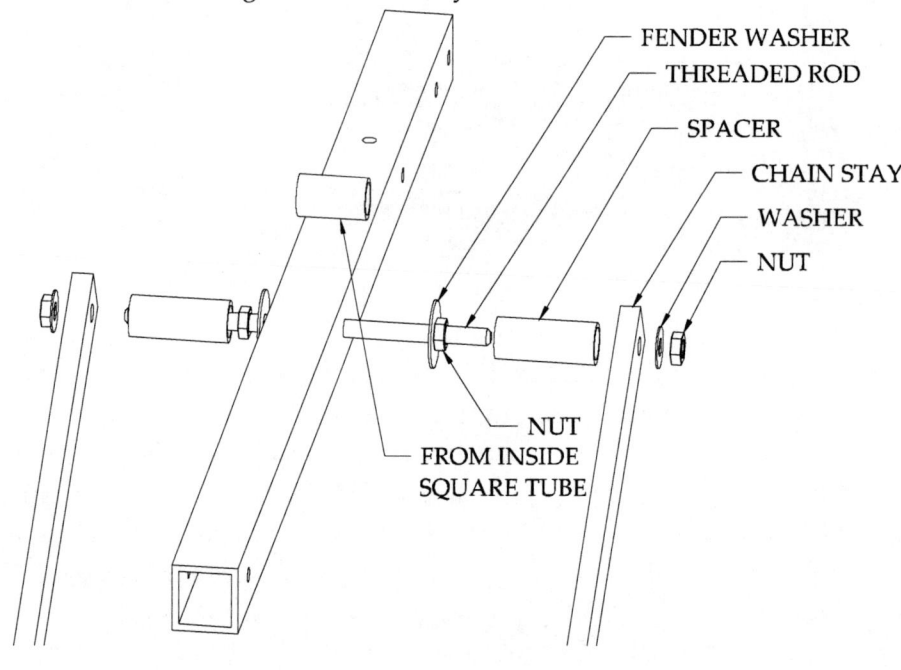

FENDER WASHER
THREADED ROD
SPACER
CHAIN STAY
WASHER
NUT

NUT
FROM INSIDE
SQUARE TUBE

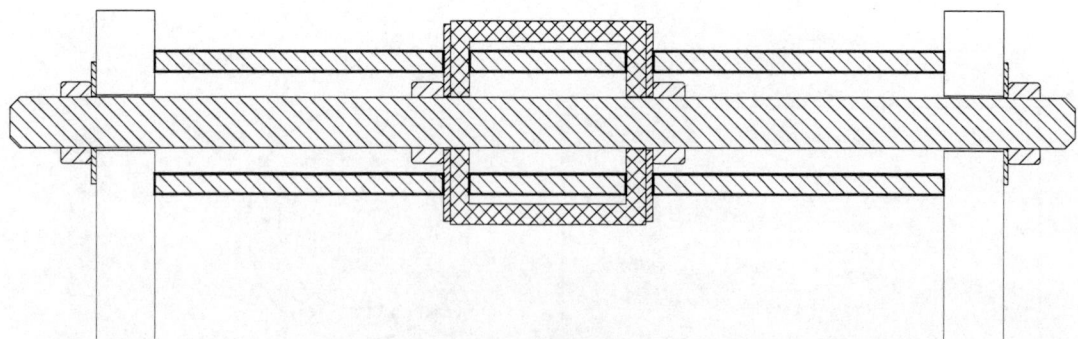

The cross section view of the top tube, 3 spacers and chain stays showing threaded rod, four 5/16 nuts, 2 flat washers and 2 fender washers.

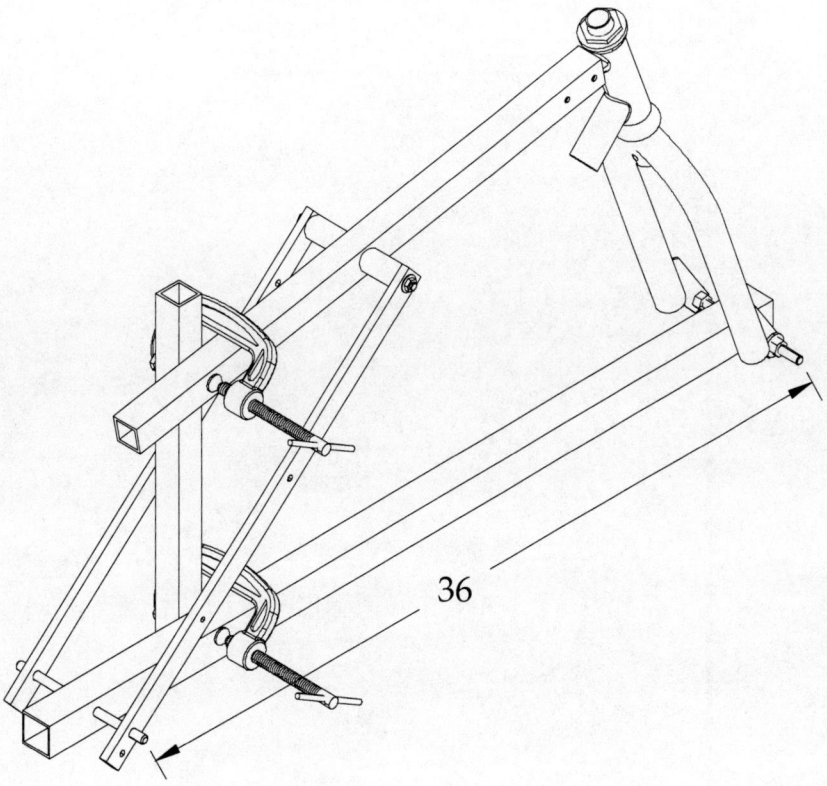

36

Before continuing with the seat stays, down tube and associated hardware, move back to the front of the bicycle and prepare the doublers for installation.

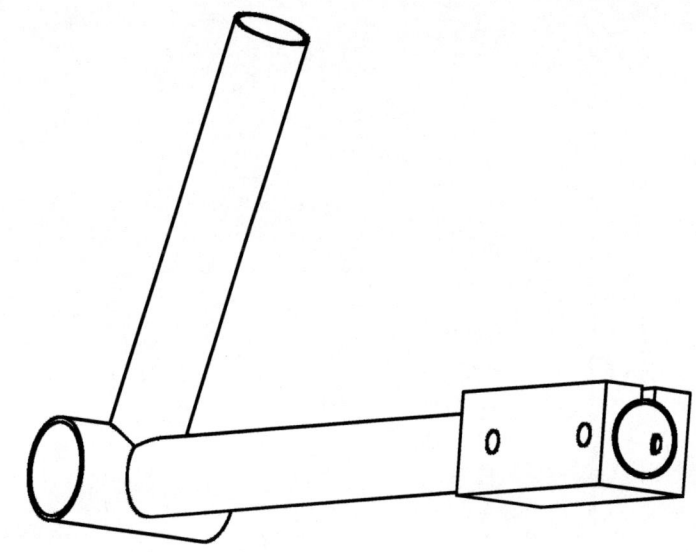

Optional square socket for mounting power system

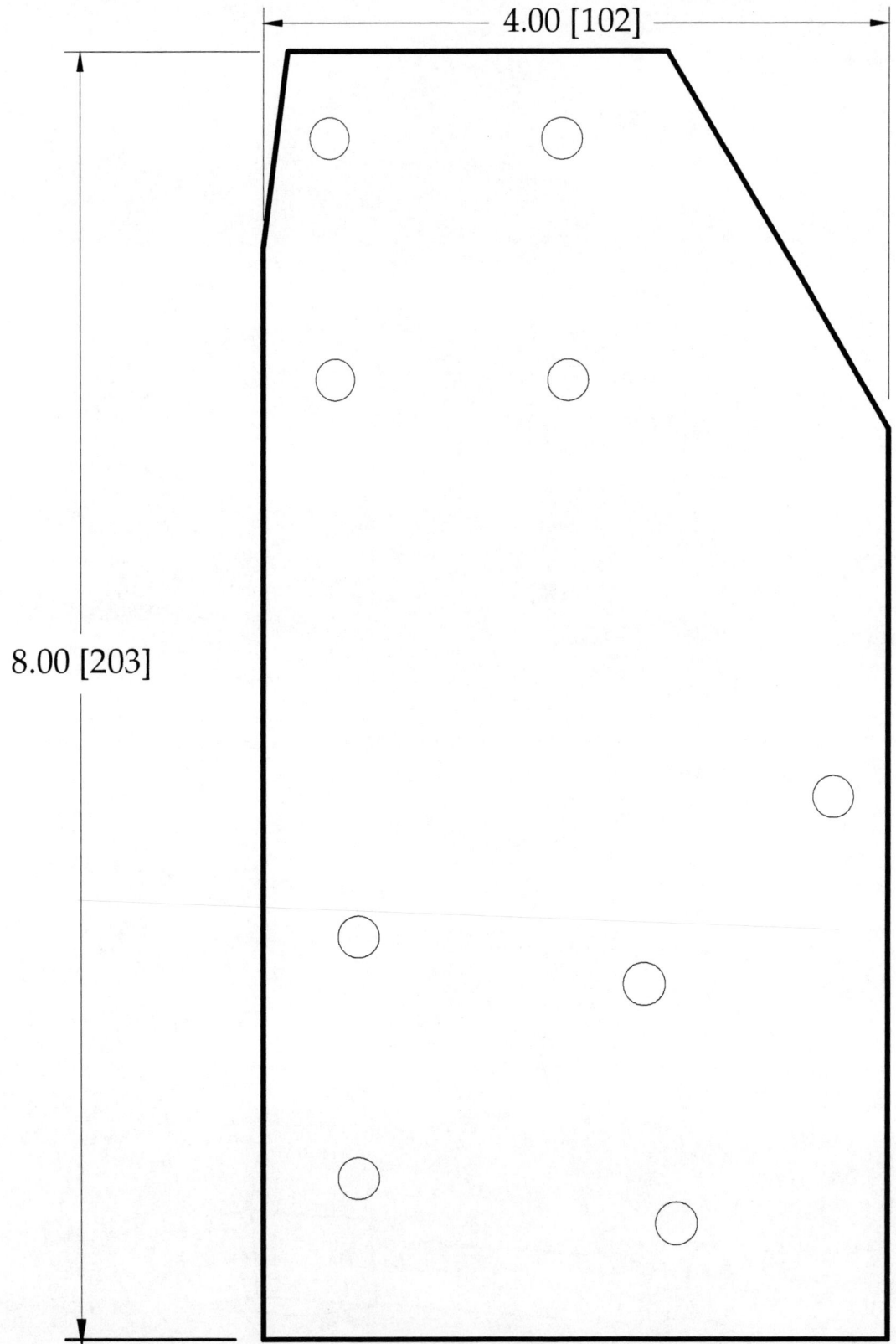

4.00 [102]

8.00 [203]

Doubler cut from 3/16 or ¼ thick aluminum plate, any alloy. Use this full sized template to layout the two pieces. All holes are 9/32 (.281) [7mm] diameter. De-burr the saw cut with a file.

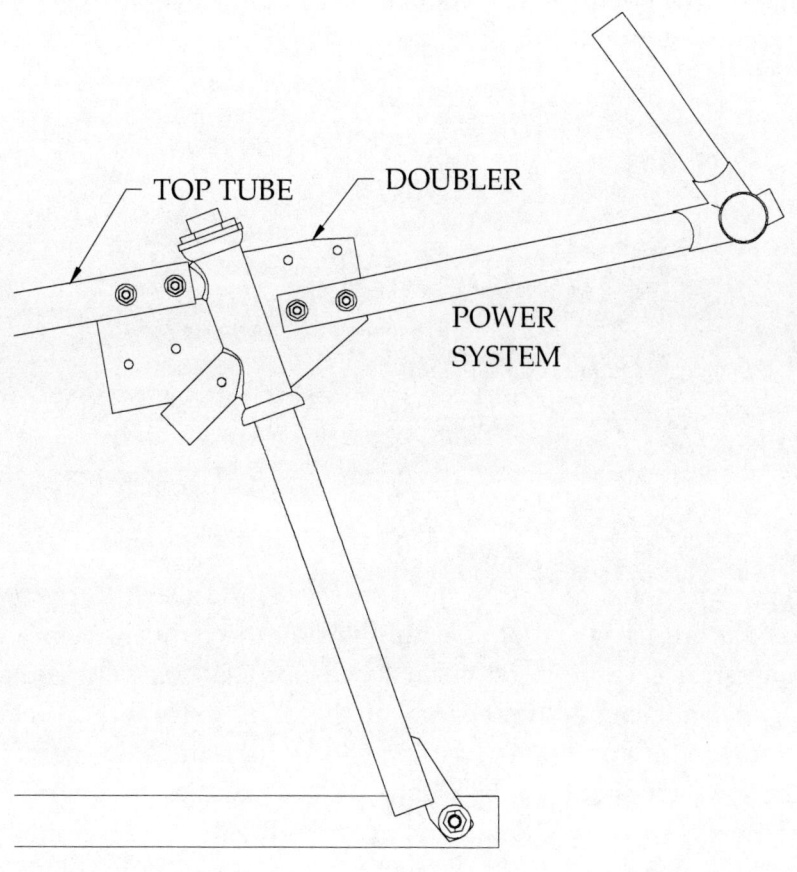

TOP TUBE   DOUBLER

POWER
SYSTEM

The Power System

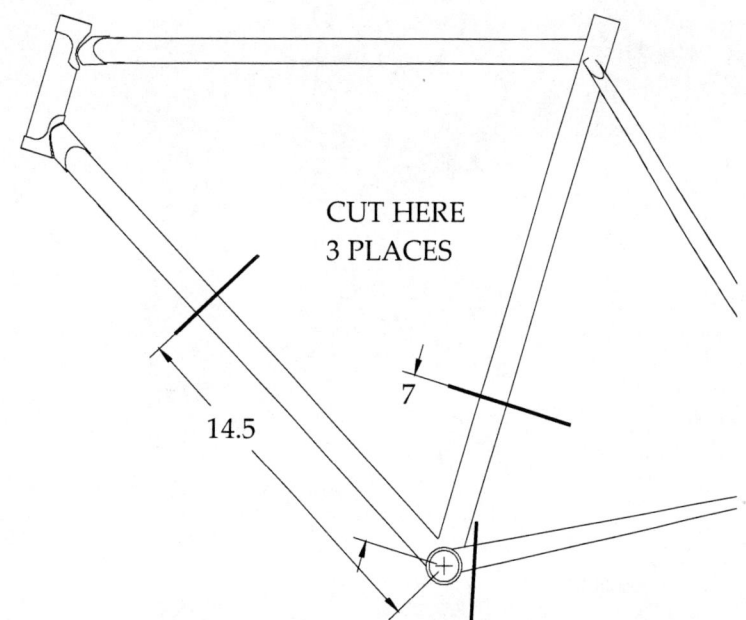

CUT HERE
3 PLACES

14.5

7

A second piece from a donor cycle is used for the power system. Using a hacksaw with a 32 pitch blade, cut the bottom bracket as shown. A road bike is used in these illustrations but you may use a BMX frame. We like the road frame because of the 3 piece crank but that is not the only reason. If you are using a derailleur on the front chain wheels, leave the seven inch cut long until you determine with some certainty that it is the correct length for your application.

Cut a 3″ length from the seat post of the donorcycle and use it to prevent collapse of the steel tube when the bolts are tightened at assembly. Install the remnant before drilling. This is a touchy operation and great care must be taken to ensure the holes are square to the bottom bracket. Drill a small hole first, check it for alignment, then drill to full size. A drill press is the best way to guarantee alignment. If you do not have one, then mark the holes very carefully and drill from each side towards the center of the tube. Center punch the holes before drilling the pilot hole.

The holes are 1½ inches apart, (38mm) and are drilled with a quarter inch drill. It is never a good idea to use zero clearance on a bolt, so you will want to run a 17/64 drill bit through this piece and the doublers after they are assembled.

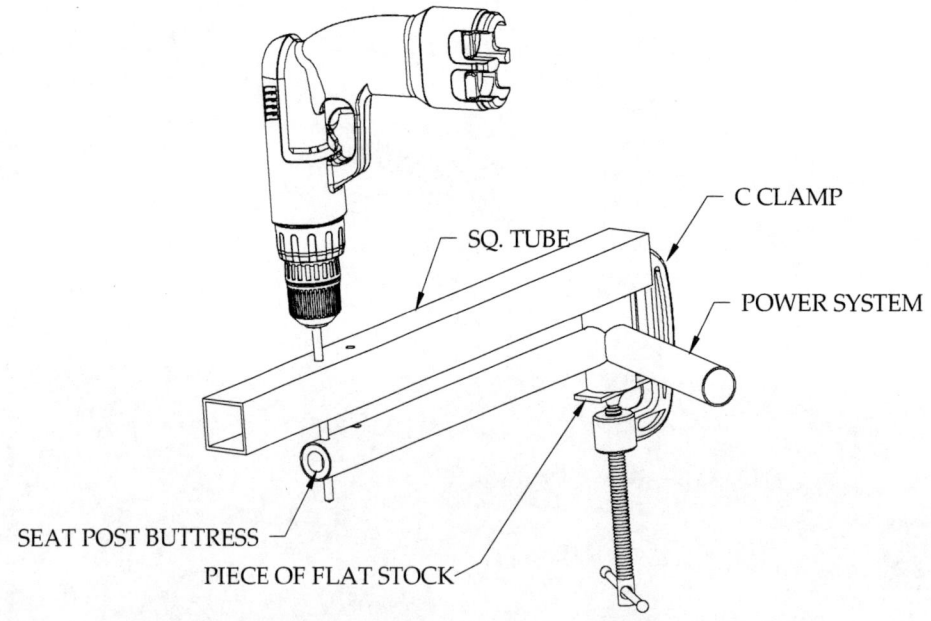

An easy drill guide, OK to use a piece from your jig

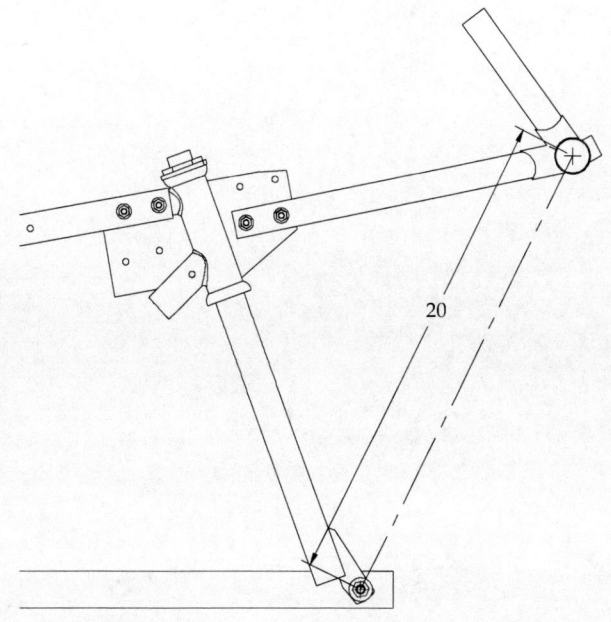

This dimension guarantees shoe clearance
Note the second pair of holes in the doubler
These are used to increase clearance

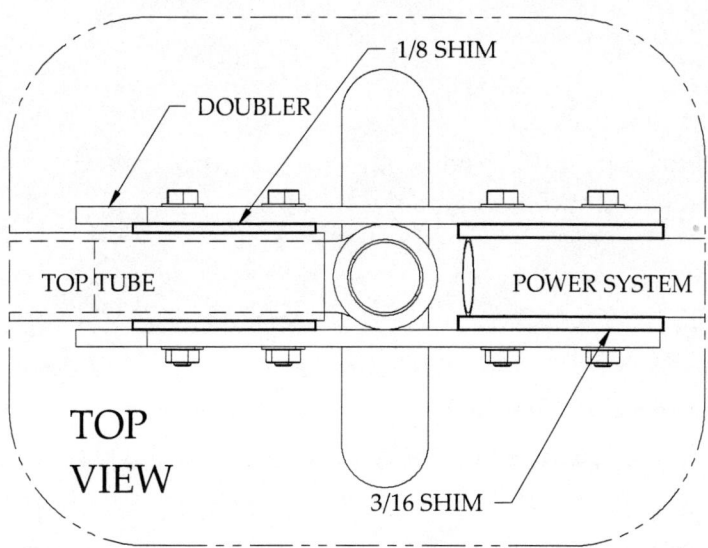

TOP
VIEW

Looking down the steering tube of the fork, it is easy to see the shims required to make this sandwich work. These values are for a head tube that is an inch and a half diameter. If your donorcycle head tube is 1.375, then the ⅛ shim becomes 1/16 and the 3/16 shim becomes ⅛. This is the arrangement you will build up as you assemble the heart of the short wheel base recumbent bicycle.

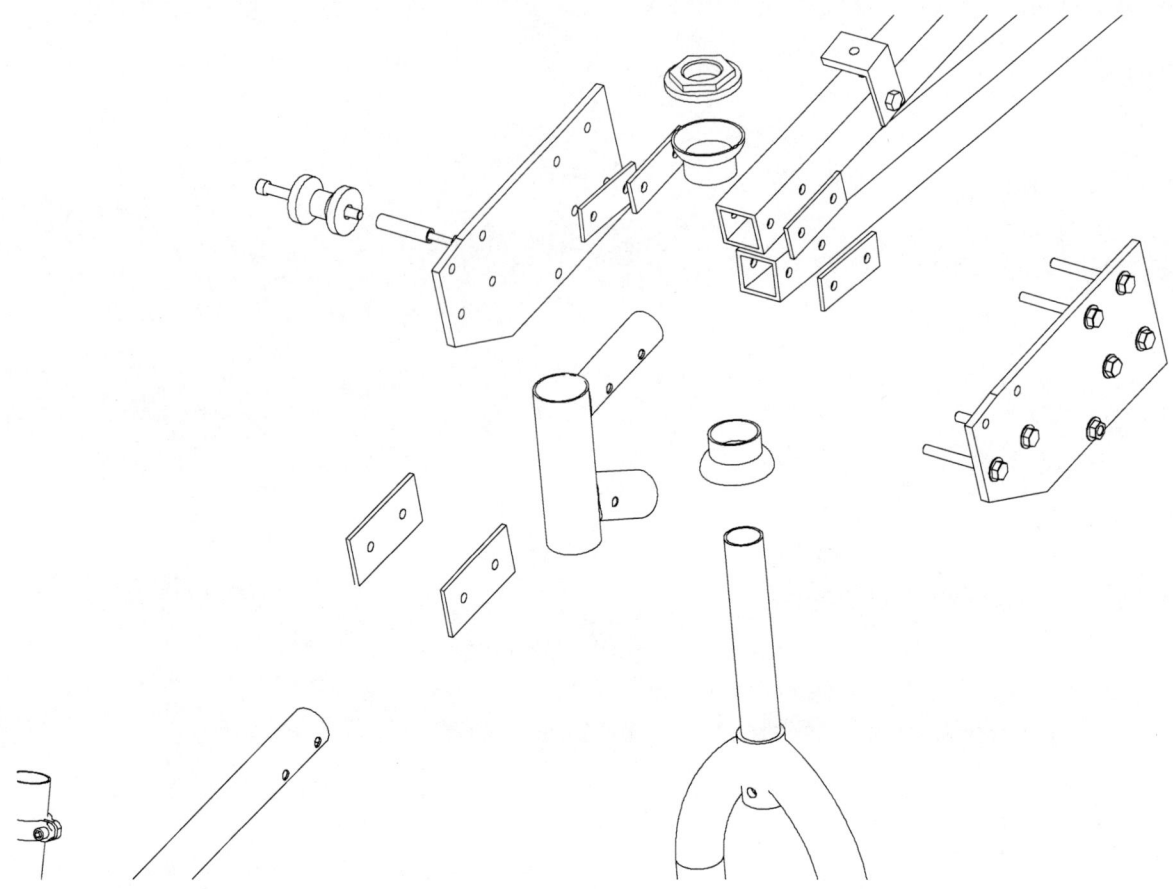

There is no need to buttress the inside of the top tube and down tube when the doublers are used. There is very little chance of collapsing either of these.

Prepare the down tube next.

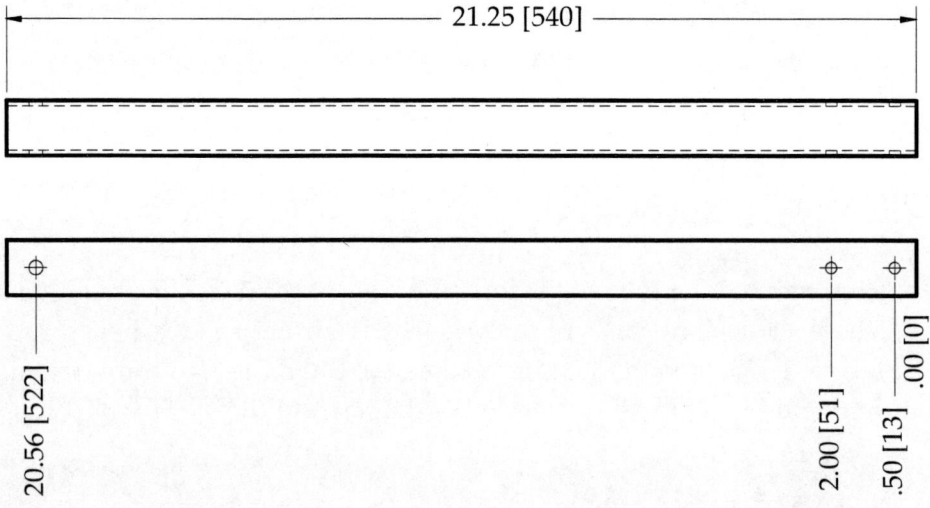

21.25 [540]

20.56 [522]

2.00 [51]

.50 [13]

.00 [0]

The down tube is cut from the same material as the top tube.

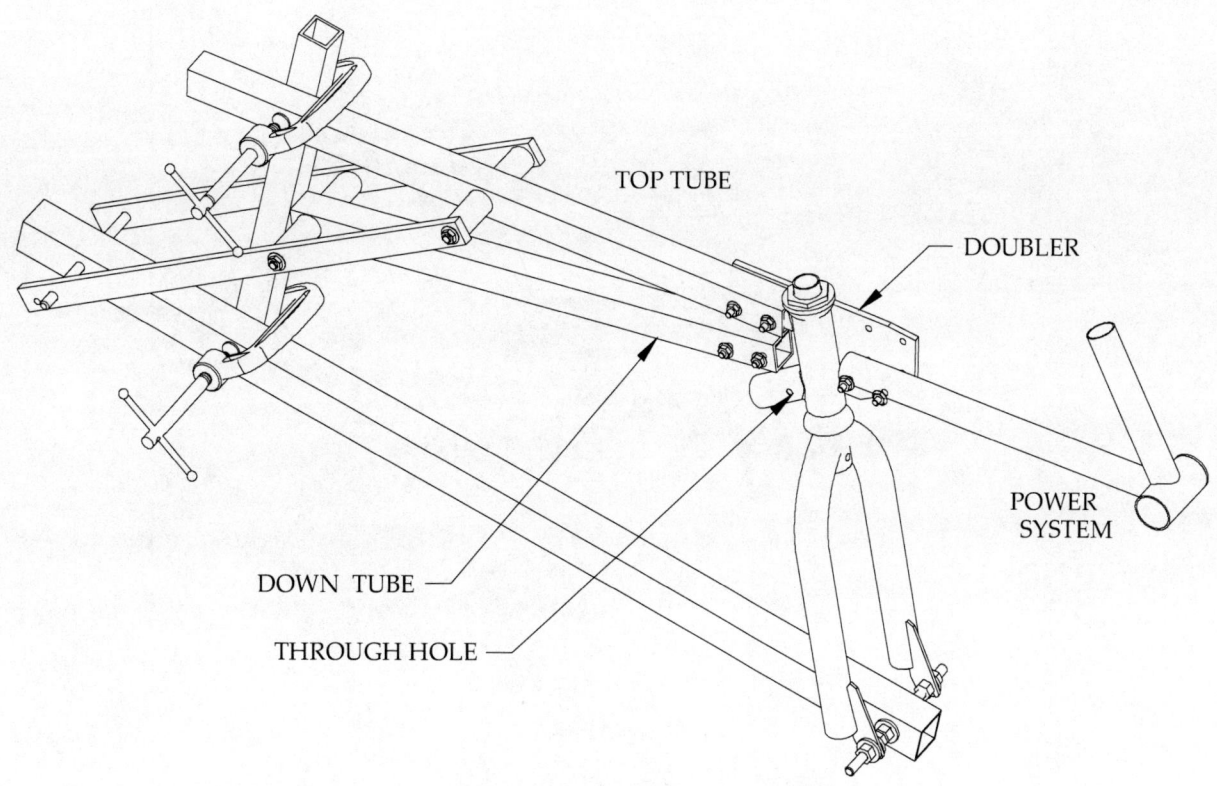

TOP TUBE

DOUBLER

POWER
SYSTEM

DOWN TUBE ─

THROUGH HOLE ─

Adding the down tube to the assembly on the jig

Once you reach this stage, install the near side shims, doubler and snug everything up. You are now ready for the seat.

The Saddle

This portion of the project is entirely up to the builder. We can offer no advice to fit every application. A scavenger and make do bike builder has very little invested in this project up to this point. Buying a recumbent saddle adds many of hundreds of dollars/euros etc to the project. The bikes we build use some kind of plastic saddle cut from a household chair. We choose the type found in schools or public offices meant for the masses. Consequently, our bikes are short on comfort and require some kind of cushion or pillow. If your project is to be something more than that, by all means, have a look around and buy or copy a recumbent saddle. If you want to build a bike meant for the short haul, then use our strategy.

Riding a recumbent can be excruciatingly painful with the wrong saddle. The lower back particularly needs to be supported and the greater the supported area, the greater the comfort. Actually, the statement should read, the less discomfort. These bikes have not found wide spread use around the world and the comfort/power issue is the reason. Ride one and see for yourself.

Our drawings show an upright position. A reclining position seems to be the more typical position chosen by most bent riders.

The square piece at the front of the bike is known as the SOCKET. It replaces the seat post used to buttress the power tube and the 3/16″ shims used to clamp the power assembly. If you have a lathe and the skills needed to make this feature, it is well worth the trouble. The outside dimensions are 1.50 inches square. Robobike makes dozens of these from time to time. Send an email message to Bingo to see if we have any available. Be sure to tell us the diameter you need.

Seat Stays

If you are using a saddle from a supplier of recumbent seats, then you will no doubt be instructed as to how to mount that saddle to your bike. There may or may not be a pair of stays involved. Chances are there will be stays. Anytime you add stays to a bicycle, you run the risk of interfering with the chain. Since that is something you don't want to happen, now is the time to install the front wheel, the rear wheel, and the crankset complete with chain wheels. The purpose for this step is to run a piece of chain from the outside chainwheel to the smallest sprocket on the rear wheel. This is the worst case for interference. How much room is there between the chain stay and the chain? As the chain is moved inboard during downshifting, it moves in and up. When you have studied the combinations well enough to give an understanding of the possible risks, mark the location for the seat stays and drill the mounting holes for them in the chain stays. To perform this step any other way is to invite rework, which is to say you will have to drill them again in another spot. It is OK to do that if you miss something, but it is just more work that needs to be done.

Another thing about the seat stays, although the drawings call for 2 pieces of ⅜ x 1 aluminum 21 inches in length, your needs may be different if you use a saddle other than the one we use in our prototypes. The length specified here works with the plastic seat we borrowed from the school dumpster, but your needs may be different. The spacers, through bolt and fender washers used for the chain stays are duplicated here at the seat stay/top tube junction.

SEAT STAY, 2 REQUIRED

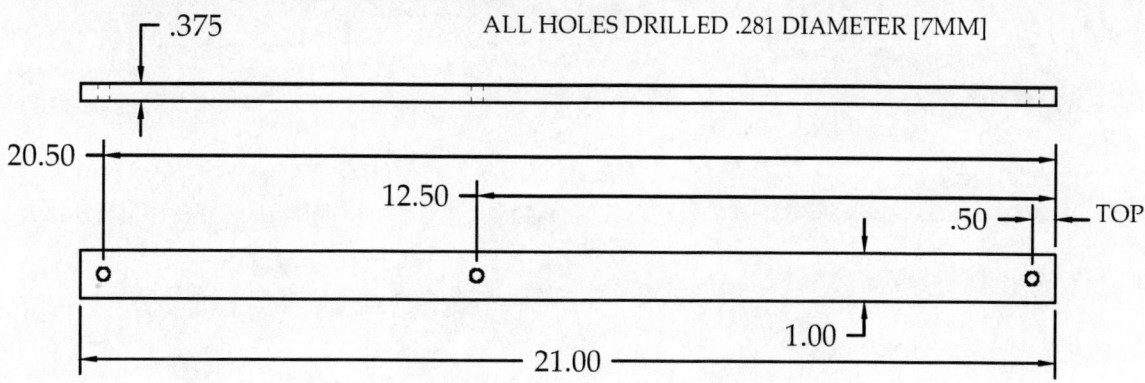

The hole on the left in this view can be tapped if you want to use that option. This is the where the seat stay attaches to the chain stay.

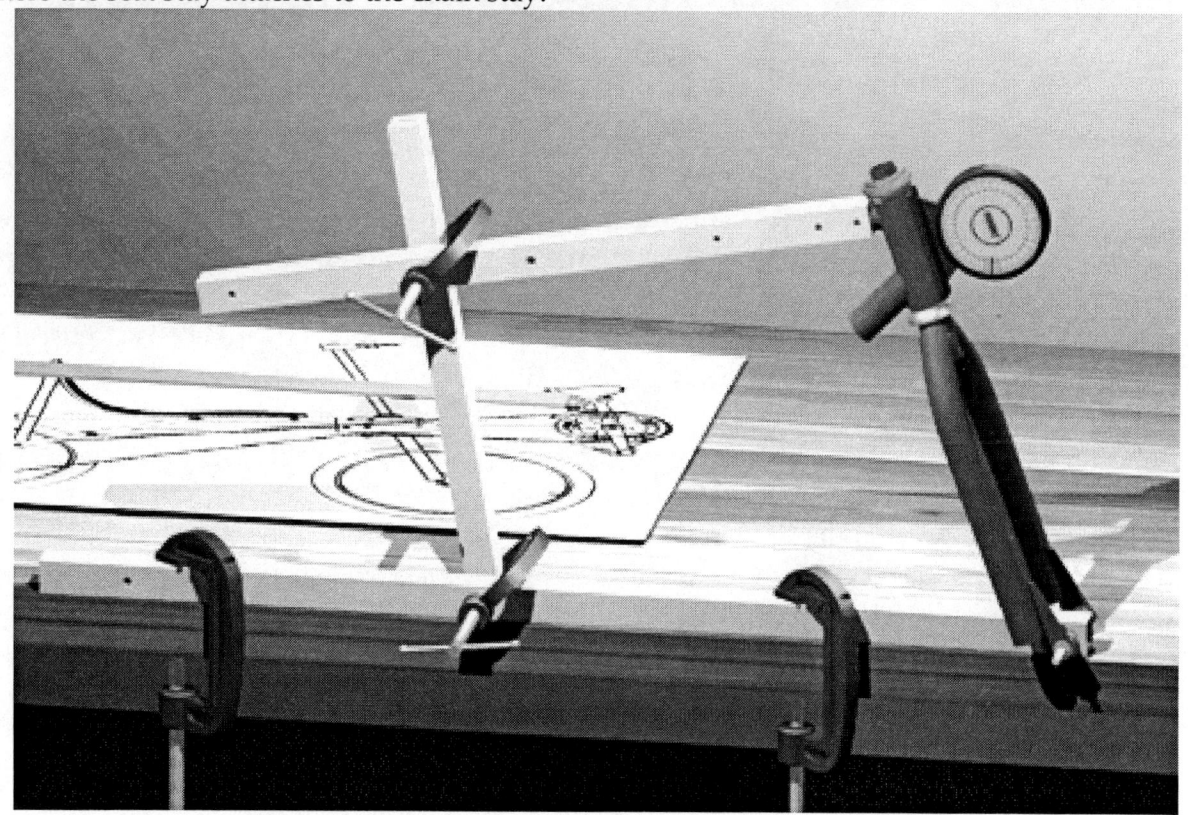

PIVOT

The seat stays can be pivoted around the bolt marked here to adjust the angle of the saddle. This arrangement is good for suspending a plastic chair. Sitting on the frame is quite uncomfortable, even with padding. It is a better ride with suspension. Store bought recumbent seats have their own hardware and instructions for mounting to a frame. If you choose to use one such saddle, keep in mind that the stay also completes the frame, making a triangle. It is acceptable to trim the seat stays above the top tube if they are not needed, but the portion of the stays between the chain stays and top tube must be there.

The through bolt connecting the seat stays and top tube is 5/16" diameter (M8).

The lower screws are quarter inch, or M6. It is recommended that the saddle to be used is attached, at least temporarily, so the holes can be drilled in the seat and chain stays. You may need to put the holes in places other than shown here.

The two pair of holes in the head tube doublers are there in case you decide to raise the power end for added clearance between your shoe and the front wheel. Most bent riders find that having the feet low is the most comfortable sitting position.

Checking for chain interference

Mounting the front end of the saddle to the top tube can be as easy as drilling a hole through both and using a long screw. We have done it this way and have found it to be perfectly acceptable. Since it is difficult to judge the riding position without riding the bike, it is the recommended procedure. You can always revise the configuration. The seat mounting at the top end of the stays is nothing more than a long screw supporting a piece of square tubing. Once again, don't spend a great deal of time on these features until you've ridden the bike and have a feel for what it is you want to accomplish.

The chain and shifting; the rear wheel

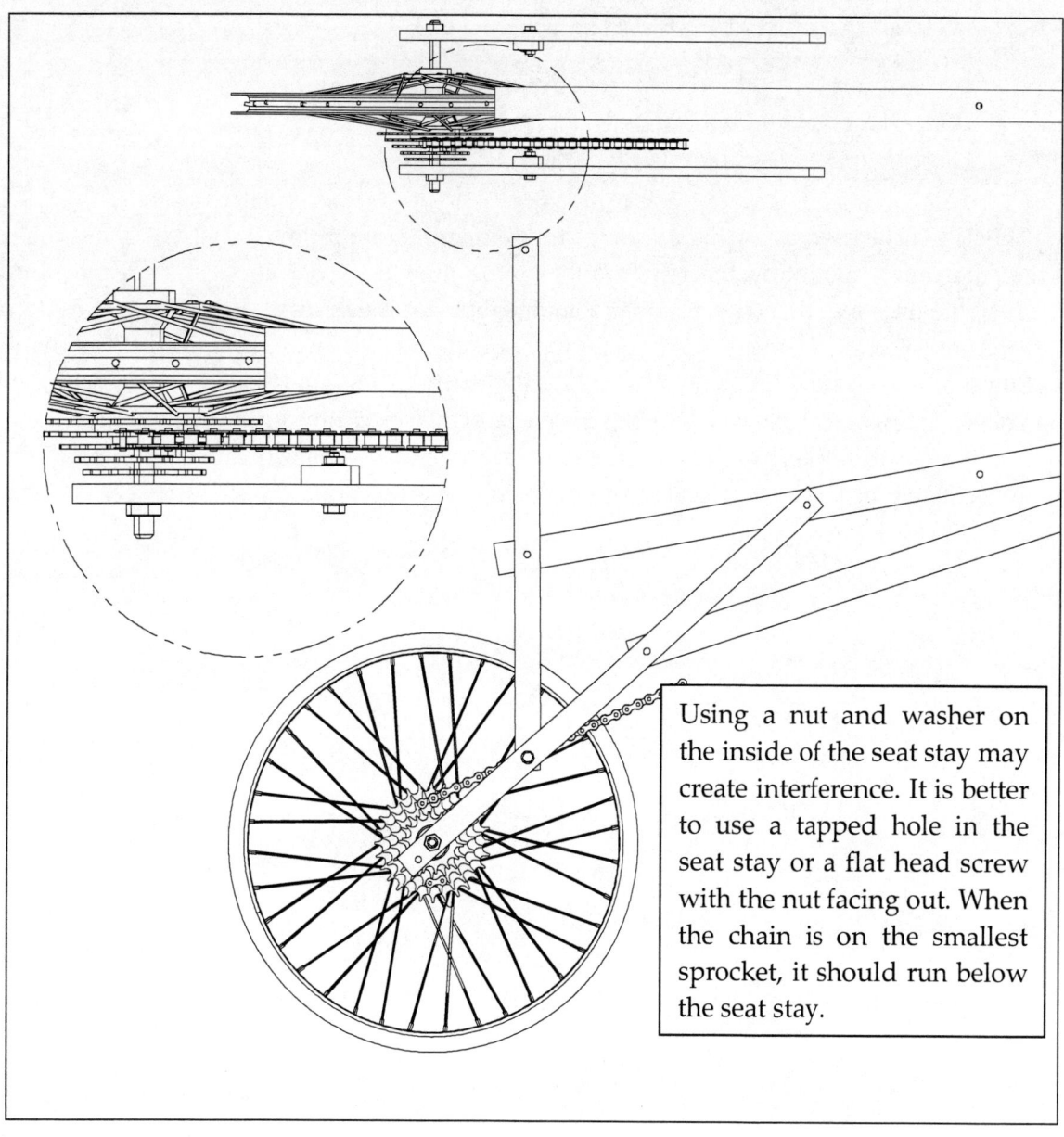

Using a nut and washer on the inside of the seat stay may create interference. It is better to use a tapped hole in the seat stay or a flat head screw with the nut facing out. When the chain is on the smallest sprocket, it should run below the seat stay.

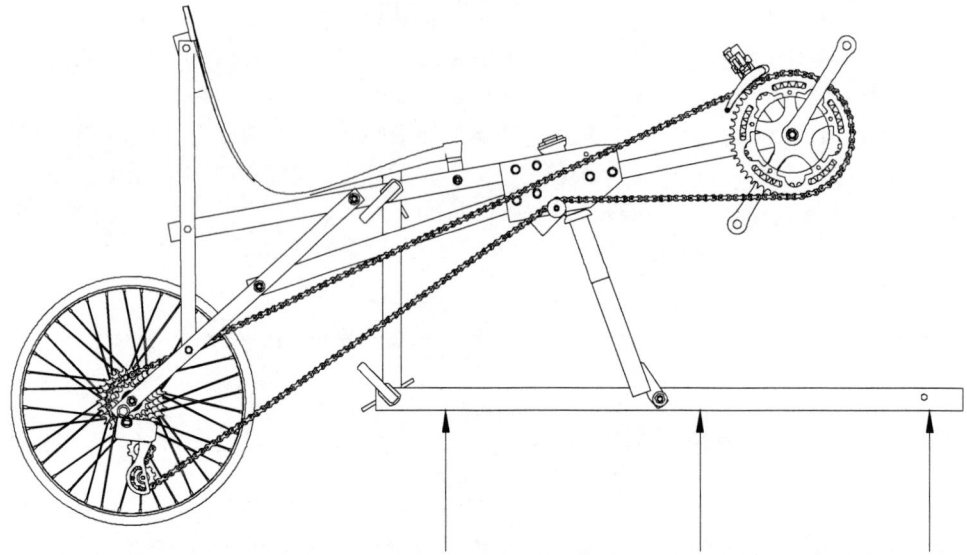

The jig is now used as a work stand for the remaining operations. What you see is the result of adding the roller, mounting the rear changer, mounting the front changer, and installing the chain. This bike uses less than two road bike chains, but not much less. The jig should be securely fixed to the top of a work bench with C clamps, bolts or lag screws. The upright is shown here supporting the bike. A new hole is drilled in the jig for the front axle. Step one is to drill the hole for the roller. The roller itself can be a single piece of nylon, aluminum, or made up of several pieces of tubing with fender washers on the end to prevent the chain from running off the edge. These are available at shops that cater to the recumbent crowd but expect to pay a lot. You can make your own for next to nothing.

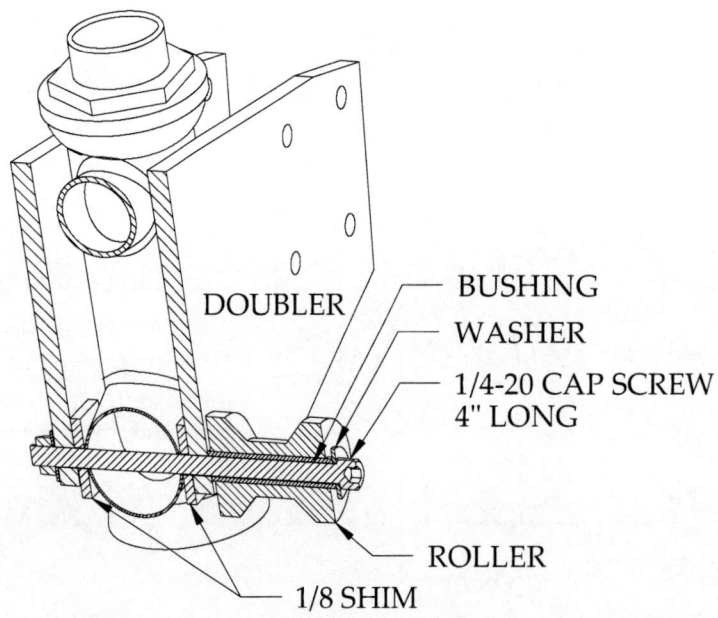

This illustration shows exactly what you want to do to make the roller work. The bushing is clamped tight to the doubler and does not move. The roller is free to spin on the bushing.

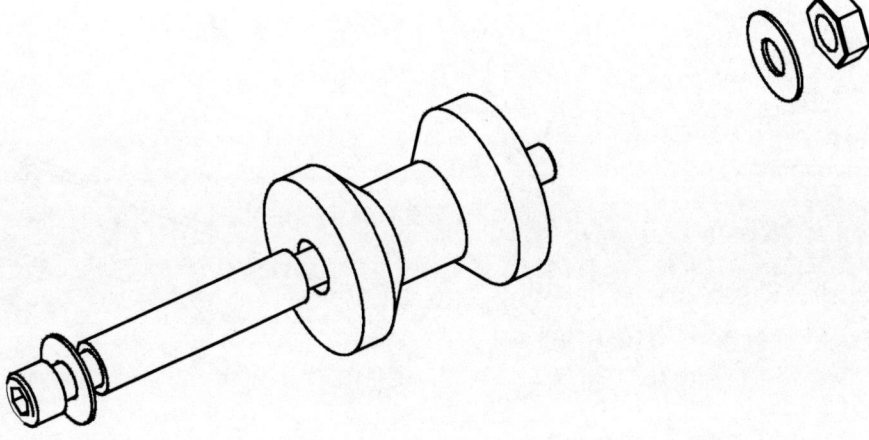

The bolt that mounts the roller bushing also clamps the head tube. It should be installed just as drawn here. There are other ways to mount the roller and if you choose another route, you must still install a through bolt through the doublers and head tube.

Notice the straight shot from the chain wheel to the rear cluster. The idler that lifts the chain past the fork is shown in the drawings as a nylon roller spinning on an axle. Though this method is fool proof and easy to build, many recumbents have refined this feature to a work of art. It is easy to imagine a classy replacement for our basic system. It is OK to guide the slack side of the chain, but never try to guide the tight side. Recumbents need every watt of power you can produce so don't burn up energy with unnecessary friction and wasted effort.

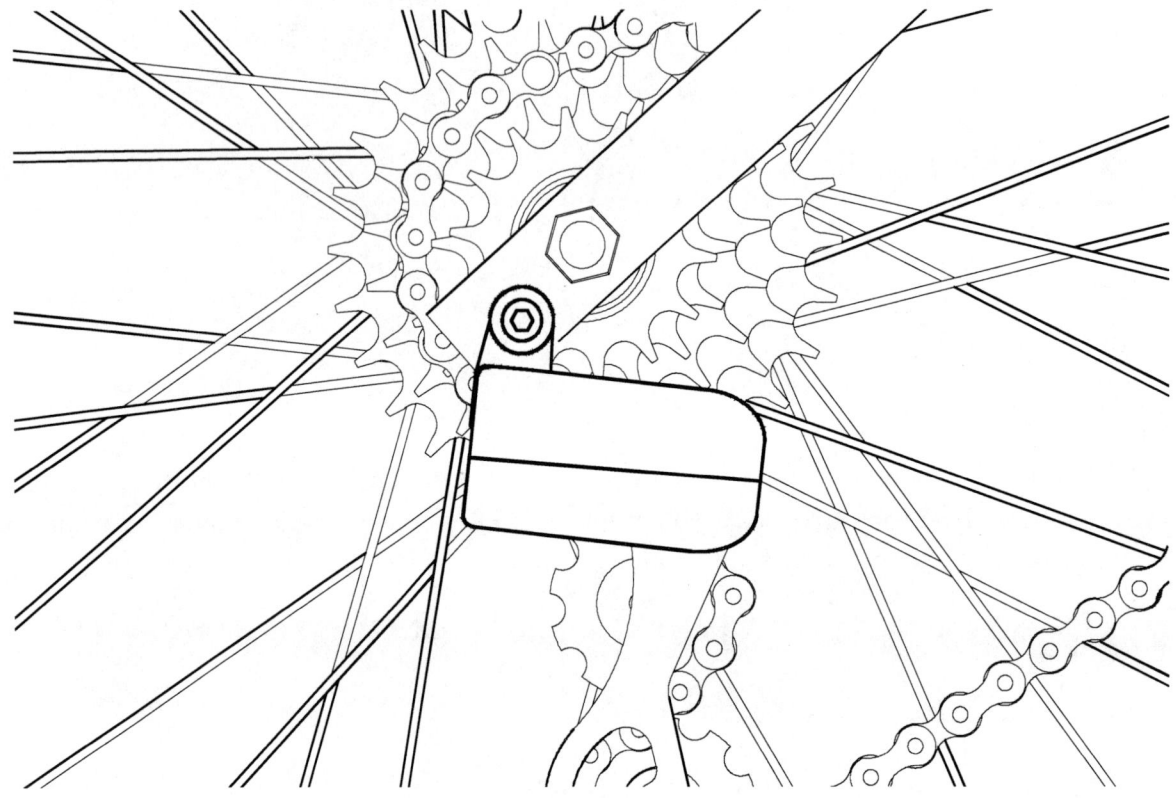

The rear changer must be mounted with a screw that clamps the changer to the stay. The swivel mechanism will no longer work if you do this but that has not proved to be a problem. The rear axle must be at least 7 inches long [17.5 cm]

Once the chain is moving like it should, then it is time to attach the control cables. That means the handle bar must be assembled and clamped in the steering tube. An extra long stem must be used. Remove the bike from the work stand and find a helper to help mount the handle bar. You must first determine the angle to cut the new stem. Grab the wedge from the donor cycle and have a look.

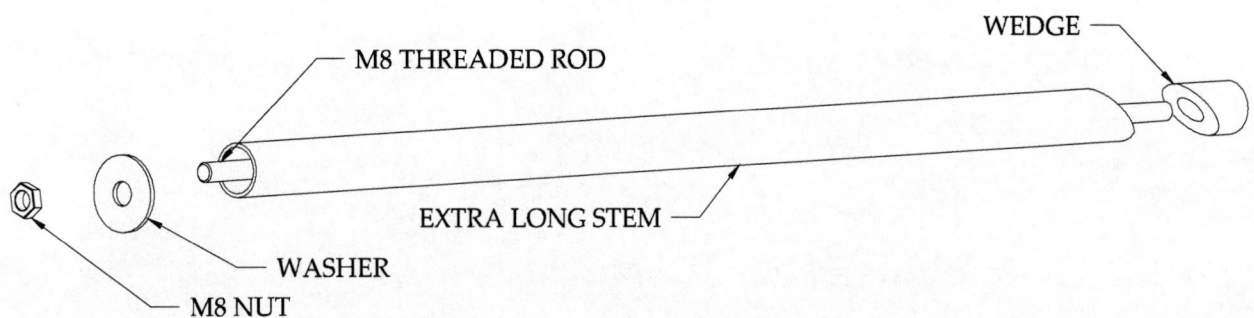

The wedge is from the donor cycle, all else is added. Buy the M8 threaded rod from an industrial supply house. Some hardware stores carry it, some don't. The length of the extra long stem is up to you.

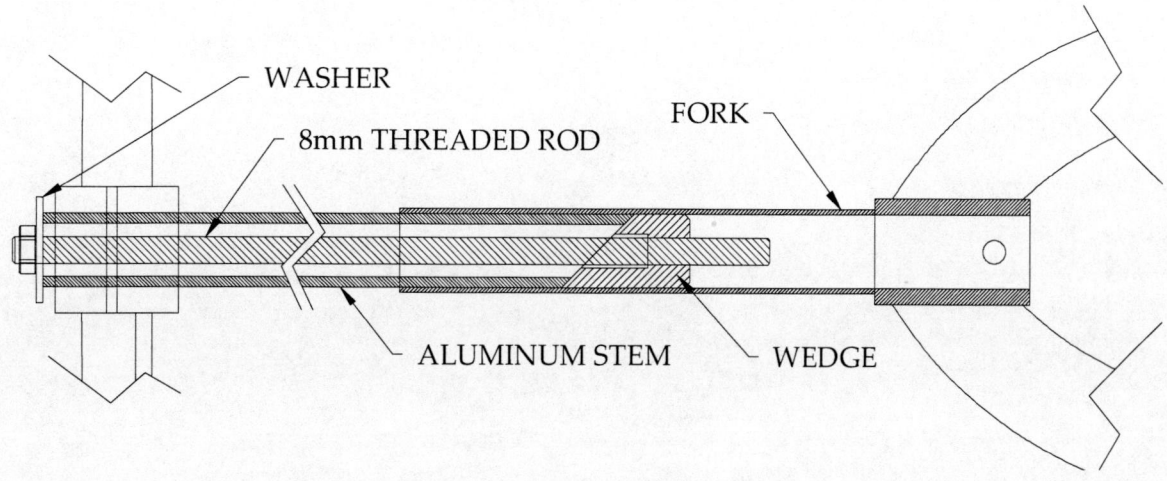

WASHER

8mm THREADED ROD

FORK

ALUMINUM STEM

WEDGE

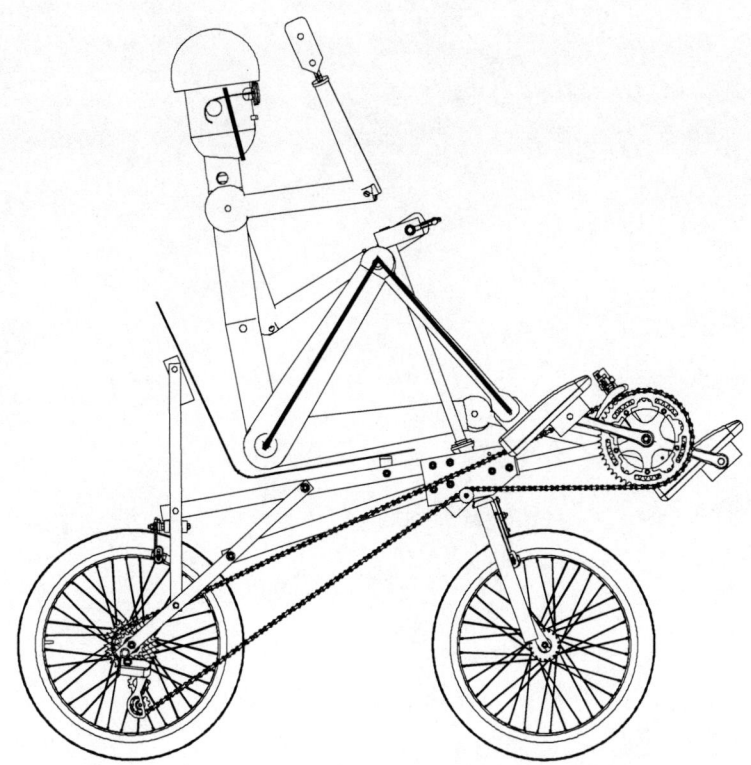

Notice the lack of seat cushions. You will want to cut the extra long stem four inches too long until you have a chance to ride. You can always trim it later. Start with a stem 28 inches long, and cut it back once you get some riding time under your belt.

The handlebar clamp is standard item though a shop made custom piece is used in all our bikes. We find it easier to make our own than to look around bike shops for what we want. This is not an option for you unless you know a machinist who can help you out with this item.

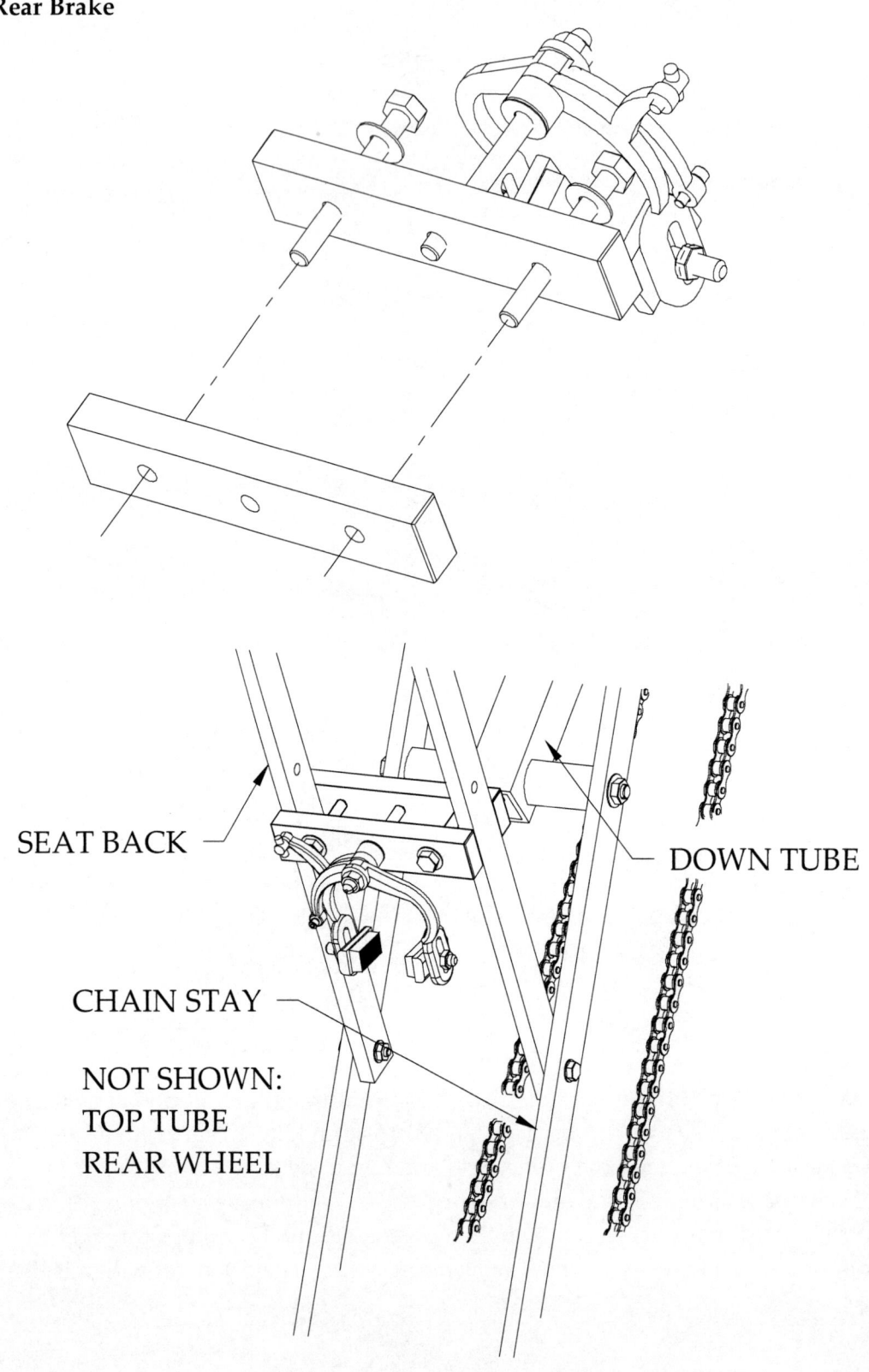

SEAT BACK

DOWN TUBE

CHAIN STAY

NOT SHOWN:
TOP TUBE
REAR WHEEL

Our frame lacks a bridge or cross piece that is used to mount most caliper brakes. A drum or disk brake on the rear wheel is certainly the easiest and cleanest solution for mounting a rear brake. If that is what you go with, smart move. Otherwise, check this out. It is a bridge clamp that supports the rear caliper brake.

Cut a couple of pieces of chain stay material and arrange them as shown in this view. If there was one and only one brake in the world, a complete universal design would be shown here. Refer to the plans for more detail. Hint: clamp both pieces together and drill them at the same time. As is the case in most bikes, the rear brake contributes only a small percentage of the total braking effort but that doesn't mean you can get by with an imperfect set up. The rear brake is important so be sure to give this bit of work all the attention it deserves. To get the length you need on the attachment bolt, you will have to use a front brake with its longer pivot bolt.

This bike looks nose heavy but it is not. The short wheel base does affect weight transfer during braking but there is no danger in locking up the rear wheel or nosing over under panic braking. If you ride in traffic you will soon be riding in the panic mode all the time so avoiding dangerous braking situations becomes second nature. Don't modify the front brake in any way and don't use aluminum fasteners anywhere on your brakes. Never use aluminum nuts or screws on your brakes. Never. Whoever thought this one up should be sent to Iraq.

The front brake is up to the builder. Never ride this bike or any bike in traffic without a front brake.

1.25 x 1.25 x .125 6061-T6 Aluminum Tube 88 inches long; this includes enough for the jig. If you choose to make the jig from some other material, then 4 feet is enough.

½ x 1 x 48 for the chain stays. This is also 6061 T6 aluminum

3/8 x 1 x 48 6061 T6 for the seat stays

.875 diameter by .125 wall Aluminum tube for spacers and handlebar stem 6061 T6

3/16 Aluminum Plate, any alloy except 1100   16 x 4 or 8 x 8 for the doublers

5/16 – 18 Threaded Rod 24"

Shim material 1/8 x 1 and 3/16 x 1 Any aluminum, steel or brass alloy

The information presented is sufficient to build the short wheel base recumbent. The staff at Robobike is not too keen on recumbent bikes, mostly because of the visibility challenge they present to motorists. We have not found them to be particularly comfortable or efficient, the two most popular reasons bent riders use to justify the seating position. Still and all, a bent is a fun project and fun to ride.

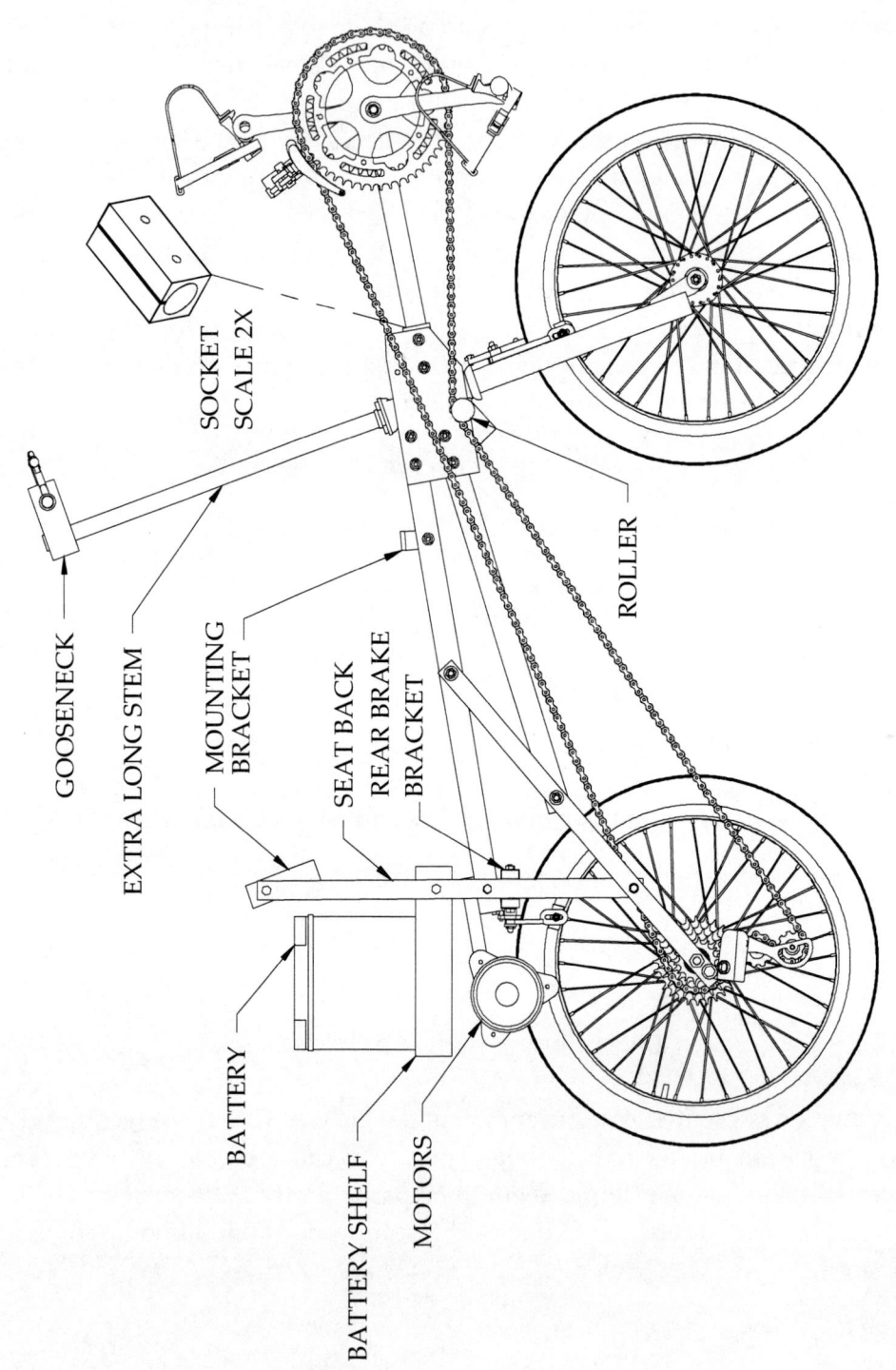

GOOSENECK

EXTRA LONG STEM

MOUNTING BRACKET

SEAT BACK

REAR BRAKE BRACKET

BATTERY

BATTERY SHELF

MOTORS

SOCKET SCALE 2X

ROLLER

Wing Nuts

Ghumal Nabi

A collection of tubes becomes a bike frame much easier and with greater chance of success if that collection is clamped and held in perfect alignment during the fusion process. A bike shop might spend tons of money and boo koo time on building a fully gimbaled jig but you won't be doing anything like that. Still, it is nice to have everything straight and true when welding.

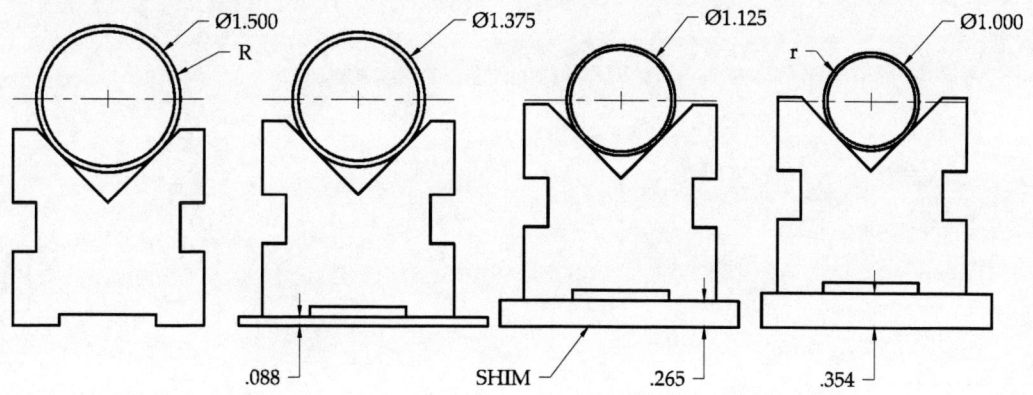

Tubes of decreasing diameter as they rest in vee blocks

Shims are needed to put each centerline the same distance above the datum surface: SHIM THICKNESS = $\sqrt{2}(R-r)^2$, a handy number to know but we find that a measurement is even better. Vee blocks are common in every professional shop but are quite rare in a typical home shop. They are expensive and not suited for most operations done around the home shop. You will need at least 7 to jig up a typical main triangle but even so, you will be limited as to the number of welding positions available with such a setup.

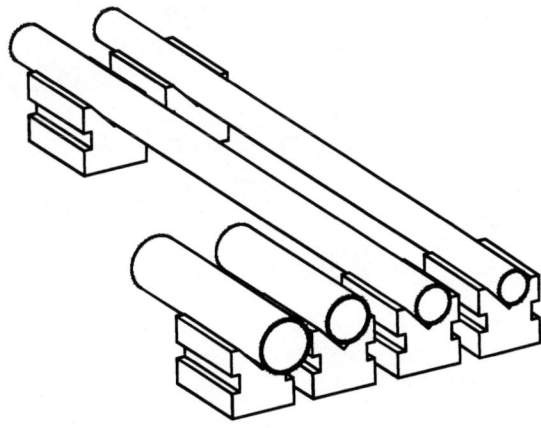

Tubes resting in vee blocks; use care that you do not crush the tube with clamping pressure.

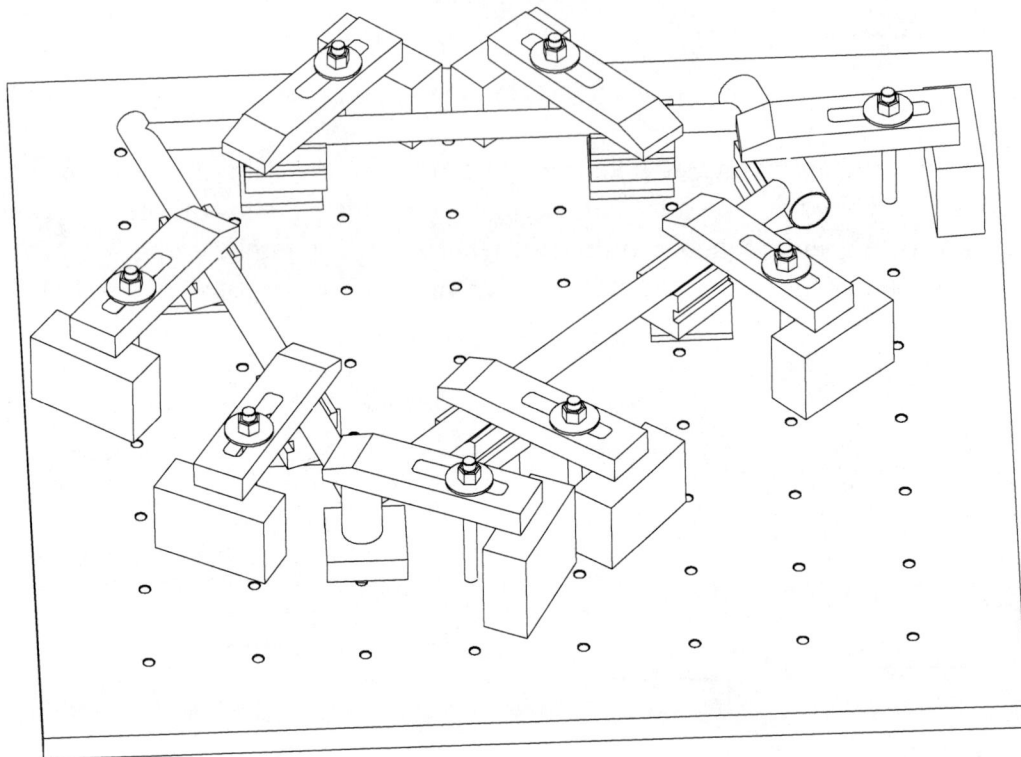

This illustration shows a main triangle jigged on a piece of tooling plate tapped with half inch holes on four inch centers. Tooling plate, known and Mic 6 and pronounced Mike 6, is cast aluminum that is Blanchard ground. It is flat as can be. The view below shows how easy it is to verify geometry with a setup like this. The frame will be checked and double checked and since this is a steel bike that will be TIG welded, the frame will be tacked while clamped. The clamps can then be removed for the final pass. The rear triangle will be jigged up in a separate set up similar to this. Your shop probably does not have a piece of 3 foot square tooling plate like this nor does it have this many vee blocks, but it is possible to simulate this set up with common hardware and C clamps.

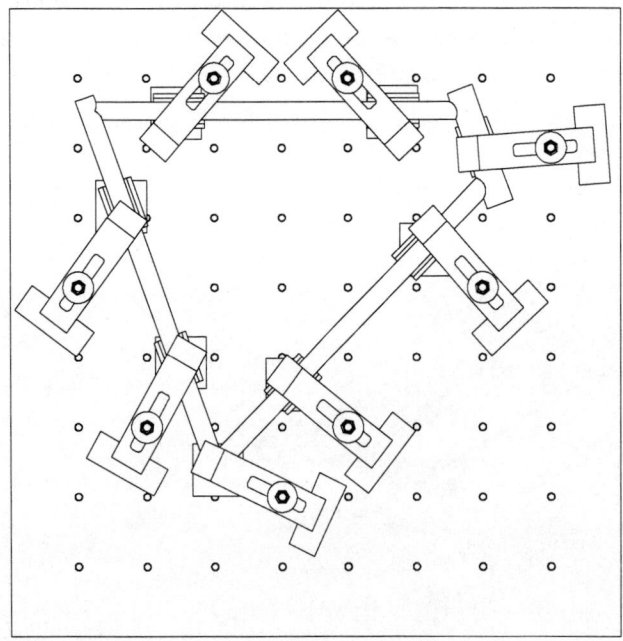

Here is a jig similar to what we use at Robobike.

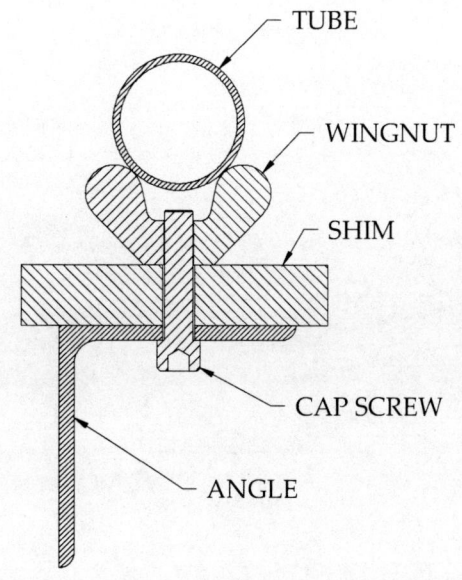

TUBE

WINGNUT

SHIM

CAP SCREW

ANGLE

You should have in your shop a collection of aluminum strips and drop offs or even flat stock sawed into convenient sizes for use as shims. All the shims in the jig are divisible by 1/16". Any adjustment smaller than that can be accomplished by filing the wing nuts or by using thinner shims.

The jig shown here is built around wing nuts clamped in such a way as to act like vee blocks. The skeptical frame builder might think that mass produced wing nuts are too crudely made to use as tooling but that is not true. Robobike ran a series of tests on a bunch of store bought wing nuts and found them to be remarkably consistent. Flaws, though few in number, are easy to spot. A file can be used to correct any flaws found in the hardware. Besides, you won't be welding anything without measuring for accuracy, right?

Joining the Seat Tube to the Bottom Bracket

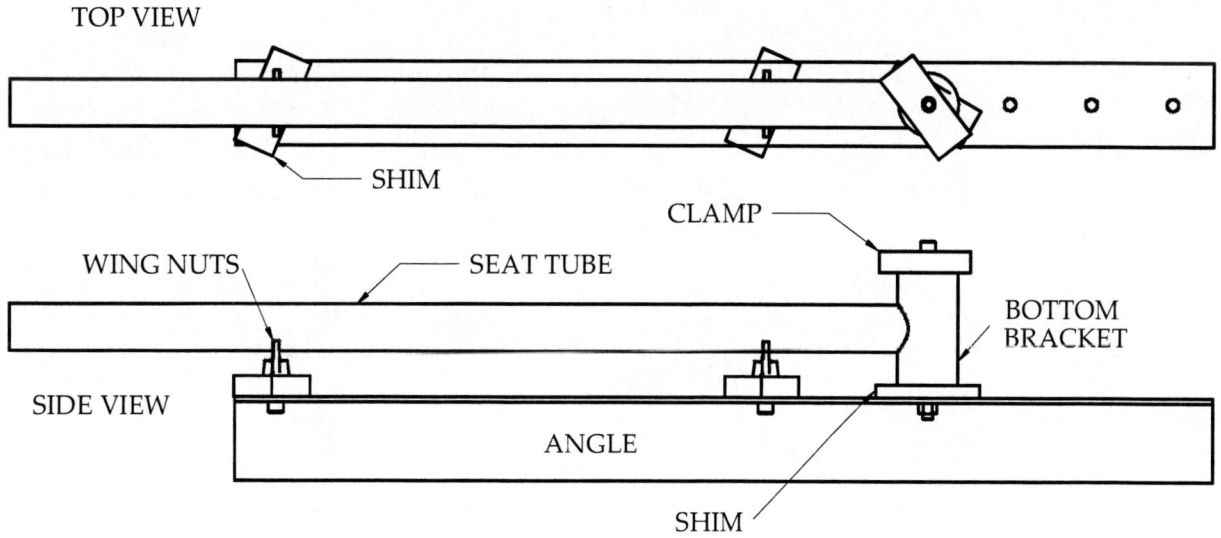

TOP VIEW

SHIM

WING NUTS

SEAT TUBE

CLAMP

BOTTOM BRACKET

SIDE VIEW

ANGLE

SHIM

The seat tube and bottom bracket are tacked in place using a setup similar to this. A small C clamp or parallel clamp can be used to hold the seat tube down on the wing nuts. Don't use a clamp without support under it otherwise the tube will bend when it gets hot.

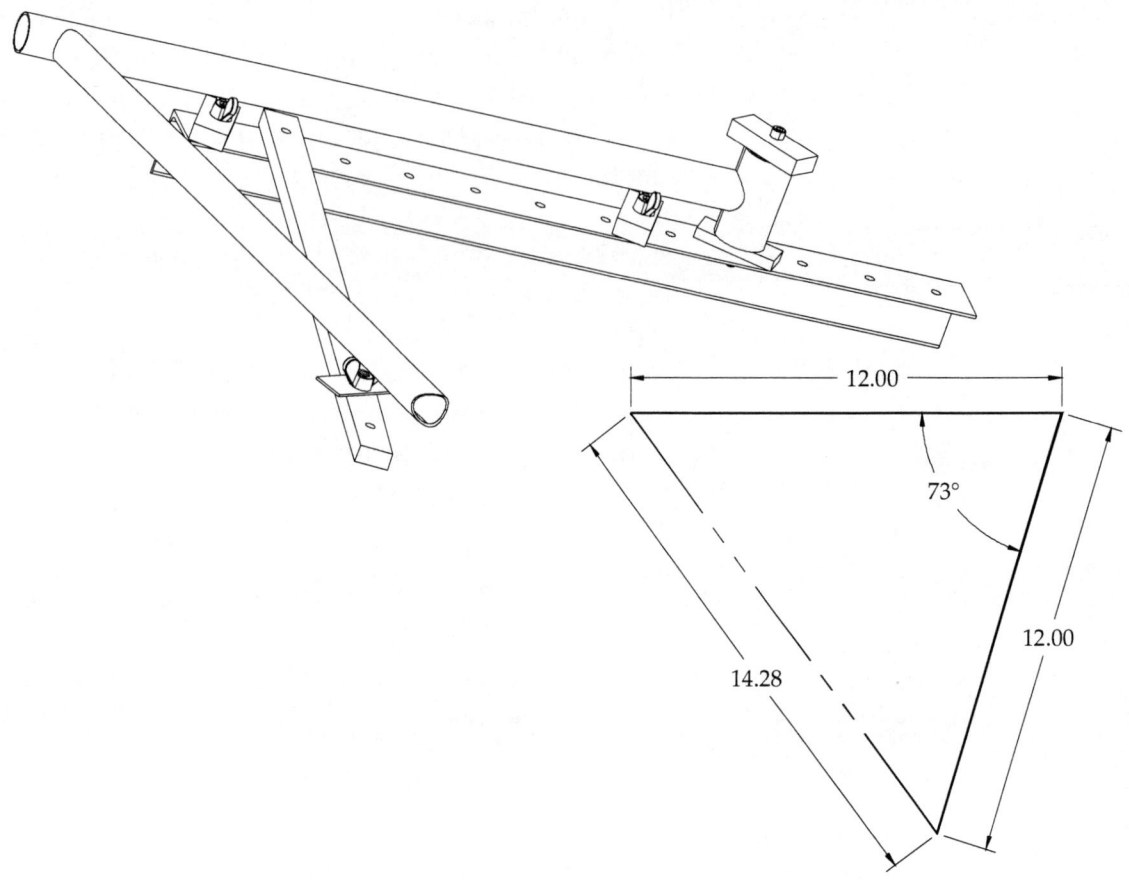

Adding the Top Tube

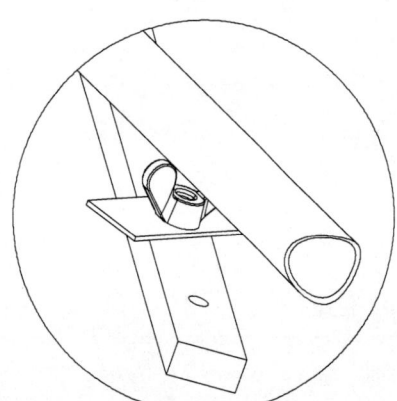

Adding the top tube involves a tack weld and a measurement. Steal a felt tip marker from a coworker and put a dot at the apex of the triangle where the center lines of the top tube and seat tube intersect. Set the angle of the top tube with a ruler. Notice the shim under the wing nut holding the top tube. The top tube is ⅛ of an inch smaller in diameter than the seat tube, the shim is half the difference.

By this time you will have found a way to make fast the angle portion of the jig to your work area using an angle plate or bench vise. That issue becomes more important as the bike grows in size and mass.

Tacking is sufficient at this time. You can finish welding the frame after pulling it off the jig and checking alignment. You can weld everything completely on the jig if you want. Whatever makes your clock tick.

Add a Second Arm to the Jig to Hold the Downtube

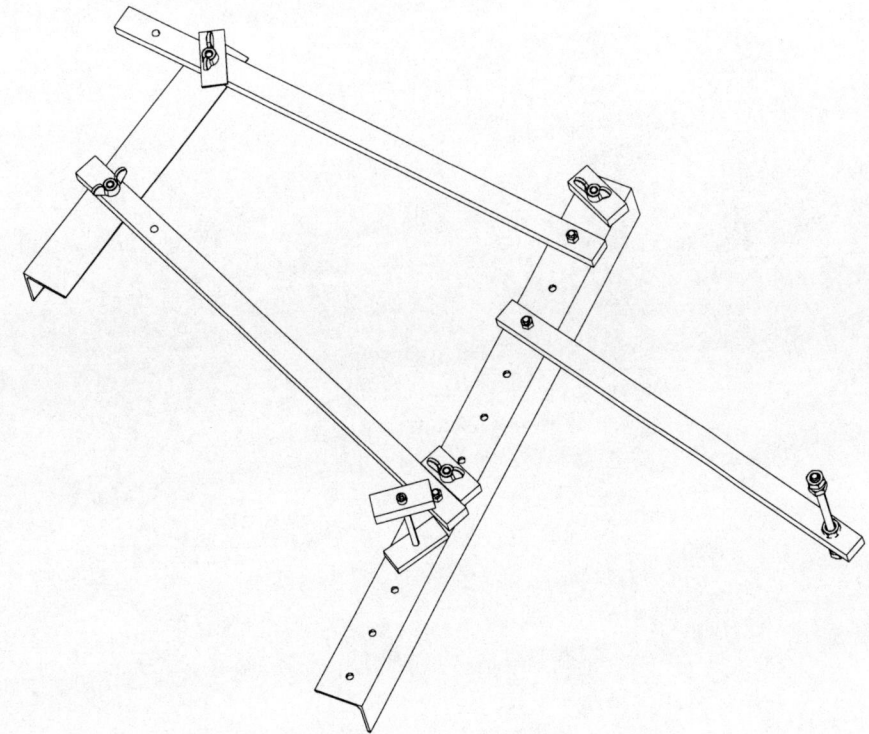

This view of the jig without the frame shows its simplicity and its adaptability to frames of all sizes. The two pieces of angle allow the jig to rest on any flat surface allowing the head tube to be set into the frame and checked for parallelism before being tacked in place.

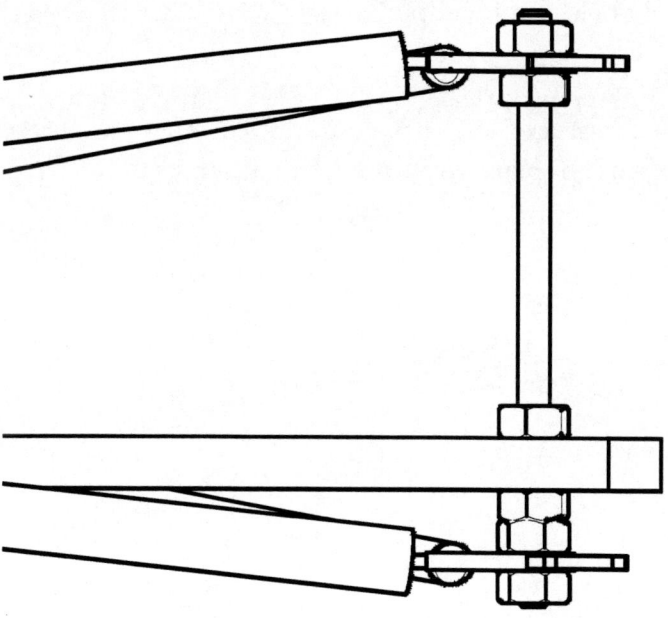

Rear drop out spreader as it is being held by the jig

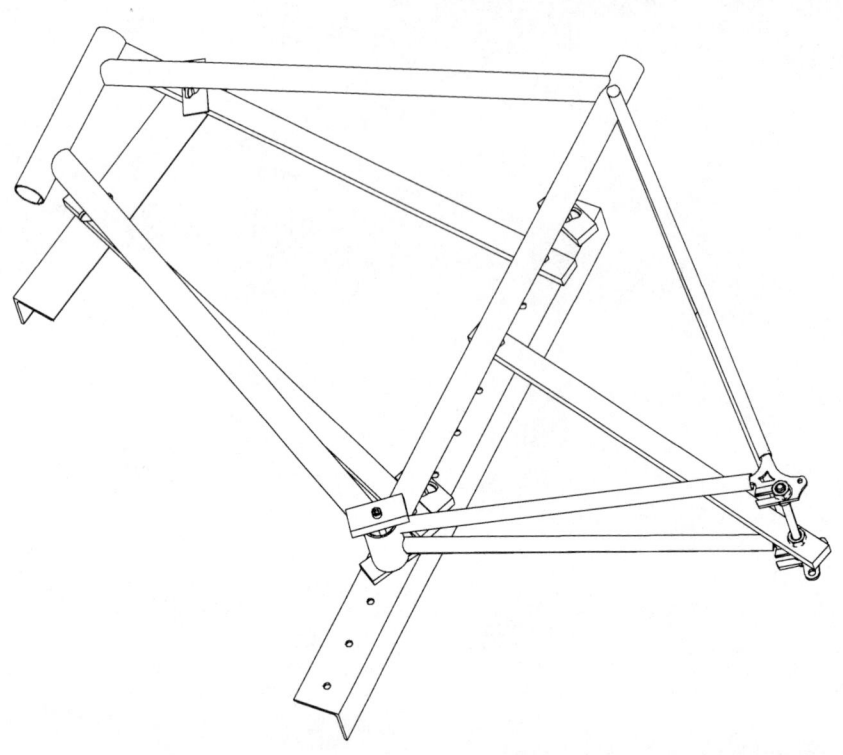

Jig with bike frame ready for tacking.
Notice the ease at which the head tube can be checked for parallelism using an indicator, depth
mic or electronic caliper.

Setting the head tube parallel to the world is very important and very easy to do. We use an
angle plate like the one shown here and rest the head tube on an adjustable parallel set at the
proper height. A small clamp will hold things in place while it is being tacked.

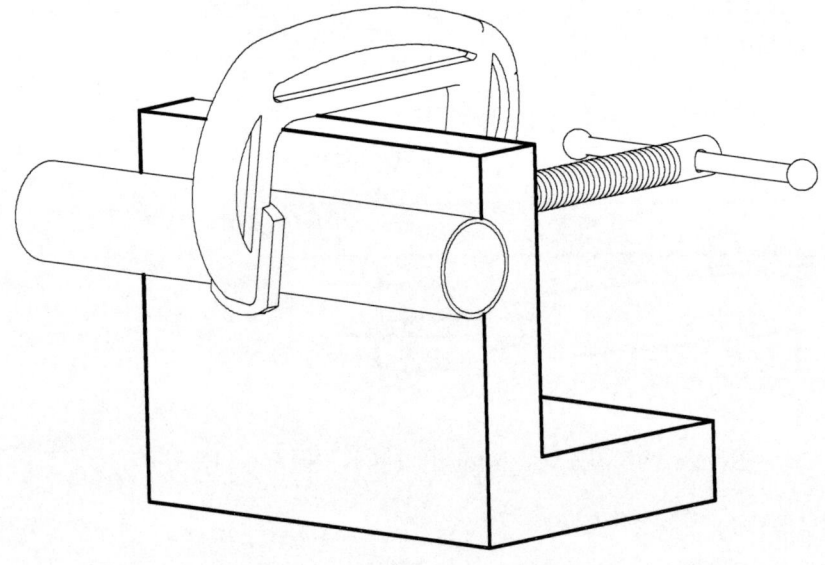

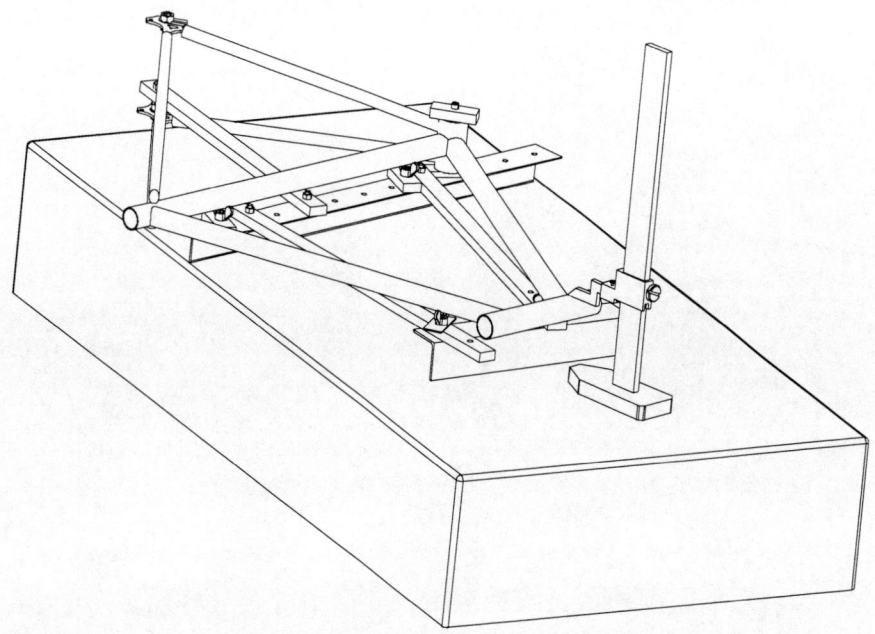

As shown in this illustration, verifying the head tube alignment is quite easy while still in the jig. That is not the case once the frame is removed.

Other inspection equipment useful here are 123 blocks and a depth mic or even a ruler. If the ends of the head tube are the same height at each end of the tube, then the head tube is parallel. Sounds simple but sometimes it is the simple stuff that gets overlooked.

While you have the frame and jig are sitting on the inspection table, verify that the dropout spacing is correct. Use the height gage to find the top of the head tube and then move the gage down by half the diameter of the head tube. This will be the centerline of the bike.

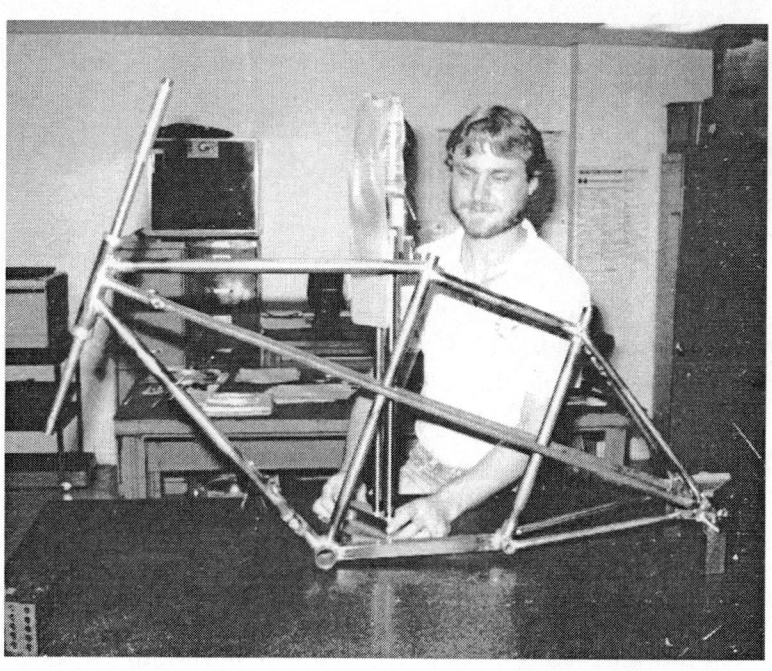

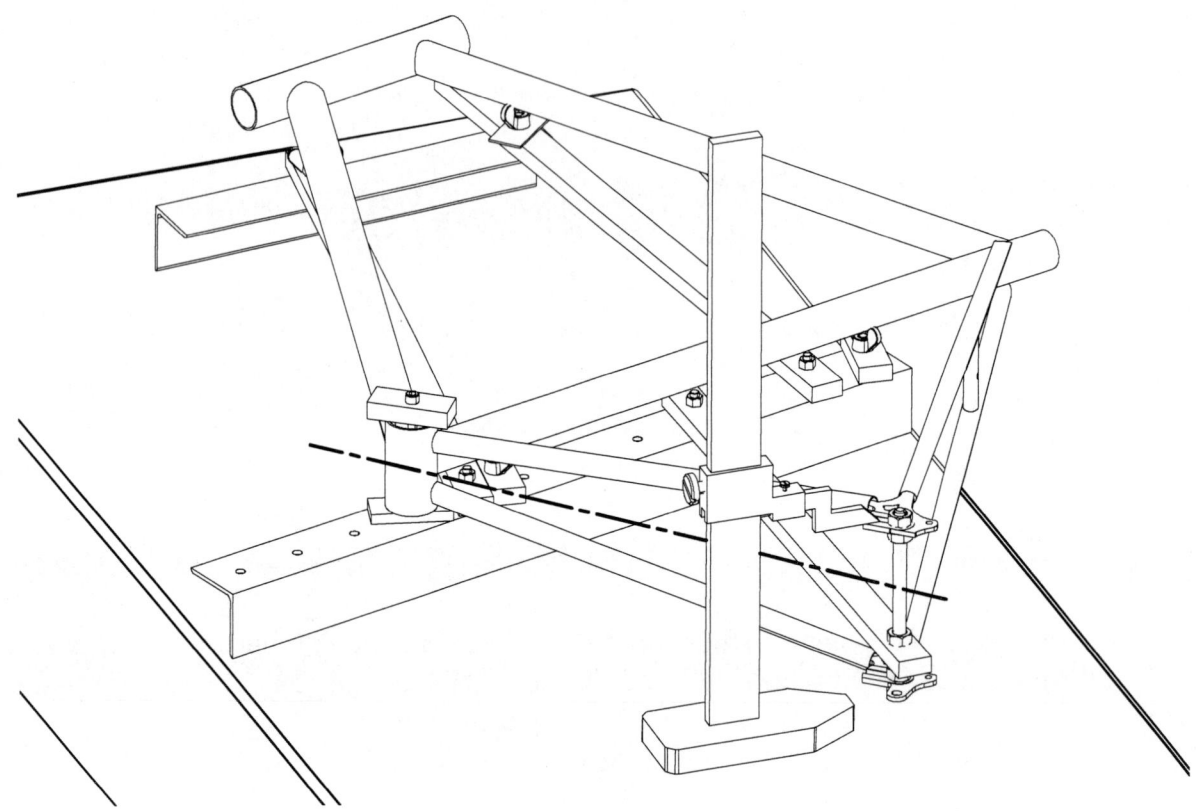

This view of the bike and frame on the table shows a measurement being taken to the outside of the dropout. Using a caliper, measure the outside to outside dropout dimension to make sure the centerline found at the head tube bisects the axle. If you do find an error, double check your figures before you begin tearing things up and fixing a non existent problem. Believe me, it has happened at Robobike.

Aluminum frames, special handling

Aluminum is a light, strong material perfectly suited for building bicycle frames. However, welding aluminum differs very much from welding or brazing steel. First of all, heat travels quickly through aluminum. Your jig needs to be aluminum so it expands at the same rate the frame does. Keep jig hardware out of the weld zone to avoid potential contamination. Even though aluminum melts at a lower temperature than steel, aluminum requires more heat during the fusion process. Aluminum will melt without much of a color change to indicate when it ready to flow but it is still easy to tell when the base material is hot enough to flow. Because of these characteristics, inexperienced welders, and occasionally an experienced welder, will ruin a project with poor heat control. It is because of that reason that Robobike has developed a few standard procedures when building a welded aluminum bicycle frame. Look at our chapter on how to buttress aluminum frames at the heat affected zone to prevent burn through and cold joints. As far as jigging and clamping goes, your aluminum bike will stay in the jig longer than a steel bike. Doing so cuts down on the amount of straightening required after weld.

Welding

Ghumal Nabi

Mr. Nabi teaches welding and American studies at the Robobike Technical Institute

There are almost an unlimited number of sources for someone wanting to learn to weld. This is not one of them. Learning to weld and building a bicycle are two different events. One is not begun until the other is well in hand. We'll show you how to increase the chances of getting a good joint using the same design tools a machinist would use to build a first class welding jig and how to put together a frame to avoid localized stress. That's it. We are not welding instructors. The best way to learn to weld is to get yourself a welder and start welding. It's like playing a piano. Practice practice practice. There's nothing hard about it. We at Robobike are welders and machinists who seldom agree about anything. One thing on which we all agree is what it takes to make a good weld joint. We also know what it takes to design some bad weld joints. We've seen some doozies. There are a lot of engineers out there who have never held a welding torch and that is really sad.

Early bicycles were built using hammers and charcoal fires. This is mighty hard to believe for someone who uses a tungsten torch and high frequency, but that was the state of the art at the dawn of the bicycle age. Though admirable as these technicians were in producing the first bikes, other solutions exist today to the problem of joining tubes for the purpose of creating a working machine.

Tube Selection

Just a word about tubes; Robobike is not in the business of building lightweight mainstream bikes. Subsequently, we use materials better suited for our needs than those found on high performance bikes. We never use steel with a wall thickness less than .040". In fact, .062 is the size we use most often. Aluminum tubes tend to go .090 to .125, mostly for welding requirements. Thinner materials require professional skills and equipment. A robot welder never takes a break, never gets tired and rarely makes a mistake. We do not have that equipment at Robobike.

The Processes

Fusion and adhesion are the two categories discussed here. The fusion categories can be described as those processes where the base metals are brought to a temperature sufficiently high that they mingle and become one. Filler rod is added and a neutral atmosphere or some other provision such as flux is used to prevent oxidation in the weld zone. The adhesion processes are similar except the base metals are not heated to such a high temperature and do not flow into one another. Soldering and brazing are the two processes important to us and are described here.

Brazing steel...never work without proper ventilation

The bronze fillets that were the hallmark of an expensive, hand built tandem frame in years past are in short supply today. This does not mean, however, that brazing is no longer a valid process for the bicycle builder. Far from it. It is easy to learn. The required equipment is readily available. It is a good choice for the home bike shop. Its biggest negative if the amount of work required to clean up after brazing.

The brazing process itself requires heat. That heat can be supplied by a torch or, in the case of mass produced factory bikes, a furnace. Furnace brazing, and I include all types of induction brazing in this category, is restricted to those bikes using doublers, commonly referred to as lugs, to join the tubes. The tubes are set in an assembly jig with a mixture of filler and flux brushed onto the ends of the tubes where they fit the lugs. They whole thing is then heated and held at a temperature high enough to melt the filler and promote migration (also known as diffusion) of the filler into the grain boundaries of the base metal. It is possible to buy a set of lugs and a tube set and put it together like a model airplane kit, but that process will not discussed. Only bikes built without lugs concern us here.

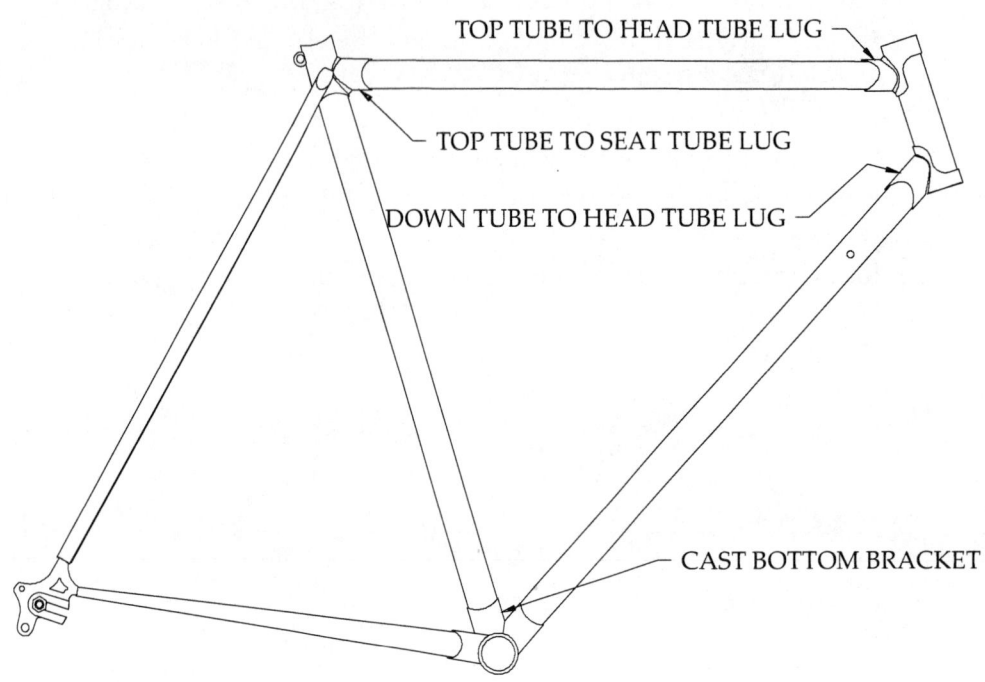

TOP TUBE TO HEAD TUBE LUG

TOP TUBE TO SEAT TUBE LUG

DOWN TUBE TO HEAD TUBE LUG

CAST BOTTOM BRACKET

Lugs for this type of construction are investment cast steel. Some poorly made bicycles have lugs made of stamped steel that are folded to resemble cast lugs.

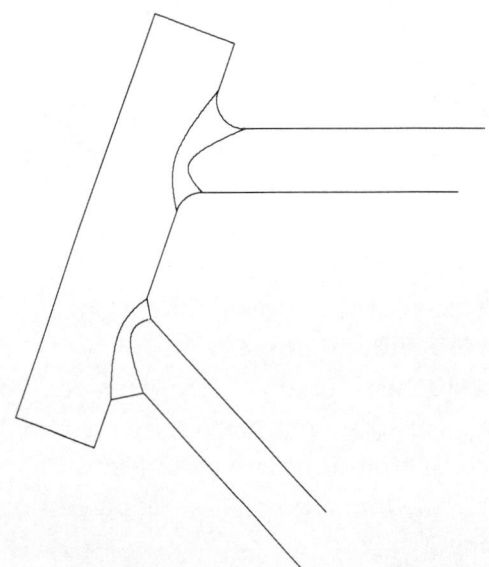

Head tube from Loveboat after much cleaning and filing

Torch brazing is similar to furnace brazing though the heating is not as uniform. Filler migration into the grain structure of the base material is certainly part of the process but the amount of base metal surface in close proximity is limited. Instead of lugs, brass fillets of substantial size are built up using multiple passes around the joint. These fillets have the same effect as the lugs and that is to spread the stresses over a larger area. Stress is defined as load/unit area. Increasing the unit area reduces stress. Reducing stress reduces the resultant local strain. Subsequently, a bike frame with large fillets is more rigid than a frame with smaller fillets. Frames with greater rigidity will not feel the effects of metal fatigue as soon as frames lacking rigidity. Keep this in mind as you design and assemble a bicycle.

Designing for the brazing process

Good designs can be identified by elegance in both meeting the design objectives and in the ease of manufacture. All welding processes create distortion and brazing is no exception. Most of the time, distortion can be ignored or corrected but in some cases, it cannot. There are ways to prevent distortion. Installing plugs or scrap head set bearings to keep the tubes round is one way of doing this as is installing bottom bracket cups during the brazing operation. The heat will draw the hardness from bearings so they must be discarded after the process.

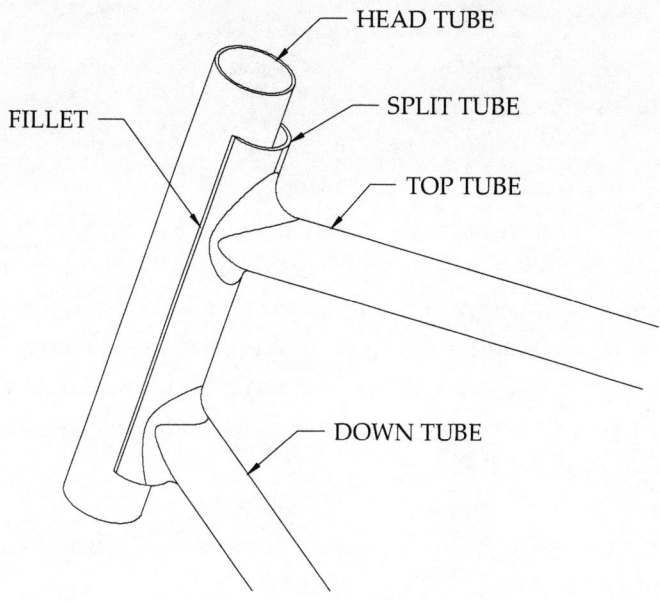

The half moon or split tube is another way to guarantee distortion free head sets. Originally used at Robobike to repair a head tube that had gone banana in a big way, it was found to be a good all purpose design gimmick, especially for prototypes that may go through several revisions. If the long fillet is prepared properly, lower temperature silver solder can be used. Silver solder requires a large contact area for a joint like this and this certainly qualifies. Here is another solution has already been discussed in Delivery Boy.

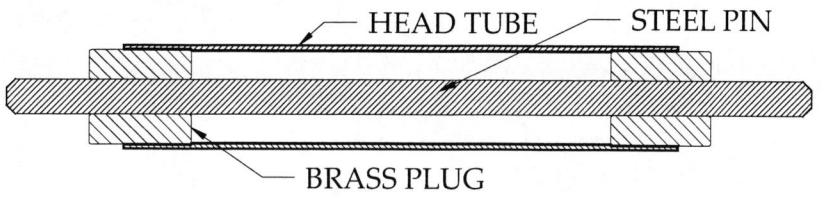

Doublers

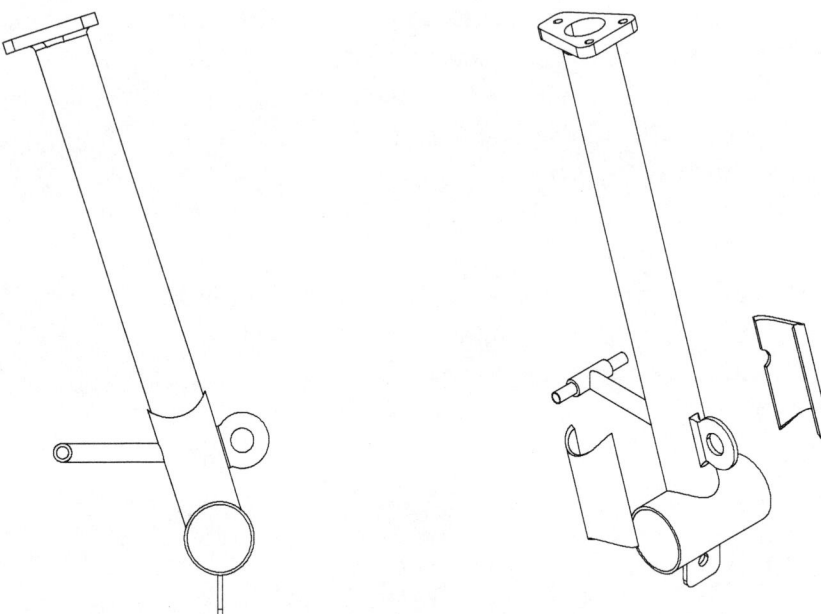

The Nile Crocodile and all subsequent travel bikes built at Robobike have this lower seat tube configuration made of steel. After brazing the entire assembly with bronze, the doublers are added and silver soldered in place. The silver solder melts at a much lower temperature than the brass so there is little danger of unbrazing what has already been done. These doublers add a great deal of rigidity to the joint. This is only one example of a doubler. Other uses are easy to imagine. Always consider whether or not one is required. They add a substantial amount of rigidity for the little work required to produce them.

In the 1930s, the Pietenpol brothers petitioned the controlling body for civil aviation in the USA for permission to use brazed joints in their homebuilt aircraft and to have them approved generally for all home built aircraft. Their petition was denied after some tests were conducted. Fatigue failure of the high cycle variety was the reason for the denial. This is the reason behind creating large fillets when brazing. The type of fatigue found in powered aircraft and in bicycles are of the same general type but differ greatly in the number of stress reversals while in service. An airplane may feel an impulse at every firing of every piston while a bicycle may count every pedal stroke. This is a simplistic explanation, to be sure, but the point is that you cannot compare the two types of structure using the same parameters.

Burning

Thin wall tubes joined in a cluster may burn if heated improperly. Flux heated to too high a temperature burns and becomes a contaminant, spoiling the operation. The zinc in the brass filler rod becomes a poisonous gas when it gets too hot. Burning can be minimized by designing tube clusters that are easy to braze. Don't direct the torch to the inside corner of a box, for example, without first heating around the area. This technique is referred to as banking heat. If the area is sufficiently hot and sufficient heat energy is stored in the surrounding area, then the heat directed at the joint does not dissipate and less heat energy is needed in the local area. Trying to braze a dirty tube may result in burning as does trying to braze a thin section to a thick section. A doubler around the thin section may be of some help here. Try to avoid extremes in thickness. They often make little sense structurally.

Flux and rod

Most brazing rod in use today is flux coated brass that has an affinity for clean steel at its liquidus temperature. **Keyword: clean** Added flux is not necessary and usually just makes the clean up more difficult. The silver solder process, however, does require added flux. Water soluble flux for silver solder is just what it sounds like. When brushed onto tubes in liquid form, it dries out as soon as the flame hits it. When it goes liquid, the tubes are very close to brazing temperature. Robobike uses silver solder for shifter bosses, water bottle cages, doublers and sometimes entire projects. It is absolutely required for tubes thinner than .032 wall thickness. Doublers are required when building with silver solder. No exceptions.

Metals other than steel

Titanium and other non-ferrous metals can be joined by brazing using various types of filler, but for our purposes, the filler should be silver solder with at least 45% silver content. Since the process is defined as being adhesive and not one involving fusion, the quality and subsequently the integrity of the joint cannot be guaranteed without testing and by that, we mean testing to destruction. Why would you want to do that? Titanium luggage racks are cool, so are racks built of stainless steel. If you insist on using these metals in a structural application, then fusion welding is the only option. Welding titanium at home is not practical.

Aluminum cannot be brazed at home in spite of what all the weld sites and text books devoted to the subject say about it. This is a process that has no application in the bicycler's world. Once again, the reason comes back to verifiable strengths and reliability. A brazed aluminum frame may be perfectly adequate but simply taking a design meant for a steel frame joined with brass and substituting aluminum is foolhardy. An aluminum frame designed for this process does not resemble a steel frame at all. Besides that, the change of state that happens in aluminum when heated to these temperatures is another black mark against brazing aluminum. We do not allow brazed aluminum in any project at Robobike.

Stainless steel should be silver soldered if used at all. Once again, testing is required so why bother. Diffusion into stainless is not always the same as diffusion into steel. The cubic structures are different, even among the group known as stainless. It is imperative that you know the difference and know what process is appropriate. Silver solder is not appropriate for structural applications rendered in stainless steel.

The fusion processes

The most popular processes are Gas Metal Arc Welding (GMAW), sometimes called MIG welding and Gas Tungsten Arc Welding (GTAW) sometimes referred to as TIG welding. A third process, Shielded Metal Arc Welding (SMAW) or stick welding, has limited use for bicycle work. Oxy-acetylene was once the only process available but it has fallen into disuse today, at least for fusion welding.

SMAW - Shielded Metal Arc Welding or Stick, is an electric arc welding process in which heat for welding is generated by an electric arc between a covered metal electrode & the base metal. The electrode coating provides shielding. The welding equipment for this process is currently the most inexpensive of the methods described here.

GTAW - Gas Tungsten Arc (also known as TIG) Welding is easily performed on nearly all metals. It generally requires little or no post weld finishing. It is an electric welding process in which heat for welding is generated by an electric arc between the end of a non-consumable tungsten electrode (the torch) and the base metal. Filler metal is added by a hand held filler rod. An inert shielding gas provides shielding for the torch and the arc. (Inert gas creates a protective atmosphere around the welding in process). This is the only welding process we do at Robobike.

GMAW   - Gas Metal Arc Welding (also known as MIG) is quick and easy on thin-gauge metal as well as heavy plate. It generally requires little post weld cleanup. GMAW is an electric arc welding process where heat is produced by an arc between a continuously fed filler metal (wire feed) electrode & the base metal. Shielding is obtained from an externally supplied gas or gas mixture. The two most common techniques used with GMAW are Spray Transfer and Short Circuit Transfer, also known as short arc. With short arc, the wire is allowed to come in contact with the work piece. This short circuit results in high current flow, intense heat and deposition of the wire into the weld zone. This happens several times a second. Short circuit transfer is not appropriate for aluminum welding. With Spray Transfer, metal is transferred across the arc creating a continuous spray of fine droplets of filler metal. These droplets are projected down to the base metal.

Generally, the work piece is prepared the same for welding as it is for brazing. Since the tensile strength of the base metal and the filler metal in the fusion processes are nearly the same, a buildup of a large fillet is not as important as it is for the brazing process. There is less chance of catastrophic failure in a fusion joint than there is in a brazed joint.

Heat Sinks and Doublers

Heat sinks are used to bank or store heat. Since aluminum wicks away heat so quickly from the weld zone, it is difficult to maintain a large area near the liquidus temperature. The heat sink is a piece of weld tooling, usually copper or steel, that is inserted into a tube so that its mass is added to the weld joint during the process. The heat sink is removed after the joint has cooled. A well designed heat sink will contribute to clamping, alignment and distortion control too.

Heat sinks are often used with designed features such as doublers. This illustration shows a tube with a doubler welded in the area where another tube joins. It has been welded with a piece of round copper bar inserted inside the tube. The small hole, a vent hole drilled through both tubes, is used in this operation and the next, which is to join the second tube.

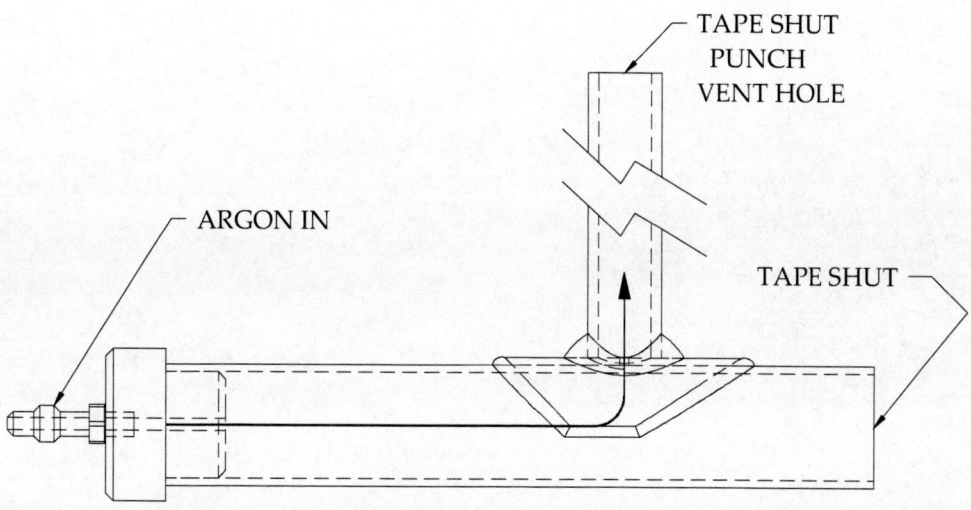

The gas backup, as it is known, is used only on the fussiest of weld joints. It prevents oxides forming on the backside of the weld joint. As with the first operation, a copper round is inserted inside the second tube during the weld operation. The copper is removed from the bigger tube after the doubler is welded. If closed and access is not possible, a doubler in the form of a small sleeve slipped into the smaller tube makes the welding operation quite a bit easier. In this case, the doubler is merely an aid for the welding operation. Its use allows the frame tubes to be a lighter gauge than what would be possible without the doubler. What is the point of using aluminum tubes in your frame if the welding process demands a heavier wall thickness than the anticipated stresses require?

We have already mentioned that aluminum has a high thermal coefficient. Not only does this complicate the welding process, but it influences the safety equipment needed to handle aluminum at elevated temperatures. Dark glasses should be worn under the hood to protect the eyes when the hood is raised. Gloves are absolutely necessary. As far as that goes, all exposed skin needs to be covered. This applies not only to the welder, but anyone in the vicinity acting as support or observing. It is possible to get a severe burn from aluminum in the weld shop. Please pay attention. Burning from both infra-red and ultra-violet is a very real hazard and cannot be ignored.

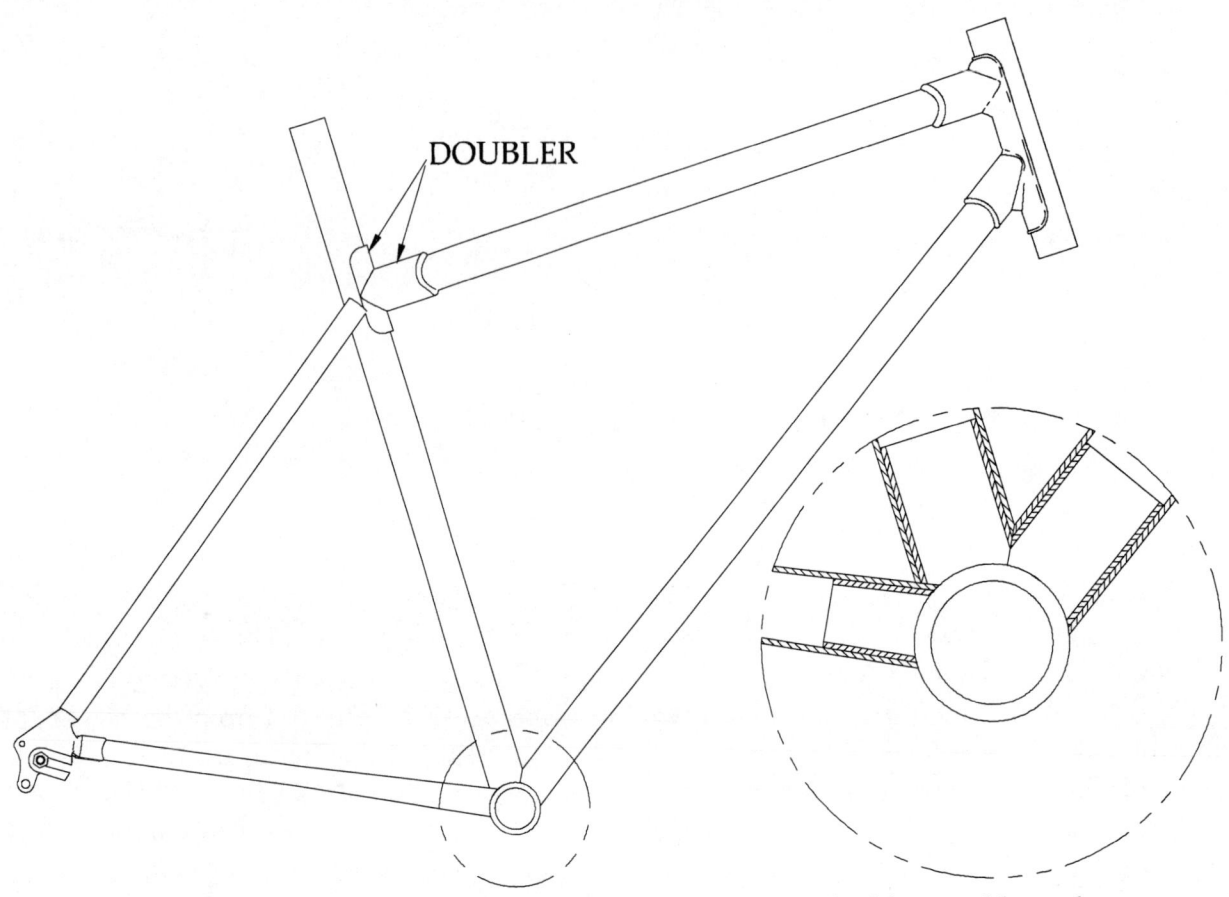

DOUBLER

An aluminum frame showing both external and internal doublers and how they are used. The bottom bracket is the most massive part of this frame and takes more heat during the fusion process than any other area. Subsequently, distortion can be a big problem in this area. Skipping around is one way to control distortion and to ensure the joint is heated equally. The head tube is filled with a steel or copper heat sink, both to prevent distortion and to maintain roundness. The rear triangle presents its own special problems. The biggest is the tubes burning away at the ends. Once again, the answer is a doubler. Shown here is an external doubler at the drop out and an internal doubler at the bb. Check out bikes you see on the street and in bike shops. There are some clever designs in the world today.

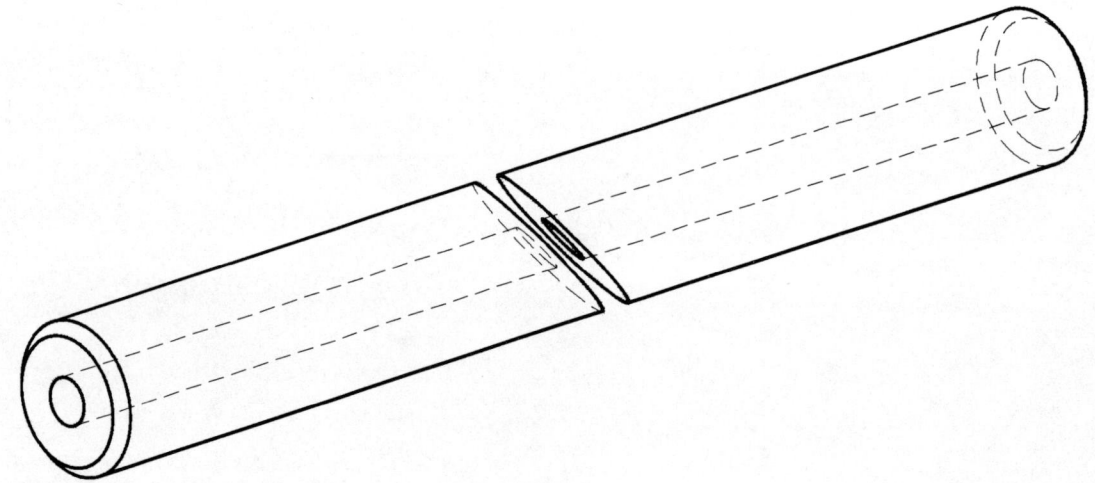

This two piece heat sink is made of steel. Notice the 45° cut between the two pieces. The outside diameter is .020" smaller than the head tube. A through bolt draws the two pieces together. The two piece construction aids in removing the heat sink after the welding operation. A single piece of steel that fits the head tube tight enough to do any good cannot be removed after the distortion kicks in.

The process of choice for aluminum is Gas Tungsten Arc Welding, or TIG. AC is used always for aluminum and argon is the shield. The rod is chosen for resistance to cracking, or hot shortness as it is known. Weld metal cracking can usually be prevented by welding with a filler metal of higher alloy content than the base metal. 6061 alloy, which contains 0.6% silicon, is crack sensitive when welded with 6061 filler metal. However, when welded with ER4043 filler metal, which contains 5% silicon, it welds quite well with high resistance to cracking. The filler metal melts at a lower temperature than the base metal and stays liquid longer. This plastic state allows the joint to yield relieving stress that causes cracking during the cooling phase. Both 6061 and 6061 should be welded with ER4043 while 7005 aluminum is best welded with ER5356. Check with your local neighborhood weld shop for advice on other alloys.

Also, be aware that the welding process changes the mechanical properties of the tubes. If you don't know what that means, you should take a minute to consider whether or not you should be welding with aluminum. Robobike uses 6061 exclusively and sends everything we do to the heat treat shop, mostly because the heat treat shop charges by the batch. Using doublers and extra heavy wall thickness will go a long way to eliminating this need, but if you are using heavier tubes than necessary, why are you building an aluminum bike?

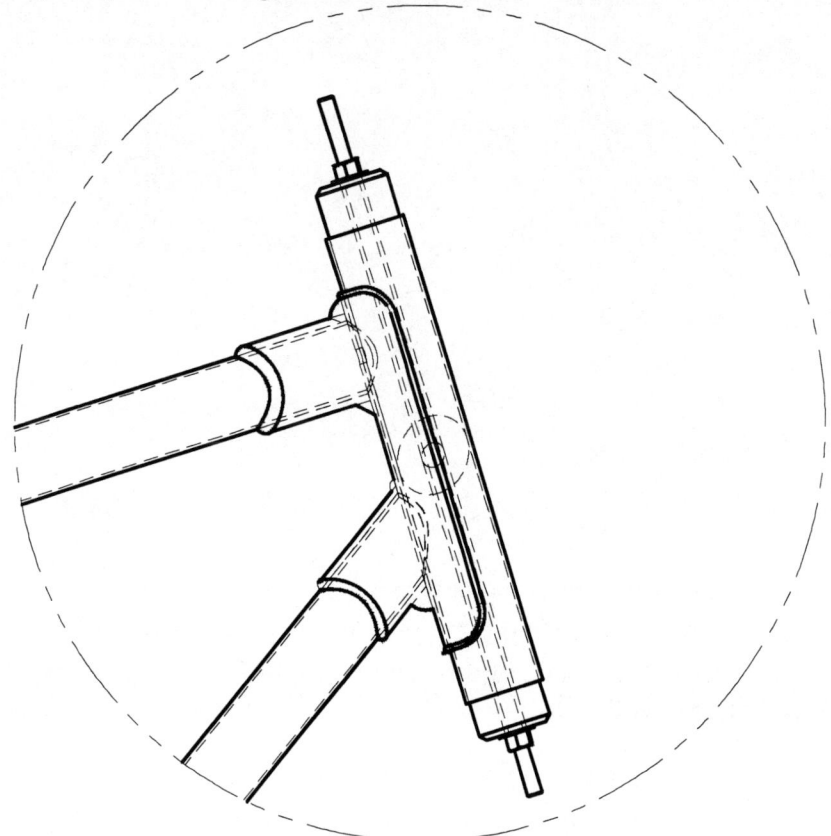

Heat sink installed in a heavy duty aluminum head tube

Shop Tips

Bottom Bracket

The bottom bracket is one of those things that requires a lathe. There is the tap option but we at Robobike have never used it. Apparently, a pair of taps running on a hardened axle is available for those who build bikes the conventional way. Robobike is not in that category. We use a lathe. Take a look at the drawing of the bracket and notice a few things. The minor diameter is bored to 1.335 inches. There is also a thread relief shown at the end of the thread. This is done for two reasons. It allows the unloading of the tool at the end of the cut and gives the finished bracket somewhere to move during the straightening process after welding. We'll get to that later. The thread relief is where the tool begins its cut when cutting the left hand side of the bracket. Set up a stop or indicator so you know where it is. Also, you will find that threading a steel tube of this diameter works best at a speed higher than what you learned in shop class. You need an indicator to know when to pull the half nut.

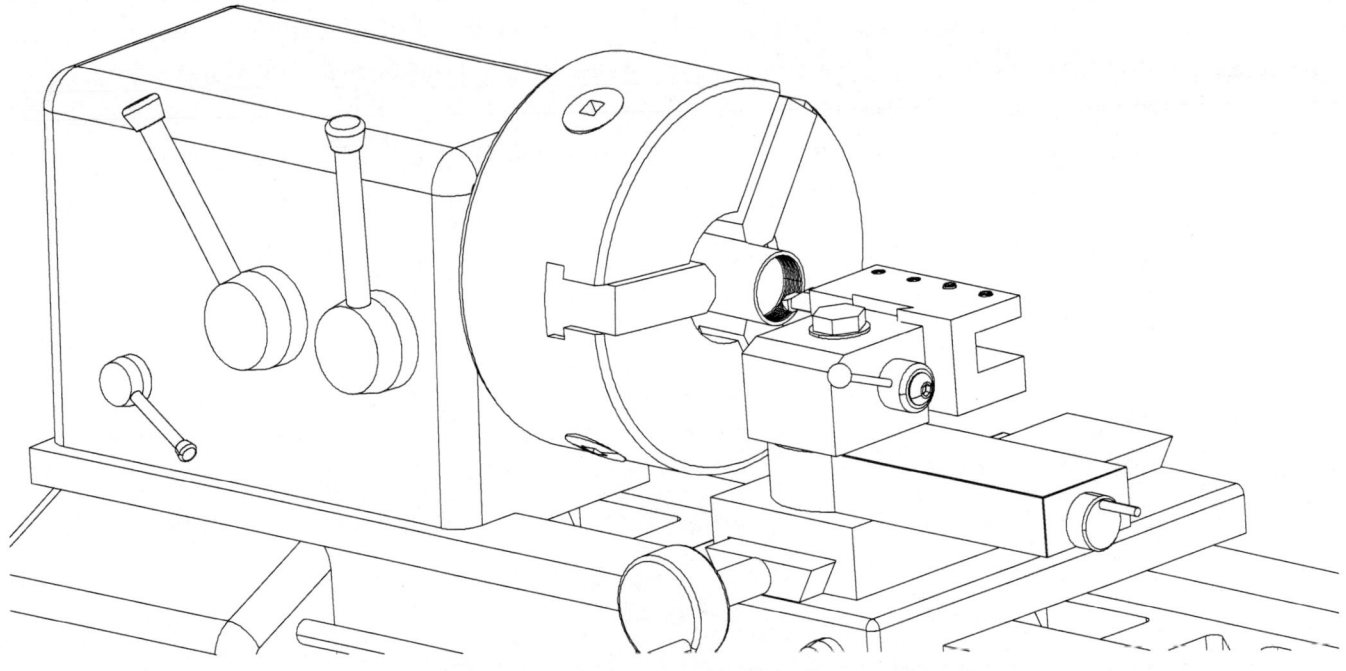

Bottom Bracket in 3 jaw chuck during the threading operation

The best reason for chasing the threads with taps after brazing (welding) is to correct out of round condition. The heat from the fusion process will distort the tube, even if welded with scrap bearings installed. Subsequently, some rounding up is required. The best way to guard against having to rework your frame with a hacksaw is to thread the bracket so that the cups spin freely when installed before welding. That will guarantee success in the rounding process. The bracket will move around its thinnest section, the thread relief. You will simply squeeze the bracket in a vise or specially made fixture until the outside diameter measures round again. It is quite a simple process.

Though we generally thread both ends in a 3 jaw, threading a spud with a MT3 taper on one end that fits the headstock spindle taper is actually the most accurate way to do this. It all depends on if you feel like removing the chuck. Most of the time, we don't.

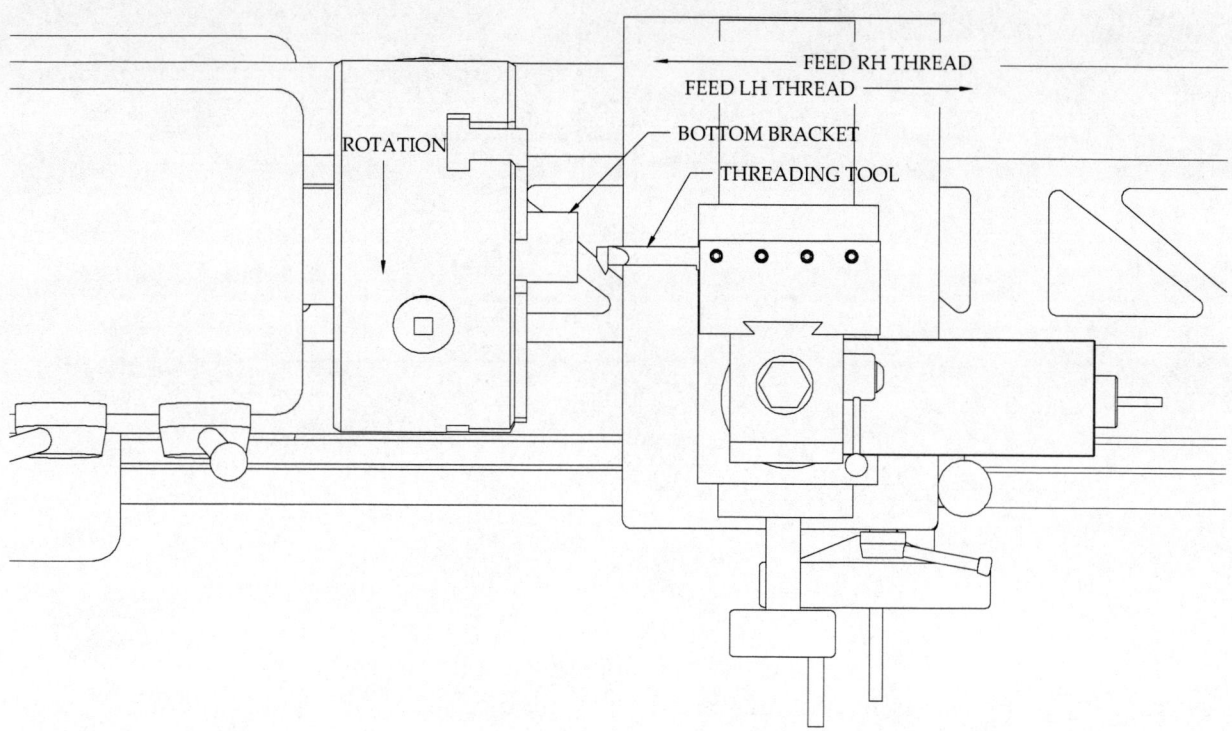

Top view of the threading operation

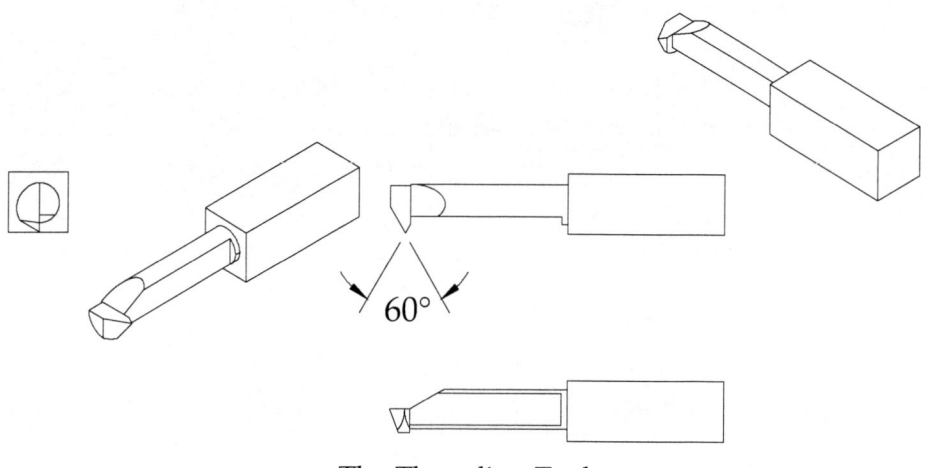

The Threading Tool

The tool is ground from a piece of good HSS steel, preferably a tool that contains cobalt. M2 is a good choice. The cobalt helps the thin point resist the cutting forces and the high heat generated whenever steel is cut.

Finally, if you are building an aluminum bike, make a couple of thread inserts that press into a smooth bore. A pair of bronze inserts pressed into a smooth aluminum bb ensures you won't scrap a lot of work because of stripped threads.

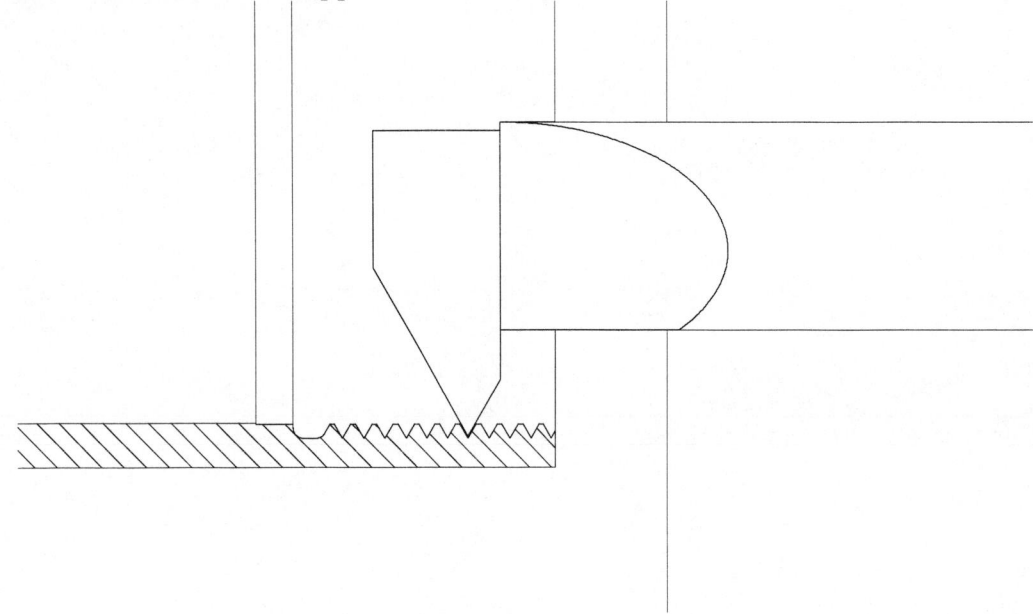

View showing thread cutting tool as it forms the thread

Use an indicator or stop at the end of the cut and a high enough cutting speed to ensure a good finish. Running the lathe too slow results in tearing and a bad looking thread.

Measuring wheel spacing

There exist a number of standard size wheel spacings in the bicycling world. Since you are building your own bike, you are not obliged to use any of them. You should, however, know how to master the process and fit a bike with a wheel that makes it go down the road reasonably straight. Even more important, you should have an idea of what to do when things go wrong.

An alternate method of measuring wheel spacing is to use a truing stand, the choice of most bike mechanics everywhere. That seems so obvious and it should go without saying but Robobikers are an odd bunch.

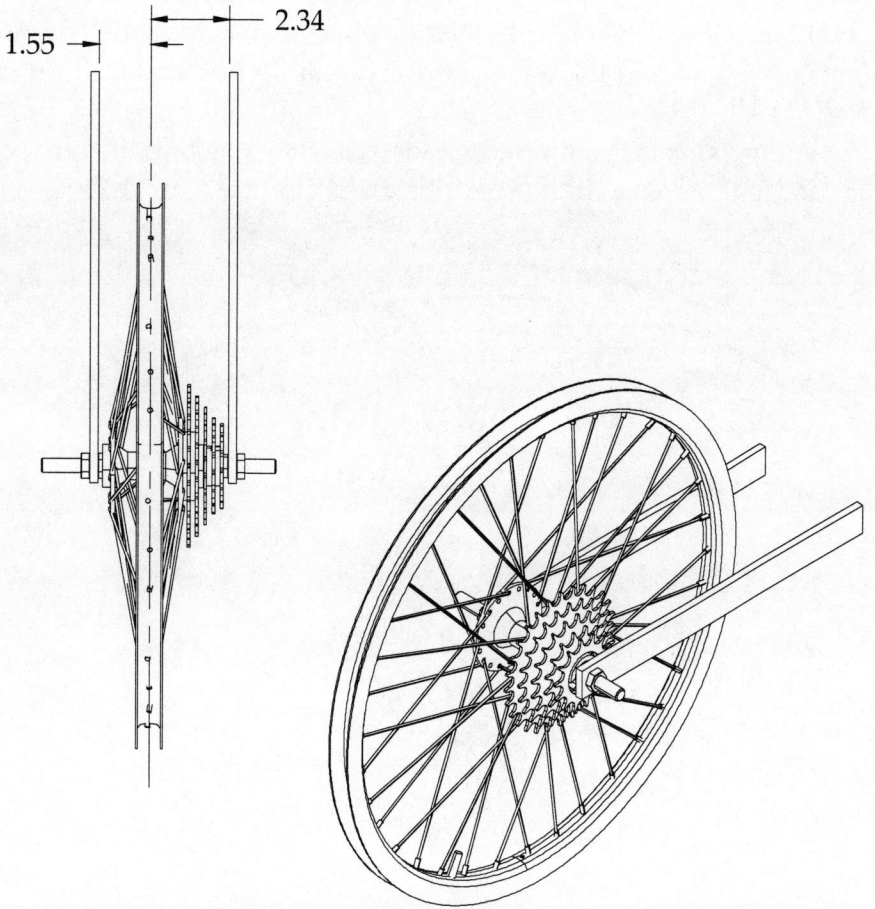

Step one in controlling your world, specifically the rear wheel drop out spacing, is knowing what the wheel measures over the locknuts. Robobike uses a lot of weird wheel combinations like lacing a rim from a small motorcycle to a BMX hub for example. We lace bike rims to motorcycle hubs. We learned to ignore the rules a long time ago especially since the rules are arbitrary anyway. You can buy a bunch of stuff already built but if all you want to do is spend your money at the bike shop, why are you reading this? Cut two pieces of flat stock and drill a hole for the axle at one end. This allows you to accurately measure the rear wheel without disassembly. Since you want to wind up with roughly a five inch spacing, you can add shims in the form of washers until you get there. This is not a new concept and has been done since bicycles were all home-made, one of a kind machines.

In the example shown here, adding a ⅛″ (3mm) spacer on the freewheel side and .92″ (23.5mm) on the other will get you real close. Remember, the rear wheel spacing should be less than the frame unless you like to struggle with your wheel every time you install it or remove it. The frame spacing can be measured with a ruler directly.

Wheel Building

May the Lord have mercy on anyone who is given the task of collecting all that has been written about building bicycle wheels. It's just a wheel, for heaven's sake, not some kind of transcendental, magical, other worldly experience. You take a hub and connect it to a rim with a bunch of spokes. That's it. Take a look at this example. We are putting a BMX rim on a 36 hole hub from a disk brake equipped battery powered motorcycle. Step one find the hole for the valve stem (it's the big one) and put a spoke in the small hole next to it. Fill the hub as shown and take a break.

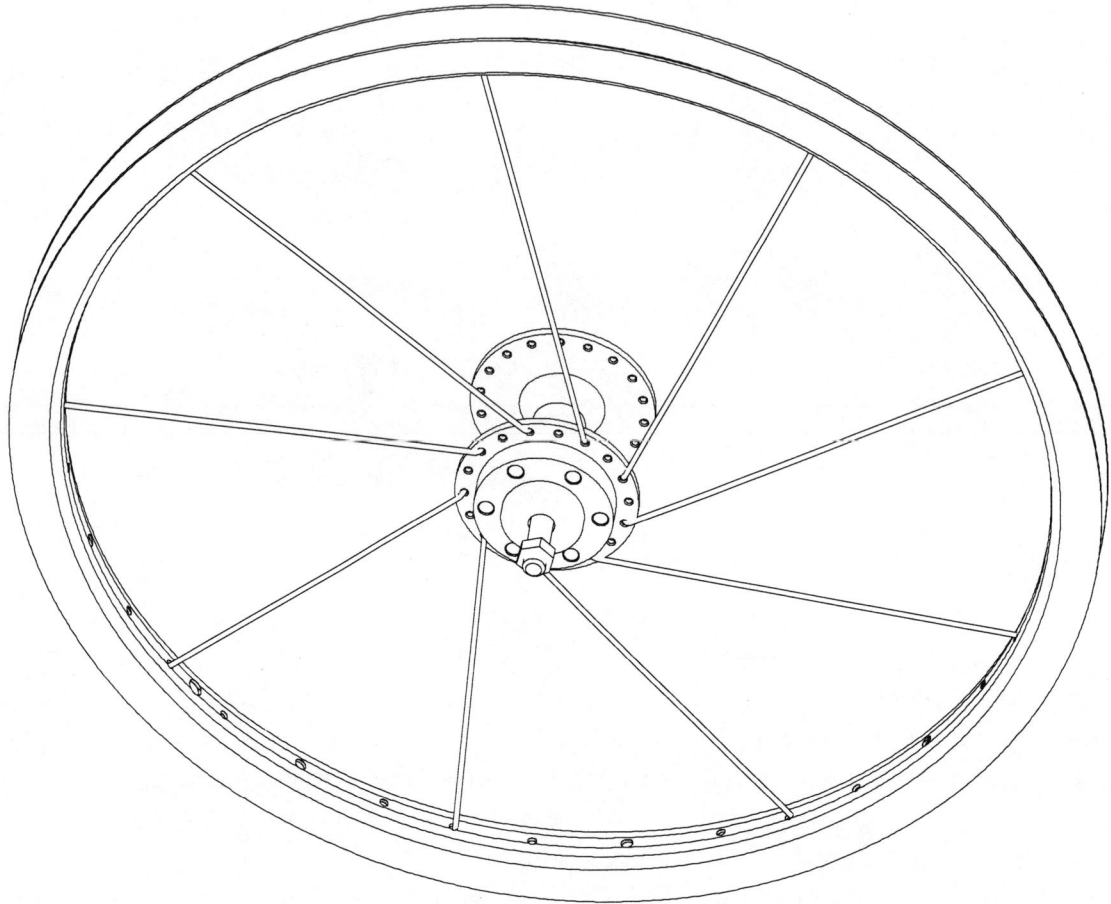

You don't want to block pump access to the valve stem hole so be sure to give the hub a twist (clockwise in this view) that opens up the space around the hole. We are making the big assumption that you know the proper spoke length. If you don't, then start looking around. Spoke calculators are a big help but most of us don't have one. If you are lacing up an oddball combination, they won't help anyway. Start measuring bike wheels similar to what you want to accomplish. How many crosses? In our example, each spoke crosses another twice. This is known as a 2 cross wheel. It is a perfect example of making do. Two cross wheels are not mainstream but is a good compromise of what is best and what is possible. If you are halfway through the building process and realize the spokes are short, then start over and do 1 cross. If too long, try 3 cross. There's not much difference between the three on a wheel this small. You will find that determining spoke length is probably the most difficult part of building a Robobike wheel. Not because the length is hard to determine, but sometimes a trip to a bike shop to talk to some prissy know-it-all is required. My apologies to all you prissy know-it-alls out there.

Software can be used to determine length but it's not for everyone. We at Robobike build virtual wheels before buying spokes. Not everyone has these skills but with the advances in online services, it won't be long until a photo of the hub and rim is all you need to arrive at the proper length.

Wheel building is one of those things you cannot learn from a book. We cannot emphasize enough the importance of hands on experience when it comes to producing a good wheel. Build a few and you'll know what I mean. It is not hard but neither is playing the piano for my buddy Mike.

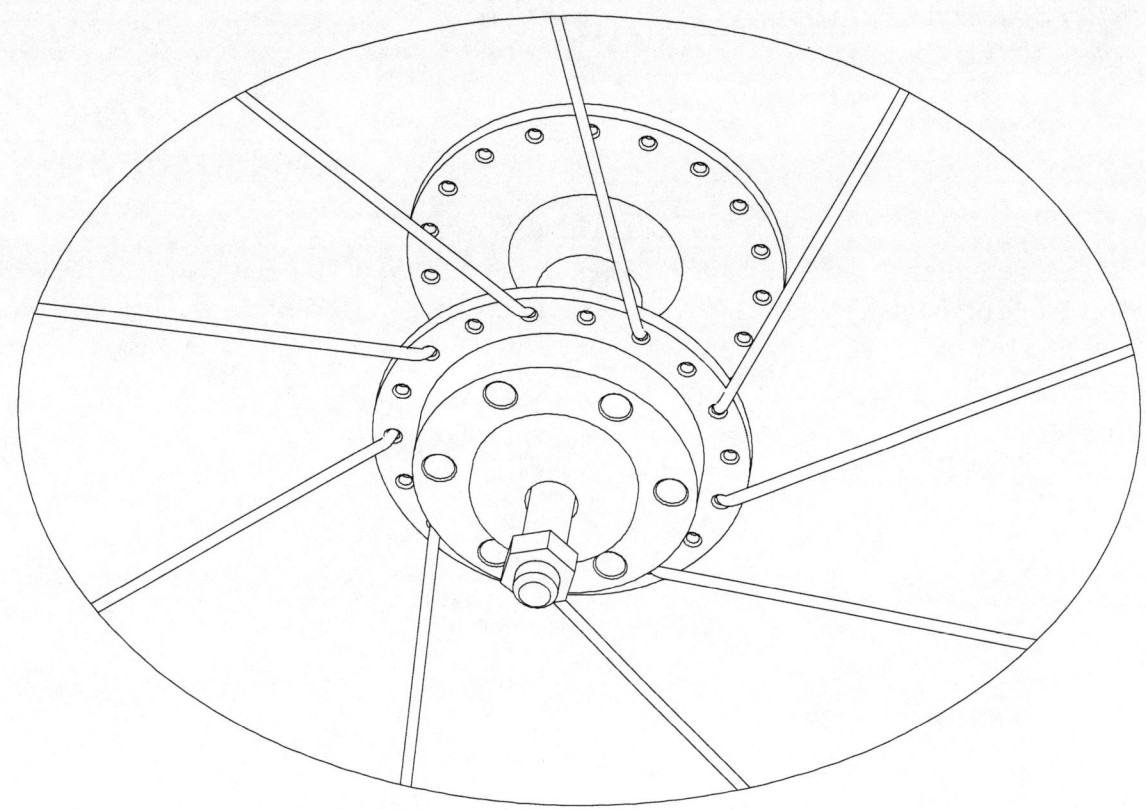

The first nine spokes installed through the hub

The first nine spokes are quite easy and not a challenge, even for first time wheel builders. The second course, however, reveals the complexity involved in building a properly tensioned bicycle wheel.

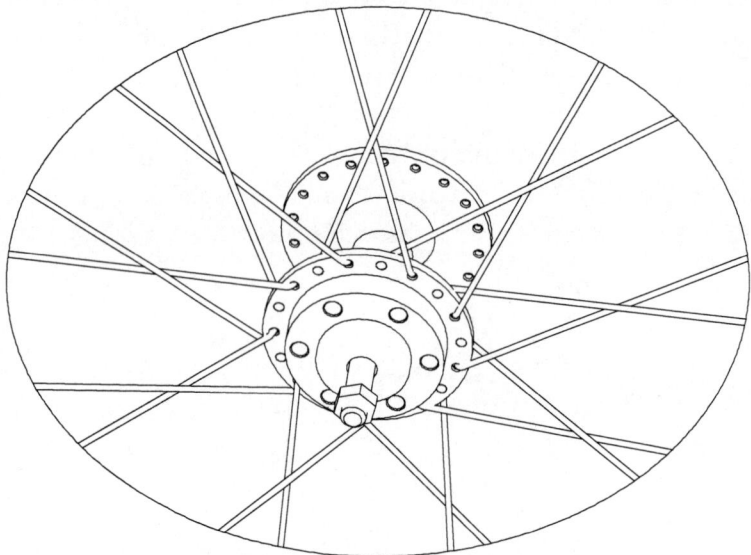

The second nine spokes

Please note how the second course passes to the outside of the first course at the second cross. This is one of those things that everyone does. Robobike cannot detect any advantage or gain in rigidity from using this technique, but we do it anyway. The second course of nine spokes ends the easy portion of the wheel building process.

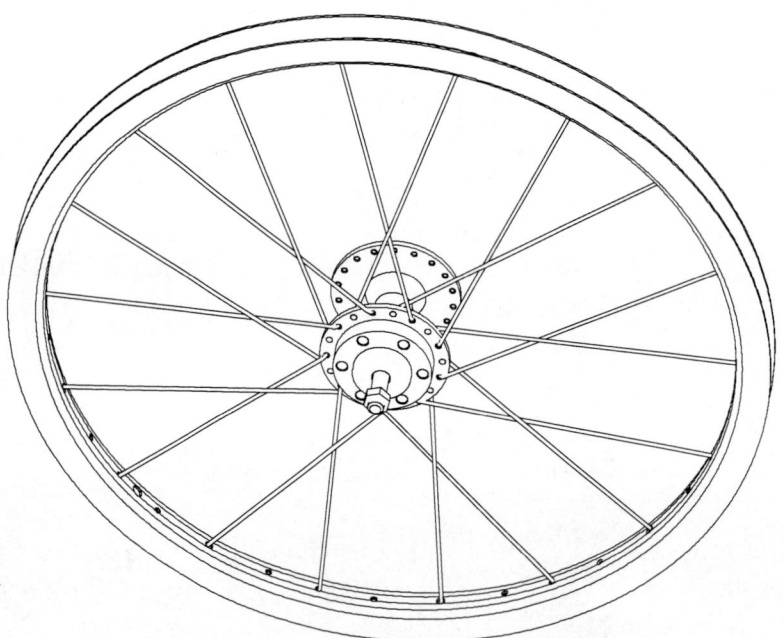

The second group of nine spokes

The spokes are installed with the spoke nipples screwed on just enough to capture the nipples. Torquing does not begin until all the spokes are in place. Use washers under the nipples if your rim does not have grommets or some other means of buttressing the area around the spoke hole. It is best to avoid using a rim that is not double wall construction unless the wheel is being used for a trailer or some other unoccupied vehicle. When half the spokes are in place, it should be evident if the spokes are too long/short.

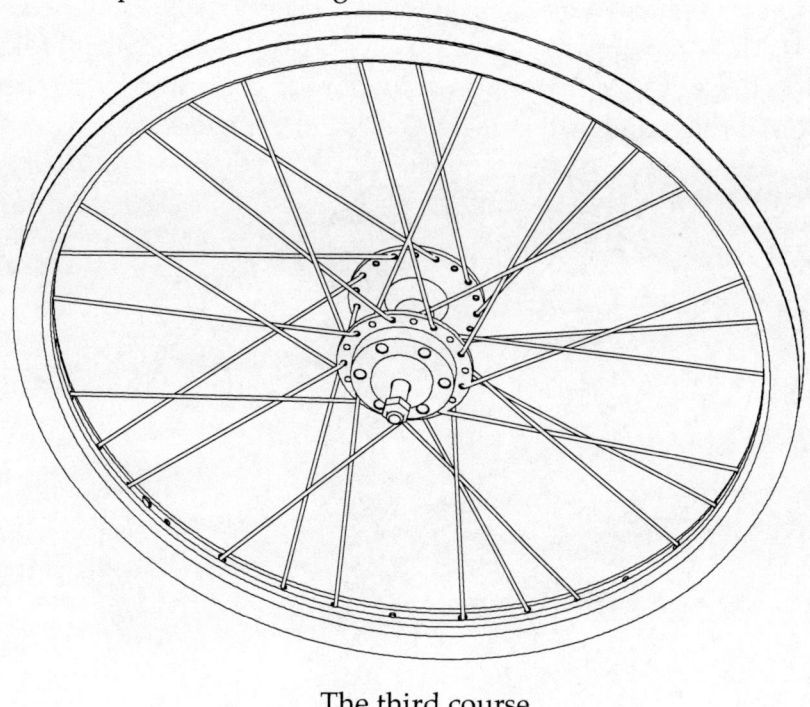

The third course

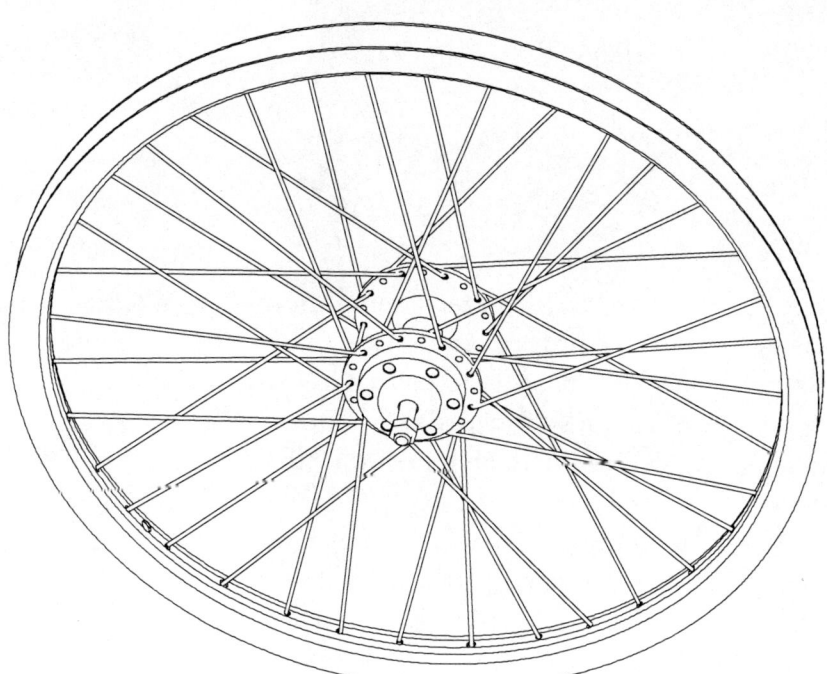

The final course is laced up by adding the row with the spoke heads towards the inside of the wheel. Don't be afraid to bend the spokes. You have to.

Truing the wheel

A wheel spinning true does not mean a wheel properly tensioned. The difference being that the wheel will not support its load unless the spokes are brought up to a minimum level of stress. Ideally, all the spokes are tightened the same amount. This is usually the case in front wheels but not so in rear wheels. Those of you with bike shop experience are aware that broken spokes on rear wheels are limited to those spokes that transmit the torque generated by the pedaling motion to the rim. These spokes are all found on the freewheel side of the wheel.

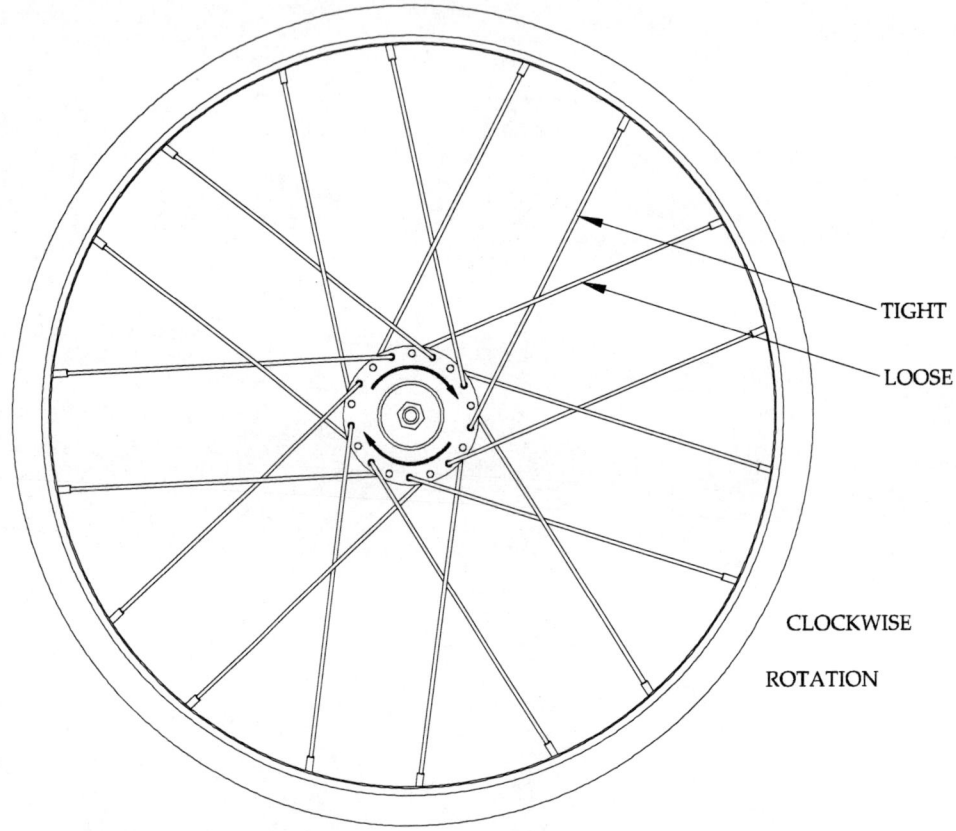

TIGHT

LOOSE

CLOCKWISE

ROTATION

We mention that because the wheel tensioning process at Robobike involves bringing the spokes up to the same tension by using a guitar pick to gage tightness. Simply pluck the spokes to get an idea how tight they are. The spokes marked TIGHT in this drawing are the spokes that gain tension, and therefore stress, as a result of pedaling torque. We tune these spokes a bitter flatter than the rest and tune the spokes marked LOOSE a bit sharp. This will help prevent broken spokes. All the spokes on the flange side opposite the freewheel get the same tension.

We won't bore you with the details of tightening spokes. Once you've done it, you see how easy it is. Until you've done it, no amount of explanation makes any sense. Find a junk wheel, unbuild it and put it back together until you've mastered the process. It is easier than you think. Don't forget to use grease on the spoke threads.

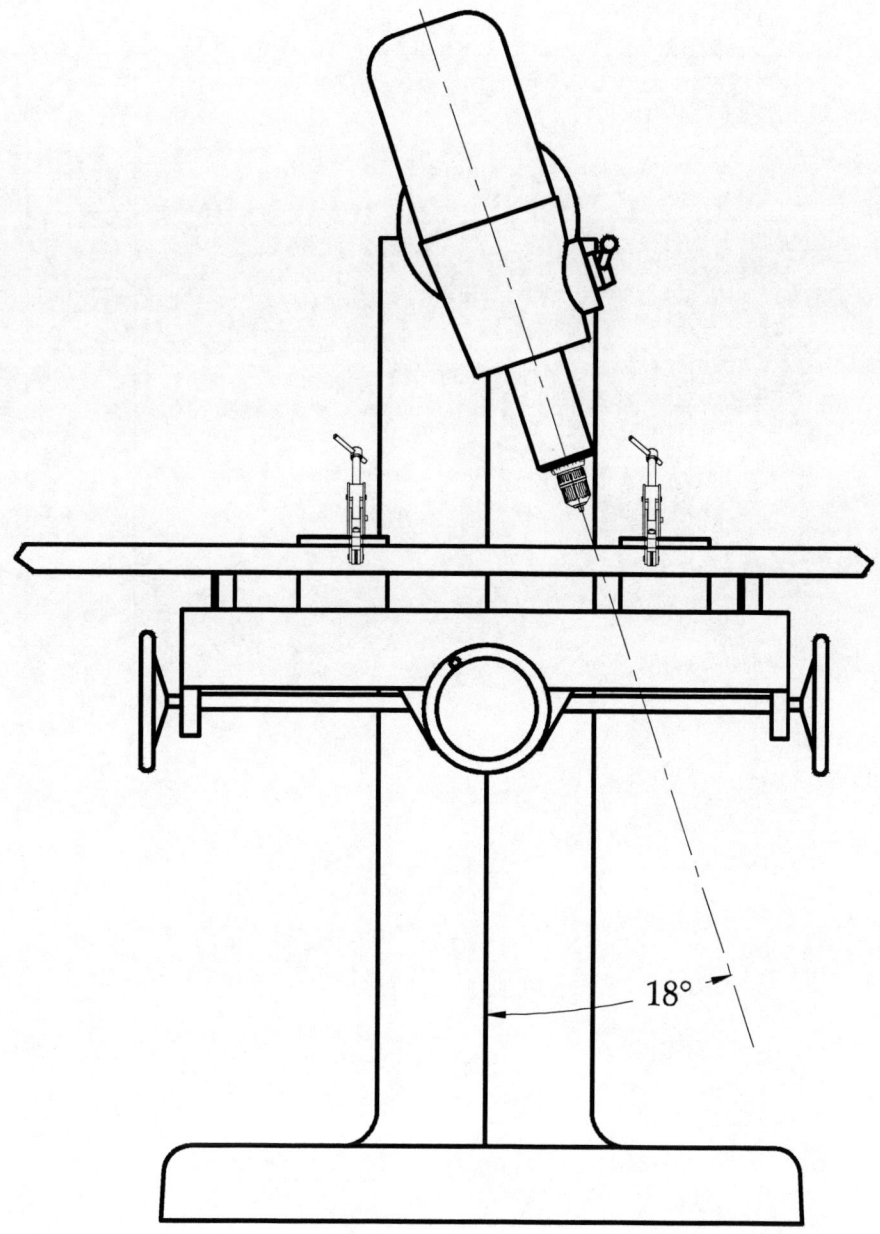

18°

    This view of a stylized milling machine set up to bore the three holes in the backbone of the Delivery Boy project. Notice how the head of the machine is kicked over to match the drawing. The hole for the steering axis is drilled and bored on location and the ends are formed for the head tube and seat tube. The backbone sits on 1-2-3 blocks and is clamped to angle plates. It is OK to add tooling holes in the backbone to help clamp the work piece. Put the holes where ever you think they might help. We put two tooling holes perpendicular to the steering axis so we can bolt the backbone to the angle plates which helps in holding the work piece in place.

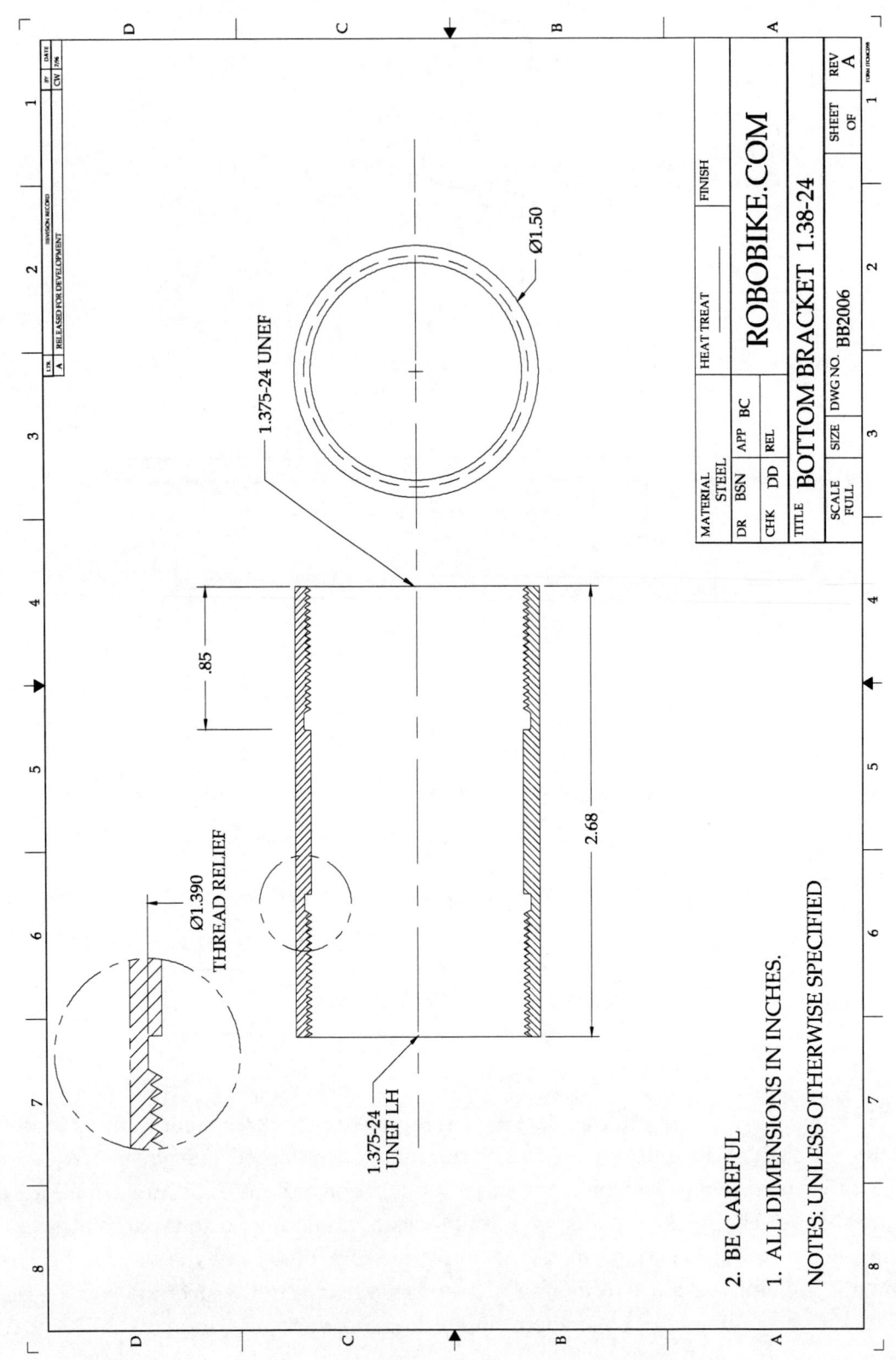

Ø1.50

1.375-24 UNEF

.85

Ø1.390

THREAD RELIEF

2.68

1.375-24
UNEF LH

2. BE CAREFUL

1. ALL DIMENSIONS IN INCHES.

NOTES: UNLESS OTHERWISE SPECIFIED

ROBOBIKE.COM

FINISH

HEAT TREAT

MATERIAL STEEL

DR BSN   APP BC

CHK DD   REL

TITLE BOTTOM BRACKET 1.38-24

DWG NO. BB2006

SIZE

SCALE FULL

SHEET OF

REV A

REVISION RECORD

LTR A RELEASED FOR DEVELOPMENT

BY DATE

CW 7/96

134

Co-axial Wheel

By Ghumal Nabi

Ghamal served as pastor at the Saints Frankie and Johnny church in New Orleans for many years. He embraced the automobile free lifestyle after being ordered to pay restitution.

Before chain drive became commonplace in the early days of bicycling, placing the crank axle and the wheel axle together was the way it was done. The direct connection certainly reduced transmission losses but the limitations of the configuration quickly made themselves known.

Power was moved from parallel shafts via flat leather belts in the days before roller chain. One exception to this rule is the first reported example of a bicycle with pedals which was not a front driver but a safety bicycle powered by turning a rotating pair of cranks and driving the rear wheel through connecting rods. The year Kirkpatrick McMillan built this extraordinary machine was given as 1840 by George Routledge in <u>Velocipedes, Bicycles, and Tricycles</u> in 1869 though the wrong builder was given credit.

A patent search for co-axial crank and wheel axles returns quite a number of hits. Most of the designs are amusing but unrealistic. Robobike was not the first to build a co-axial wheel but is certainly the first with an easy to build and useful design. Torque generated by the crank axle is transmitted via chain to a jackshaft. The power in the jackshaft goes to the wheel via chain. How much easier can it get?

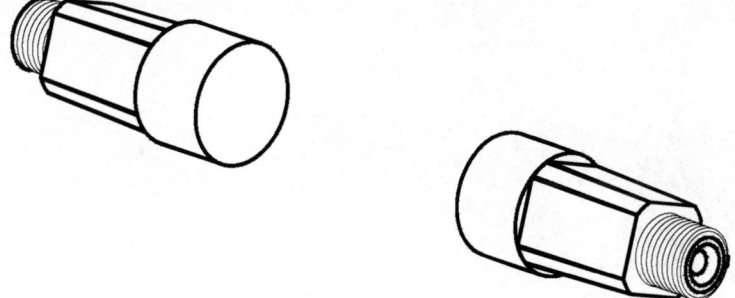

Square ends cut from conventional axle. Splined ends work just as good.

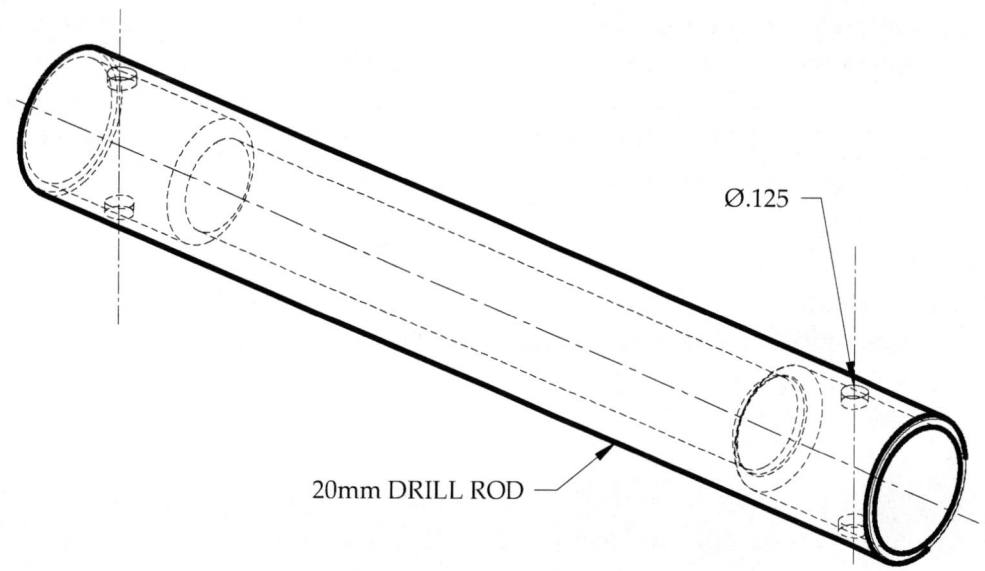

Ø.125

20mm DRILL ROD

To build this wheel, begin by putting the axle in a lathe collet and turning the whole shooting match, bearing races and all, to a nice smooth cleanup. Use a live center and take the diameter to about .625 inches. The axles are harder than Chinese arithmetic. Use 883, 895 or an equivalent grade carbide. A tool post grinder works too. You will counterbore a piece of 20mm drill rod to fit the end pieces, so don't waste a lot of time worrying about finish beyond the normal concern for doing a good job.

Remove the ends from the body of the axle. You can cut the axle with a high speed abrasive wheel but you can't touch it with a hack saw.

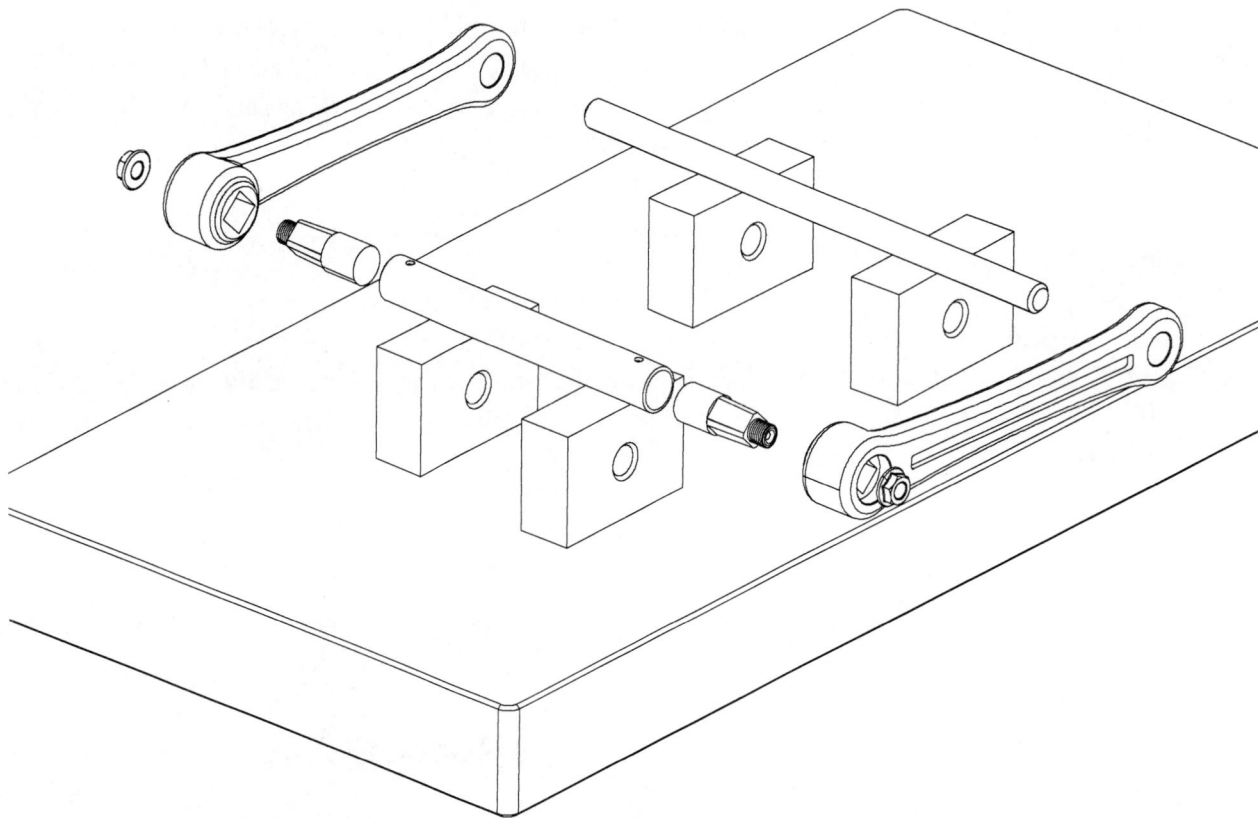

About the time our first co-axial wheel was being built, Robobike was contacted by a group that was helping people with immigration problems. Apparently, they knew of a woman from Brazil with such problems and asked us to evaluate her skills as she listed her profession as bicycle mechanic, frame builder and shop owner. What a happy day it was at Robobike when Bonita Caliente arrived at the shop for the first time.

Bonita looked at the axle then under construction and asked to have a try at joining the ends to the new axle shaft. Before doing so, however, she went to the chop saw and removed most of the round portion of the axle ends leaving only 1.5 diameters worth of length. She then sand blasted the axle ends to remove the black oxide, polished the new axle in the lathe and then fluxed the whole thing and soldered both ends at the same time. This was before we started pinning the assembly as part of the joining operation but even so, the new axle ran straight and true. She did this all by eye and with very little command of the English language.

Bonita and her little son became a presence around the shop for quite some time, and eventually she was hired as a welder at an aerospace company. Poor girl.

136

Attaching the square axle ends to the axle body

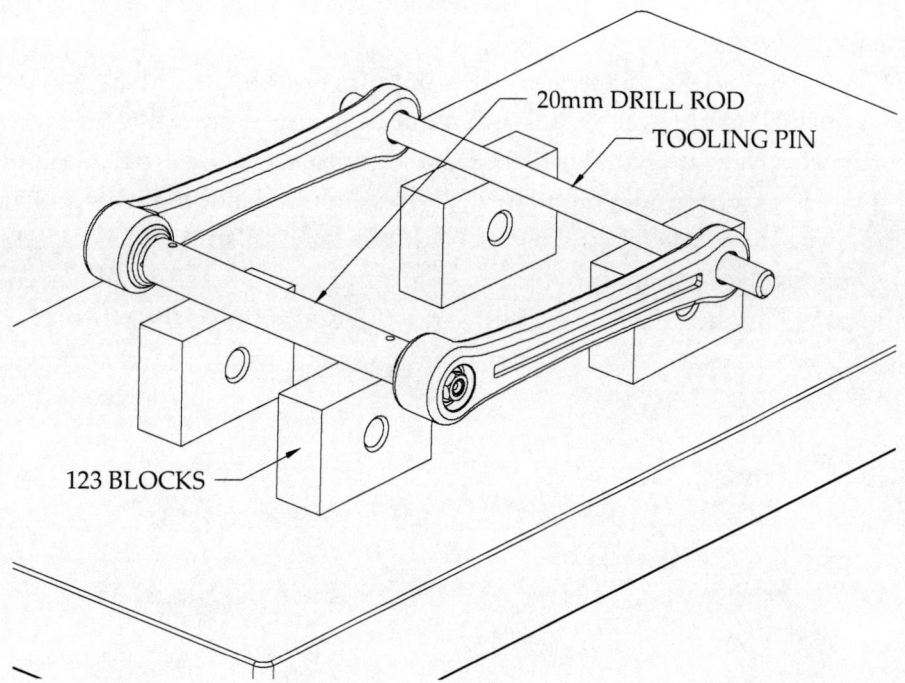

A six inch length of 20mm drill rod is drilled and counter bored to fit the square axle ends that were singulated earlier. Notice the small holes drilled near the end of the drill rod. These are for pins. Soldering the assembly as it sits is impossible. The arms are aluminum and will draw away heat faster than you can supply it with a torch. Besides, using aluminum like this is totally wrong. It adds contamination. Install the pins and solder.

The pin holes are drilled completely through. Pretty tough going that. A ⅛ cobalt bit running slow will do the job but you might need a couple of bits to finish the two holes. Run the drills no faster than 500 rpm which is about 16 feet per minute. Any faster and you burn up the bit. Any slower and the cutting speed approaches zero. Pin the assembly before silver soldering. It is usually a bad idea to combine pins and welding in a single process but it is required here.

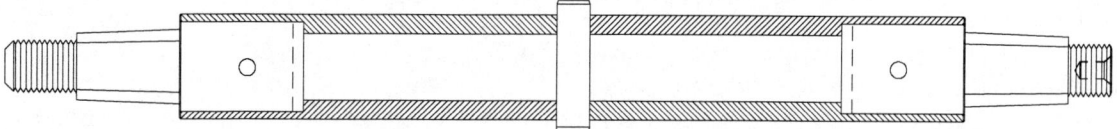

Completed axle with center pin installed

You are wasting your time if you don't use cobalt drill bits. The illustration shows the whole business sitting on 123 blocks for the drill operation. Be sure to clean the oil used in the drilling operation before silver soldering. The tooling pin is half inch diameter.

Don't for a minute think that you can put this assembly together without some type of setup similar to this. Any misalignment will haunt your every pedal stroke. If you are building this axle for use by a loved one, make it perfect or don't make it at all. There are a few things in life more annoying than a bent pedal but it's hard to think of any right now. You don't want your favorite girl looking at you and all she sees is a crooked axle.

After the silver solder operation is finished, drill a ⅛ hole all the way through the axle equidistant from each end. Then drill the hole again to quarter inch for a one inch long split pin.

This pin will control any tendency for bearings, spacers and other features to migrate along the axle. Wheels built without center pins soon need realignment. Clean the axle, install the center pin and put the axle in the freezer.

The radius of the wheel determines the bottom bracket height above the ground. The closest thing to a normal height is realized with a Fat Boy, also known as a 24 inch mountain bike tire. Whatever rim you choose is attached to the disk with screws. A rotary table or some other type of dividing head is set up under a mill or drill press spindle and the disk is drilled and tapped around the periphery. The whole business gets balanced later on so it doesn't matter if the screws are not equally spaced. However, the bolt holes around the center hub do need to be equally spaced. These holes will mount the bearing cups and will determine if the wheel rolls true.

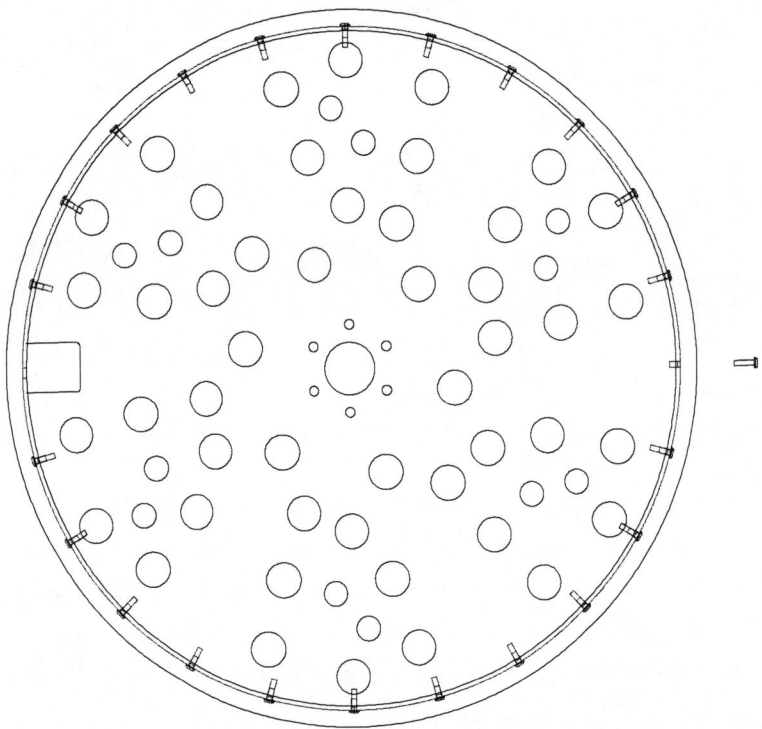

The disk is made of quarter inch aluminum. The use of a CNC mill is quite handy for making this piece. A rotary table works too if you don't have a CNC machine. Be sure to add some custom lettering to the disk if you have the chance. Whatever you do, make sure that the center hole and pattern around it are concentric with the outer rim.

The lightening holes, if done on a CNC mill, are a heck of a lot easier and nicer looking than if done by hand on a rotary table or by layout and drill press. The cutout for the valve stem throws the whole business out of whack so a balance operation will be needed after the wheel spins on its own bearings. The easiest balancing method yet devised is to let the computer figure the number of holes, their size and placement and figure the center of mass. Adjust the holes in the CAD model until the center of gravity is coincident to the center of the wheel. All up to date CAD programs can do that. Lacking that, spinning the wheel and drilling a hole on the heavy side works too. Wheel balance is quite important on this or any other bike.

Bearing cups

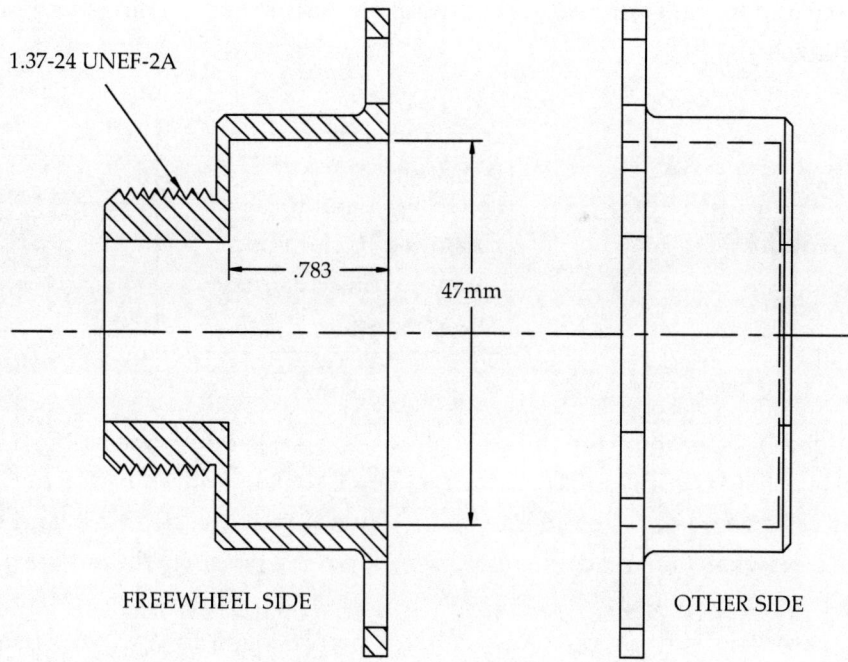

Two bearing cups, each containing a shielded double row angular contact bearing, squeeze the wheel disk between them. The cups are 6061 aluminum. Other than the bearing diameter and depth, the dimensions are left to the builder. Be sure that the depth of the bores are a couple of thousandths less than the actual thickness of the bearing. The diameter should be a slip fit. The bearings are made fast when the cups are tightened against the disk.

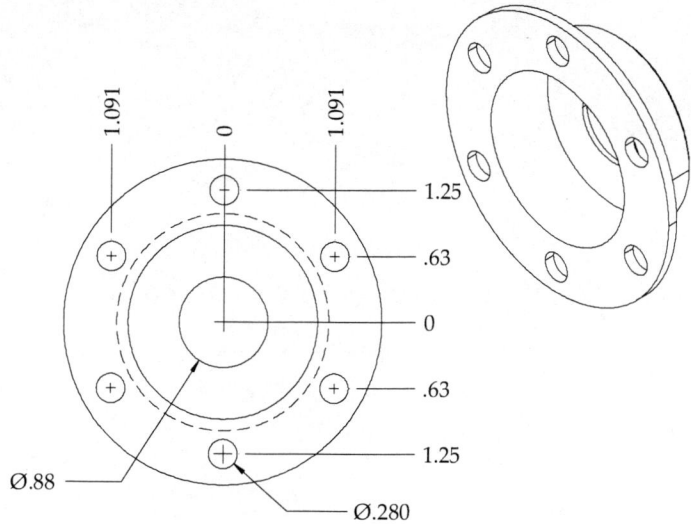

With the axle silver soldered, the rim attached to the disk and the bearing cups finished, it is possible to begin assembly. Warm one of the bearings over the toaster, in an oven or on a coffee warmer to approximately 140° F. You don't want to cook the lubricant, just warm the bearing. Remove the axle assembly from the freezer and rub some grease on one half of the axle. Slide a bearing onto the axle and drive it home using a piece of aluminum tube that is at least 20mm but less than 21mm on the inside diameter. Tap the bearing using this tube and a hammer until the bearing is driven onto the axle all the way to the center pin. Now put the axle back in the freezer, warm up another bearing and repeat the whole process one more time. Don't forget, however, to slip the wheel disk onto the axle before driving on the second bearing. Neither bearing should require much force and might even slide on without any effort at all. Things will get tight when the temperature stabilizes.

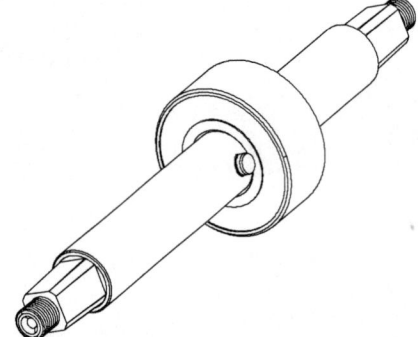

Angular contact bearings need to be installed back to back. Double roll balls may also be used.

Every assembly operation on this wheel has a disassembly operation. Most require jack screws or some kind of custom puller. Bearings, even sealed and shielded double row angular contact bearings, require periodic maintenance. This involves cleaning and renewal of the lubricant. In spite of what you read in the papers, there is no such thing as a maintenance free bearing.

When disassembly is desired, the wheel disk can be used to draw the bearing off the axle using a home made puller.

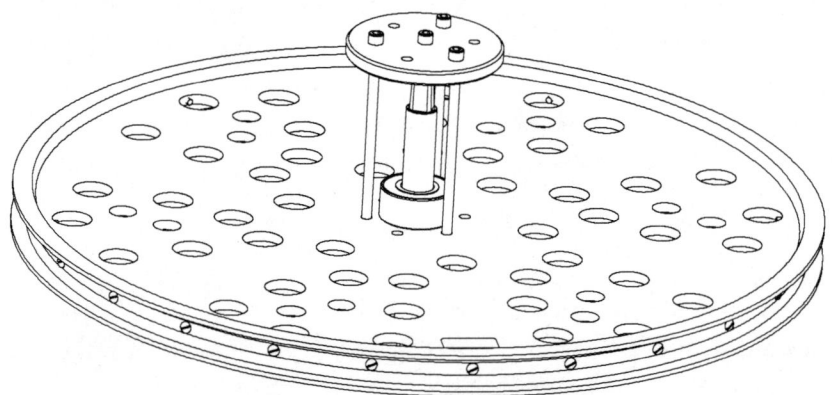

Install the bearing cups and the hardware used to secure them. Give the wheel a test spin and put a critical eye on the rim. It should spin straight and true with no wobble, just like a real bicycle wheel.

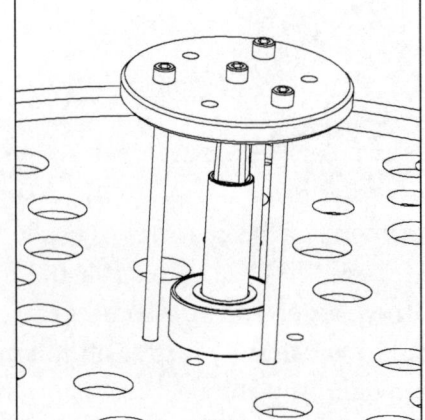

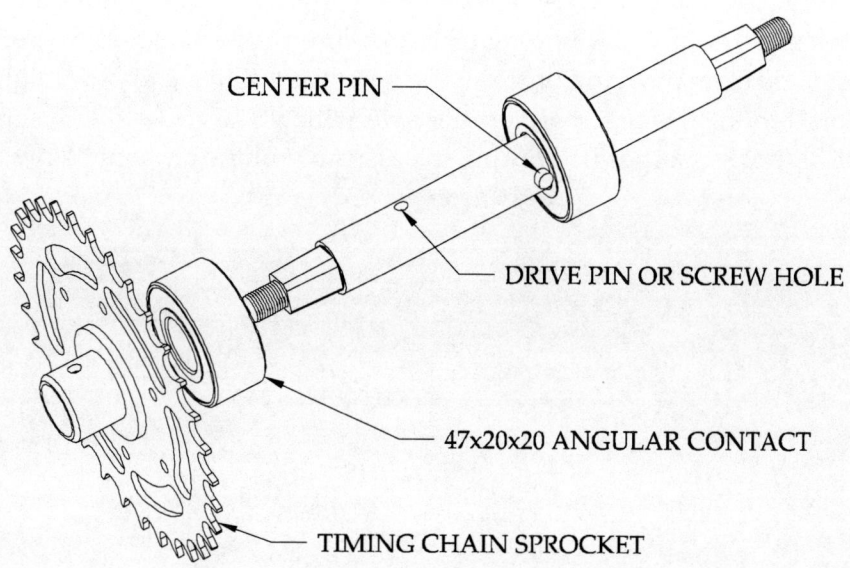

CENTER PIN

DRIVE PIN OR SCREW HOLE

47x20x20 ANGULAR CONTACT

TIMING CHAIN SPROCKET

The final bit of fabrication for the co-axial wheel is a means of transmitting power from the crank axle to a jackshaft before transmitting it back to the cluster. This can be accomplished two ways. The first is to add a chain wheel outside the outer bearing. Putting a crank arm and spider on the tapered axle square opposite the cluster side will do that. This is the method used on the Delivery Boy project.

The second method is to attach a sprocket or chain wheel on the rotating crank axle and fixing it to that axle. This assembly is used on Loveboat, the recumbent unicycle and Max. Since disassembly is a requirement too, then this sprocket needs to be affixed to the axle with a fastener or pin. Robobike has used both and finds that a cap screw is easier.

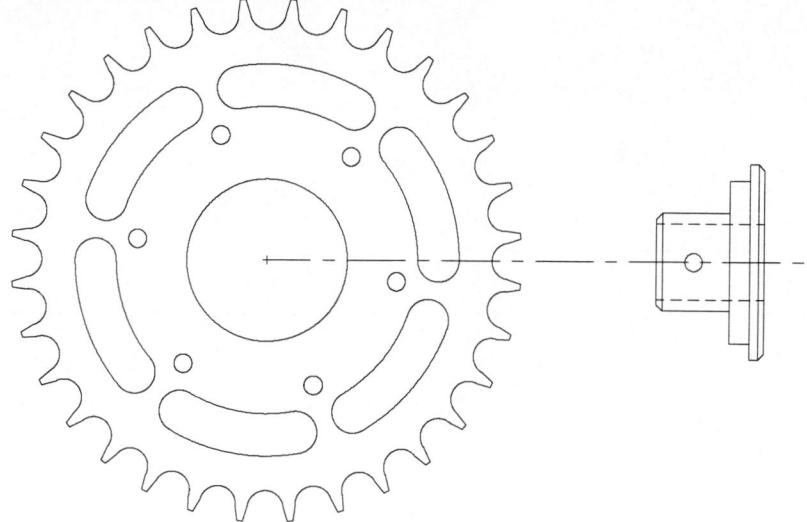

Any convenient size steel sprocket can be used for this detail though Robobike prefers using 32 or more teeth. The theory here is that any wear will be distributed among more teeth. The sprocket is prepared by boring the center to a clean up if required and by removing all plating. This last bit is important to prevent the silver solder adhering to the thin layer of plating and not to the base material itself. A hub that fits the bore of the sprocket is prepared for silver solder. The hub is made from any kind of steel. The sprocket will have to be straightened after the soldering operation. Mount this assembly on the axle with a #10 cap screw inserted completely through the axle. This hole is best drilled during the assembly phase and not before.

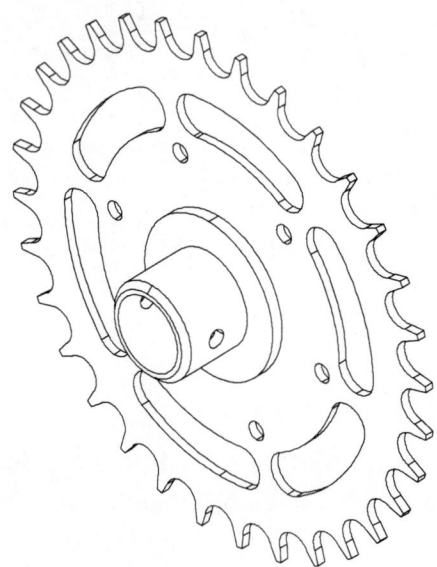

A 32 tooth sprocket silver soldered to a steel hub

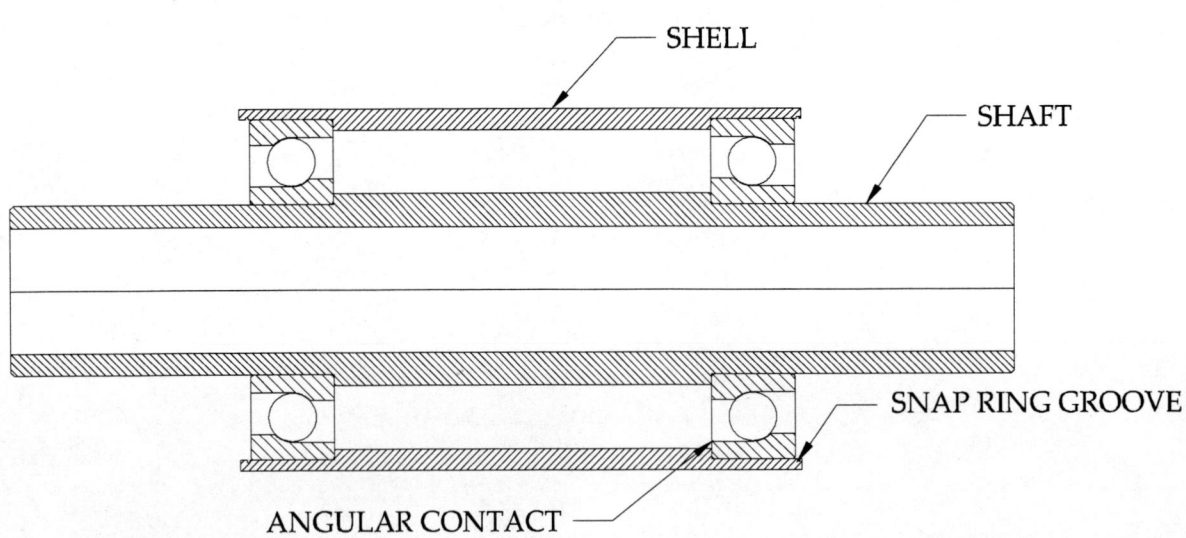

Mount Angular Contact Bearings Back to Back
to Control Both Thrust and Radial Loads.

142

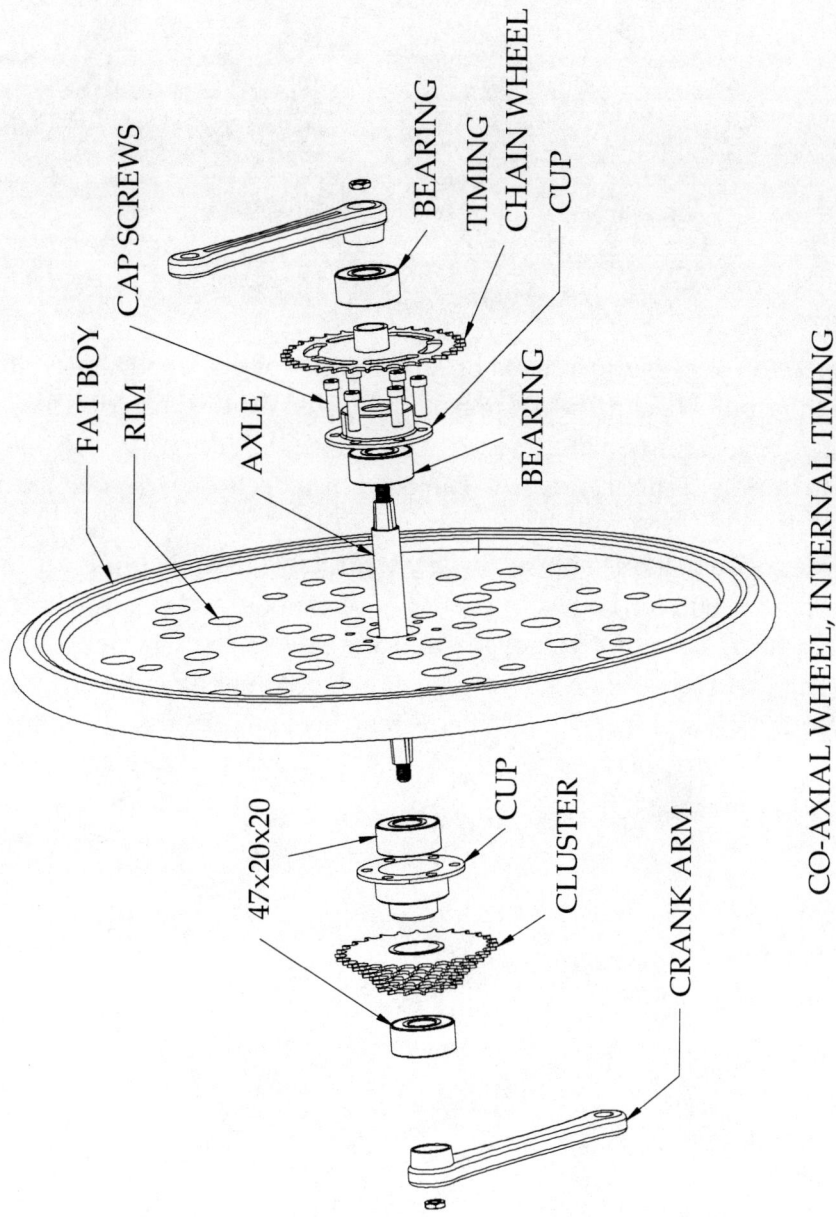

FAT BOY

CAP SCREWS

BEARING

TIMING

CHAIN WHEEL

CUP

RIM

AXLE

BEARING

47x20x20

CUP

CLUSTER

CRANK ARM

CO-AXIAL WHEEL, INTERNAL TIMING

The fat boy mentioned in the drawing is a 24 inch tire marked 32-507.

The all purpose jack shaft

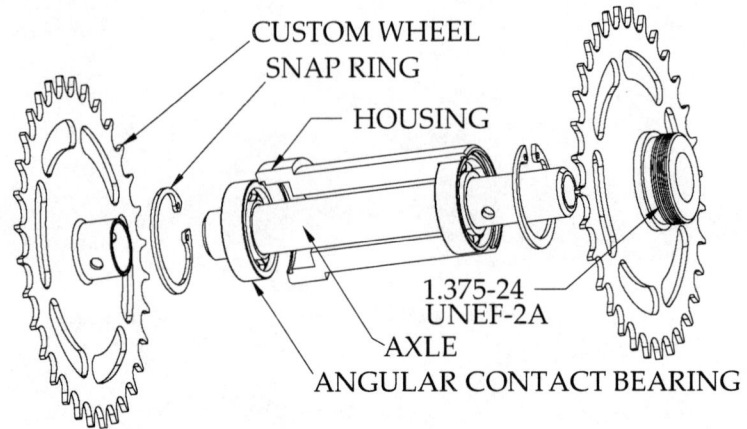

CUSTOM WHEEL
SNAP RING
HOUSING
1.375-24
UNEF-2A
AXLE
ANGULAR CONTACT BEARING

This piece of work is much used on Robobike projects. The Delivery Boy, Max, recumbent unicycle, and the front wheel drive recumbent all used a derivative of this basic design. One of our battery powered bikes uses two of these.

Construction is straight forward. The custom wheels shown here are large steel sprockets soldered to a hub.

You will notice that one side of the jackshaft has a threaded hub for mounting a freewheel which is especially useful for battery powered applications. It is possible to drive the shaft with a motor and then have the motor removed from the power circuit when coasting. Take this chain wheel off the shaft and reverse it. The freewheel then becomes a driver and not a driven side.

Another option is to install a left hand freewheel on either side as either a drive or a driven sprocket.

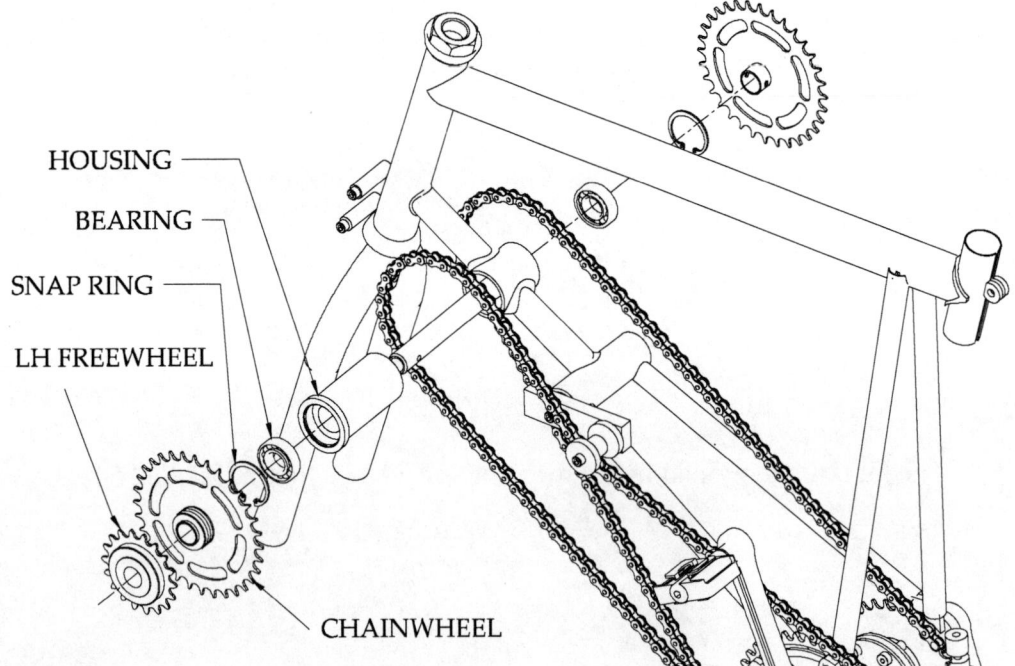

HOUSING

BEARING

SNAP RING

LH FREEWHEEL

CHAINWHEEL

Delivery Boy

A load carrying homebuilt project for the metal worker with skills at the master level

This all steel project revolves around the coaxial wheel first used in the Loveboat. The 50.25 inch wheel base Delivery Boy is intended to be built by an expert metal worker who has access to a machine shop with a milling machine, a lathe with at least a 7/8 collet, a welding or brazing set up and all the necessary clamping and jigging skills. The bike has a battery power assist option. If the world ever truly embraces efficient energy use, this type of utility bike and its derivatives will be pervasive. Let's start with the rear drop outs and the beginnings of our assembly jig. The jig is built as the bike progresses. Do not attempt the building of this bike without a jig unless your goal is to build a circus bike.

The Dropouts: Braze, Drill/tap, Cut, Clamp and Bore

Two inch diameter by ⅛ wall is the tube size used for the dropout clamp assembly. The rounds are half inch diameter. The piece of quarter inch at the top of the assembly in this drawing is where the stays are attached. Use a moderately high temp (1500° F) brass rod and join the pieces.

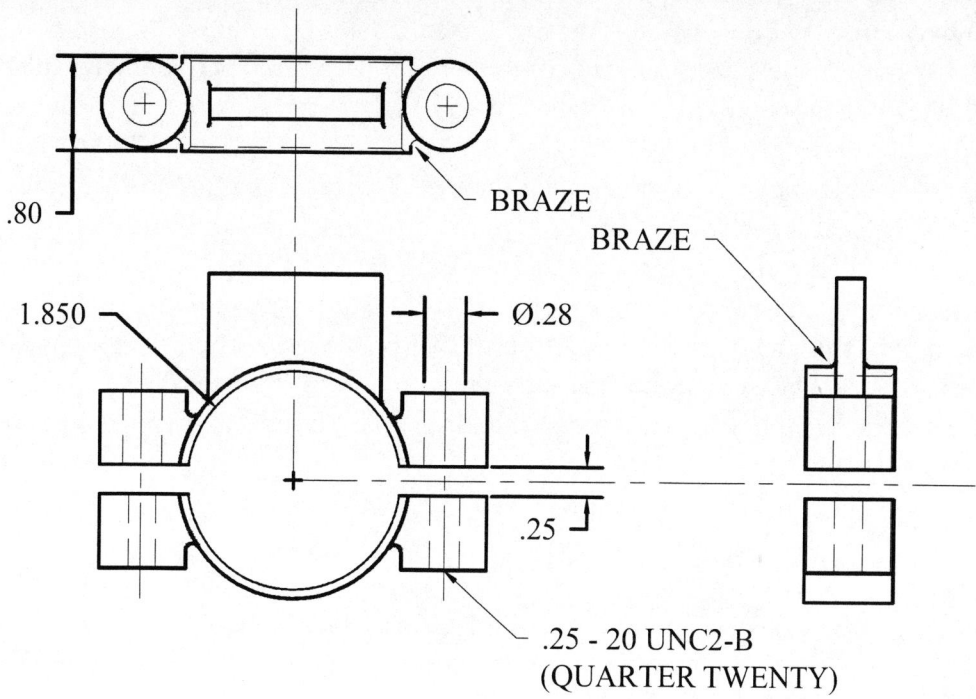

The rounds are drilled and tapped for ¼-20 screws. The bottom half is drilled to .281 and the tapped hole is the top half. Cut the dropouts and mill to the dimensions shown. Be sure to mill the .25 gap and install a shim before clamping the two halves together for the finish bore operation. Hold the 47mm diameter to plus .002" minus .000". If you screw up, reduce the thickness of the shims and bore again. The same shims will be used on the bike to set the clamping pressure on the double row balls. Any kind of steel will suffice. Once they are finished, begin preparation of the all aluminum jig. The first piece of the jig, the DUMMY AXLE to which the dropouts are clamped, acts as a heat sink preventing subsequent brazing operations affecting work already accomplished.

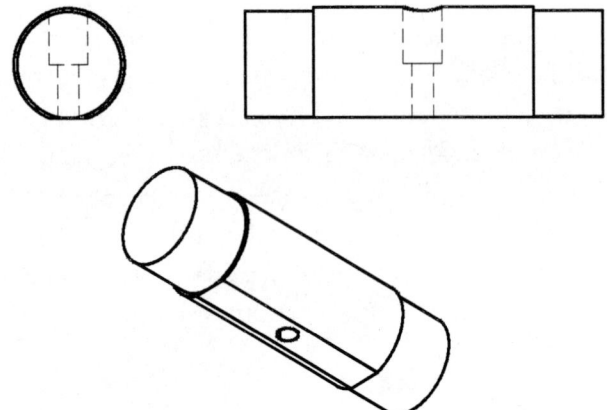

This piece of tooling begins the alignment process. It is used to assemble the dropout and stays, acting as a heat sink to bank heat during the brazing or welding process. It guarantees the dropouts stay round during this process.

The dummy axle

The Backbone

The backbone is the structural focus of this project. Use a 1.5 inch diameter tube with either a .06 or .08 wall thickness. The lighter will work for delivering flowers, the heavier for bags of concrete.

Bore three holes at an 18.5° angle, one for the head tube, one for the steering tube and of course, one for the seat tube. You can either kick the head over or clamp the work at the required angle. Kicking the head is the preferred method as the work piece can then be set up square to the table. Bore a ¾" radius for the head tube, drill and bore a one inch diameter hole for the steering apparatus and bore the backbone for some kind of seat post clamp. The backbone is actually quite an easy piece of work. Once cut, don't braze anything to it until it is fitted in the jig. Select the fork and the head set you want to use. Add optional tooling holes to the backbone for the mill operation if you want to.

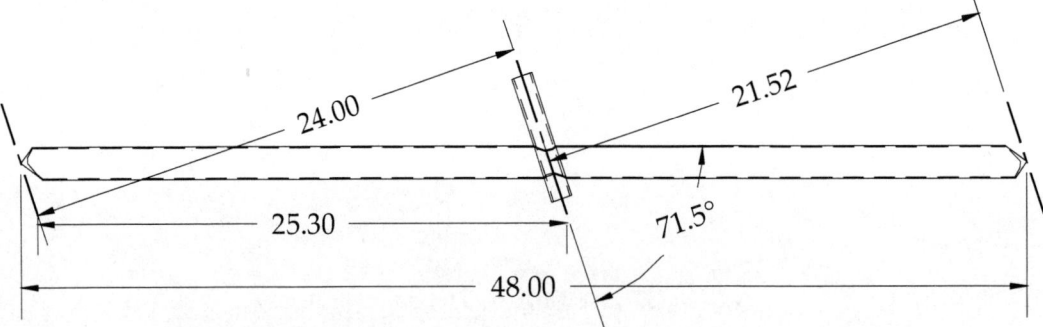

The backbone of Delivery Boy showing the ends prepared
and a hole bored for the steering tube.

The head tube will be cut from the same material as the backbone itself. It will have to be bushed depending on your choice of headset cups and cones. Since you already have selected the fork, go ahead and prepare the head tube (facing, boring and bushing) but leave out setting the cups and cones until after the brazing operation. There are an infinite number of headsets on the market so the choice of headset and fork is left to the builder.

The one inch diameter tube that will be used to support the steering axle is shown in this drawing but fitting and brazing of this detail is done later in the project. Just punch a hole in the backbone for the time being. This item requires fitting, measuring and clamping as the bike frame nears completion.

The tail end of the backbone is for the seat tube and seat post clamp. It too will be fit up later. This detail is one of those things best left to the very end of the project. That way, you have time to develop ideas for customizing to give the bike some flair. If you have access to a CNC machine with a fourth axis, this clamp is a perfect candidate for some custom engraving.

Jigging and Clamping

The view of the jig looking forward shows a 2x3 aluminum tube, a piece of 5/16 threaded rod used as an axle for the front fork, heat sink (dummy axle) bolted in place and dropouts clamped onto heat sink. The 2 x 3 tube is 60 inches long. All that is needed to complete the jig are some pieces of either rectangular tubes or angles and some C clamps.

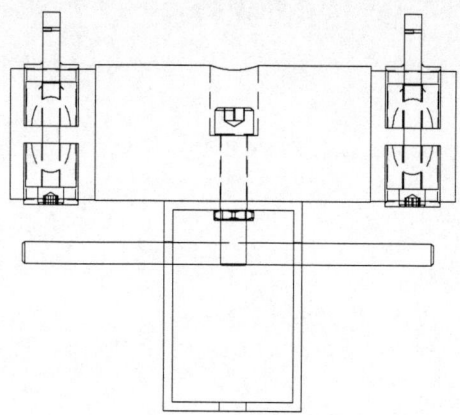

Rear view of jig, with dropouts clamped in place, looking forward

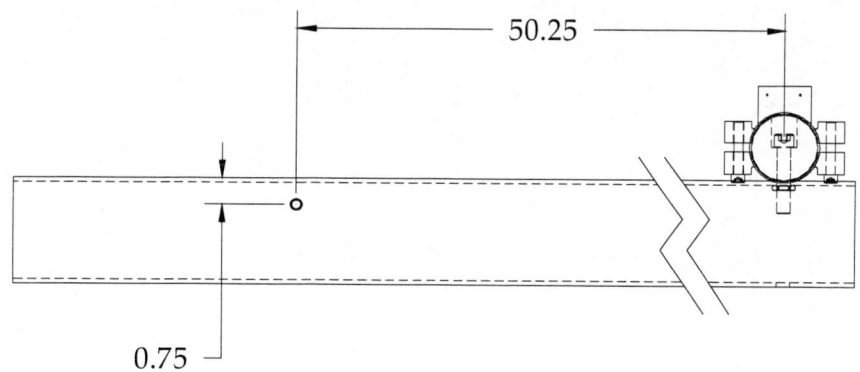

Side view of jig, with dropouts clamped in place.

There is nothing to prevent us continuing with the next big step in the fitting up of the frame. A picture's worth a thousand words so here's a whole bunch showing the fork resting on the 5/16 pin used as the front axle, two cones used to center the head tube on the fork, the backbone clamped to the jig using four C clamps, and two uprights of 2" angle with quarter inch shims to take up the difference in the backbone diameter and the width of the jig. The one inch tube used for the steering axis is used here for eyeball check and not brazed at this time. Pin the stays to the dropouts if you want to. It makes life easier until you decide you want to remove the stays at a later date. Do not use hardened pins for this reason.

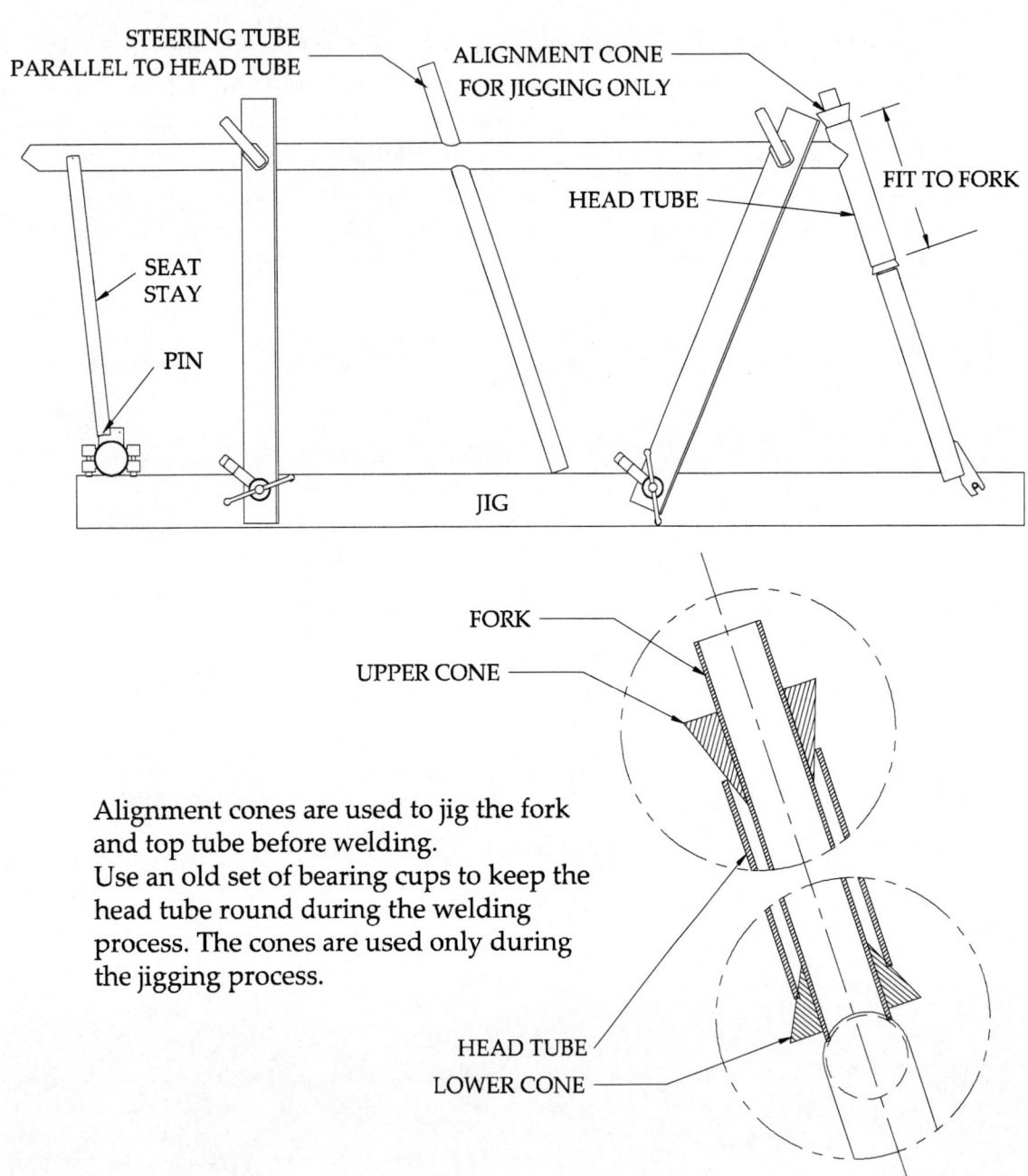

Alignment cones are used to jig the fork and top tube before welding.
Use an old set of bearing cups to keep the head tube round during the welding process. The cones are used only during the jigging process.

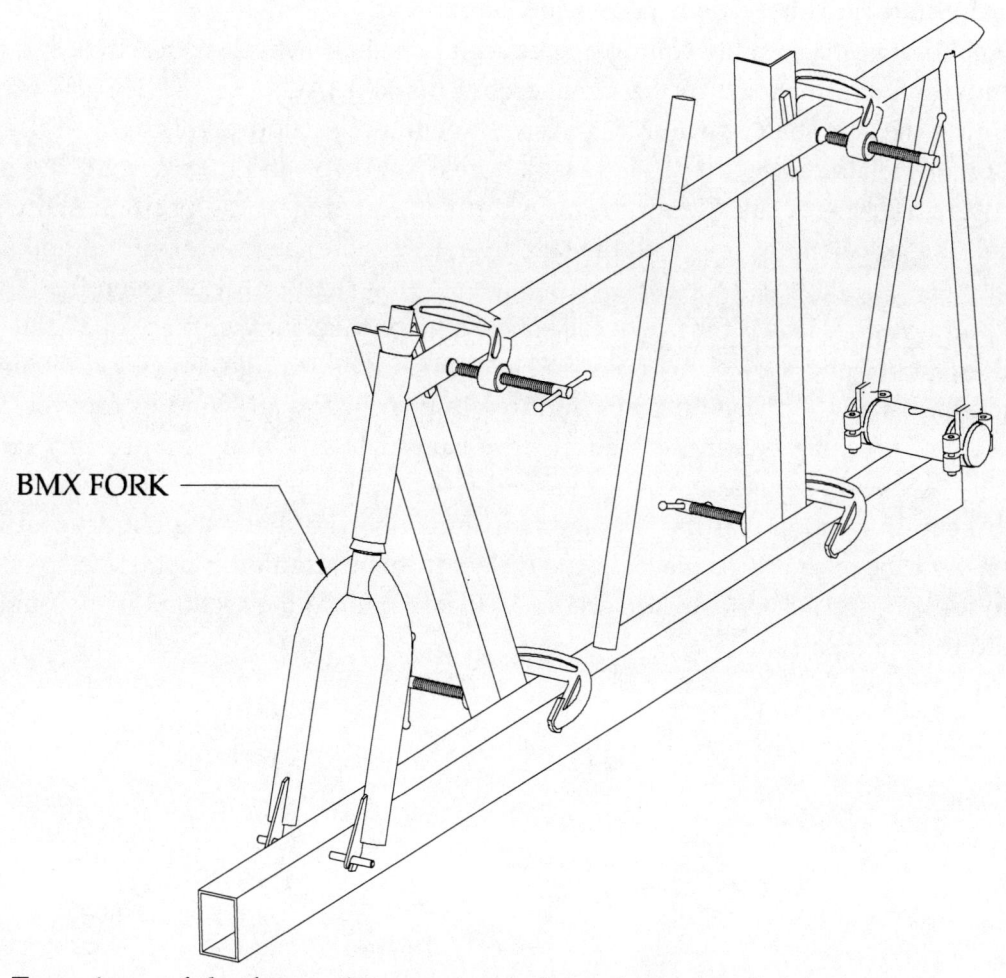

BMX FORK

Two views of the frame shaping up on the welding jig. The center of the backbone is 18" above and parallel to the top of the jig. Note the ¼" shim between the upright and the backbone and the cones used to center the head tube on the fork.

The seat stays shown on the jig are Ø.75 x .050 wall 4130 seamless tubing, the backbone is also chrome-moly. A good source for these tubes and nearly all your bicycle building needs can be found by doing a search of the homebuilt aircraft websites. We here at Robobike have a short list of preferred vendors but rather than publishing a list that is not updated, it is best that the builder do this work.

Tack everything together with just enough fillet and penetration to hold it in place.

After doing all that, it is time to consider the next sub-assembly. The down tube along with the jackshaft housing, chain stays and cross piece are all jigged up next.

The Jack Shaft Housing, Down Tube and Chain Stays

The Jack Shaft is an assembly comprising at least two chain wheels, 2 bearings and an axle. It is built on its own and installed in the circular ring marked JACK SHAFT HOUSING in this drawing. Building the jack shaft assembly is covered in another section of this book. Take a piece of the dropout material (Ø2" steel tube x .125 wall), bore it to Ø1.76" and trim it to 2.875" long. Tap two holes as shown in the detail. Clamp the jackshaft support ring at the position shown in the drawing. Install the jackshaft housing with the tapped holes for the set screws pointing down.

Take a piece of 1.00 x .06 tube (or 1⅛ x .06 if you prefer) and fit it between the head tube and the jack shaft housing. This is the down tube shown here. Take another piece of 1" tube and fit it between the backbone and the jackshaft housing at approximately a right angle to the downtube. This is the jackshaft stay. Go ahead and tack all three in place using any kind of rod you want. If the head tube is not finish bored for the headset, why isn't it? In any case, you are only tacking at this point. A heat sink will be used later for the semi-finish and finish passes on the head tube. A good point to keep in mind is that the average machinist does not have the cutters required for finishing the head tube once it is in place on the frame. If it is brazed after being cut to size, then certain precautions must be used to ensure accuracy. Please refer to the section on shop tips for an insight on head tube heat sinks.

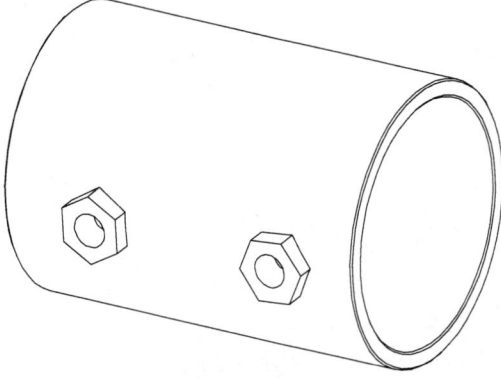

Jackshaft housing showing two 1/4" nuts brazed to outside for set screws. The all purpose jackshaft is slipped into this ring and held in place with the set screws.

The chain stays attached to the dropouts and the associated cross piece are shown in the illustrations. Fit them up any way you feel is best. Tack everything. You may modify this part of the design, the stays and the crosspiece, any which way you want, but it is recommended that you wait to do so until the rear wheel is fitted into the dropouts for a clearance check. Remove the frame from the jig. Check everything for straightness on and off the jig. Try the wheel. Measure and fit the cross piece used to mount the brakes between the seat stays or set the brake rotor and the disk brake caliper and check for clearance. Straighten what you have to. Go ahead and braze what you have so far but only to give it a root pass. The rule is, until you've checked and measured everything twice, don't weld anything today that you don't want to take apart tomorrow.

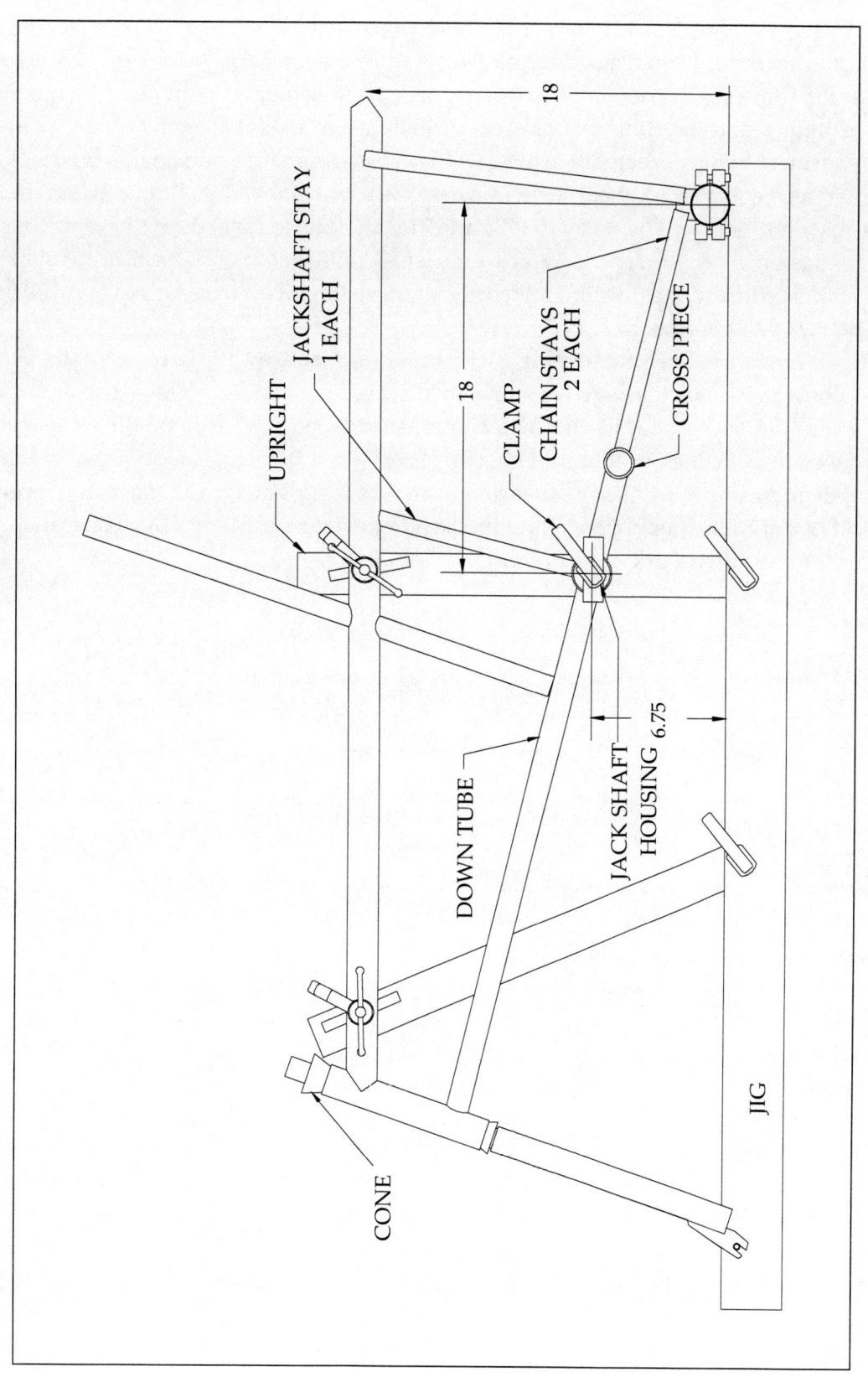

UPRIGHT

JACKSHAFT STAY
1 EACH

CLAMP

CHAIN STAYS
2 EACH

CROSS PIECE

DOWN TUBE

JACK SHAFT
HOUSING 6.75

CONE

JIG

18

18

151

Fitting Up

The Delivery Boy is ready for some finish work. Just a bit of explanation about fitting up. This term is something I came across while working in a ship yard years ago. It is actually very hard work for someone whose job description was fitter's helper as mine was. Imagine shearing, bending, grinding and beveling bits of steel, usually quite massive, and holding them in place while an enormously fat, perpetually drunk welder with disgusting personal habits yells at you to move faster as he blasts at them with a wire feed machine. Our fitting won't be quite as reprehensible, but there will be many details and bits and pieces fabbed on the spot. These bits are difficult to document so some experience with steel fabrication is helpful. You may choose a different path as you add the finishing touches, but those described here work very well.

The Head Tube

Finish braze the head tube using a generous fillet and multiple passes. The joint is only lightly to moderately loaded but give it some good size fillets none the less. Move around like you should, never getting one spot too hot while another remains cold. It is possible to face and bore the head tube after brazing but if brazed properly, you won't have to. Robobike has a pair of gages that use dial indicators to measure distortion after brazing and we manage to eliminate both banana and out of round conditions using the technique described here. This is hardly production tooling but for prototype work, it is cracker jack.

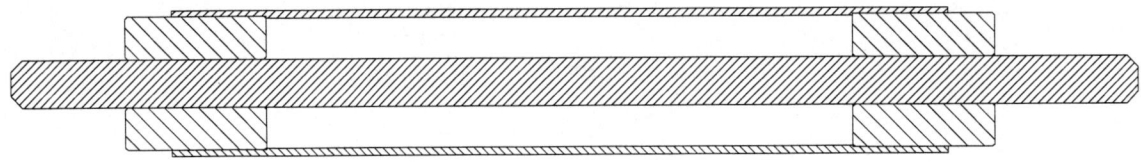

Weld tooling used to prevent banana

Shown in section is the head tube, two plugs turned to the bearing cup diameter and reamed to fit a pin, and a pin to keep everything straight. If possible, make the plugs from brass to ease disassembly. The plugs should fit the tube with an easy press fit which in this case is .000 to .001 clearance. Believe me, they will be plenty tight after brazing. Avoid using steel plugs. You'll never get them apart without a big hammer. Aluminum works OK for plugs but can be balky. Braze until you get tired and then clean everything before moving on. There is nothing else to braze at this end of the bike so go ahead and fit the headset and mount the fork, keeping in mind that it will be disassembled a number of times before the maiden ride.

The Steering Axis

The steering axis doesn't require a heat sink but does require care in assembly. Riding the Delivery Boy is easy once under weigh, but the tricky part is handling all that mass when you are at a standstill. Those of you with tandem experience know how much stress is directed through the captain's handlebars at rest. Subsequently, a good remote steering design isolates the steering mechanism from the strain that occurs as a result of bike handling. This bit of the bicycle must have extraordinary reliability and strength yet work smooth under all load conditions.

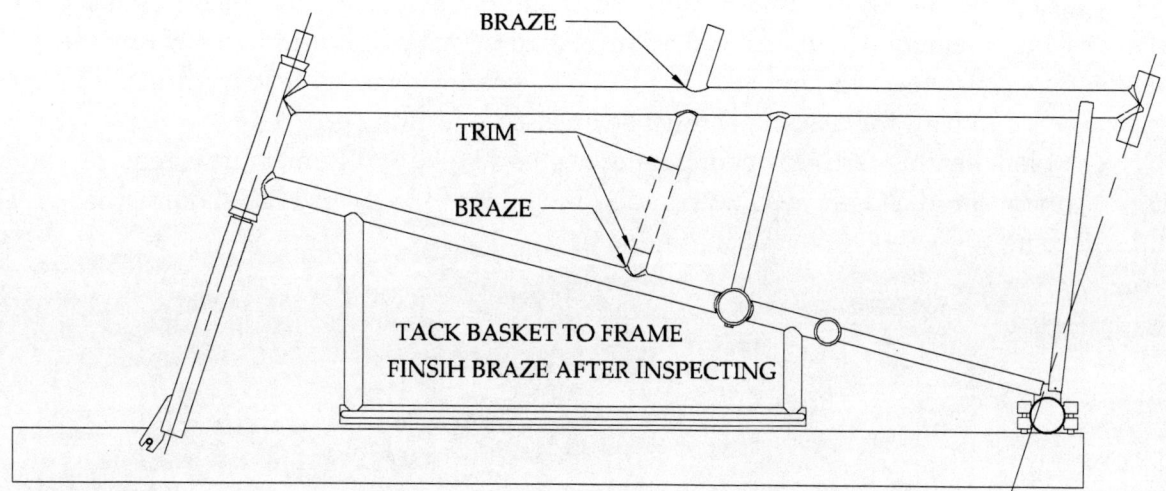

BRAZE

TRIM

BRAZE

TACK BASKET TO FRAME
FINSIH BRAZE AFTER INSPECTING

Trim a piece of one inch diameter tube and face both ends to 14 inches. Braze it all around where it passes through the backbone and again where it butts up against the down tube. Trim with a hacksaw where the dashed lines are drawn.

The steering axis is fitted with a massive angular contact bearing at the top and a plain bearing at both the down tube socket and the end of the steering tube where it is trimmed. This arrangement gives a hefty lever through which the bike can be controlled around the longitudinal axis.

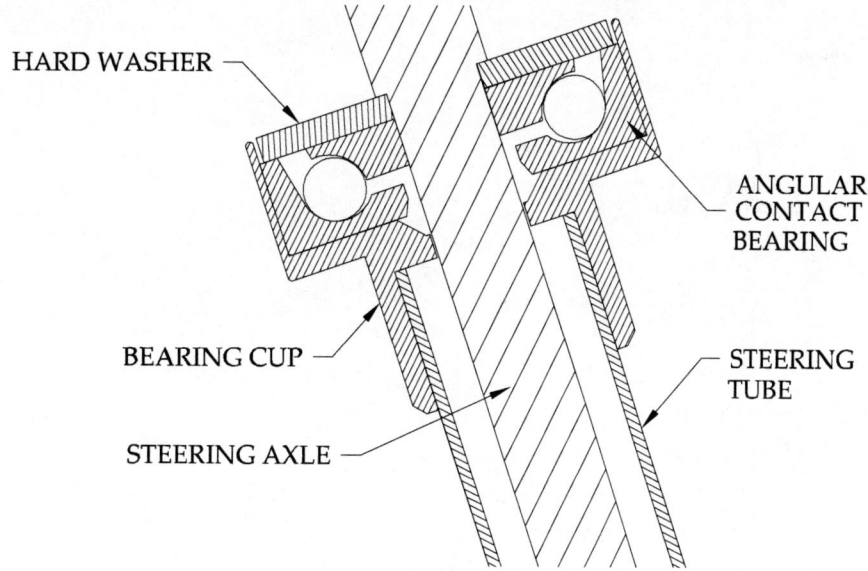

HARD WASHER

ANGULAR CONTACT BEARING

BEARING CUP

STEERING TUBE

STEERING AXLE

Schematic section view of the steering tube, upper end, showing the steering axle with the turned shoulder to bear against the hard washer.

A locking collar should be added if the post is made of aluminum. It is not needed with a steel axle. Also shown is the bearing cup, a custom piece which is a nice bit of lathe work. The bore where the cup is pressed onto the steering tube requires a bit of care as does the bore supporting the outer diameter of the angular contact bearing. During assembly, the cup is drawn down onto the frame tube using a piece of threaded rod through the entire assembly.

The angular contact bearing controls thrust and radial loads so it is heavily loaded at times. That's why the assembly is so massive. This combination makes for a smooth steering mechanism. Add the two plain bearings and fit the fork and steering post with lever arms. The pinning operation sets end play and absolutely must be precise.

The plain bearings are easy enough, the push pull tube and Pitman arms require a bit more thought. Spherical rod ends screwed into a tube and attached to levers with shoulder bolts is about all there is to it.

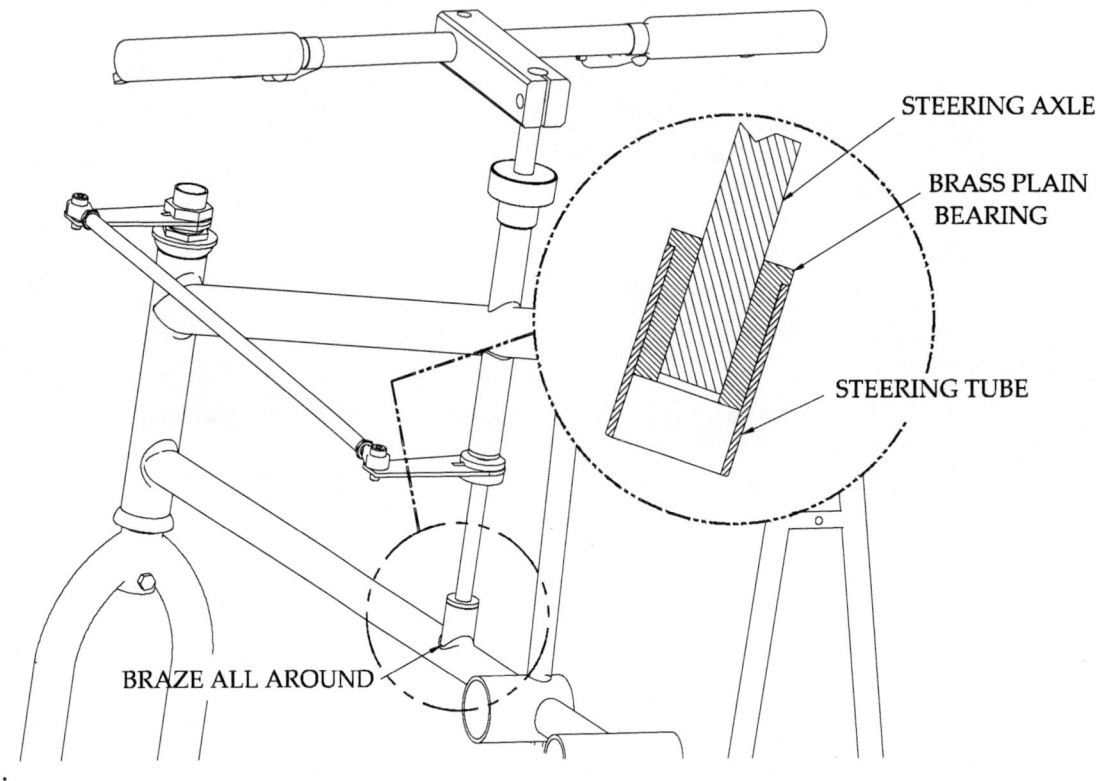

STEERING AXLE

BRASS PLAIN BEARING

STEERING TUBE

BRAZE ALL AROUND

One important detail left to the builder is to decide whether or not to braze a sleeve to the inside of the fork steering tube. It is recommended. The pin through the fork and steering lever is .1875 diameter. A sleeve assures complete control even after the front end has been crashed or worn from normal wear. Do not use a roll pin.

When the steering is finished, install the wheels and check for play in the steering mechanism. There must not be any. In the early days of tandem bikes, this type of steering was common place as it was assumed that the lady rode in front and the man did the steering. What a great idea. Having the stronger rider nearer the drive wheel reduces the loads on every part of the structure. Inputting the steering and bike handling forces between the riders instead of at one end makes perfect sense. Today it is rare to see a tandem bike with stoker steering.

Decide what you want to yield in a crash. We do not pin the gooseneck connection where it clamps the steering axle. This is where our bike will give way in a crash, preventing damage to rider and steering linkage caused by extreme stress on the components.

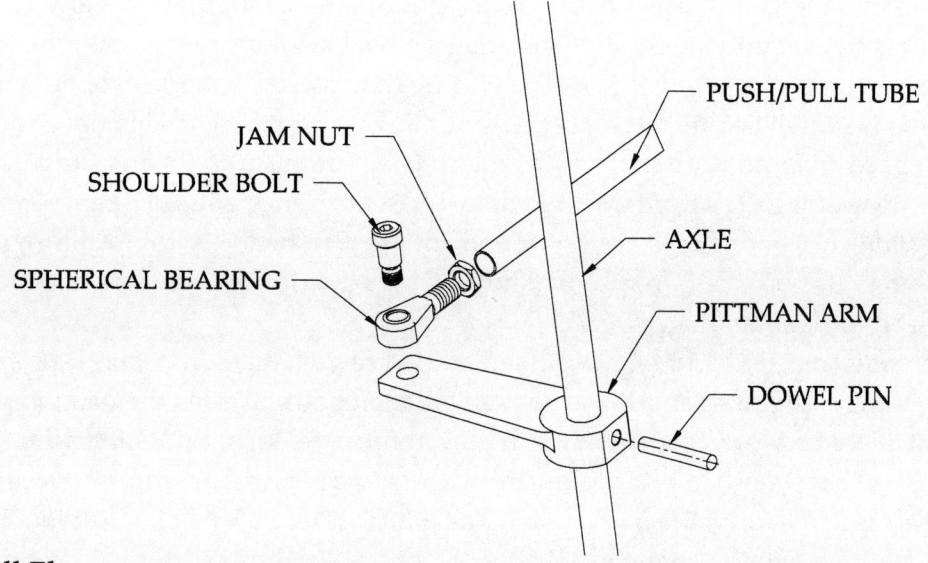

JAM NUT

SHOULDER BOLT

SPHERICAL BEARING

PUSH/PULL TUBE

AXLE

PITTMAN ARM

DOWEL PIN

All Else

Another design strategy to discuss before we add the cargo rack is our decision of where things are attached to the structure. Adding tubes to an existing cluster of tubes can be done but should be avoided. It is far easier to braze two tubes together than a tube to a cluster of tubes, mostly because the heat energy directed into the joint is greatly reduced. This results in less distortion, a cleaner looking joint and increased satisfaction when all goes together nicely.

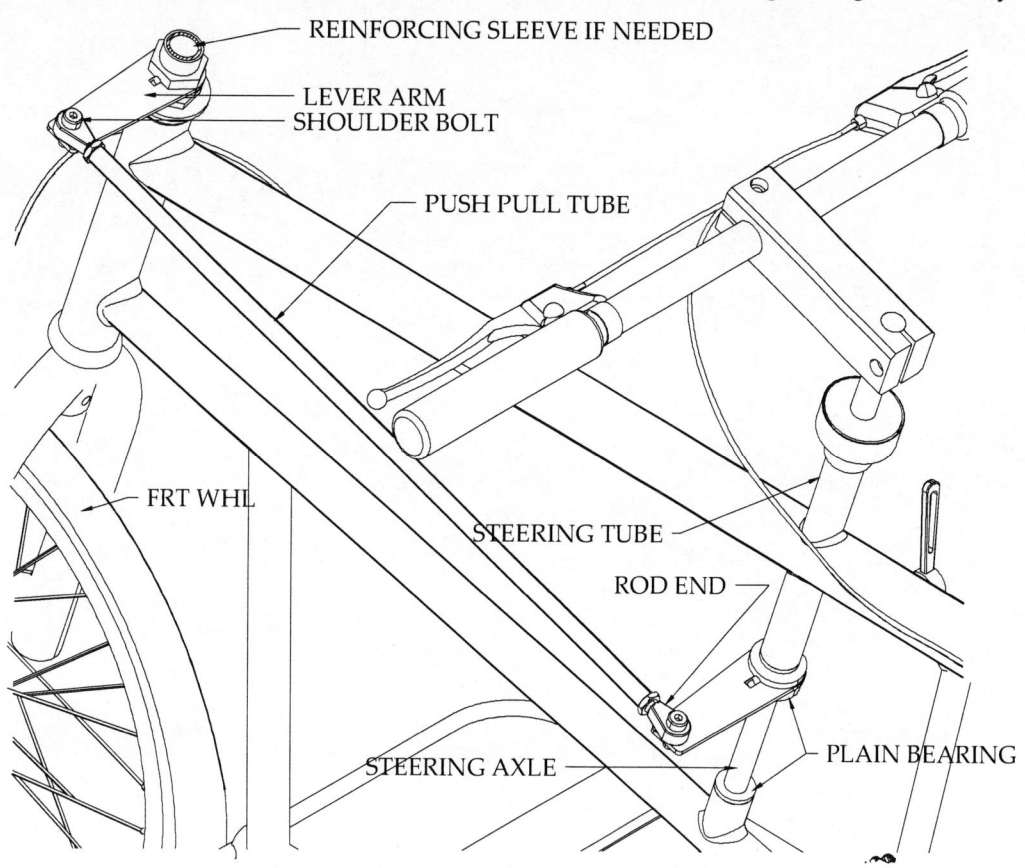

REINFORCING SLEEVE IF NEEDED

LEVER ARM
SHOULDER BOLT

PUSH PULL TUBE

FRT WHL

STEERING TUBE

ROD END

STEERING AXLE

PLAIN BEARING

Remote Steering Assembly

The load carrying rack or basket is up to the builder. The configuration shown works well for most loads but is not the only possibility. Put the bike back on the jig when building the basket to keep everything square and symmetrical. The electric motors and batteries are not shown. The type of service this bike will see dictates a series wound motor as these things have more torque pulling at slow speed than any other type of motor. They are also known as universal motors because they run on AC or DC current. Most people have experience with these motors but aren't aware of it. A vacuum cleaner has a series wound motor. Personally, I think the motor(s) is a wonderful addition to this bike but unless you know how to care for fifty pounds of batteries, start with something a bit less demanding.

The jackshaft is installed and likewise the modified rear changer. Most critical observers of this bike see two things. The first, and it is true with all homebuilt bikes, is the paint job. Even the most magnificent piece of work incorporating highly refined features will suffer the slings and arrows of the masses that choose to offer comments if there isn't at least an effort to put some paint on your bike. ***Paint is dumb but do it if you must.*** The other object noticed by observers is the class of rear changer. High end classy changers don't work on this bike because the crank arm has to swing and clear the changer. Subsequently, only low end steel changers can be made to work as they hang nearly straight down. Most have some type of parallelogram mechanism but they certainly aren't the latest and greatest. Never mind that they work without a hitch, are cheap and indestructible, they are simply not what is stylish these days. You will need an angle bracket to mount the changer.

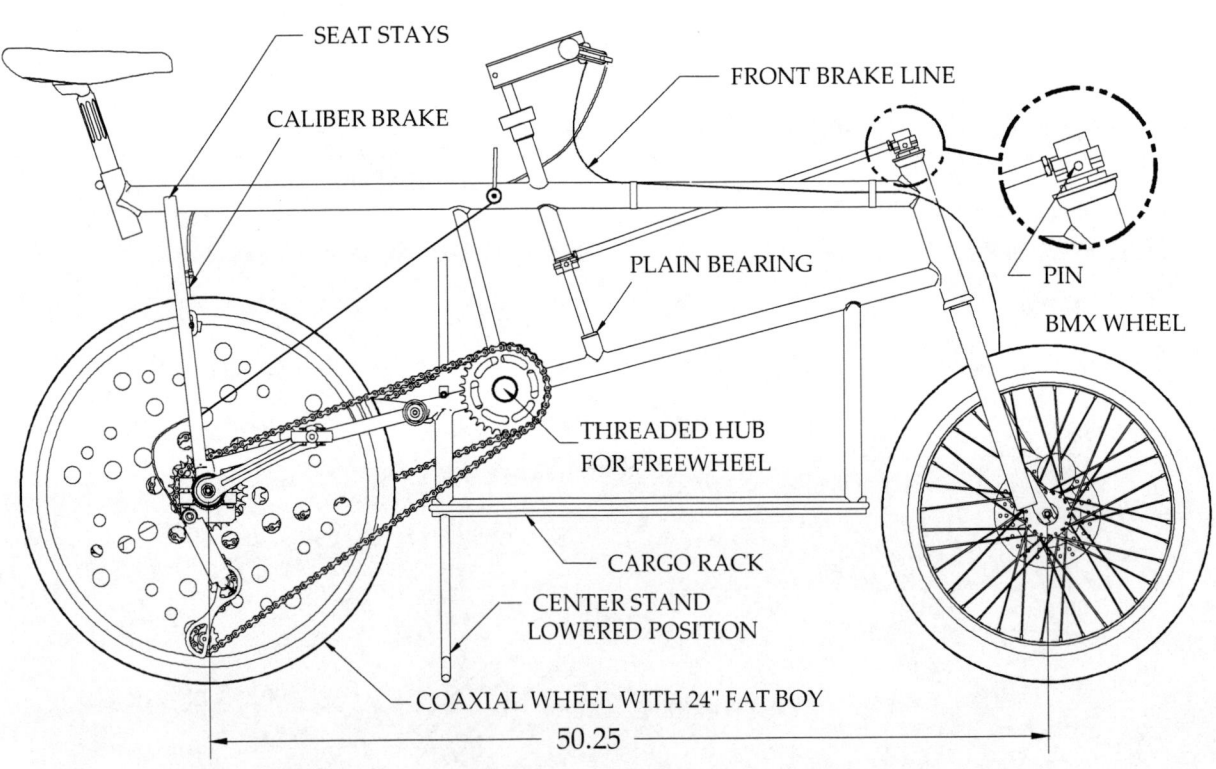

SEAT STAYS

CALIBER BRAKE

FRONT BRAKE LINE

PLAIN BEARING

PIN

BMX WHEEL

THREADED HUB
FOR FREEWHEEL

CARGO RACK

CENTER STAND
LOWERED POSITION

COAXIAL WHEEL WITH 24" FAT BOY

50.25

Finally, since the rider sits over the rear wheel, it is very easy to do wheelies when empty especially if that is your goal. Powering up hill with the front wheel just off the pavement is quite a sight to see. A touch of the rear brake brings all back to earth but just to make sure, if you choose to go without the electric motor option, carry 10 pounds of ballast securely attached to the front of the frame if you choose to ride the bike empty.

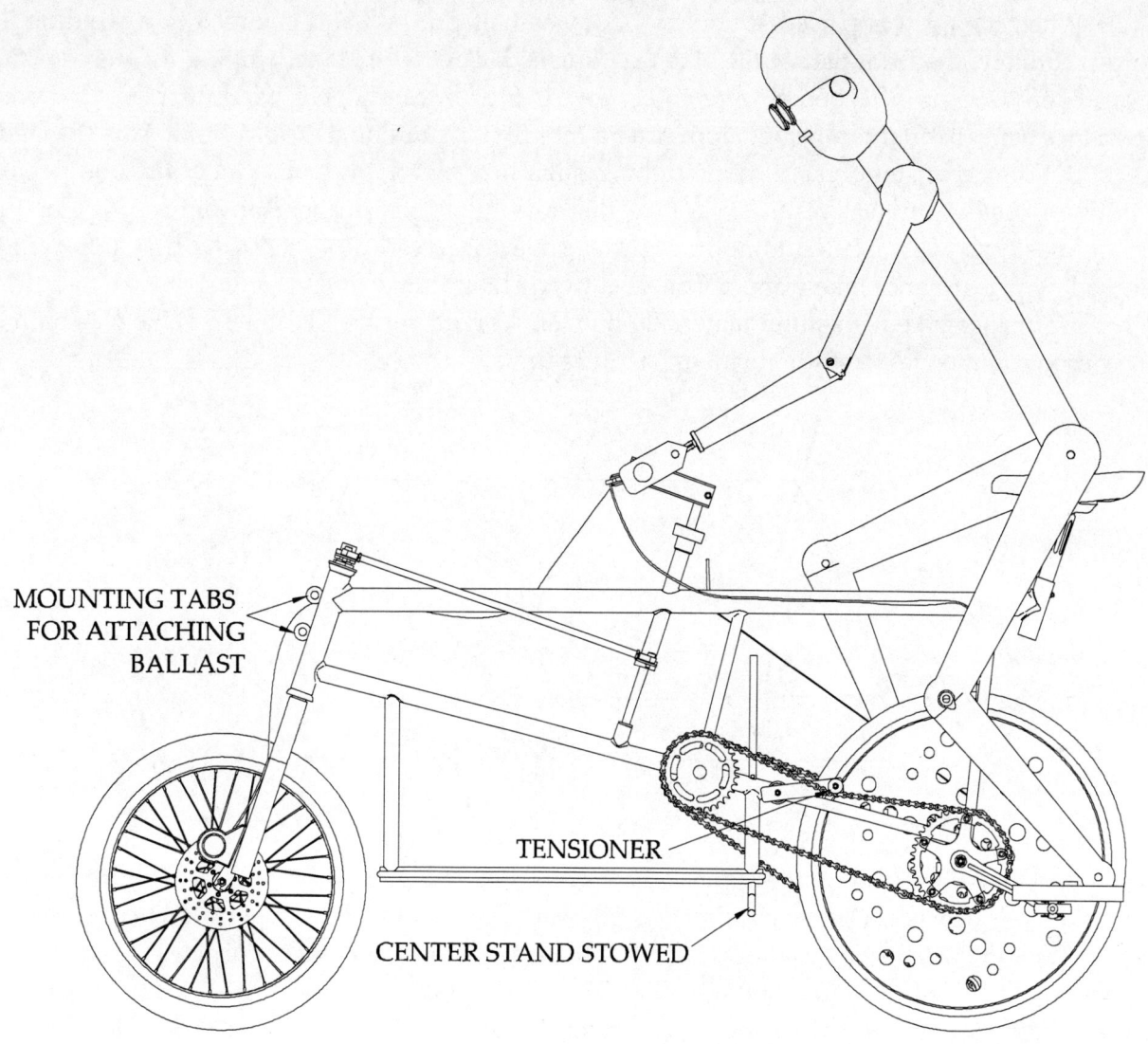

MOUNTING TABS
FOR ATTACHING
BALLAST

TENSIONER

CENTER STAND STOWED

RIDE SAFE

The Loveboat

The fastest, most efficient tandem bicycle ever built and how it came to be.
Master level skills required

Some projects begin as sketches and tables of load calculations while some projects begin by changing the blade in the hack saw. Loveboat began with a personal ad.

When the ad was placed, a tandem bike was half finished and clamped in a welding jig. More accurately, the front half of the bike was finished. The rear half sat waiting for the selection of a stoker. Dozens of women were interviewed. Stoker candidates with no prior bicycling experience were given top consideration. After a month of marathon dating, a stoker was selected.

Building a custom bike, if done right, results in a bicycle that absolutely fits one person. Building a custom tandem results in a bike that absolutely fits one person times two. For this reason, mostly, it was decided to approach this project in a series of steps; the first step was to build a low performance bike from carbon steel to work out the geometry and step two, to build a high performance bike with stiffer material. The plan worked very well. The first bike was built of low carbon commercial steel square tubes, an odd but valid choice.

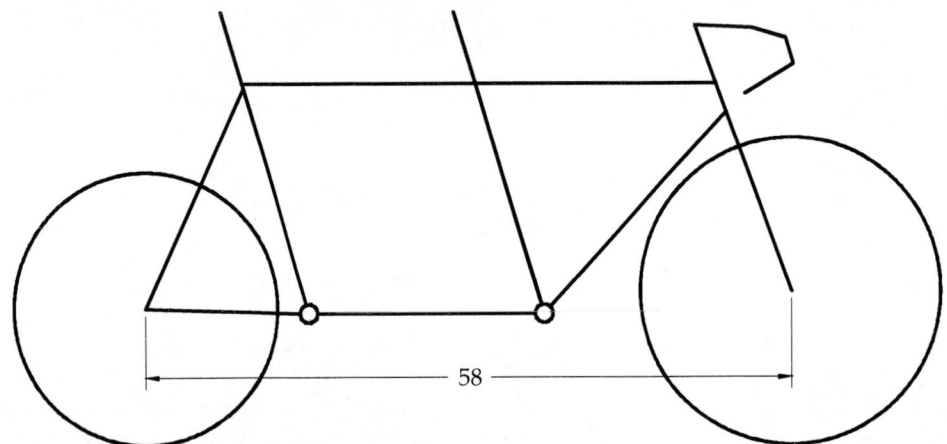

This illustration shows step one as first proposed and subsequently built. The front wheel was a high performance 27 inch clincher and the rear wheel a 24 inch high performance clincher of the type Junior USCF racers used in the 1980s. The rear rim was laced to a Sturmey Archer 3 speed hub that had been gutted and modified with a TIG welder to accept a five speed cluster. The choice of the smaller rear wheel was made in an attempt to shorten the wheelbase. A smaller wheel is easier to bring forward. Doing so moves the center of gravity aft. The bike rode fine.

The specs for the **step one** bike were:

Wheelbase 58 inches
Front wheel diameter 27 inches
Rear wheel diameter 24 inches
Captain has control of single caliper brakes front and rear
Shifting with downtube shifters, Captain
Conventional ten speed gear arrangement

This bike was the first Robobike project to use the half moon head tube and the second to use vertical drop outs. The half moon was used to fix the head tube angle which was brazed incorrectly. After a year of regular use, the first tandem bike in the series was scrapped when it was discovered that the wheelbase had grown due to the forks yielding. What a scary revelation. The forks used on the final rendition of the Loveboat are a direct result of this and other performance data being rolled into a new revision. The total lack of emergency braking power from the two caliper brakes, though they performed well, was another reason for abandoning the first bike.

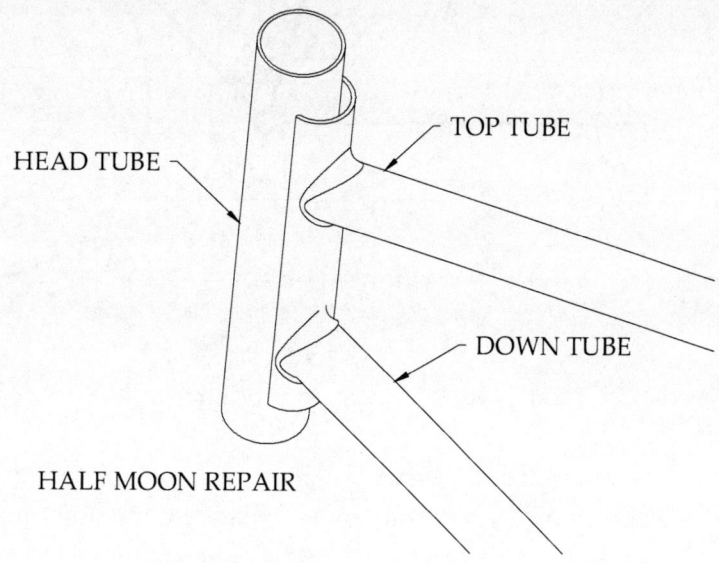

The scorecard for the first tandem for Team Loveboat was mixed. The bike performed well in spite of 5 inches of trail, had room enough for the stoker by conventional tandem rules, had good weight and balance characteristics and always answered the bell when it came to club rides. On the minus side, the frame absorbed power at an unacceptable rate, the timing chain was a nightmare and the bike met with derision from the crowd who looks at a bike and sees only a paint job. Not only that, the bike was the source of jokes among those who measure the value of a bicycle in kilograms.

Step two saw the first co-axial wheel in the Robobike stables. Searching for a way to give the stoker an additional 10 inches of room without increasing the wheel base or destroying the balance of the bike, we drew up a radically different tandem. The bike built for step 2 later became known as the Fiasco.

Step two

Step two is a whole new bike. The primary design goal is giving the stoker more room. This is to be done without increasing the wheelbase. The only solution to this design goal is to make the axle of the rear wheel and stoker's crankset co-axial. The wheelbase remains unchanged at 58 inches and the stoker has more room. Way more.

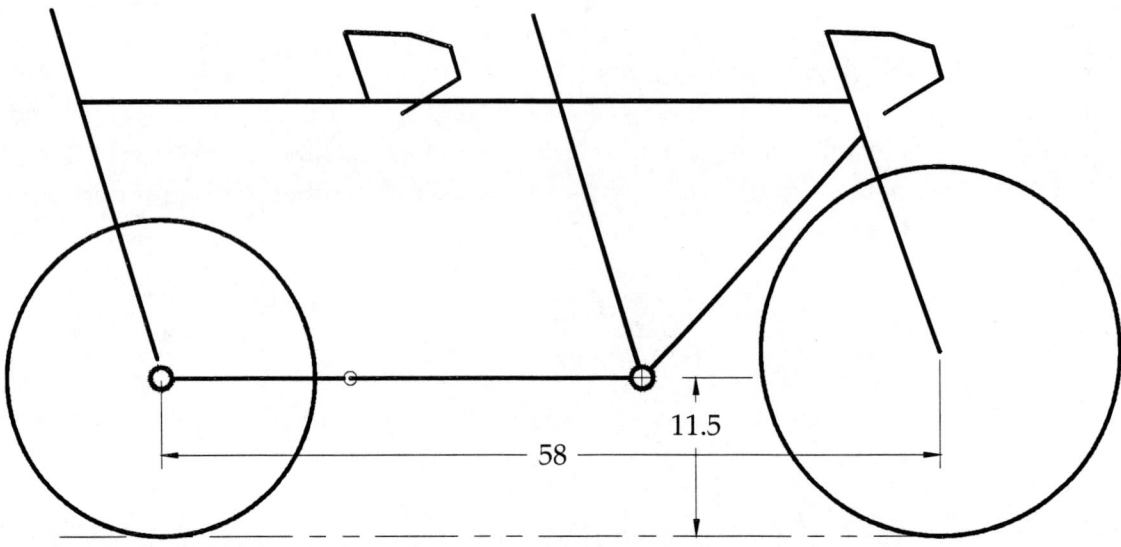

Our first coaxial tandem

The rear wheel is not hard to visualize if you think of two pairs of bearings each performing a unique task. One pair supports the wheel disk and the other pair supports the axle.

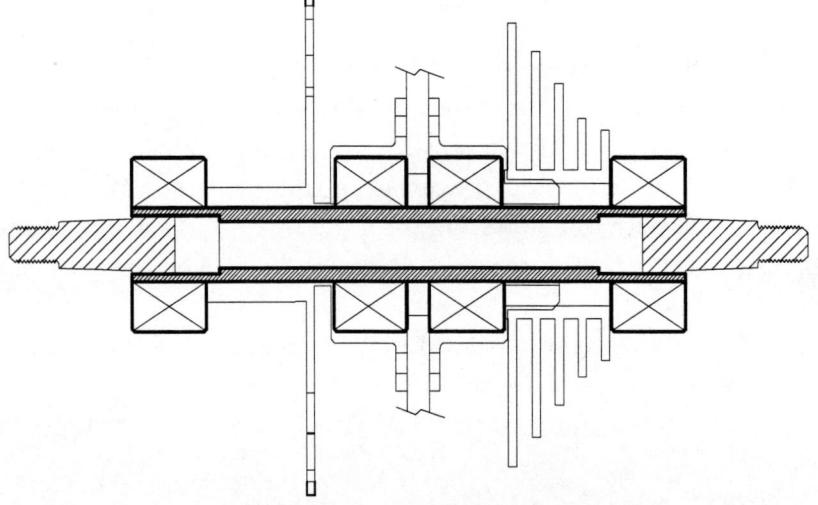

Our first co-axial wheel axle

Step two was ridden all of 2 miles before it was returned to the shop, cut up into bin sized pieces and scrapped. Why the bike was a total failure is easy to see now that we have years of experience with Loveboat.

The frame was so flexible that when turning a corner, the stoker, being behind the wheel contact patch, would accelerate away from the center of the turn while the captain would move towards the center as is the case in normal bicycle maneuvering. The magnitude of these opposing forces and their consequences were not anticipated. When the bike recovered from turns, the energy stored in the frame would unwind and cause the rear wheel to jump off the ground. Not only that, but oscillations similar to those found in tail heavy airplanes made control impossible. For those who have never flown a tail heavy airplane, the whole business is downright terrifying. After two miles and a dozen turns, the crew dismounted and walked home. So what was wrong?

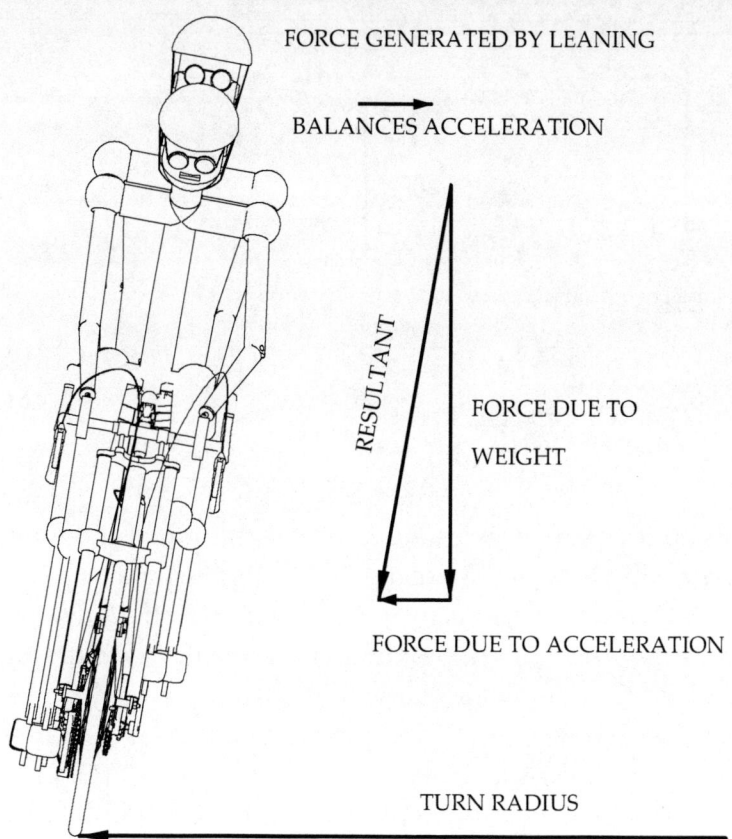

FORCE GENERATED BY LEANING

BALANCES ACCELERATION

RESULTANT

FORCE DUE TO WEIGHT

FORCE DUE TO ACCELERATION

TURN RADIUS

The bicycle was built with chrome moly steel. The diameter and wall thickness were typical for bicycle construction and if anything, the tubes were a bit on the stout side. The problem must lay elsewhere.

A steady state turn with constant radius and constant velocity produces constant acceleration and easy to control forces on the bicycle itself. Making a big wide sweeping turn is easy and can be done with no control input whatsoever. Key word: equilibrium.

In this illustration, a sudden stop without straightening the bank angle results in a crash towards the inside of the turn because the force due to acceleration drops to zero. Conversely, straightening the bank angle without stopping the turn results in a crash to the outside of the turning circle. The point is, a steady state turn is a maneuver that puts very little stress on the bike frame resulting in very little strain.

A steady state turn is a mild maneuver, to be sure, but its execution requires dynamic stability. Therein lies the problem in regards to the step two bicycle. The transition into the turn requires accelerating two separate and distinct mass centers (a couple) in opposite directions around the rear wheel contact patch. These opposing accelerations create opposing reactions. The frame must oppose these ractions. The only way the frame can counter these opposing forces is to twist about the longitudinal axis. It actually twists around a bunch of different axes that are too numerous to analyze without more empirical data. This became apparent immediately with the Fiasco. It is unbelievable just how much a steel frame can flex in its effort to control such opposing forces. Even scarier is just how fast a frame can release the energy stored this way.

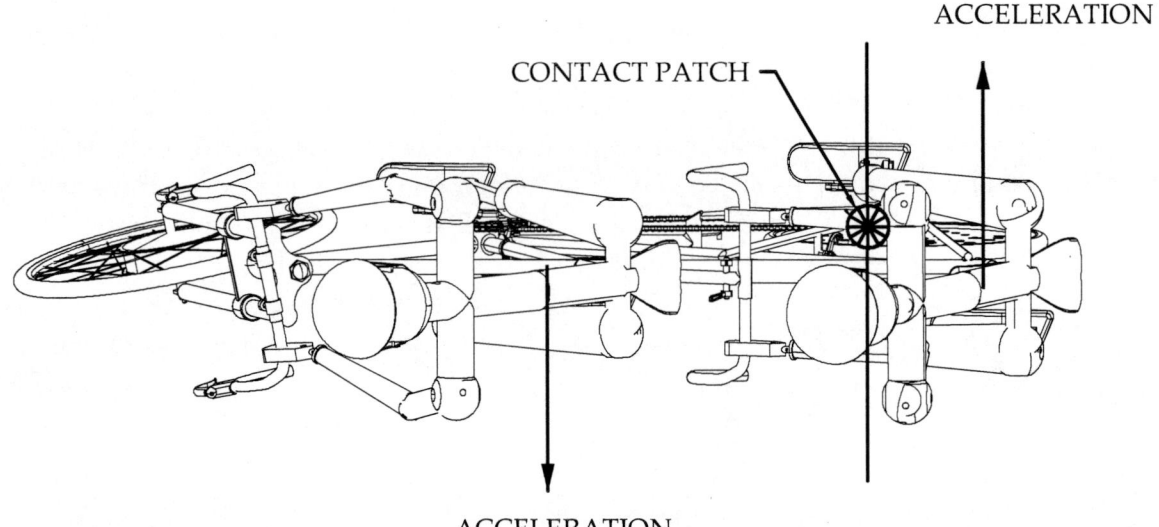

ACCELERATION

CONTACT PATCH

ACCELERATION

TRANSITIONING FROM STRAIGHT AND LEVEL TO A STEADY STATE TURN REQUIRES

MOVING THROUGH THIS PHASE

The top view of the bicycle as it begins the turn is useful to show the forces involved. Turning a complex set of force vectors into a simple 2d problem only begins to illustrate how and why a frame could be tweaked so severely. The frame, like any mechanism, has strengths and weaknesses. It is tragic that Robobike didn't take this opportunity to analyze the frame in greater detail. It was felt that the risk just wasn't worth any benefit gained from continuing with this obviously unsafe machine. It cannot be emphasized enough; this frame had widowmaker written all over it.

Although these illustrations show a drum brake on the front and a disk wheel on the rear, these features were not present on step two. They were first introduced on the final rendition of Loveboat. After the complete and absolute failure of step two, a regrouping was in order. It was decided to try again but instead of finessing the control of these forces, the brute force approach would be the order of the day. We at Robobike had confidence in the design.

About this time, attention was redirected to the stoker candidate who had put her faith in the designers and builders at Robobike. There was no hiding the fact that she was asked to ride a bicycle that was short on stability and long on hazard. The captain of the Loveboat began a blitzkrieg campaign involving champagne, candlelight and bubble baths, along with moonlit picnics and a few symphony concerts. A mutiny was prevented. The stoker was soothed sufficiently to restore faith in the effort.

These two circles show the relative size of the top tubes used in the development of Loveboat. The profile on the left is the step two bicycle that was such a failure and the profile on the right shows the brute force approach used on Loveboat. Both are 4130 normalized steel with a published yield strength of 90000 psi, modulus of elasticity of 30,000,000 and an ultimate tensile strength of 105,000 psi. The smaller of the two is 1.125 outside diameter by .040 wall and the bigger tube 1.25 by .08 wall (28x1 and 31.3 x 2). The cross section of the smaller tube is .1363 square inches and the bigger tube is .2941 square inches. The bigger tube is 2.2 times as massive. The top tube, the boob tube and the uptube are all made of this heavier material. The stays are all ¾ diameter by 1/16 wall. This is indeed one massive frame.

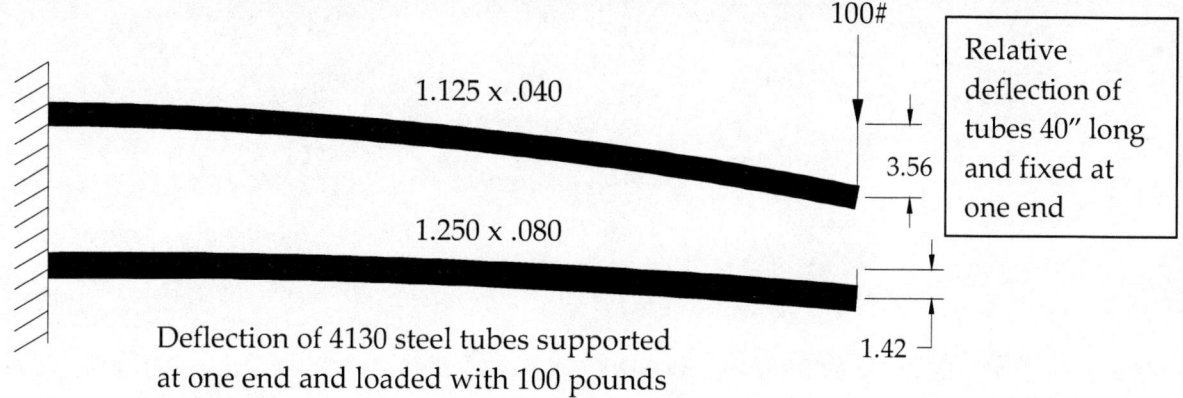

Deflection of 4130 steel tubes supported
at one end and loaded with 100 pounds

While all this work was being done on Loveboat, another tandem was finished. Daisy was built as a travel tandem but never saw service in that capacity. She was ridden many many miles and was a great success. One bad thing about Daisy was the shortage of braking ability. The number one good thing was the incredibly good handling. We at Robobike saw this latter quality as being the result of the motorcycle style front end built entirely of aluminum. It was decided that Loveboat would have the same style of front end but instead of a custom design, the front end from a Honda CB 350 motorcycle was selected. All the heavy steel suspension parts from the motorcycle were discarded and aluminum fork tubes substituted. The drum brake and hub were retained. Special spokes had to be made to fit the hub but that wasn't such a big deal.

When we say special spokes, what we really mean is regular old bicycle spokes made of steel that have been adapted for our application. Since the rim requires standard gage spokes, that aspect could not be changed. The flanges on the motorcycle hub were several times thicker than normal bicycle hub flanges so bicycle spokes wouldn't do the job. Also, the spokes had to be short. Our solution was to determine spoke length, mostly by trial and error and to bend a standard issue 14 gage spoke to a specific length. A new head was formed by brazing a tiny flat washer onto the end of the spoke. This method does not require rolling a new thread onto the old spoke after trimming it to length. It worked well.

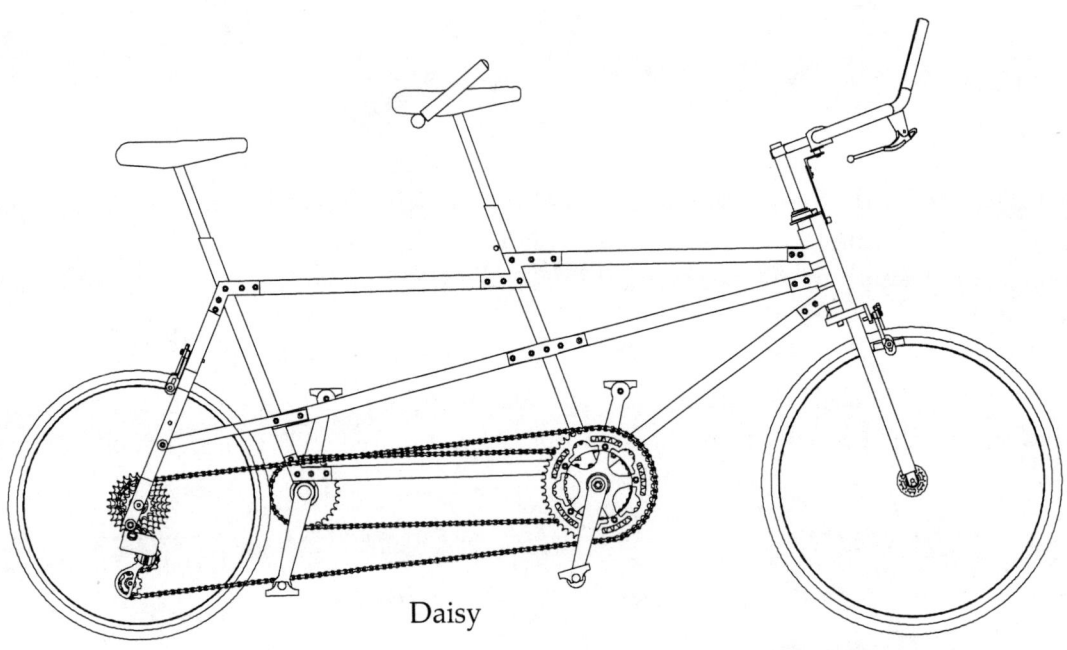

Daisy

When the final design was finished on what was to become the 'Boat, approval was given to build the welding jig. It took many months to finish the jig. It has leveling screws, pads for transits and lots and lots of clamps. Work then began on the bicycle itself.

Building Loveboat

One of the constraints assigned to the project from the very beginning was a 58 inch wheelbase. The goal is to build a tandem bicycle with more room assigned to the stoker than is considered normal. This was to be accomplished without increasing the wheelbase. The design weight of riders and frame was to be 350 lbs (160 kg) although the final rendition with all the cables, water bottles and everything else that makes a bicycle exceeded that figure but not by much. The design predicts a balance point at the 42 inch station. The finished bike has never been weighed to determine the actual balance point but it is thought that the actual figure is very close.

The rear dropouts are made first. They are then clamped around the dummy axle in the jig.

LOVEBOAT

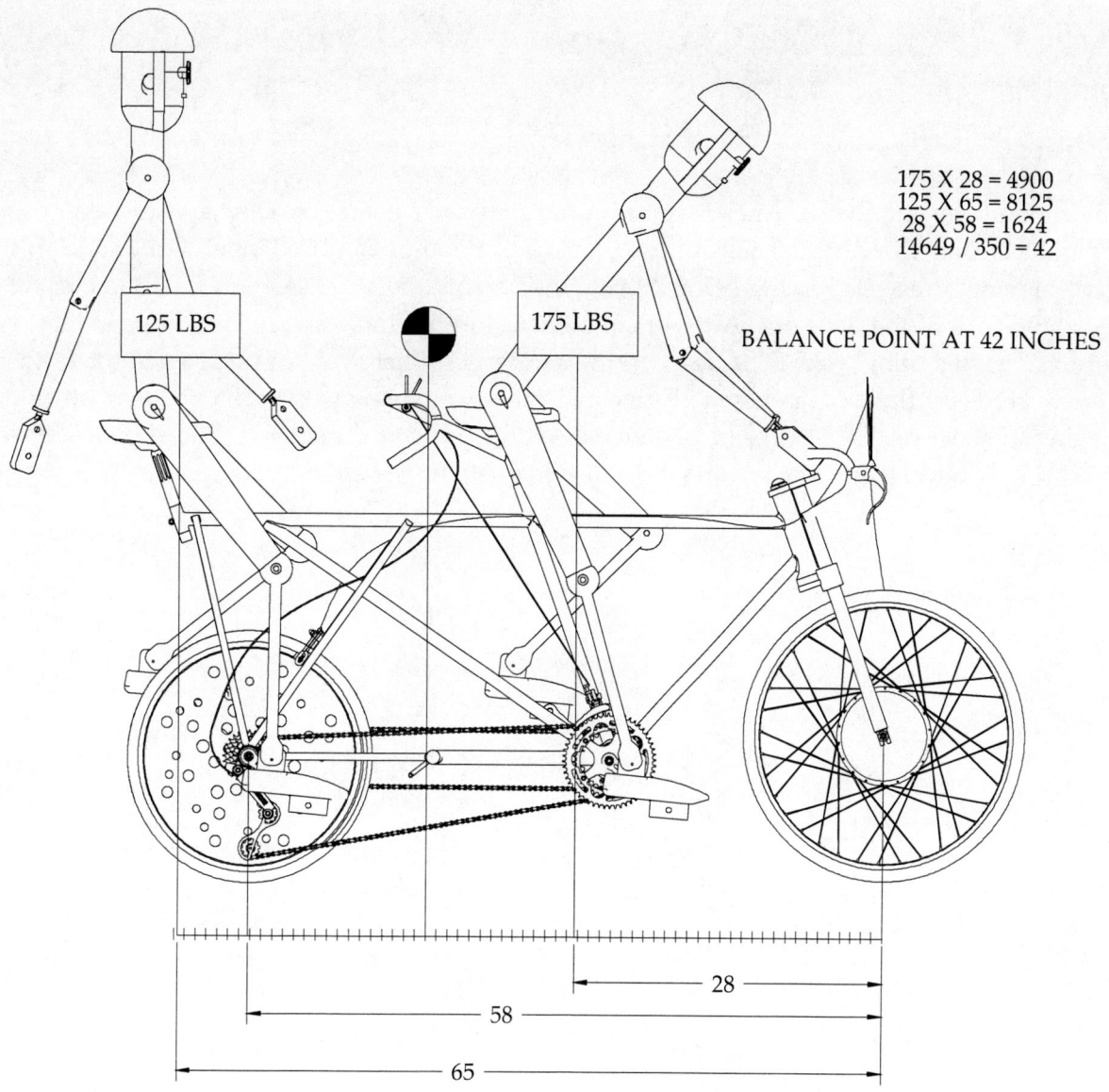

175 X 28 = 4900
125 X 65 = 8125
28 X 58 = 1624
14649 / 350 = 42

125 LBS

175 LBS

BALANCE POINT AT 42 INCHES

28

58

65

Weight and balance calculations of the Loveboat during the design phase. The finished bike is very close to these estimated values.

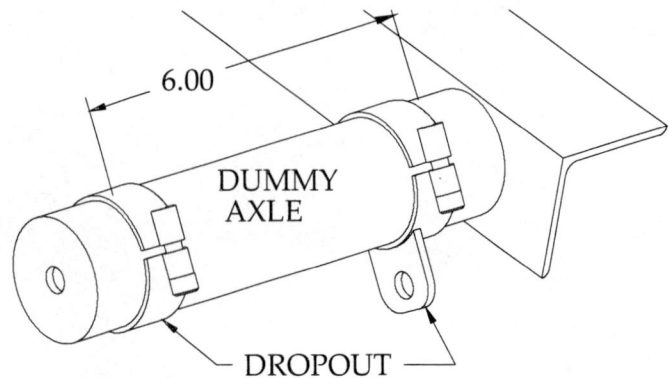

6.00

DUMMY
AXLE

DROPOUT

The dropouts are simply two rings that clamp the crank axle bearings. They are split clamps. Any type of steel will work here. The round features are made of ⅜ round steel. Drill and tap these before brazing. Braze everything before boring the bearing diameter. A two inch diameter tube or pipe is the core of the drop out. After brazing but before boring, saw the assembly in half. What really makes this thing work is to clean up the saw cuts so that at assembly, two ⅛ thick washers inserted between the two halves will give the screws something to tighten down on without crushing the bearing. Bore the bearing diameter with these shims installed. You should not clamp the bearing without them. The bearings will turn to dust very quickly if you do.

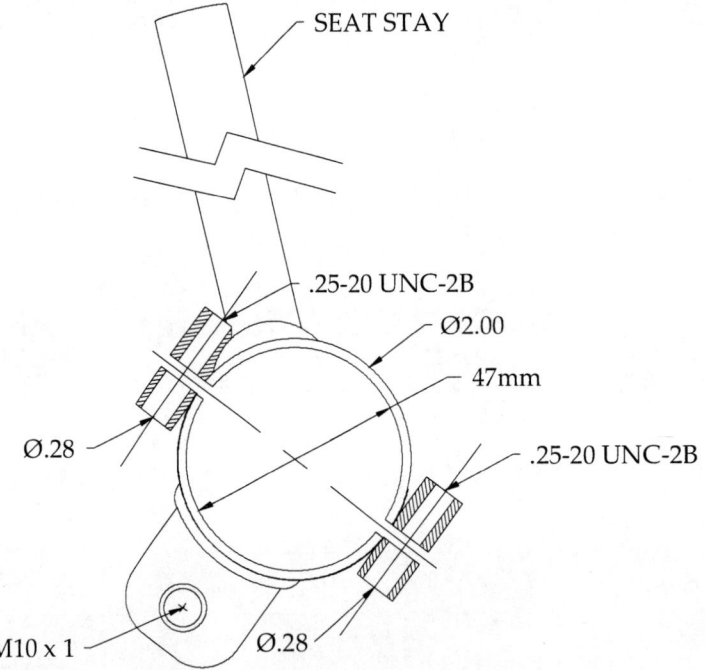

SEAT STAY

.25-20 UNC-2B

Ø2.00

47mm

.25-20 UNC-2B

Ø.28

M10 x 1

Ø.28

The ⅛ spacers can be a few thousandths thicker or thinner to fix the pressure. If you can spin the spacers after the bearing gets tight, then increase the thickness of the spacers. If you can move the bearing after the spacers are tight, thin the spacers in .001" increments until all feels right. This is something you want to save until the very last so don't get in a rush to finish. The tab with a M10 tapped hole for mounting the derailleur is added later.

For now, having the dropouts in the jig is what you want to do. The next step involves a great deal of work.

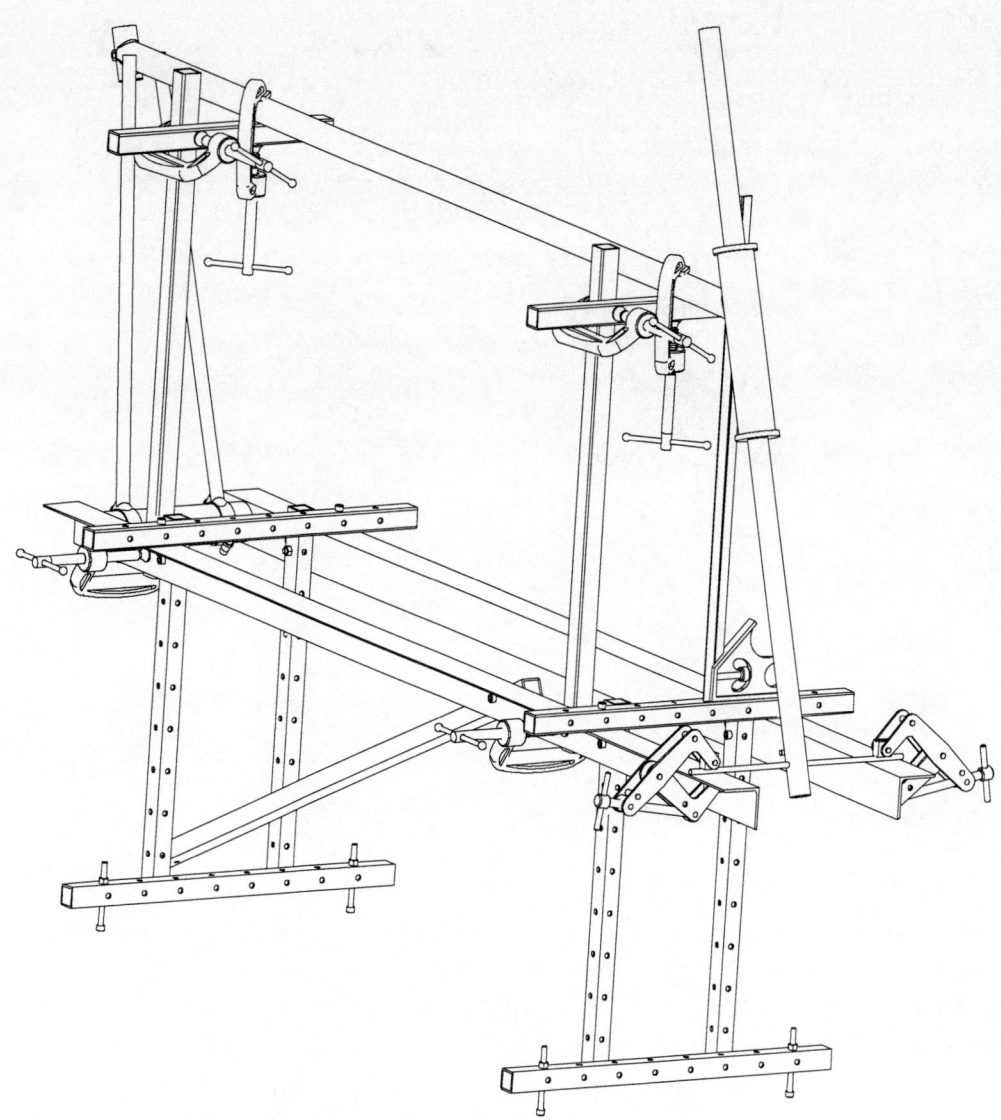

Loveboat takes shape on the welding jig

Jigging the Frame

The top tube is mitered and joined to the head tube using two tack welds at the sides to permit easy manipulation while on the jig.

Two bushings turned to fit the inside of the head tube and drilled to fit the alignment tube are fitted as shown.

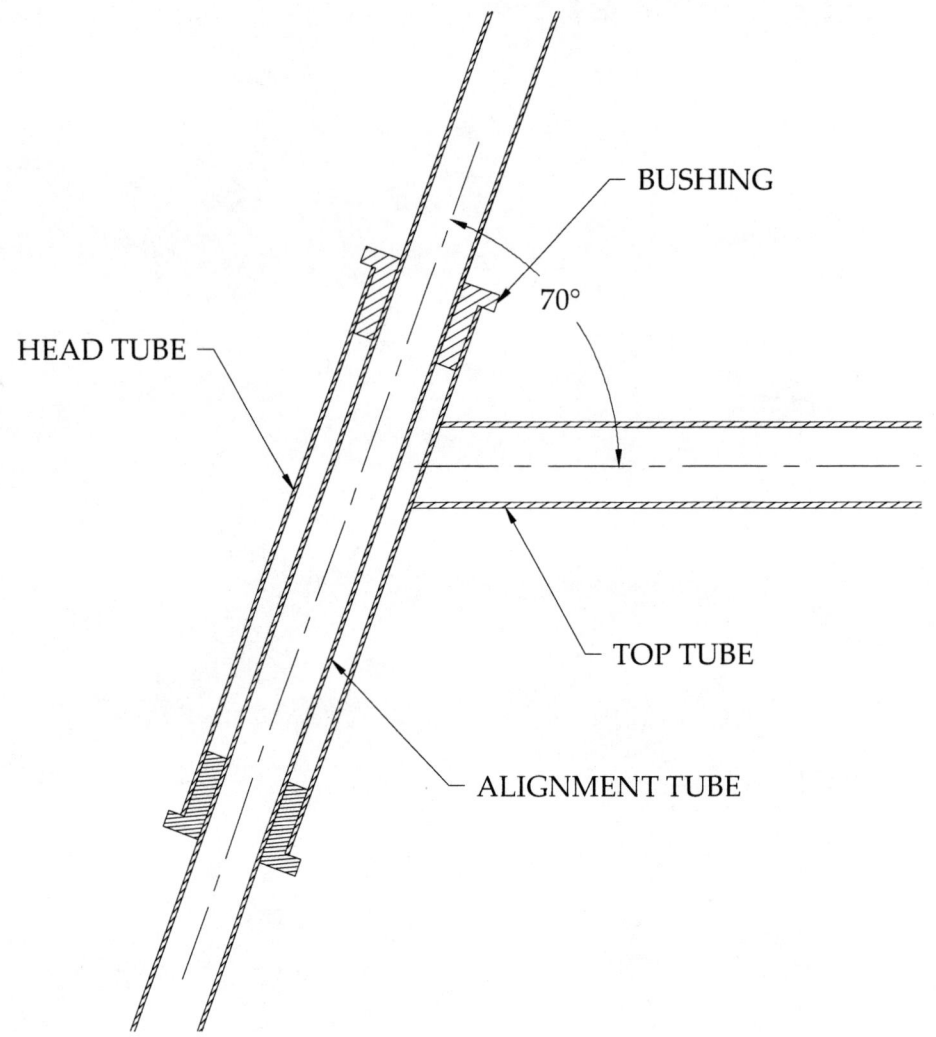

BUSHING

70°

HEAD TUBE

TOP TUBE

ALIGNMENT TUBE

The head tube itself can be of any convenient size as long as it will work with the chosen front end. Loveboat has a front end pilfered from a Honda CB 350 motorcycle. If you have trouble finding such an assembly, keep in mind that any scooter or small motorcycle will work as long as it has a substantial brake. The head tube on Loveboat was cut from an automotive shock absorber found lying alongside the road. If you live in an area where there are automobiles, these kinds of things can be found along the road quite easily. Loveboat was built in Phoenix, AZ in the USA, a city where everything winds up on the side of the road eventually. Lacking that resource, choose the head tube that works for you. We will cover the finer points of the front end, steering and brakes in a bit. Since this project is done entirely by brazing, keep in mind that the braze fillet at the head tube/toptube and head tube/down tube will be massive so don't select a piece of tubing for the head tube that is thin walled. There will be distortion caused by the brazing process and a thin walled tube will go banana on you. The salvaged tube we used measured 1.75 diameter by .06 wall.

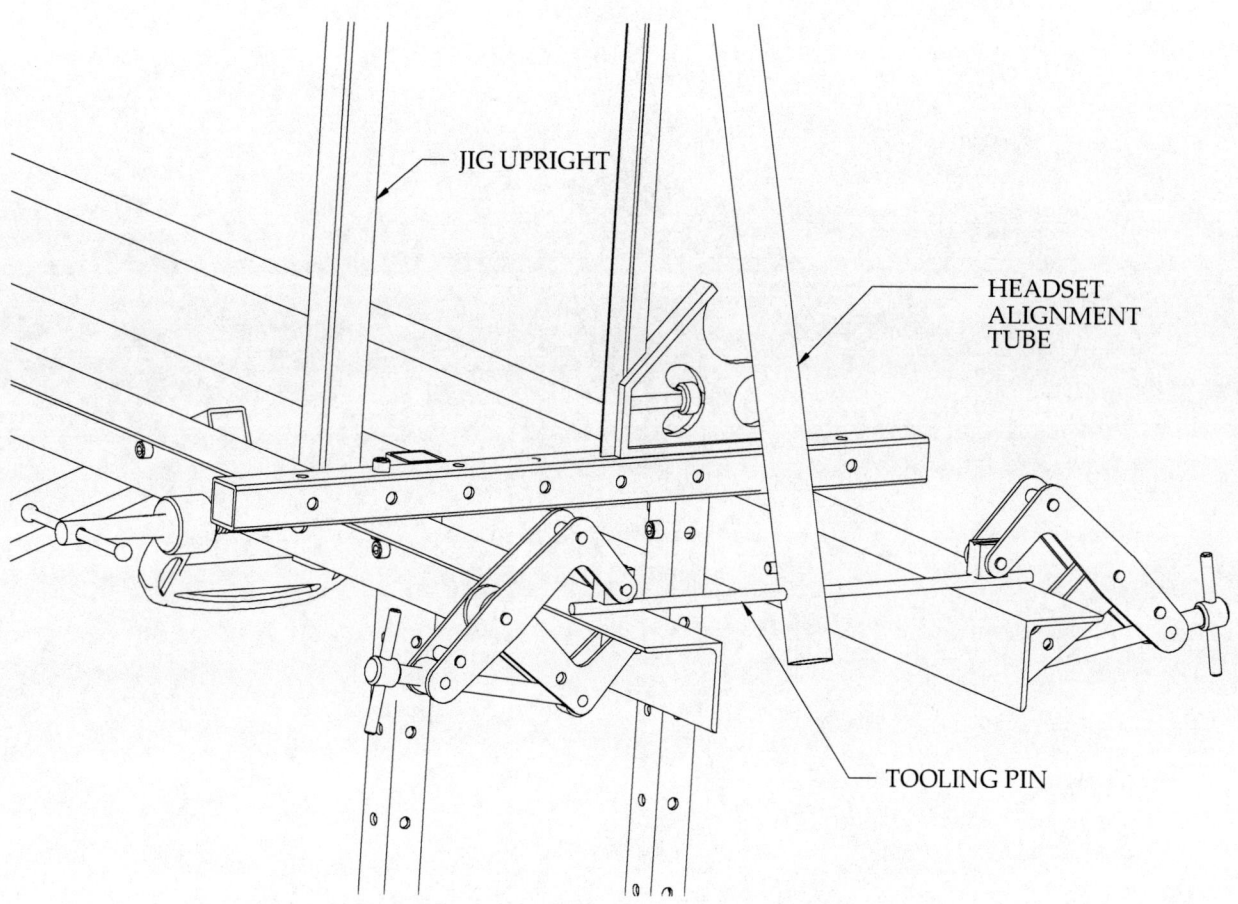

JIG UPRIGHT

HEADSET
ALIGNMENT
TUBE

TOOLING PIN

The TOOLING PIN through the alignment tube is clamped to the top of the jig. The dimensions that follow only work with a jig made from 2 inch angle.

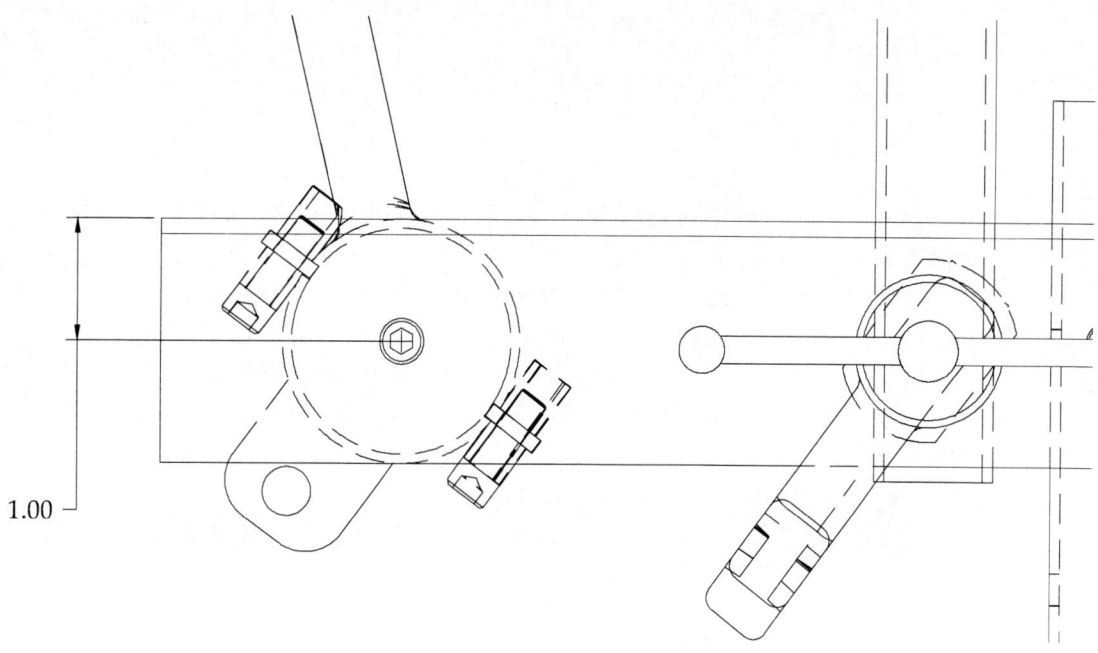

1.00

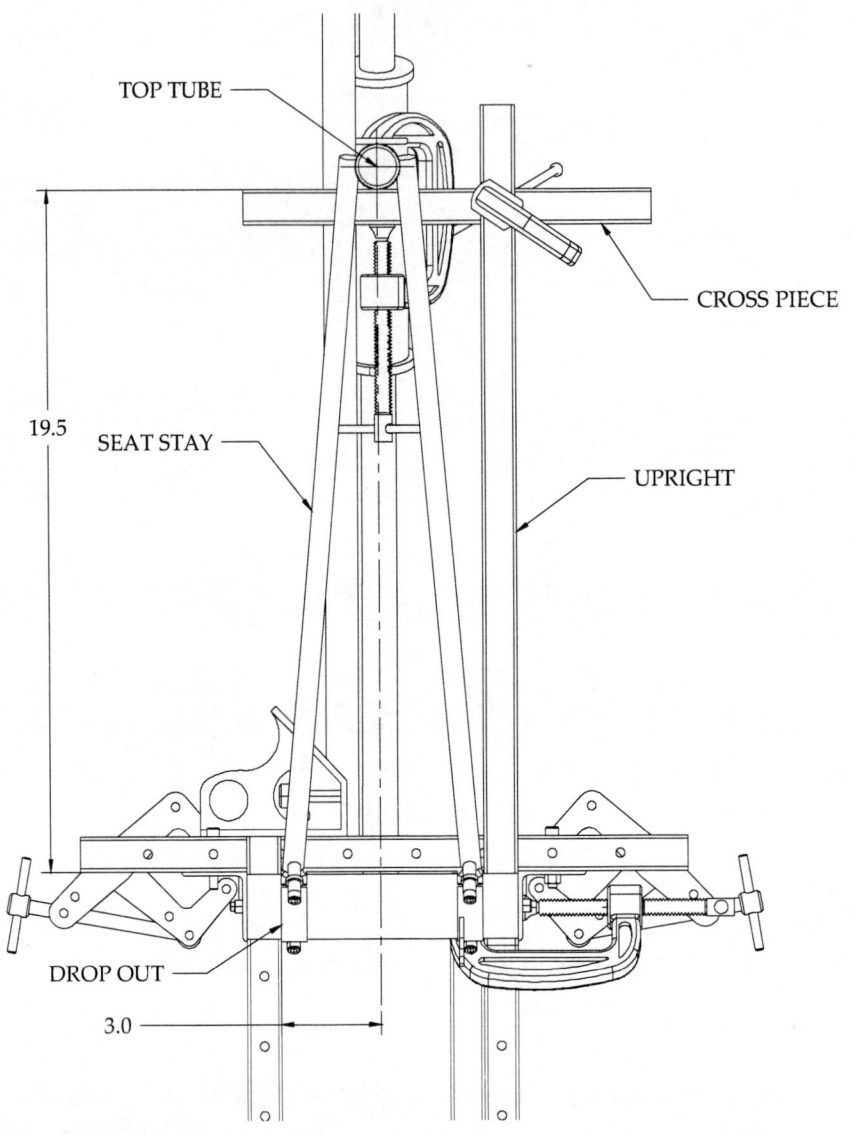

TOP TUBE

CROSS PIECE

19.5   SEAT STAY

UPRIGHT

DROP OUT

3.0

This view of the proto frame on the jig is from the back looking forward. The upright and cross piece support the top tube while the seat stays are tacked in place. It is best to use just enough filler to hold the stays in place just in case the stays need to be repositioned.

The upright is made from square tube and clamped to the side of the jig. Leveling screws on the feet of the jig are used to level the jig in all axes while the uprights and crosspieces are themselves set with a level. The dummy axle to which the drop outs are clamped is 8 inches long. The spacing of the rear dropouts is 6 inches outside dimension. Using one inch square tubing for the uprights and crosspieces makes measuring a bit easier.

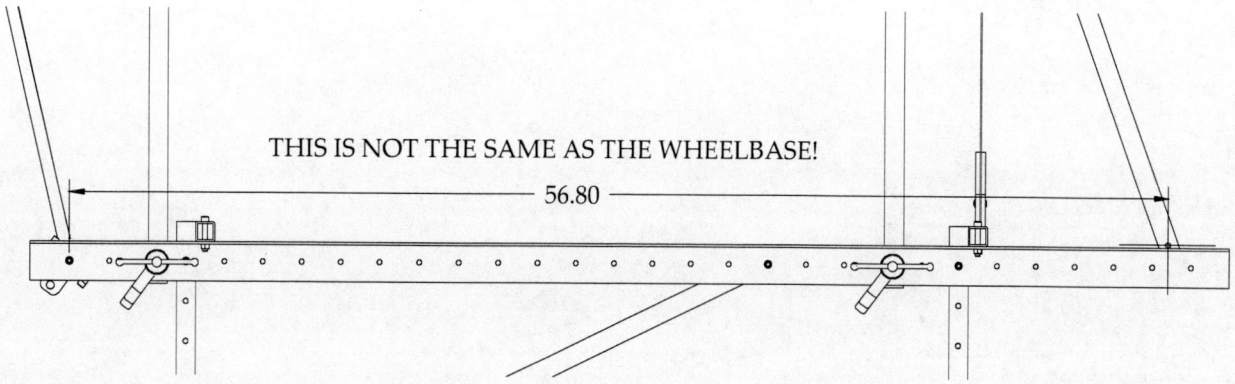

THIS IS NOT THE SAME AS THE WHEELBASE!

|← 56.80 →|

The location of the tooling pin through the alignment tube that rests on the jig is shown in this view. The clamps that hold it in place are not shown.

The front bottom bracket is held in an eccentric for the purpose of tensioning the timing chain.

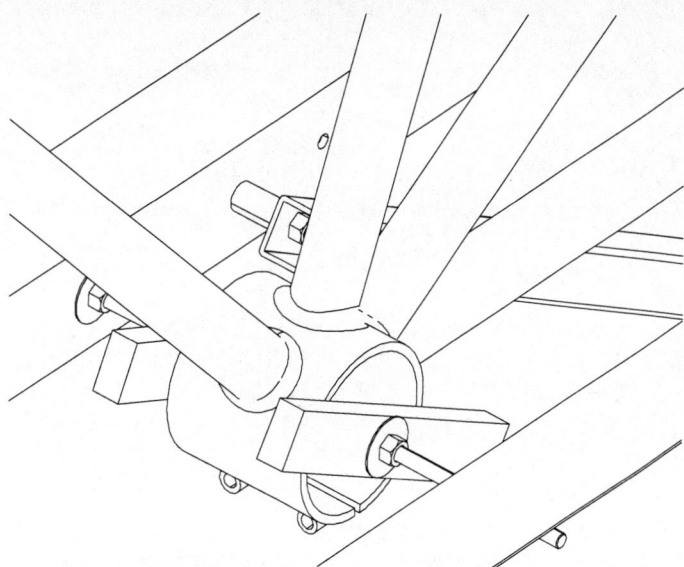

The shell clamped in the jig. It has already been brazed to the boob, down, seat and uptubes.

The eccentric shell is made from a 3 inch diameter tube with a .06 wall 2.6 inches wide. The eccentric is 2.68 inches wide. Clamp it into the jig using the arrangement shown here. Loveboat uses a conventional bottom bracket axle and bearing cups so the spacing is what you would expect. Also shown here in this view are the boob tube, uptube, seat tube and down tube joined to the eccentric shell. Once again, fit everything and tack it together with some small tack welds using a bronze rod. There is no need to clamp the eccentric tight around a round piece of stock during the tacking operation but you will need something when it comes time to do the root and finish passes. The eccentric itself is made from aluminum.

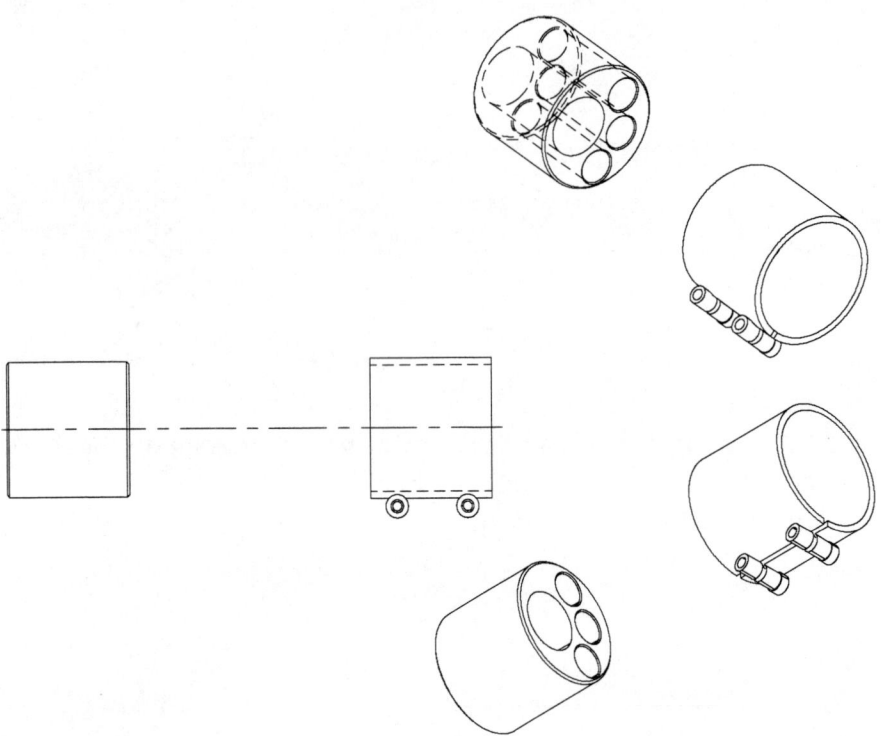

The aluminum eccentric and steel eccentric shell, also known as a clamp
This is the same method used on mainstream tandems

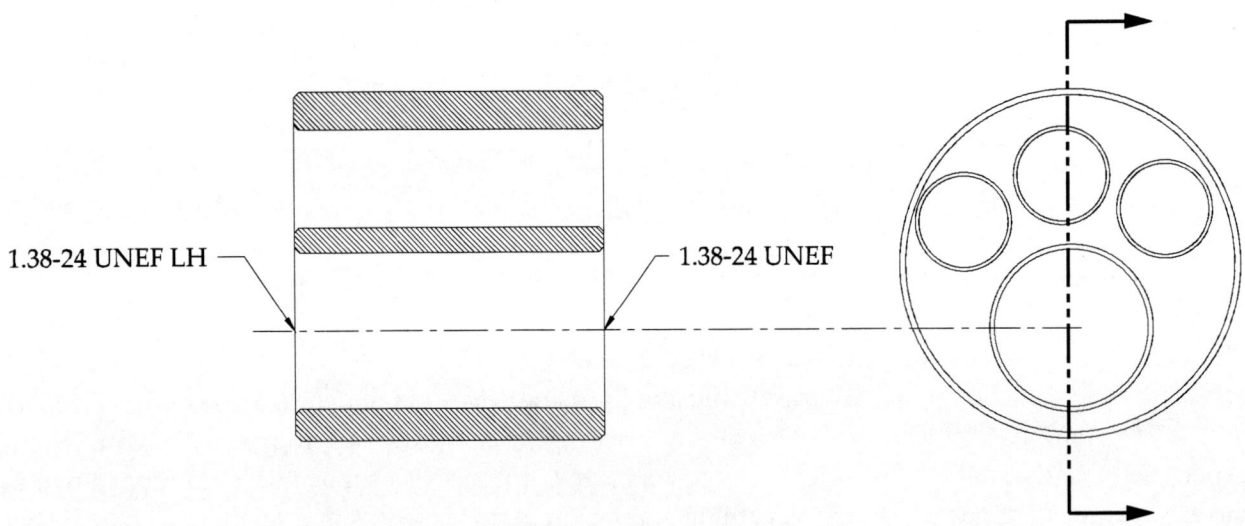

1.38-24 UNEF LH

1.38-24 UNEF

The eccentric, made of aluminum, showing the threads for the cups and the lightening holes.

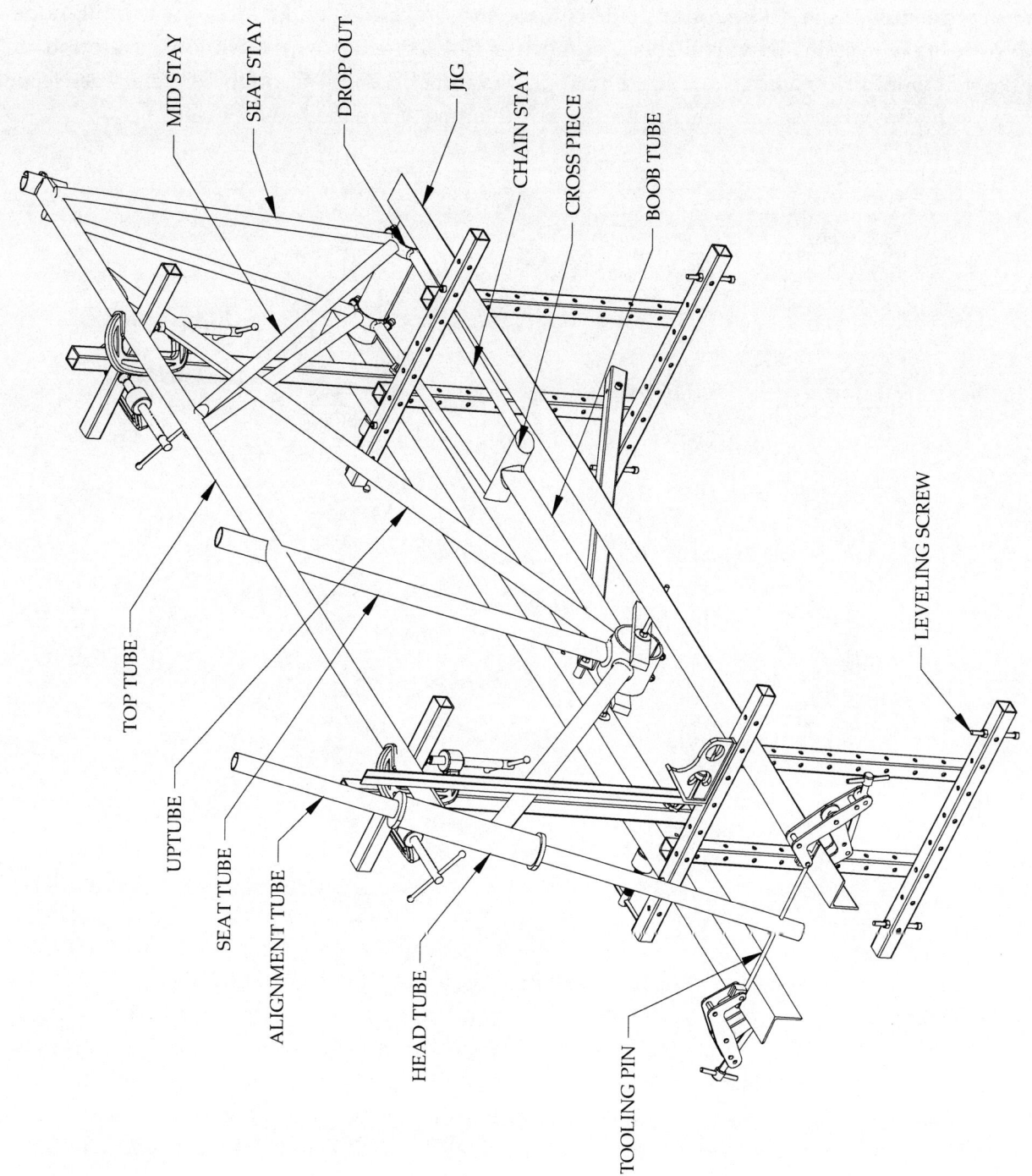

MID STAY

SEAT STAY

DROP OUT

JIG

CHAIN STAY

CROSS PIECE

BOOB TUBE

LEVELING SCREW

TOP TUBE

UPTUBE

SEAT TUBE

ALIGNMENT TUBE

HEAD TUBE

TOOLING PIN

The Front End

As mentioned before, the front end of Loveboat is pilfered from a Honda 350 motorcycle. The tubes, springs and shocks of the motorbike are replaced with aluminum tubes, 1.25 diameter. Aluminum drop outs are fabricated and glued to the new fork tubes. The reason for all this motorcycle stuff is the desire for absolute control and brakes. When Loveboat was built, none of the disk brake systems now available were in use. Subsequently, when we looked around for a brake that would stop a Loveboat sized mass accelerating downhill through 10 meters per second, motorcycles are what we saw. The triple clamp is retained as are the head set bearings.

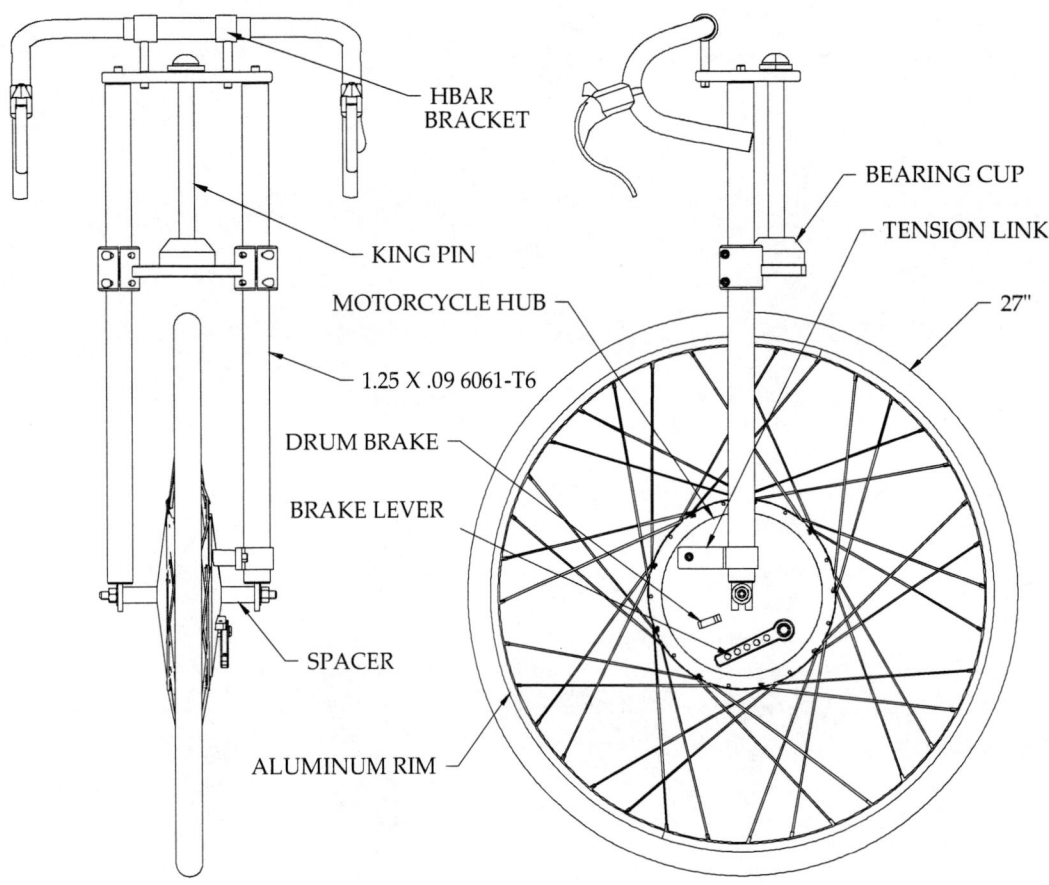

A bit of calculating went into determining the new spoke length. Luckily, the Honda has a 3 cross front wheel so extending the spokes to meet the new rim was pretty easy to visualize. Since conventional spokes would not work with the thick flanges of the wheel hub, it was decided to make what we needed by bending 14 gage spokes and forming a new head.

Each spoke is bent in a jig and a small washer brazed in place using silver solder. The hub and rim are set up so that there is no dish in the wheel and all spokes are the same length. This arrangement works quite well. The spoke enters the rim at a pretty extreme angle but that has not proved to be an issue.

174

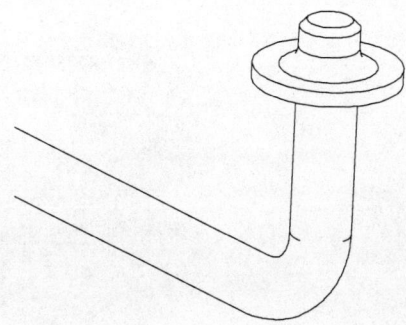

Spoke with washer soldered to formed end

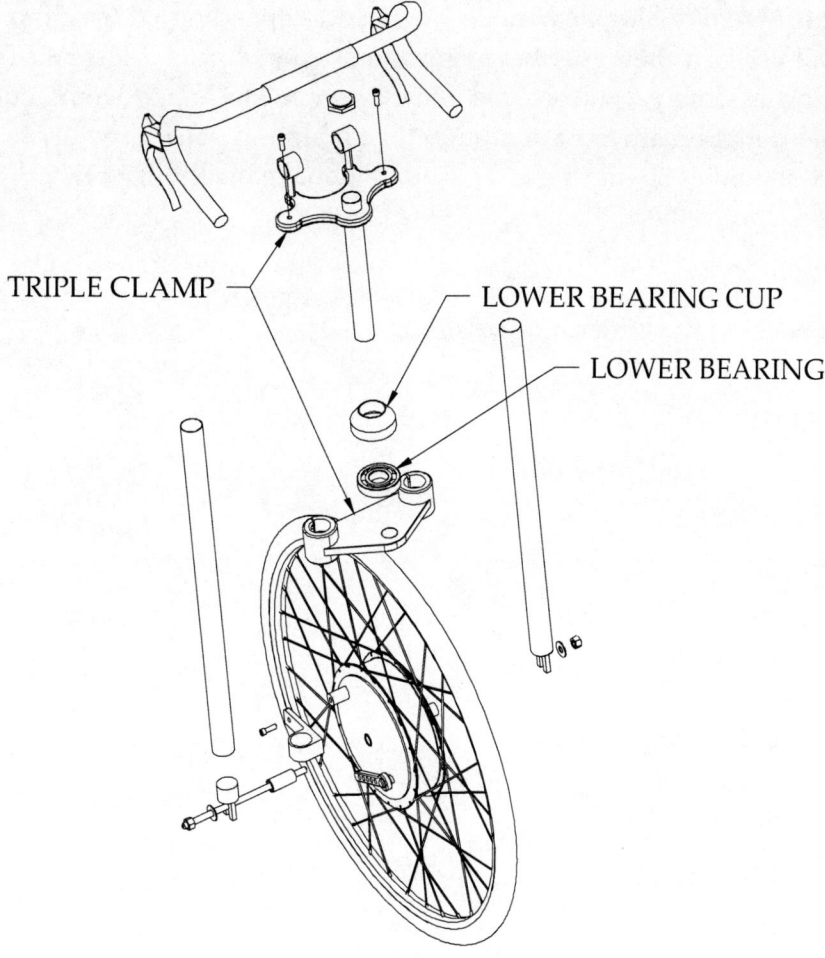

TRIPLE CLAMP

LOWER BEARING CUP

LOWER BEARING

The original motorcycle lower bearing cup adapts the new head tube for use with the existing bearings in the steering assembly. The upper bearing was used for another project so it had to be replaced by a simple single row radial ball bearing.

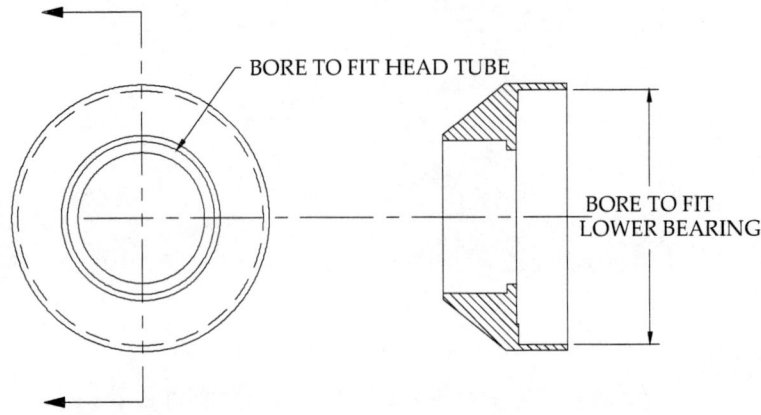

The lower bearing controls radial loads as well as thrust loads. Fit the bearing in the cup so that it is a slight push fit. A zero to .001 clearance works good depending on the fit to the steering king pin. The radial ball used for the upper bearing is mounted in a similar fashion. The domed nut on the Honda steering assembly controls end play through lock nuts, shims and washers. Each application will no doubt be different and other than adapting your assembly to fit the head tube of the frame, there shouldn't be much effort required to make the thing work.

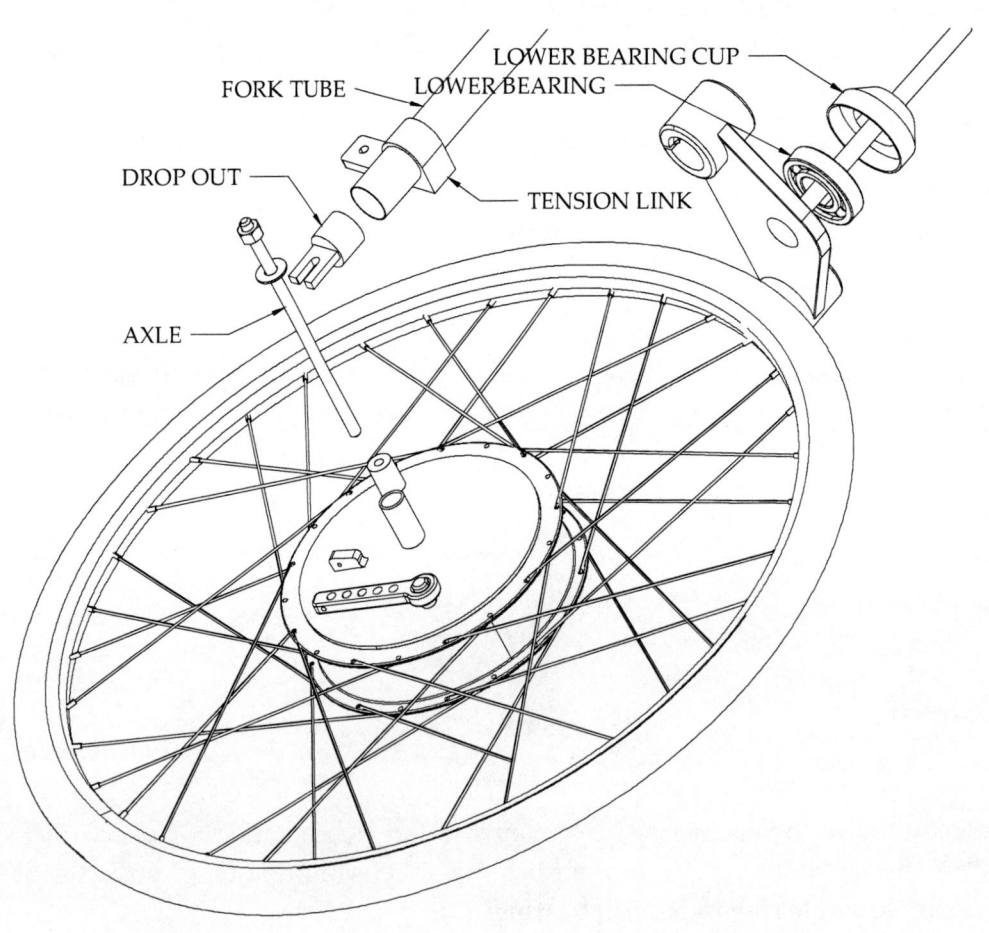

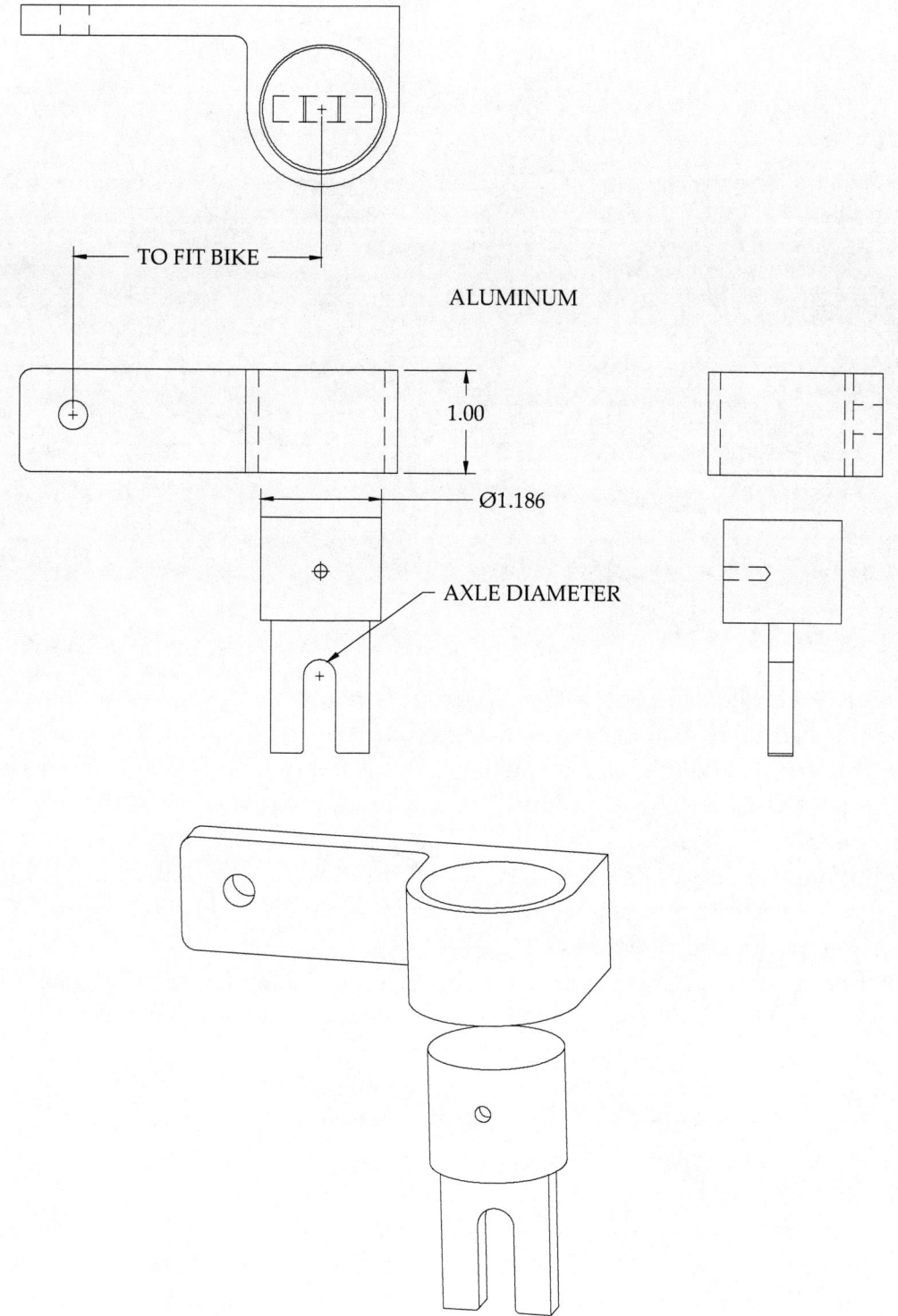

TO FIT BIKE

ALUMINUM

1.00

Ø1.186

AXLE DIAMETER

Three custom parts complete the front end assembly; a tension link and two drop outs.

The tapped hole in the drop outs anchors the drop out in the fork tubes. The tension link, like the original motorbike, prevents the shoes from grabbing the drum and rotating with it. The original link is a steel strap of substantial proportions but ours is aluminum. Loveboat reaches speeds of over 50 mph from time to time and the comfort and security of the pilfered front end and brake is welcome indeed. Nearly everyone who sees it asks "Isn't it heavy?" the answer is, naturally, "YES". And that's a good thing.

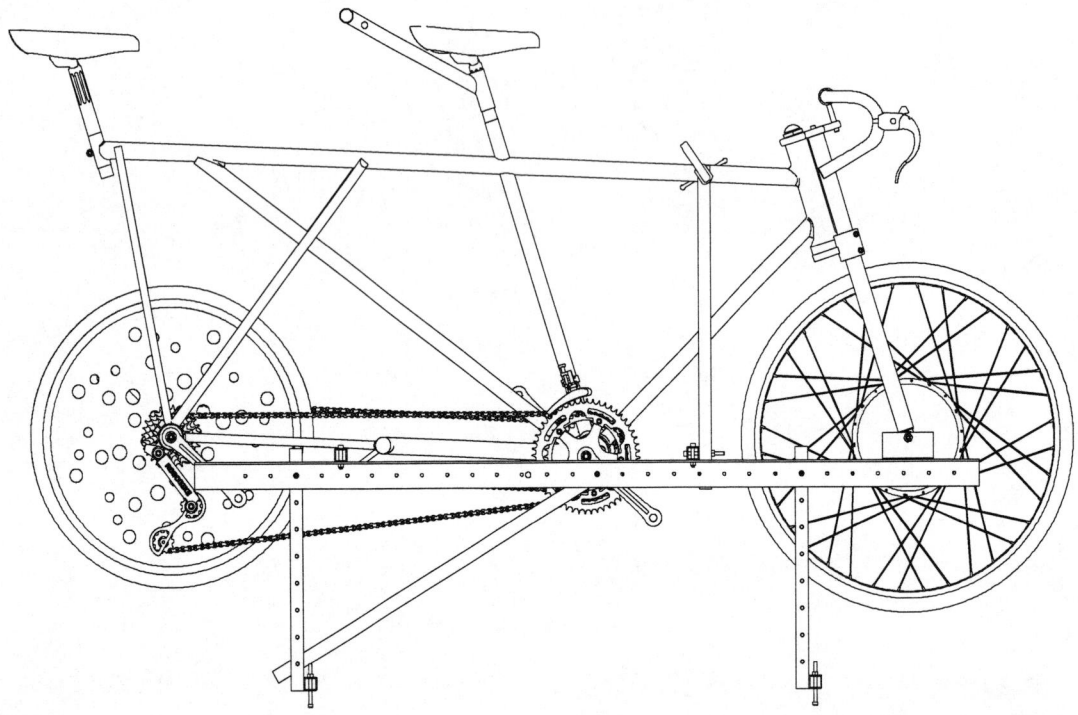

Once the frame is finished, the assembly jig is reconfigured to double as a work stand. As with all the coaxial wheeled bikes at Robobike, hanging a rear changer is a bit more work than finding something that can handle the selected ratios. The stoker's right side crank arm must clear the changer. It is OK to mill off 3/16 of an inch on the inside face of the crank arm to create clearance. There are a number of derailleurs around that hang straight down. These changers are usually steel and are found on lower end bikes. We have found a number that work well and further details on how to modify a changer are included in the plan set for this bike. Contact Robobike to get a copy if you want more information.

The front brake should be tested thoroughly before riding. If a conventional bicycle brake lever is used, and there is no reason it can't be, then a custom ball end will most likely have to be attached to the cable to make it work properly with the lever mechanism. If a disk brake is chosen, then follow good workshop practice in bringing this online. There are enough places on the rear wheel to mount multiple caliper brakes. Loveboat has two caliper brakes on the rear and one of these is energized by the stoker.

The stoker is also given the assignment of handling all the gear shifts. It takes communication and a lot of practice to work together as a team in this regard. The job is much easier if the captain communicates his intention. Clear and concise keywords eliminate confusion. SHIFT UP and DOWN SHIFT are clear and concise. Likewise with braking and moving through traffic. The crew of Loveboat uses the words NO and CLEAR to indicate when it is safe to change lanes, turn, or perform some other maneuver. These commands should be practiced and agreed upon. No conversational queries or instructions should be issued when underway. If you are an experienced tandem crewmember, then you know what I mean.

Above all else, Ride Safe.

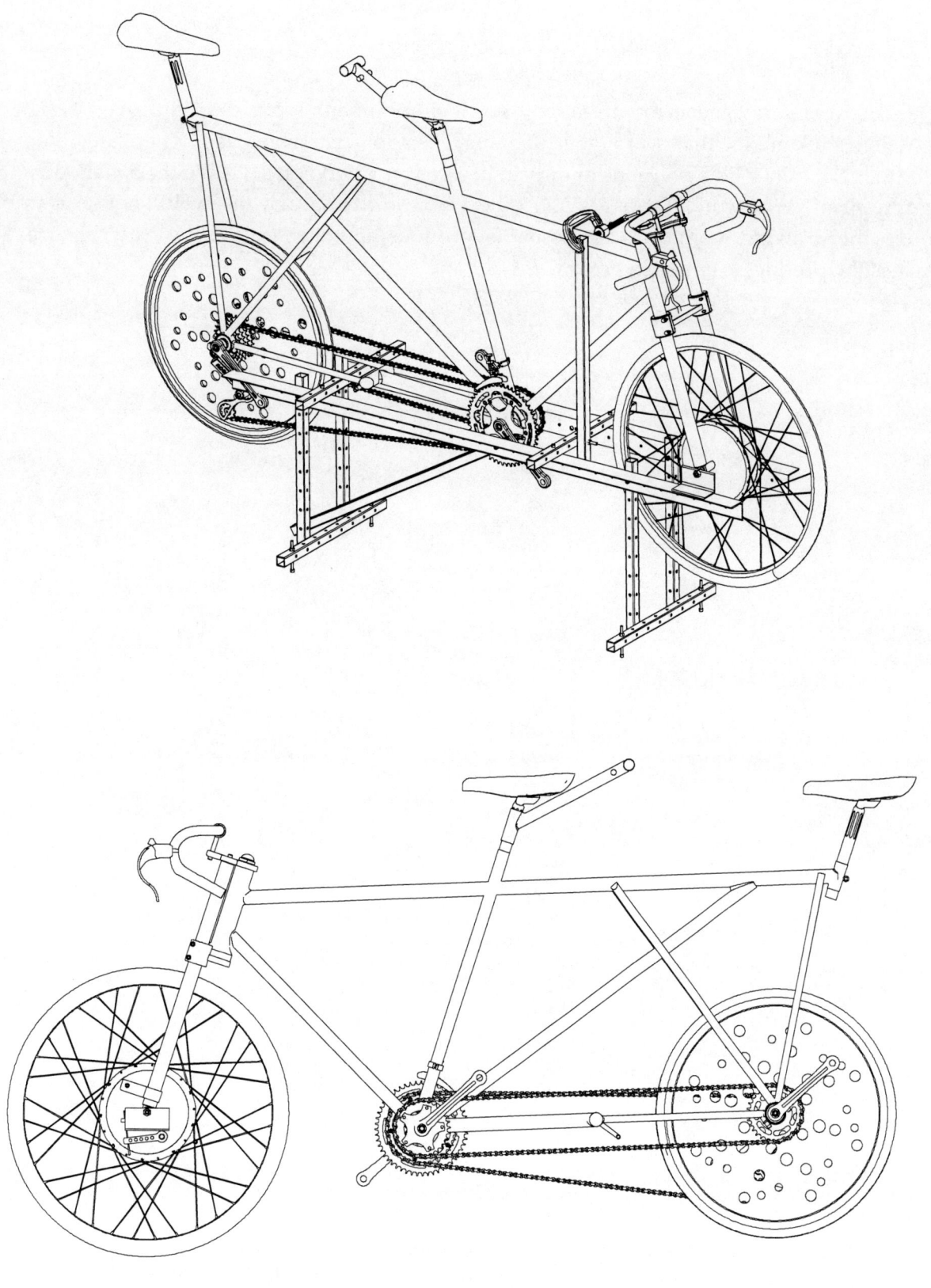

Max

Bingo Sun Noon

There are craftsmen who are happy producing numerous copies of a proven design and who delight in knowing that every move they make is appreciated by a user. There are others who prefer to make minor little revisions to proven designs and by doing so, leave their mark on a truly magnificent piece of work. There are still others who drift through the weld shop and wander through the drawing room with no desire to produce anything except the truly bizarre. This bicycle is the product of one such person.

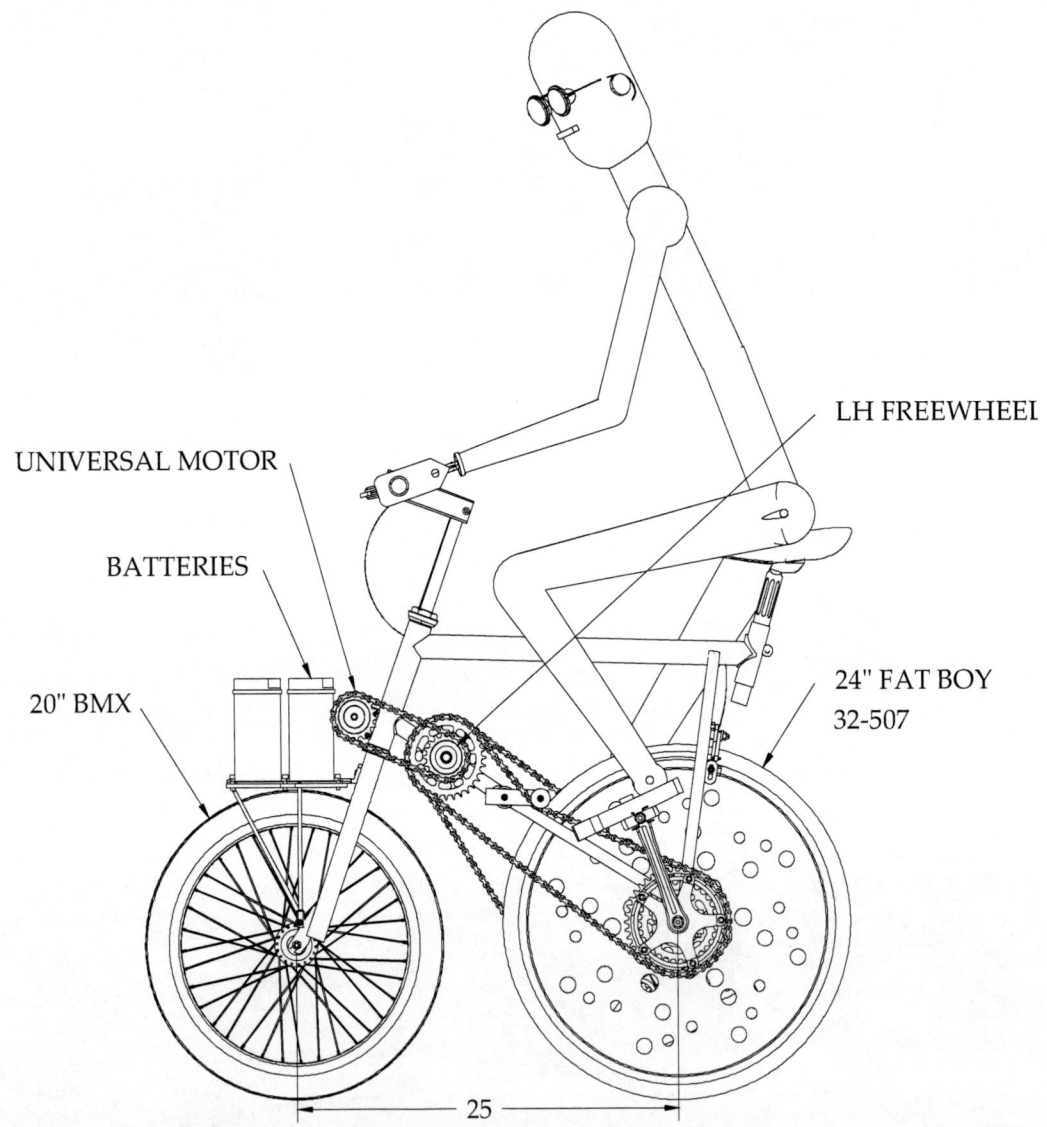

UNIVERSAL MOTOR

BATTERIES

20" BMX

LH FREEWHEEl

24" FAT BOY
32-507

25

Though originally built to travel easily on public transit, Max has never been used for that. Max has never really been used for anything except to occupy the idle hands and minds of the staff at Robobike.

When Loveboat was first built and rebuilt using a number of different coaxial wheels, there remained a pile of discards that were hardly landfill material but lacked an application. Such items clutter the shop and if not hidden from view, attract the eye, the brain and the attention of everyone around. The co-axial wheel is truly remarkable. The concept of co-locating the pedal axis and the wheel axis is a good one. A rider sitting behind the rear wheel is certainly a challenge but Loveboat and Delivery Boy proved that sound engineering practices and perseverance will pay off with a decent and quite stable bicycle. Both Loveboat and Delivery Boy are long wheel base bicycles. It is relatively easy to imagine a solution to their unique requirements in regards to stability and control. So what happens if these solutions are applied to short wheel base bikes? Max can answer that.

Max was first built with a fixed gear and no brakes. It was a circus bike. Hopping around with the front wheel off the ground was easy. In fact, keeping the front wheel on the ground proved to be a bigger accomplishment. The only riding position that worked was standing up and leaning forward. Forget about riding it anywhere. The finished bike sat in the back of the shop for quite some time.

The next time Max saw life was on a test track to work out a speed control/motor combination. Putting a sizeable battery pack on a front rack made the thing safe to ride. The motor made it easy. In fact, the bike is so much fun to ride, it's a problem to take it anywhere. Everyone wants to have a go.

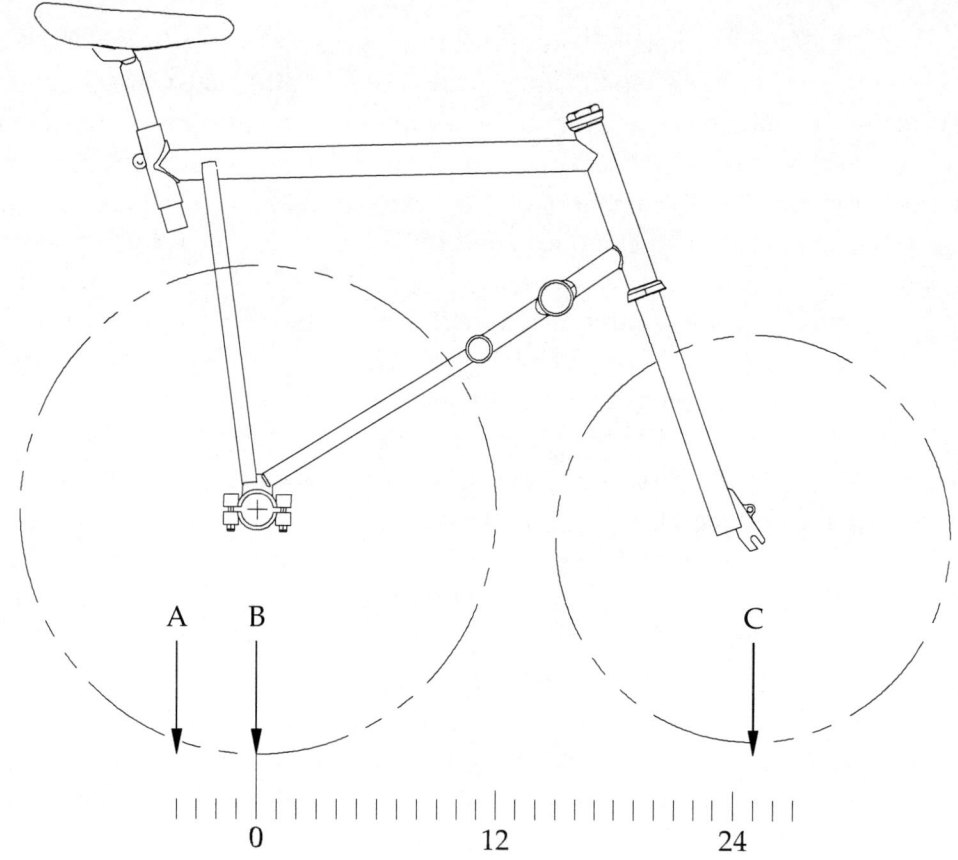

Put a big guy on this bike. His center of gravity falls on the number line at Point A, four inches aft of zero. If this big guy weighs 170 pounds, then a moment of -680 inch-pounds is generated.

181

Total moment at Point B is zero with 20 pounds of bike found here. Moments at Point C is 500 in-lbs. Another twenty pounds of bike here. These moments are in a positive direction. Total moments are -180. Divide this by total weight and the balance point is found to be just aft of the rear axle. It needs to move forward 12 inches.

Adding a single 30 pound battery 23 inches forward of the rear axle contributes 720 in-lbs. of moment in the positive direction. The balance point is now forward of the rear axle but just barely. The calculation stands at 540 in-lbs/240 lbs = 2.25 inches.

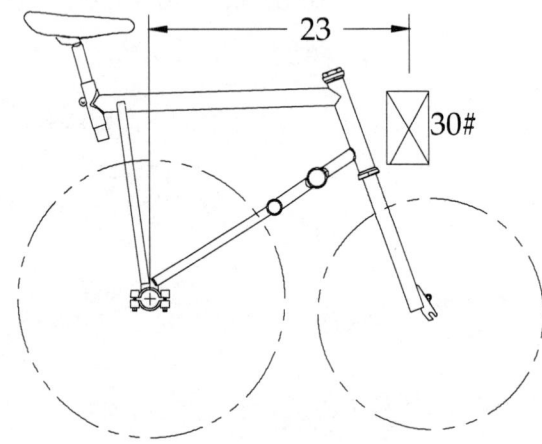

What good is a 30 pound battery without a motor?

Add the motor, chains, jackshaft, associated brackets and hardware. The electric motor comes from what is commonly known as an outboard motor (actually an engine) like the type used on boats. The bit we use is the motor that raises and lowers the assembly out of the water. It is a series wound motor identical to those found in old technology vacuum cleaners.

The jackshaft is a Robobike standard item but with a left hand freewheel fitted for this application. As we add these to the bike and record their weights and arm info, the balance point slowly moves forward. A five pound jack shaft at 15 inches, a five pound motor at 20 inches and another 30 pound battery at 27 inches adds 965 in-lbs of moment and 40 pounds of vehicle weight. Those devices and the chains and racks that go with them move the balance point to six inches forward of the rear axle. That's not good enough. We cheat and move both batteries forward two inches by extending the rack. The center of gravity with a 170 pound rider sitting upright is seven inches forward of the rear axle. That will have to do.

As it turns out, the bike is quite comfortable and handles well with this configuration. We use it on the flat. The brakes are somewhat light but it is geared quite low. With this much battery and with such a small motor, the thing will run all day without a charge. We ride it at the beach, thru the park to the supermarket to take advantage of its wagon towing ability but never try to mix it up with vehicular traffic. The motor and jackshaft adds complexity and requires greater rigidity in the frame. The left hand free wheel allows for motor engagement without powering the pedals. This seems like something that is taken for granted, but that is not always the case in a chain drive ebike. It's just one of those things you learn the hard way.

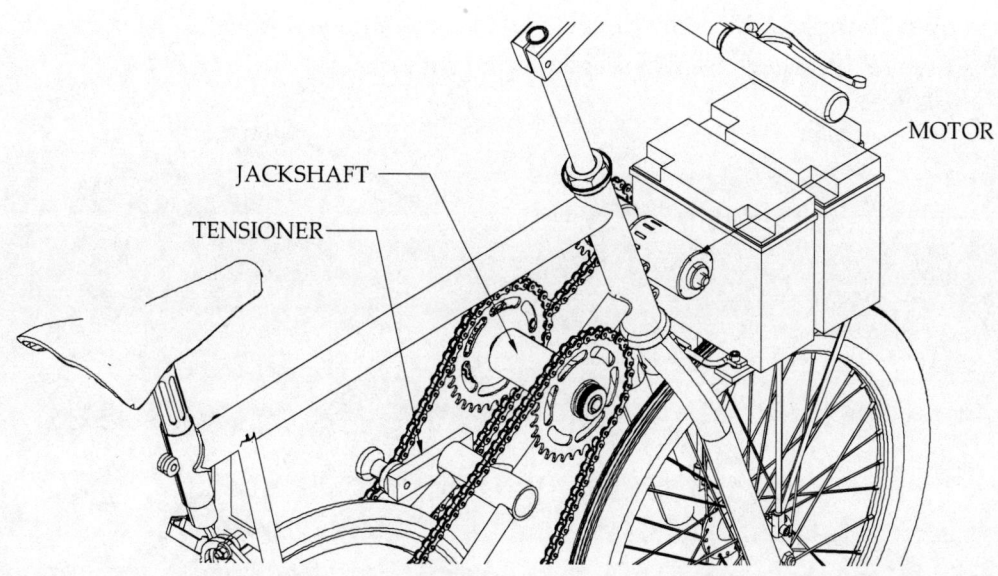

JACKSHAFT

TENSIONER

MOTOR

The tensioner is a simple roller spinning on a bushing and secured with a cap screw. Nothing too exciting here. The motor is rated 12 v and 15 amps. We have used two of these on this bike with two switching arrangements. For starting, the motors are switched on and run in series. For cruising, the motors are run through another set of contacts that put them in parallel. In series, each motor uses half the line voltage and the current is reduced. In parallel, both motors use full line voltage and run stronger. We did this to prevent burnout and brush wear. This series-parallel switching can be done with one device, a DPDT switch. Even so, a second switch should be installed so the whole business can be switched on and off. Since that time, the bike has been restricted to flat land applications and is not run in traffic. Given that, the rider can pedal it from a dead stop to prevent a long, high amperage drain so we removed one motor. The motor is fused at 30 amps. The motor is not very efficient but the size of the battery pack needed to keep the front wheel on the ground takes care of that problem. Efficiency is usually not given high priority when discussing transportation and sadly, this set up is no exception.

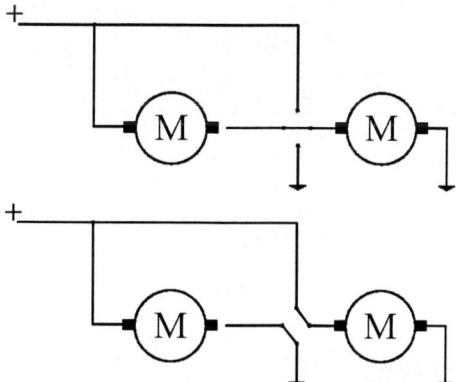

A single switch moves from motors in series to motors in parallel

The speed control tested earlier on this bike used a resistor-capacitor cascading into a 555 timing chip to generate a digital pulse. This then drove a transistor bank for powering the motors. There are a number of high amperage semiconductor devices now in use to drive motors. It is a fascinating subject and far too complex to discuss here.

Max is now being run without a speed control but the size of the motor guarantees it doesn't run over 10 mph. A bit more development work directed towards Max might start a whole class of short wheel base bicycles. Then again, it might not.

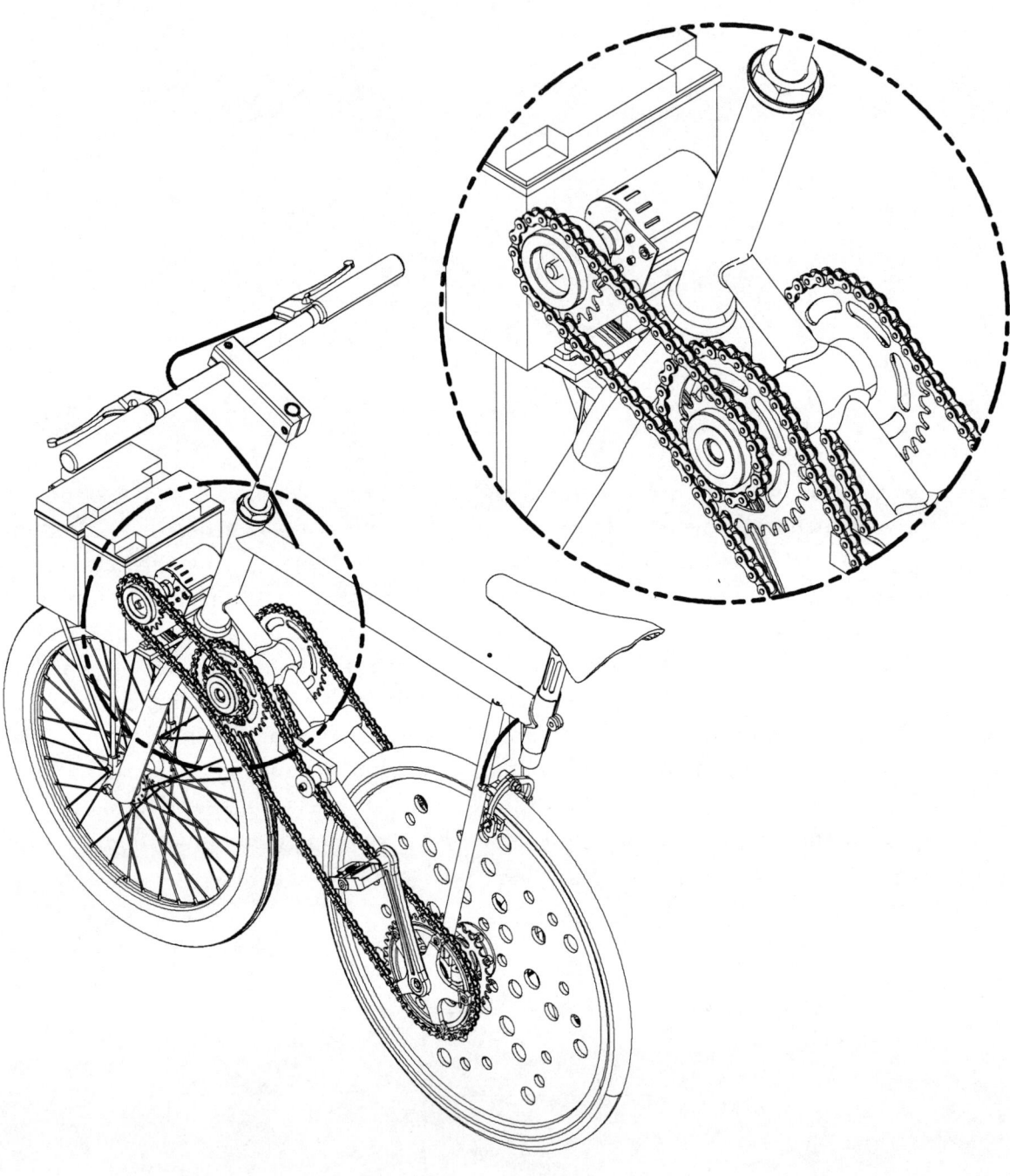

Robobike Wichita

The year is now 1980. All the players that will come together to form Robobike are in transition. Krilson left Montreal and after a period of hitchhiking to all corners of north America, has taken a job in Wichita, Kansas as a machinist building the Beech Starship and King Air B200s. When Ronald Reagan's tax on private airplanes takes effect January 1, 1982, he and everyone else who works at Beech, except those who have been there forever, are fired.

Bingo Sun Noon was passed over by the communists whose job it is to decide who needs to attend re-education camps. Bingo kept a low profile, hid his mother, and made a modest living building wheelchairs and artificial limbs for those unlucky enough to have first hand experience with US land mine technology. Twelve months after the abandonment of Saigon by the Americans, he builds a bicycle rickshaw and pedals with his mother to the coast. There, he builds a boat and shoves off. He is picked up by the US Navy after a week at sea. He is barely alive as was his mother and 15of 18 other people in his little boat. They are all moved to camps in California. After three years in the camps, an agreement with the US government moves Bingo and his mother from the camps to Wichita. The US government agrees to buy missiles they don't want or need from Beech Aircraft if Beech agrees to give jobs to refugees from Vietnam. Bingo completes an apprenticeship and is fired in 1982. Krilson is his mentor in the program.

John Shewmaker is working as a machinist at some nondescript machine shop in southern California. He parties like it's 1999. Life is good for the former marine.

By some odd twist of fate, they all wind up in Arizona working in the same machine shop. They start hanging out and begin building bicycles in a hangar at the Chandler airport. Strange bicycles, but bicycles none the less. The first was the Flyer, a bike that went along in the luggage compartment of a Skylane.

Travel Bikes

The bicycle that is now our one and only travel bike wasn't always such a hot ticket. It did not come to us in a dream. Born of a need to carry a bike in a Cessna 182 luggage compartment, its evolution was long and tortuous. There were a number of revisions, four complete rebuilds, hundreds of miles of testing, and plenty of opportunity for doubt. What made it all the more difficult is the fact that there is no shortage of good quality travel bikes available. So why build our own?

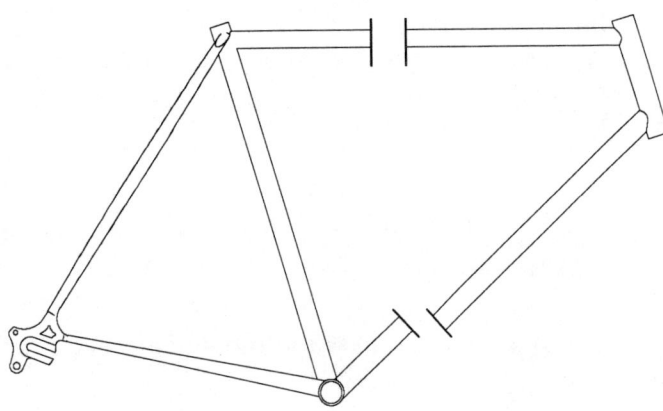

Schwinn bicycles of Chicago, Illinois, supplied our first travel bike in the form of a yellow Varsity. In order to fit it into the airplane, we cut it into two pieces. This was a fairly easy operation owing to the fact that the top tube was cut first and two flat plates brazed to the ends. These plates had holes drilled around the edge for the purpose of rejoining the frame. The same was done to the down tube. Our first bike, which we named the Flyer after the Wright brothers' biggest selling bicycle of 1901, was a piece of crap and was abandoned at a remote airport in the Arizona desert. We hope it found a good home. It must be pointed out that the bike was a piece of crap before we modified it so don't think we go around destroying perfectly good bicycles.

After disposing of both the Flyer and the Cessna 182, the emphasis switched to building a travel bike that went as checked baggage. We liked the idea of maintaining full size and the performance that goes with it but our experiences with putting bikes in cardboard boxes for transport were not good.

A New Design

It was decided to treat our next effort as a real design project with design goals and prioritized emphasis on the various systems. Keep in mind at this point that the objective is to design a single bike. Our design process goes like this:

1. Make a list of all the desirable characteristics you and your buddies can think of
2. Prioritize that list and name it "design goals"
3. Sketch all loads and hard points
4. Sketch possible solutions to load control
5. Determine manufacturing methods

Desirable Characteristics?

First of all, any bike that isn't a good ride isn't worth packing around, no matter how convenient. Full size comfort, rigid structure and good handling are not only desirable but absolutely necessary. Ease of transport in a stowed position is highly desirable as is ease of assembly. Snap together or folding capability is good but not absolutely necessary. Lightweight goes without saying. Survivability when in the baggage handlers evil grasp is more important than you would first think. Small size when stowed and being able to pass as a normal piece of checked bagged is very desirable. Ease of manufacture, in this case, is not so important.

These are then listed in order of importance
1. Comfort, rigidity and handling are all tied for number one on the priority list
2. Small size when stowed
3. Lightweight when packed
4. Luggage is small and unobtrusive, taxi cab friendly
5. Ease of manufacture

It is time to let our imaginations go as the design process continues. Having accepted that this bike will be powered by leg muscles and will have the usual configuration of bottom bracket between the wheels, we can sketch the four hard points that need to be connected. It is important not to latch onto a preconceived layout before looking at all the options. Though the wheels sketched here are the same size, that was decided not to be a constraint.

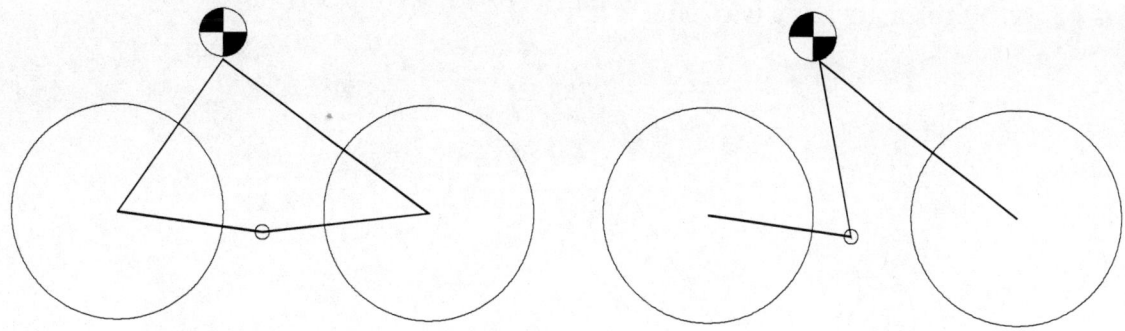

Our first two abstract concepts, with possible folding action, start the list. Kind of weird but certainly valid if all accepted notions about bicycle construction are set aside.

Since our design goals do not include trying to convince the world just how clever we can be, we decided to drop the abstract approach and stick to a more conventional design while aiming for as little structure as possible.

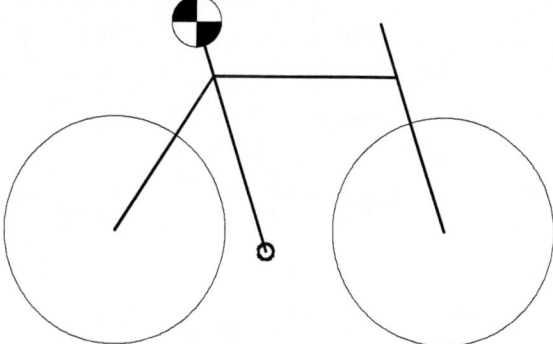

Remove the wheels and you have a compact frame readily foldable. However, all design work involves compromise but the compromises required to make this minimalist bicycle survive rough roads with a big guy at the controls are unacceptable.

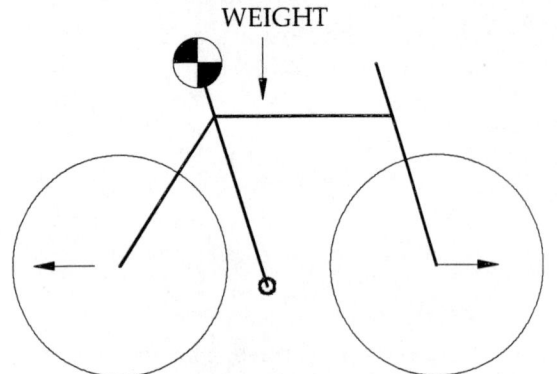

WEIGHT

This bike was actually built and sold in the late 19th century!

Add the weight of the rider to the sketch and it becomes apparent that the frame will have to be quite massive. This is true only if we don't add structure to control the reaction to the load and insist on building the cantilevered frame. Since the most efficient arrangement is to add steel loaded purely in tension, two pieces of wire are added to our sketch. Keep in mind, however, that real world bicycles are exposed to stresses that cannot be represented easily in a 2d sketch on a piece of paper. Nevertheless, add two lengths of wire.

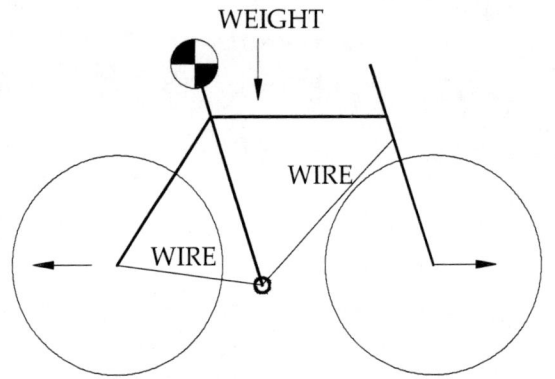

WEIGHT

WIRE

WIRE

Adding wire certainly does control the reaction of the frame to the weight of the rider and a piece of steel wire loaded in tension is absolutely the most efficient use of structure possible, however, when the top half of the drive chain is loaded in tension as a result of pedaling, then the wire no longer looks so attractive. The rear wheel moves away from the front wheel when the frame supports the weight of the rider but moves closer when the rider supplies a propulsive impulse. Subsequently, the wire used on the rear section of the bike only works part of the time. A tube will control both tensile and compressive loads so that substitution is made. Our bike is looking more and more like a plain old store bought bicycle. Maybe this is the reason bikes are the way they are. Recognizing this fact, we switch from a revolutionary to an evolutionary approach.

The evolution of the single

The second bicycle in our series of travel bikes, named Grasshopper, was built from a Miyata 710 frame that had been ridden at high speed into a road barrier, crushing the front end. We managed to salvage the rear triangle, the seat tube and bottom bracket and a few other bits and pieces.

Grasshopper

The top tube and the seat stays have been moved to a central spot to concentrate stress allowing a single massive joint being constructed at this point. Doing so avoids creating a couple that works to bend the seat tube. Bending the stays makes the rear triangle easier to pack. The top tube is large diameter titanium, the head tube an aluminum hog out. The front wheel is a very light 24 inch rim and tire made popular by its use on custom bikes designed for women, by women. It is a nice wheel. The rear wheel is a plastic BMX 20 inch rim and tire. Gearing is a conventional 12 speed set up. A weldment makes assembly a simple matter of screwing two flat plates together with four number ten cap screws.

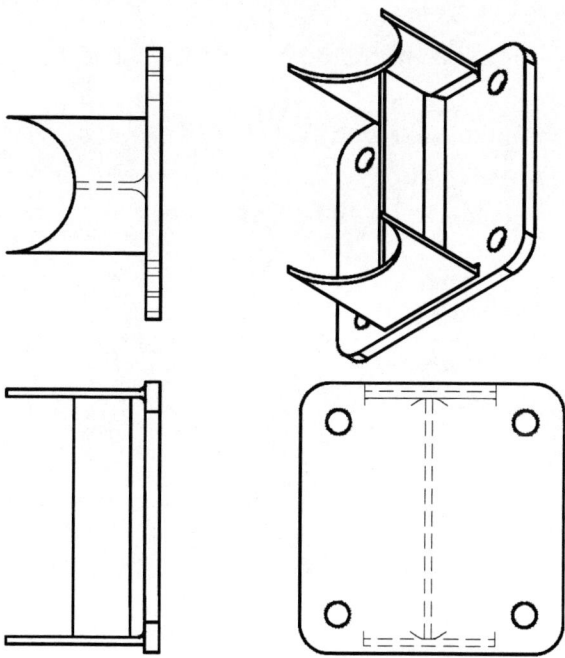

The flange weldment that made the bike work. And it worked quite well.

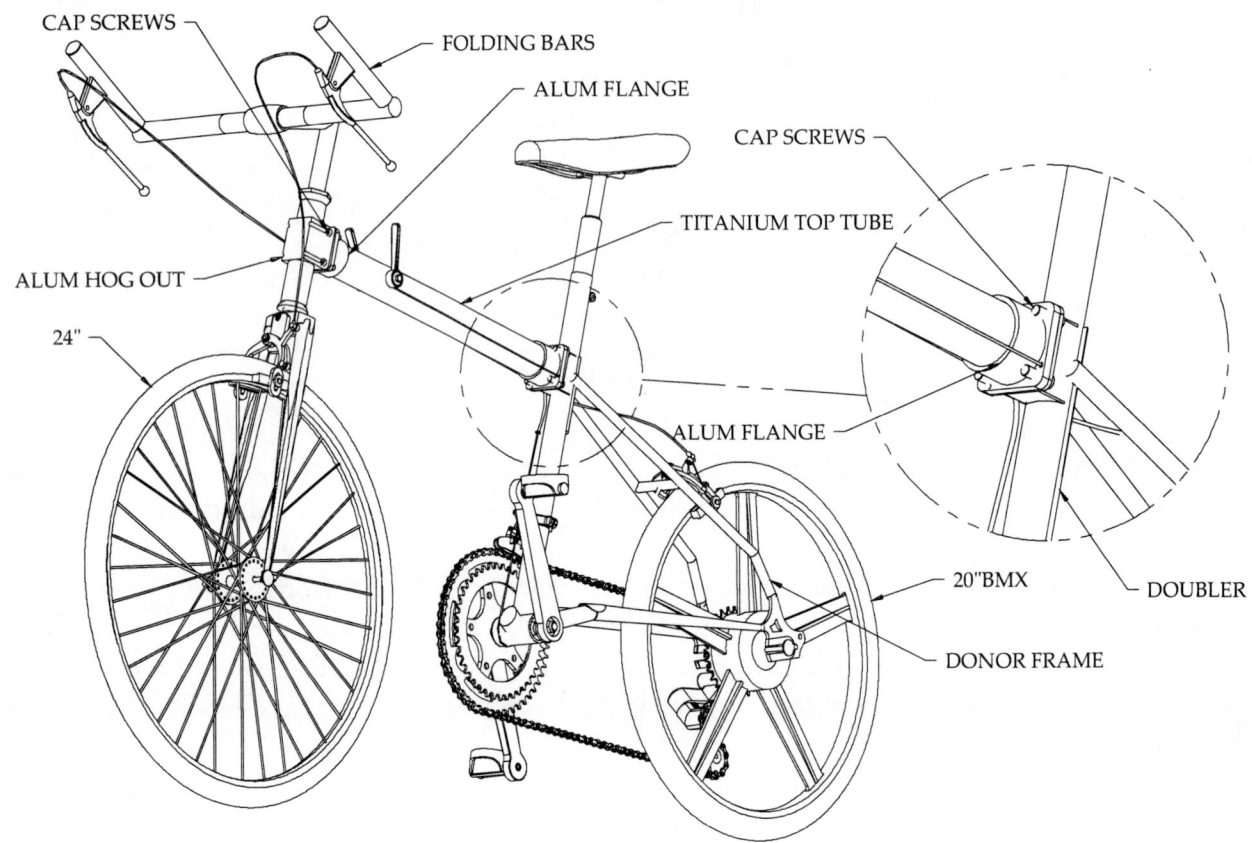

CAP SCREWS
FOLDING BARS
ALUM FLANGE
CAP SCREWS
TITANIUM TOP TUBE
ALUM HOG OUT
24"
ALUM FLANGE
20"BMX
DOUBLER
DONOR FRAME

Grasshopper as it existed just before being scrapped

The rear portion of the bike, salvaged from a wrecked road bike, was just too difficult to pack in spite of being more compact than a full size rear triangle. This part of the bike was replaced with the next generation rear triangle on the third bike in this series of travel bikes, the Nile Crocodile.

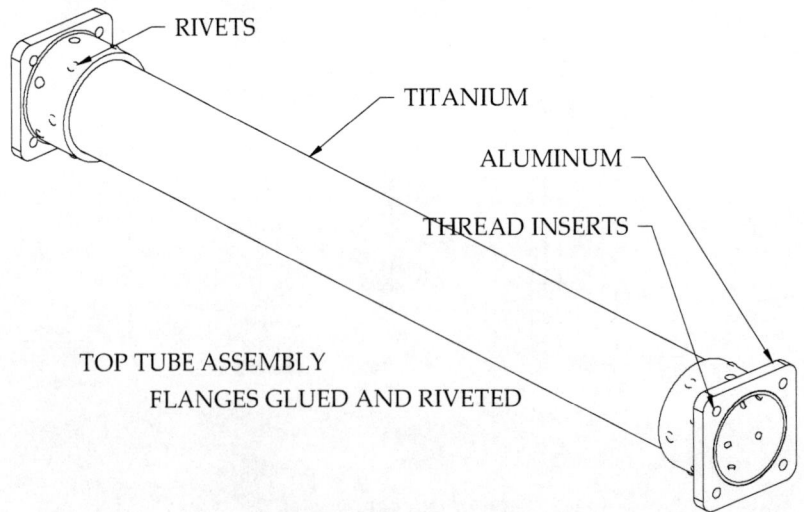

RIVETS
TITANIUM
ALUMINUM
THREAD INSERTS

TOP TUBE ASSEMBLY
FLANGES GLUED AND RIVETED

Top Tube used on both Grasshopper and the Nile Crocodile

The top tube was salvaged from an air duct pulled from a DC-10. It worked OK but was eventually replaced with a steel top tube. Steel is much better than titanium for bicycle work for lots of different reasons. The 24 inch front wheel was also replaced. A 20 inch wheel is much easier to pack than the larger wheel. Not only that, it is unrealistic to expect to find a replacement tire in remote bike shops around the world unless an easy to find size is used. Having a high tech, high performance travel bike is really cool until a flat tire puts it out of service.

The Clipper

The Clipper is the same bike as Crocodile but with a geared rear hub instead of the 12 speed, a steel top tube and a turnbuckle to prevent inchworming. The Clipper is the same as our current bike except for the front end and the brakes.

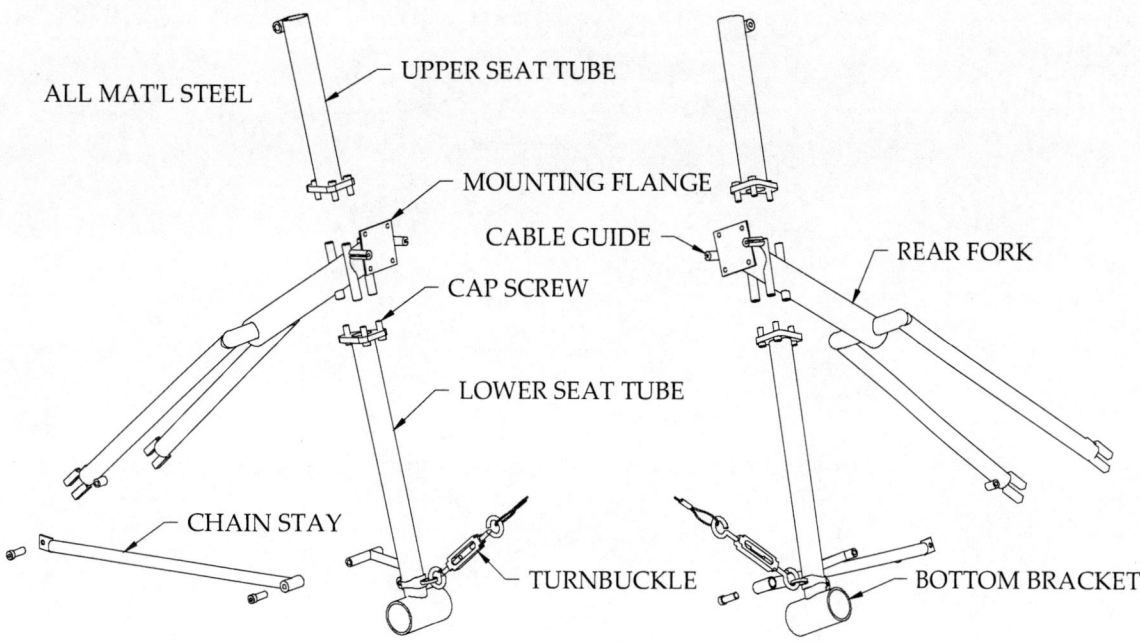

This exploded view is the new rear triangle showing how the various pieces are assembled. Both the lower and upper seat tubes were made of 1 inch diameter tubes with a .040 wall thickness and both broke after being in service a short while. They were replaced with 1.125 diameter x .064 tubes. The rear fork broke too exactly where our calculations predicted. It broke where the cross piece joined the leg opposite the chain side. This was our first case of using software to do a structural analysis and because of this, a whole new concept of bike design was embraced at Robobike. We now do complete finite element analysis on all our designs. A second chain stay was added as the result of this first analysis.

After the Flyer, Grasshopper and Clipper, our bike morphs into what we now know as the Tandem unless it is assembled to ride solo and then it is known as the Single. Not very catchy but certainly accurate.

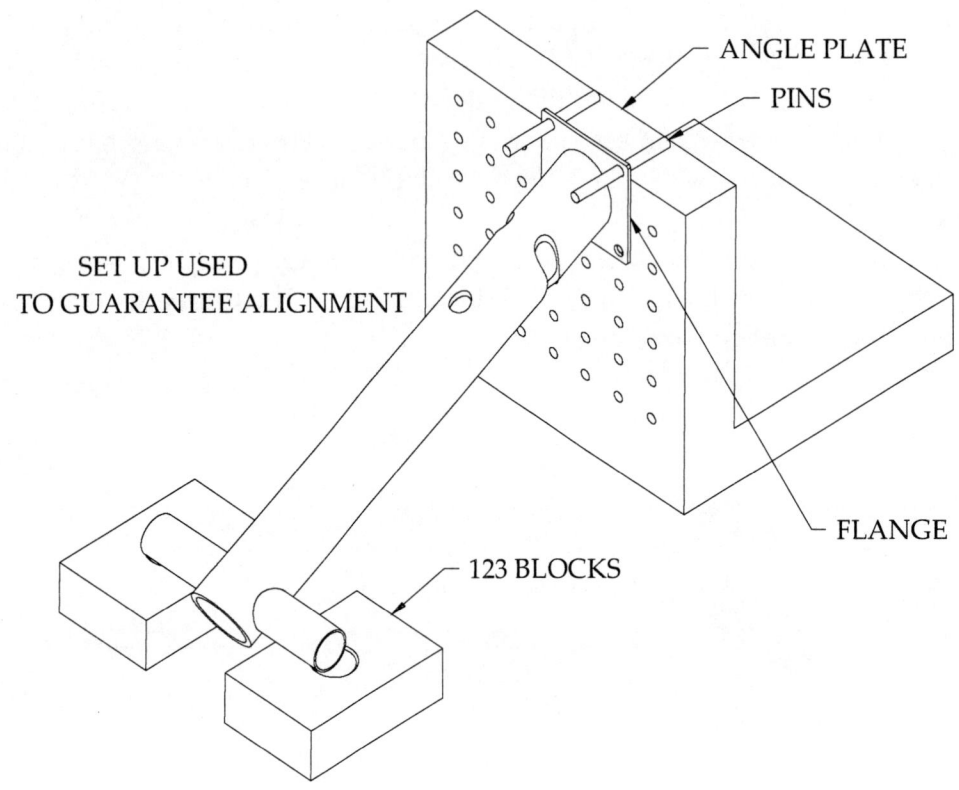

ANGLE PLATE

PINS

SET UP USED
TO GUARANTEE ALIGNMENT

FLANGE

123 BLOCKS

Details, rear fork
Set up for brazing operation above; seat tube mounting details below

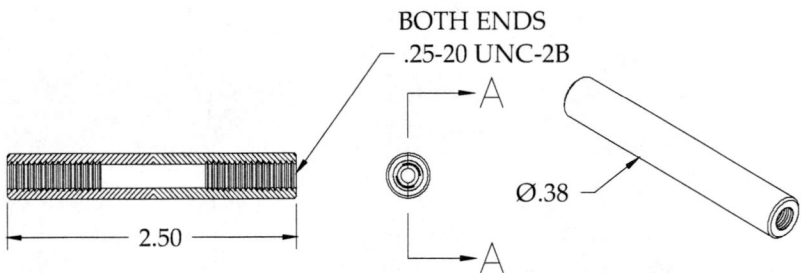

BOTH ENDS
.25-20 UNC-2B

A

A

Ø.38

2.50

Three pieces required

The rear assembly

Chain stays, lower and upper seat tube and rear fork comprise the rear assembly. The order of operations for building is important. Complete (or at least tack together) the rear fork so the lower seat tube can be installed. Only then can the stays be fitted. Wheel clearance, foot clearance and chain clearance all figure into the design. There was only one stay originally and that was on the power side. Great idea but we realized that the off axis stress created by pedaling and transmitted via chain requires a more massive structure. That is why we use the symmetrical arrangement we have now.

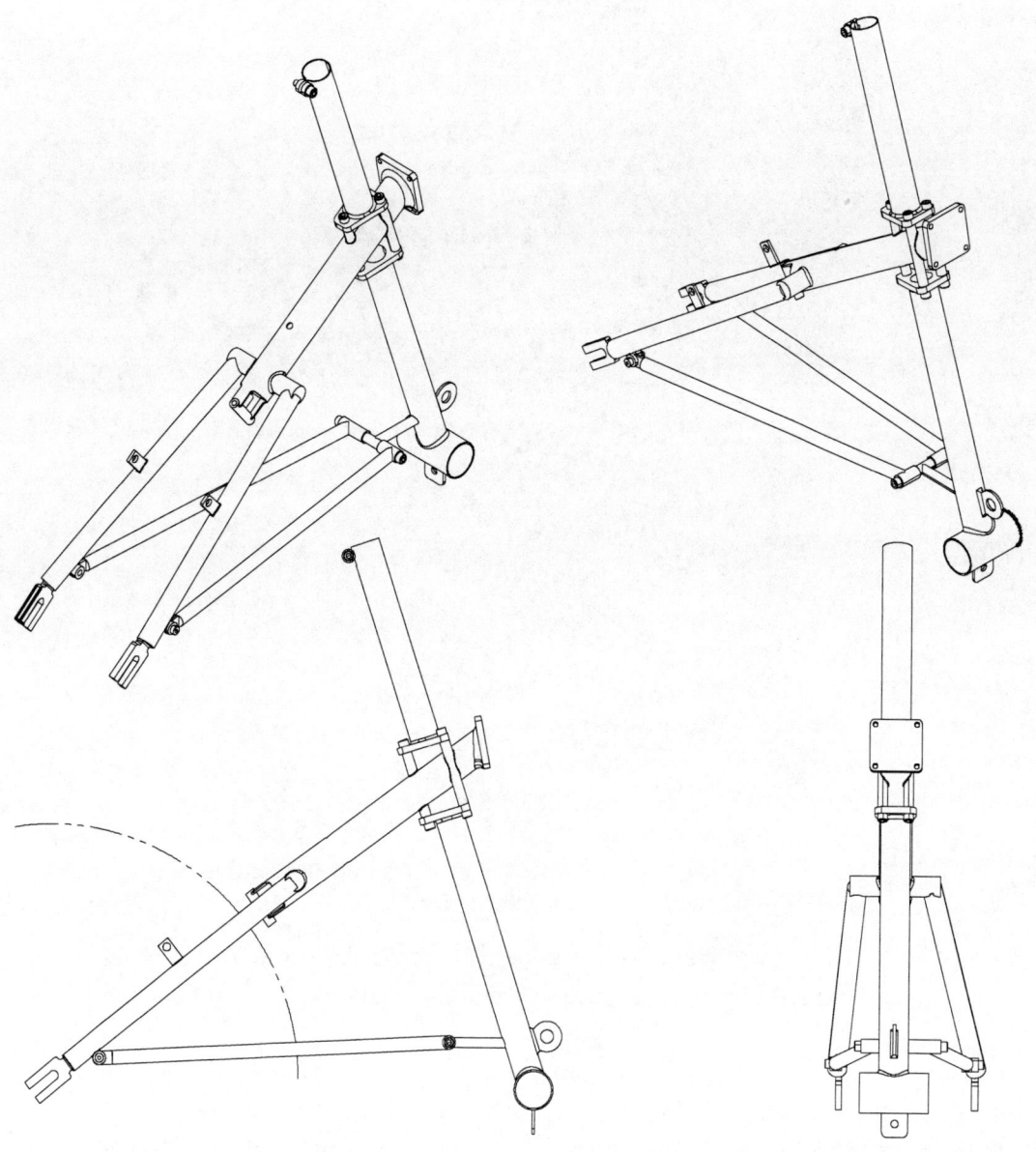

Rear Triangle: Rear Fork, 2 Stays, Upper and Lower Seat Tubes

Although it seems a trifle, chain stay to wheel/heel clearance cannot be taken for granted. Build the rear fork and lower seat tube, mount the rear wheel and then fit the stays, in that order.

If you are building this project as a torch brazed assembly, keep in mind that the TEE that joins the stays to the lower seat tube is loaded both in compression and in tension each pedal stroke. There is a bias towards tension because the weight of the rider is taken in part by the stays. Still, the stress reversals on this part of the assembly are the classic scenario for high cycle fatigue failure. Be sure to make the braze fillet massive. In fact, make all the braze fillets massive if you want a large safety factor, which you should. Use a doubler at each end of this TEE to handle the concentration of stresses. It does not have to be a big doubler. It does not have to be a work of art though it is easy to build in some artistic flair. It does, however, have to be.

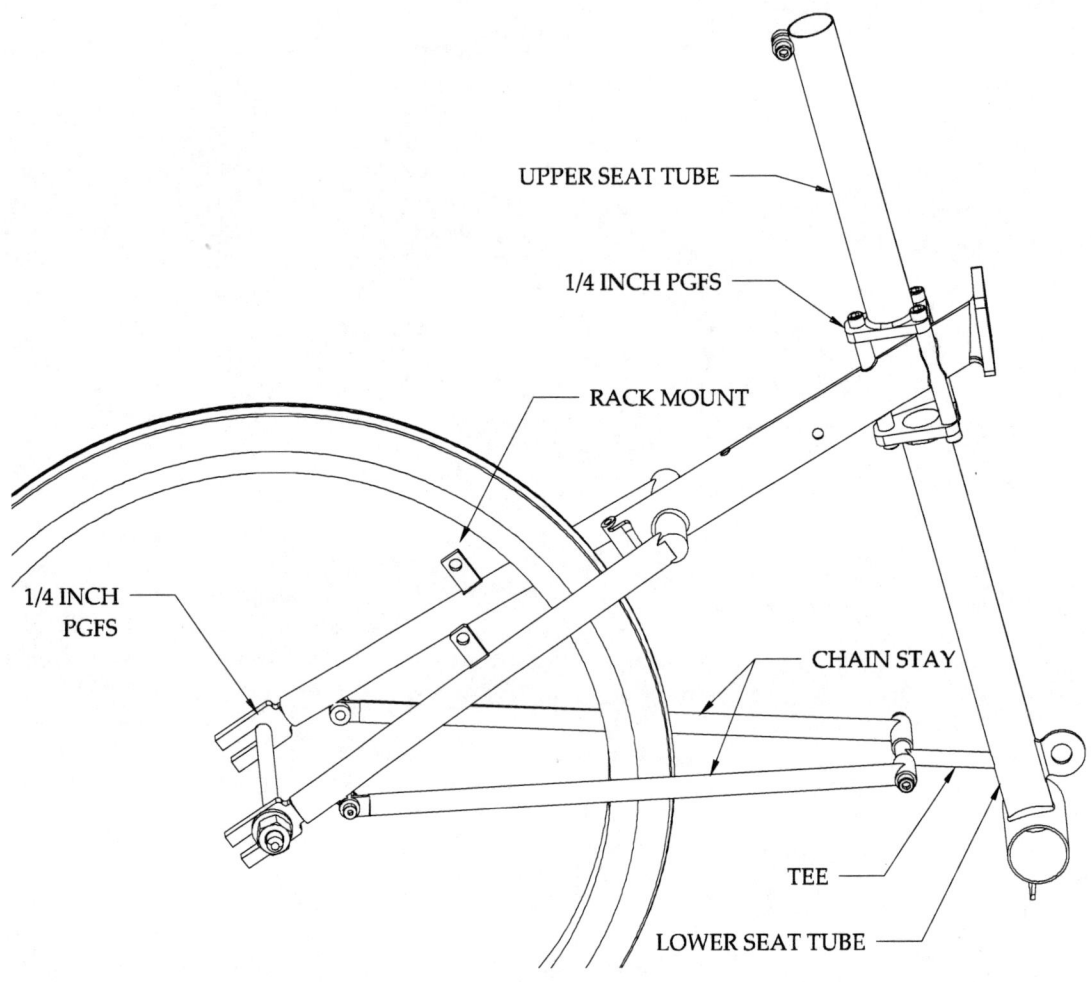

UPPER SEAT TUBE

1/4 INCH PGFS

RACK MOUNT

1/4 INCH PGFS

CHAIN STAY

TEE

LOWER SEAT TUBE

If you are welding this bike, then the usual rules apply
For brazing, make liberal use of doublers to increase the bond area

The round feature ahead of the bottom bracket is the alloy steel hard washer used to anchor the turnbuckle on the prototype. It is located opposite the TEE and is part of the load path. It is not difficult to imagine a replacement for this ring but keep in mind that its placement is important. You do not want to create a couple that might shear the seat tube. If you plan to exercise the tandem option, by all means add a doubler at the seat tube where it joins the bottom bracket. The doubler should have small holes drilled in several spots to allow penetration of the filler material. The doubler should be silver soldered. If you are welding, the doubler should be trimmed so that you do not create a weld fillet that circles the seat tube. Add a bit of obliqueness.

The rear dropouts are cut from quarter inch precision ground flat stock. If you are using a geared hub, the width of the slot is quite important. Have a look at the anti-rotation feature of your hub before committing the drop outs to the welding torch. It is always a good idea to pull the rear fork assembly off the welding jig after tacking to make sure everything works and to straighten any distortion. Generally, distortion comes later but it never hurts to have a look. We at Robobike use air hardening tool steel for our drop outs. This stuff gets a bit hard when welded but not so hard that you can't cut it with an end mill. The material designation is A2.

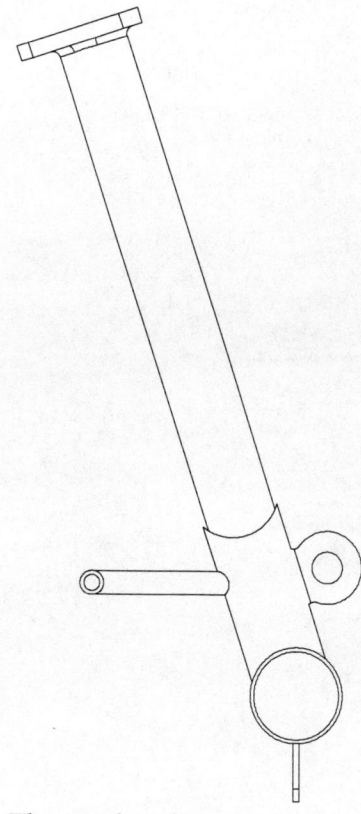

The tandem lower seat tube.
Notice the doubler

The mounting plates at the ends of the seat tubes are also cut from precision ground flat stock. The flat stock is quarter inch thick, just like the drop outs. The upper tube, since it is unsupported by a stay, has a doubler on the inside of the tube where it joins the plate. The tube size is 1.125x.06, a common size found in bike construction. The seat post is 25.4mm or one inch diameter. Wall thickness always has an effect on the seat post diameter so be careful here. You don't want to use a tube size that does not have a corresponding seat post.

Another point to watch is the features used to anchor the chain stays where they attach to the rear fork legs. The feature that works best is a piece of flat stock that is shaped to fit and drilled/tapped after the joining operation. These should also have a substantial fillet with a large surface area. We use silver solder for this operation but only because we make the surface area large on our bikes.

As already mentioned, both stays and the TEE should be clamped up and fitted as an assembly. It takes a great deal of care to do this but there is nothing out of the ordinary required other than patience and the desire to do a good job.

Our current tandem bike is this bike plus a middle half, all reinforced and buttressed for extra duty. In order to show why this evolved the way it did, we need to look at the history of the travel tandem that never went anywhere.

A Bicycle Built for Two (or One)
The Clipper morphs into the tandem Clipper
Master level skills

Robobike's travel bike packs away easily, rides good, and can be assembled several different ways to fit the needs of the user. It is not a folder nor is it suitable for commuting if portability is required. As a single, though, it fits, minus the wheels, into a backpack.

This is absolutely not a project for the beginner. Master level machinist skills are required. Detailed construction plans and instructions are available from Robobike.

Daisy

Before we can describe the current travel tandem, we have to look at what came before. Built of aluminum and joined with fasteners, Daisy was meant to be a bike that you take with. Later, with some minor changes, provision was made so that it could also be assembled as a single. It was ridden as a single across the Navajo reservation in Arizona. Daisy as a tandem never left home. The bike had little success as a single but worked perfectly as a tandem. It was designed first as a tandem and adapted to work as a single. Our current bike started life as a single and evolved into a tandem. Some clear differences are apparent when the two are compared side by side. The biggest of these is the center of gravity.

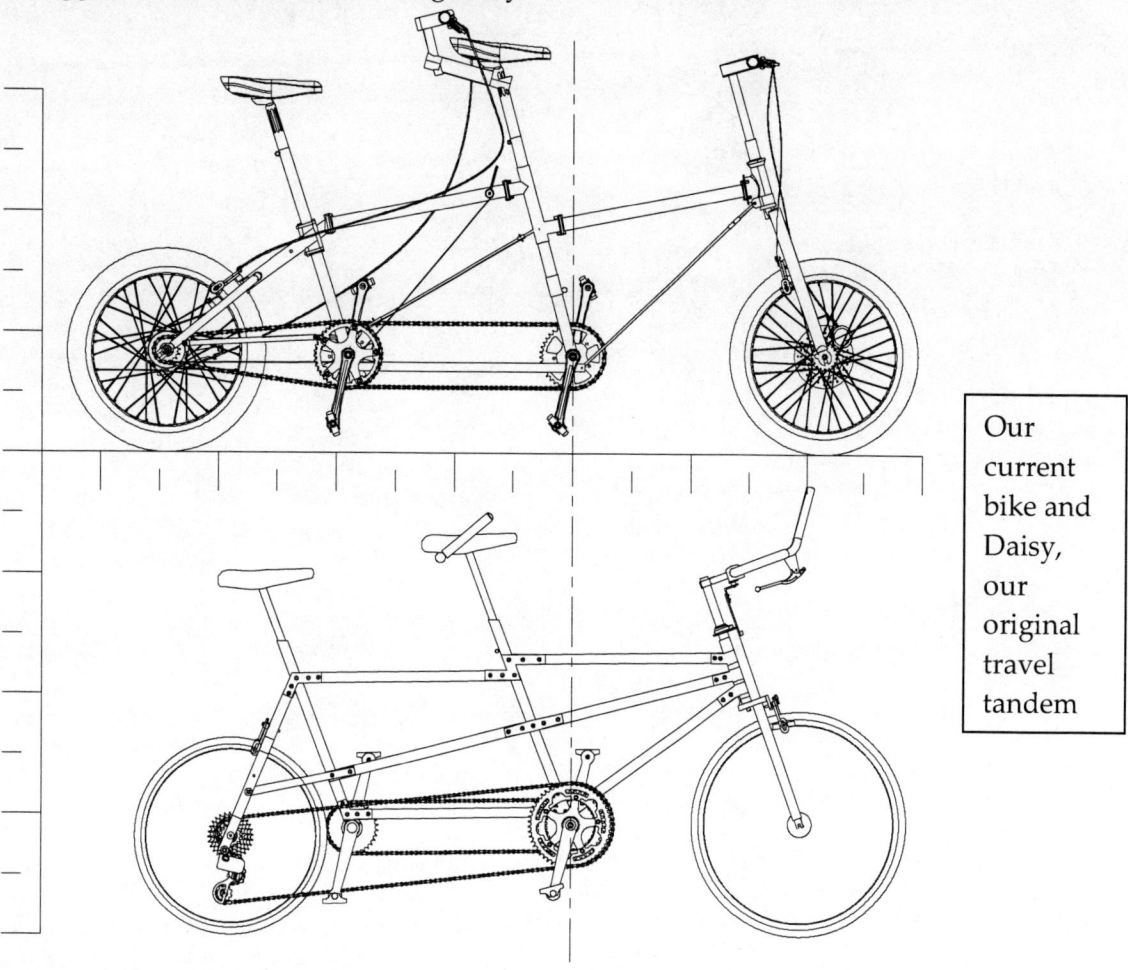

Our current bike and Daisy, our original travel tandem

Both bikes balance 39 inches aft of the front axle but because Daisy is so much shorter, the percentage of the total weight carried by the rear wheel is 68%, quite high for a tandem. The current bike carries 58% of its total weight on the rear wheel. These figures are for two riders who weigh 180 and 130 pounds with the heavier serving as the captain. The drawing above shows a six inch grid.

Daisy has a number of interesting details. Both bottom brackets are hogged out of chunks of aluminum. The head tube was an aluminum hog out too. All the doublers are 7075 aluminum except for the mid tube doublers which are steel. All the square tubes have inserts to prevent collapse when the bolts are tightened. The front fork is a lightweight copy of a motorcycle fork, all custom made from aluminum.

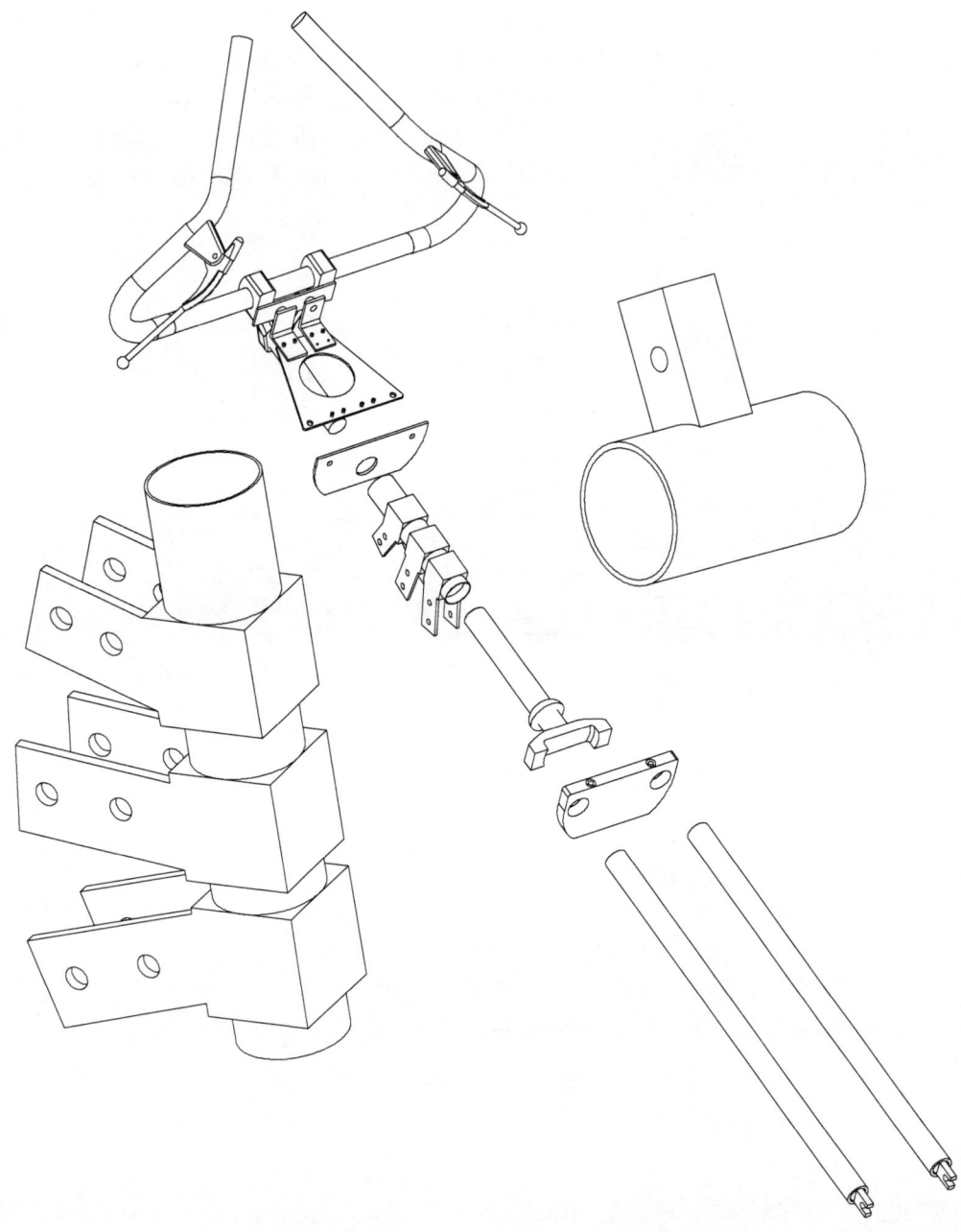

The head tube on the left and on the right, the bottom bracket. These two hog outs from Daisy are shown with an exploded view (not to scale) of the custom built fork assembly. It must be remembered that the builder of this bike is a professional machinist with many years of experience. These work pieces are not a challenge for such a person. If you do not have this experience, then this type of work is probably not for you.

The fork assembly is rigid, solid and easily adjustable. It was built like this to come apart easily for packing. When it came time to build another travel tandem that was actually useful for travel, the fork was re-examined. It was not copied for our current travel bike but many of the features are used on Loveboat. Loveboat has a complete front end pilfered from a Honda motorcycle. It is easy to see the similarities between this fork and a motorcycle.

Daisy now has a battery powered oven in place of the stoker's station and is used for pizza delivery.

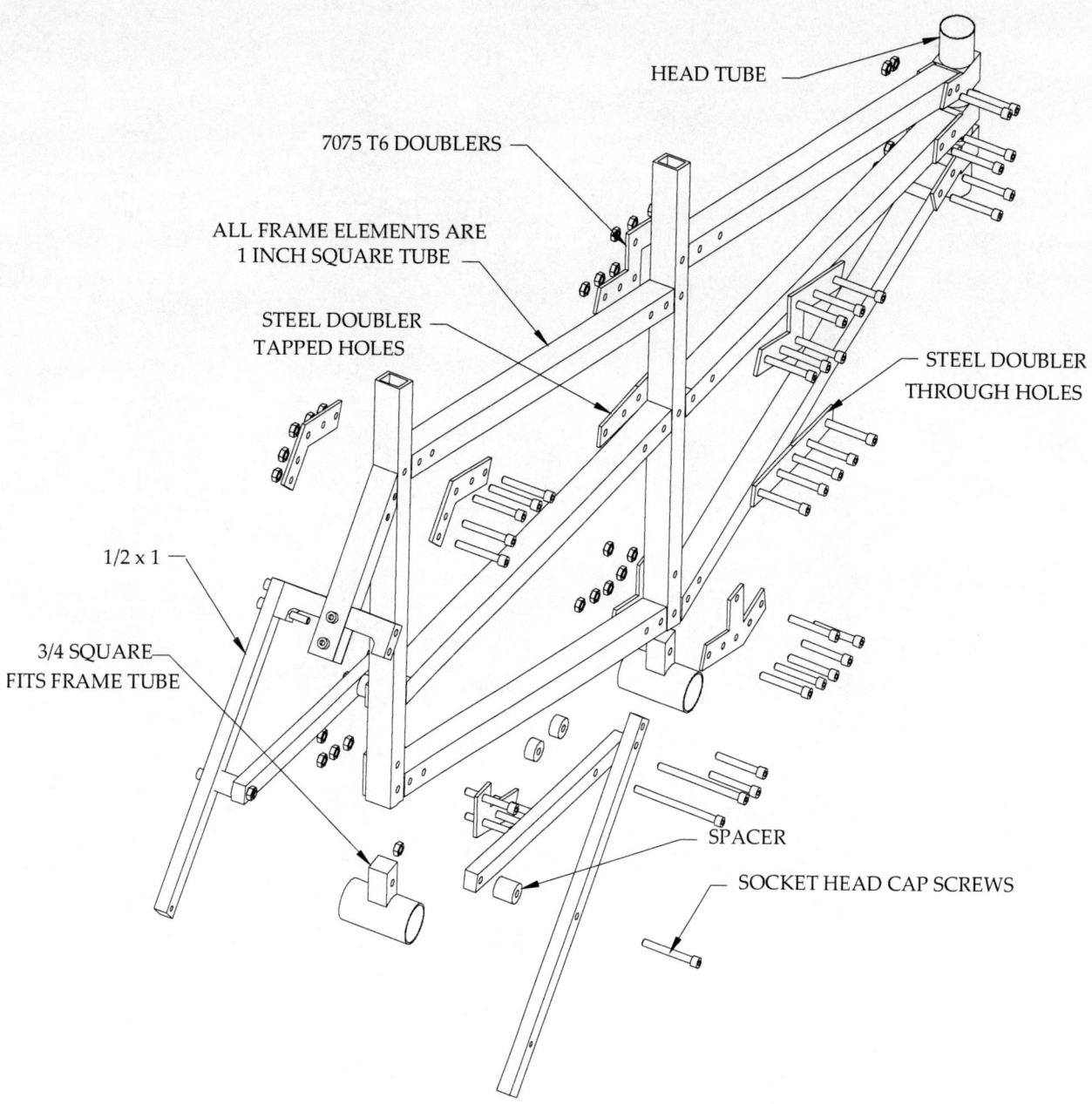

HEAD TUBE

7075 T6 DOUBLERS

ALL FRAME ELEMENTS ARE
1 INCH SQUARE TUBE

STEEL DOUBLER
TAPPED HOLES

STEEL DOUBLER
THROUGH HOLES

1/2 x 1

3/4 SQUARE
FITS FRAME TUBE

SPACER

SOCKET HEAD CAP SCREWS

Exploded view of Daisy's frame showing unusual construction method

Though Daisy's intended use was travel, its complexity and time for assembly was prohibitively high.

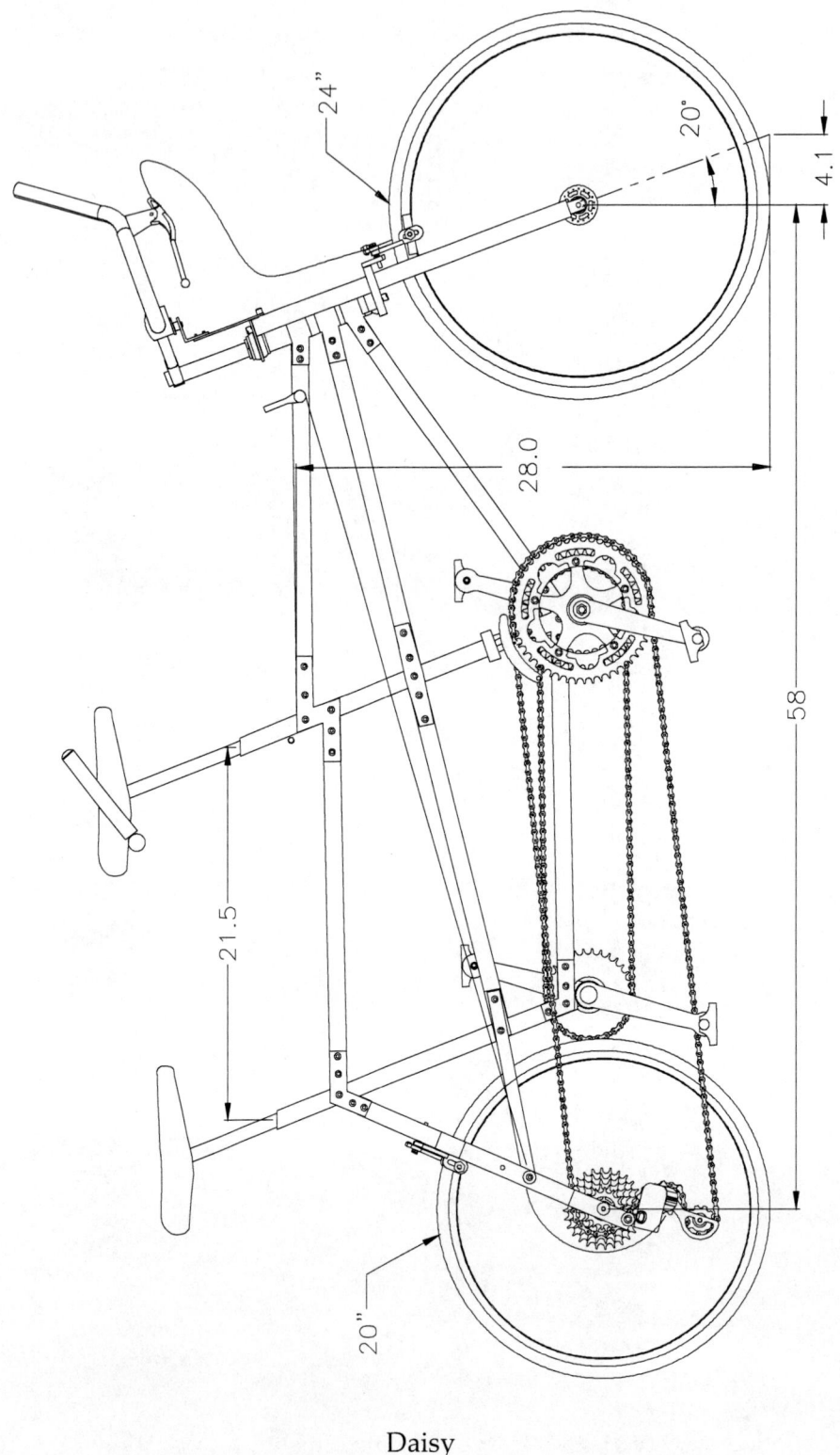

Daisy

We continue our design project by taking the Clipper and making it suitable for two riders. A long courtship and wedding prompted this requirement.

The middle half

The single becomes a tandem with the addition of two weldments and a BOOB TUBE. Without a doubt, building the weldment requires the most work. Here's the easiest of the lot.

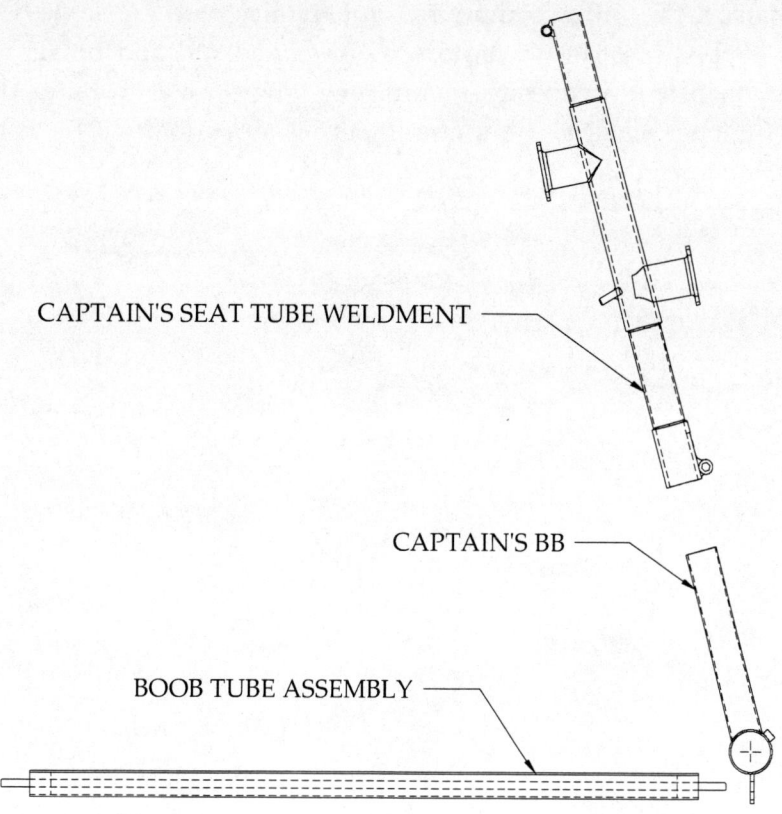

CAPTAIN'S SEAT TUBE WELDMENT

CAPTAIN'S BB

BOOB TUBE ASSEMBLY

The Boob Tube

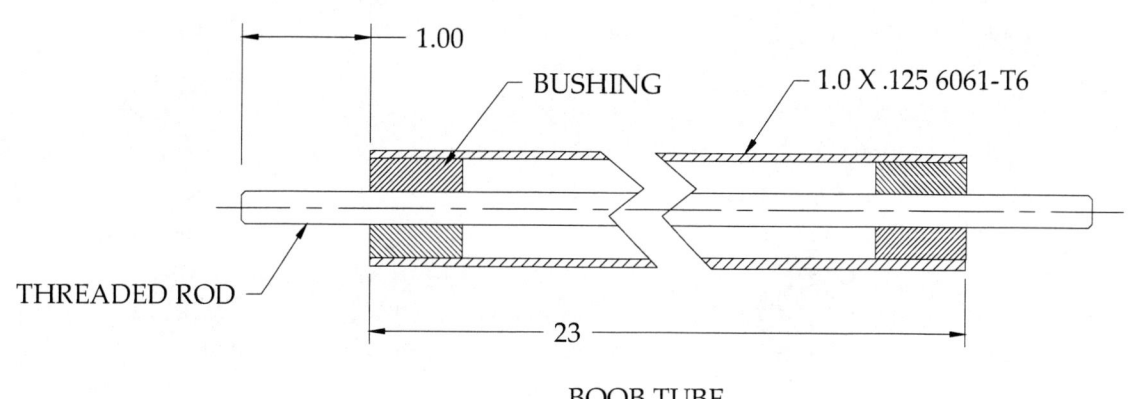

1.00

BUSHING

1.0 X .125 6061-T6

THREADED ROD

23

BOOB TUBE

The threaded rod can be eliminated if the bushings are built with thread inserts and the bushings themselves pinned to prevent their pulling out. The boob tube is loaded in both compression and tension. The tensile loads are the result of the rider's weight bearing down on the frame. The compressive loads are the result of pedal impulses and/or frame alignment. We have built this tube with both pinned bushings and threaded rod and prefer the threaded rod mostly because of the simplicity of field repairs. Our tandem has been to some primitive places. We've seen bike shops equipped with only a pair of pliers and a charcoal fire. What kind of bike repairs require a charcoal fire, I don't know but apparently there are some. One or both of the bushings should be tapped in order to capture the threaded rod and prevent its becoming lost when packed. Other than that, it doesn't require anything special to build this. Be warned of building this tube of thinner material. Columnar failure is a possibility if the tube is built too thin or if the rod is tightened too much.

The captain's bottom bracket

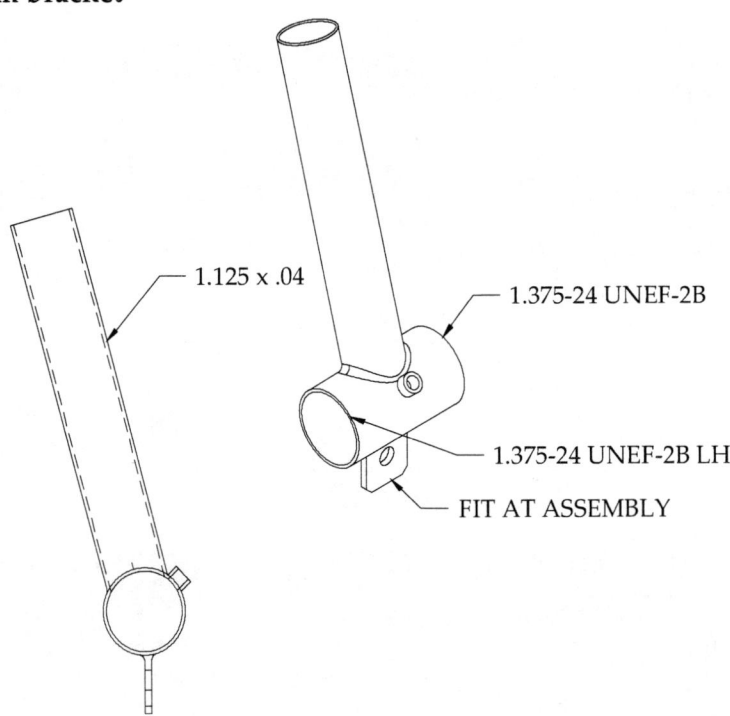

The shell is made from 1.5 x .085 steel, bored and threaded in the lathe before the weld operation. If you are welding, then you may come up with enough distortion to prevent assembly of the cups after weld so be sure to thread the cups for a loose fit. The cups should spin freely when installed in the shell. Weld the shell with old cups installed to help keep things round. The brazing operation usually doesn't result in much distortion but thread the shell on the loose side just in case. We usually bore the minor diameter to Ø1.340 and thread in a 3 jaw. Be sure to perform the welding operation on a jig to keep things square. The plate that hangs down to mount the boob tube should be done after the bottom bracket is assembled to the bike frame. This is one of those fitting operations that requires a nice touch with the torch. A bit of stitch welding will get you through without much problem. If brazing, tack with bronze then finish with silver. The silver does dilute the bronze but that's a good thing. We usually add a doubler in the form of a round disk that has been hammered to fit the shell. Cut it into two pieces and add to each side of the boob tube mounting feature. The round feature shown in the isometric view is for fitting the turnbuckle. Tap it ¼-20 left hand and buy some LH threaded rod to make a turnbuckle. We'll get to that shortly.

The captain's seat tube

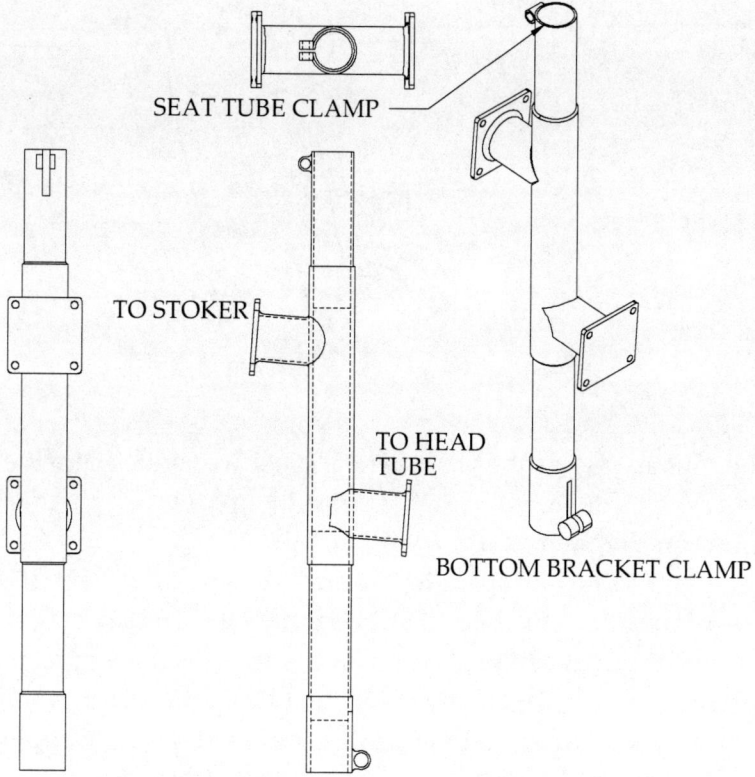

SEAT TUBE CLAMP

TO STOKER

TO HEAD TUBE

BOTTOM BRACKET CLAMP

There is no need to build a jig for this weldment but keep in mind that the faces of the square flanges and the hole patterns have to be spot on, as they say around the snooker table. Since the top tube flanges have tapped holes, all the flanges here have clearance holes. Those clearance holes are .030 oversize. That seems like a lot for a #10 cap screw but believe me, you will be glad once you put this together. Once again, use a massive brass fillet for the bosses and silver solder for the telescoping features. The plans set has a detailed blue print showing all pertinents.

The seat clamp and bottom bracket clamp use nuts or rounds welded or brazed to the tubes. A saw cut or better yet, a ⅛ wide mill cut gives the thing some room to move. Remember that this type of clamp needs to breathe so carry the cut well beyond the clamp screw or you will break the clamp features. Once again, keep things primitive if you expect to travel to the undeveloped parts of the world. Our prototype broke on a recent trip to the tropics and we managed to find a local with a hand held drill so we could put a bolt through this weldment and the seat post. It removes the adjustment feature of the seat tube but what are you going to do? Make your fillets big ones and you won't have to deal with these issues.

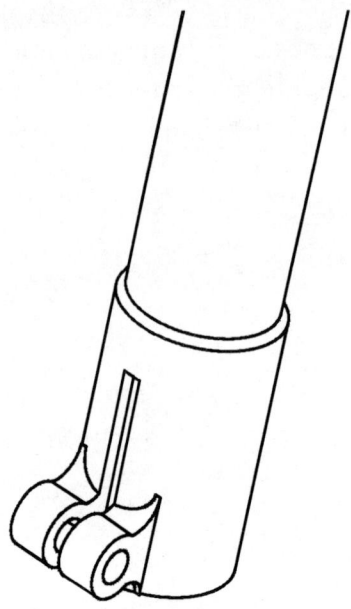

View showing the captain's seat tube weldment at the lower end where the captain's bottom bracket plugs in

A load distribution diagram

Robobike knows the folly of spending heaps of time doing a static analysis of bicycle structures. We've done a number of them. Fatigue is by far a much bigger concern to the bike builder than load bearing capacity while at rest. Controlling the amount a bike can flex, especially at the joints, is the primary task to which any competent designer directs her focus. Redundancy is another task given high priority. If something breaks, can the bike be brought to a stop safely and under control?

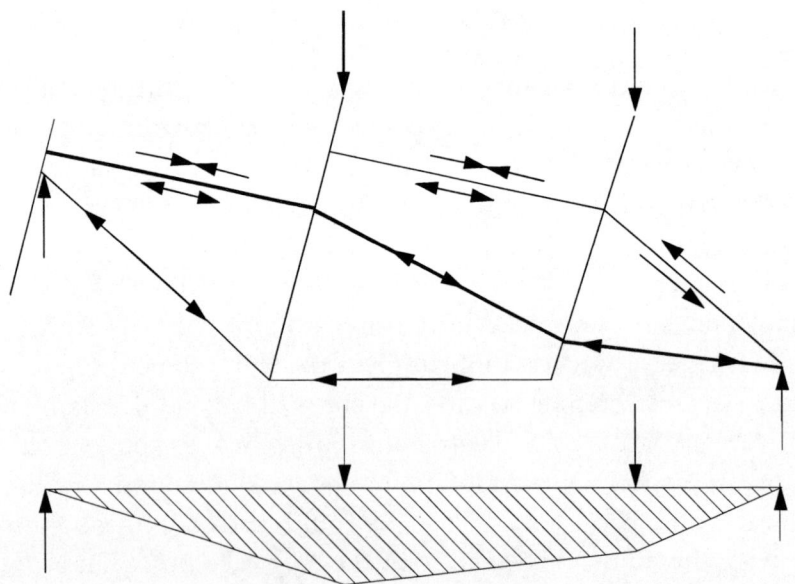

A rudimentary load diagram to help visualize needed truss work

Don't forget also that loads are 3 dimensional. You can't represent the real world on a flat piece of paper. Still and all, a sketch like this shows blatant faults rather quickly.

What happens if you hit a huge pot hole and break both chain stays at the same time? Ever heard of dominoes? How do you design for catastrophe? The answer is: massive structure and a good size braze fillet with doublers where appropriate. A big fillet will survive long enough to bring the bike to a stop whereas a small, lightweight tube and fillet will give way without a struggle. If the boob tube snaps off where it joins the bottom bracket, the turnbuckle saves the day. Load path redundancy is a good thing. It is impossible to design for every scenario and no one does but it is possible to foresee a number of failure modes. The experienced designer will do just that.

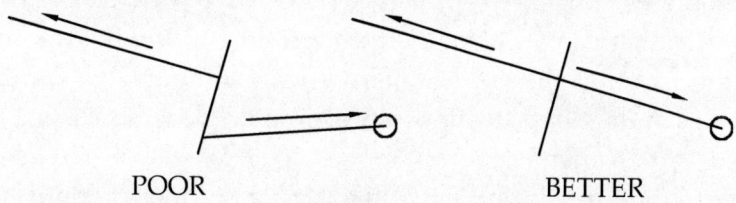

POOR   BETTER

This example is pretty straight forward. Nobody would build a frame like this but couples may exist without your knowledge.

Turnbuckles

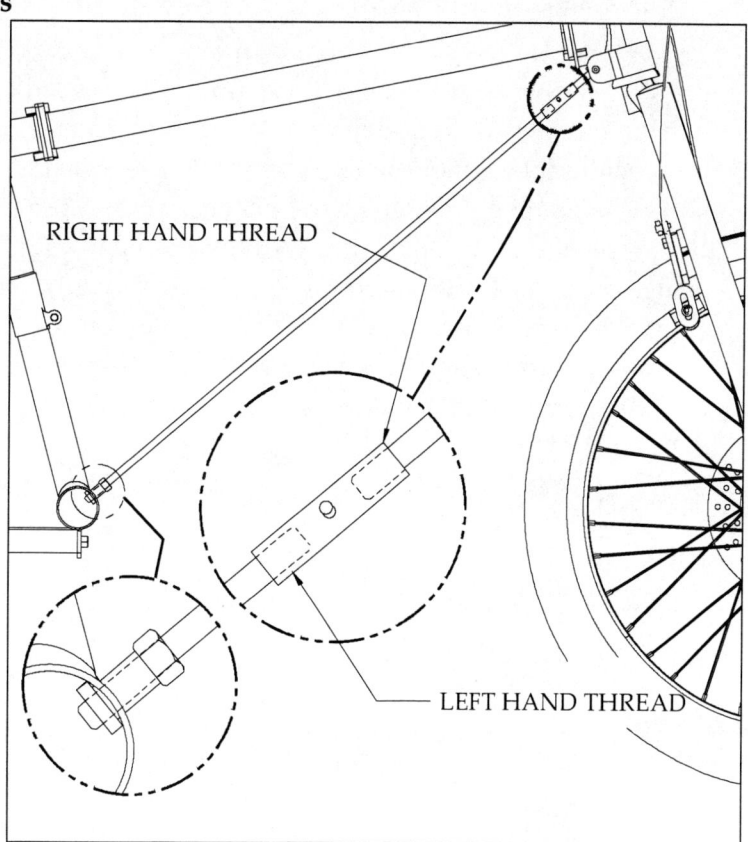

RIGHT HAND THREAD

LEFT HAND THREAD

The "Ivel" tandem from the late 19th century used the turnbuckle method for bracing. The reasons we use it are every bit as valid as they were then. Steel loaded in tension is the most efficient use of structure. The weight of the rider(s) is by far the most intense load the frame has to control. Draw your bike in profile, sketch the load paths, check for couples and other danger signs and look around. You will see bracing and truss work similar to our turnbuckles used on everything from railway cars to highway bridges.

A pair of turnbuckles is required for the tandem option while a single turnbuckle will suffice for the single bike. They are of similar construction, having, like all turnbuckles, both a left hand and right hand thread. We make our unions from brass to avoid similar metals being in close proximity. The arrangement shown here does not work with anything other than the old standard bottom brackets with a fixed and an adjustable cup. This bike is intended for remote and primitive locations so the decision was made to use old technology. If your choice of bottom bracket includes modern technology, then you cannot have the through bore of the bottom bracket shell impeded with a threaded button like that shown. An alternative is to attach the turnbuckle directly to the boob tube by either a manufactured detail or an eye bolt. Doing so eliminates the minor couple created by the configuration shown here.

You may reverse the threads and make the longer portion the right hand thread but since left hand threaded rod is so hard to find on the road, it is wise to take a full length at the start of a trip. Any damage can then be removed with a hacksaw and the turnbuckle restored to working order by buying a length of right hand threaded rod which is readily available.
The bike should not be ridden without the turnbuckles.

Top tube

This chrome moly steel top tube replaces the titanium top tube used on the Crocodile and the Clipper. It is easy to make but be sure to face off the flanges after the weld operation to ensure parallelism. Failure to do so will shoot down the whole project. Use a steady rest or side cut both ends with an end mill at the same time. Likewise, it is OK to drill and tap one flange before the joining operation, but the second should be done after welding. You'll never line them up if you do it any other way. The flanges are PGFS (precision ground flat stock), 1018 carbon steel which is easy to get and easy to cut. There is no pre-heat or post-heat required for this operation but do allow it to cool slowly. If you are brazing, make a root pass and at least two more buildup passes one of which can be a hot pass to make it look nice. You want a big fillet.

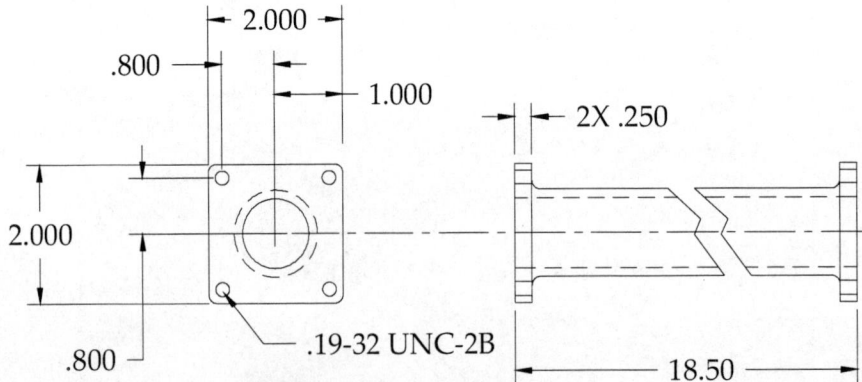

It doesn't take much to describe the top tube; it is simple as can be. The tandem has two top tubes, identical and interchangeable. Since we have the ability to turn a length of steel tube this length, we use the same material for the top tube as we do for the bottom bracket which is Ø1.50 x .08 wall. We usually turn the tube to Ø1.45 thus reducing the wall to .055. The tube is stressed most heavily at the ends so we leave those at the original size. Be mindful of concentricity if you turn the tube. To do otherwise will introduce stress concentrations and weak spots.

The front end

Our travel bike has used a number of different front ends. Some were completely custom, home built and others were borrowed from other bikes. Our current design calls for a 20 inch wheel held in a fork meant for a 26 inch mountain bike wheel. The biggest piece of work on this subassembly is cutting the head tube from the donor bike and welding a 2" square plate to it. This plate will bolt up to the custom top tube. Here's what we use for the travel bike currently number one in our line up.

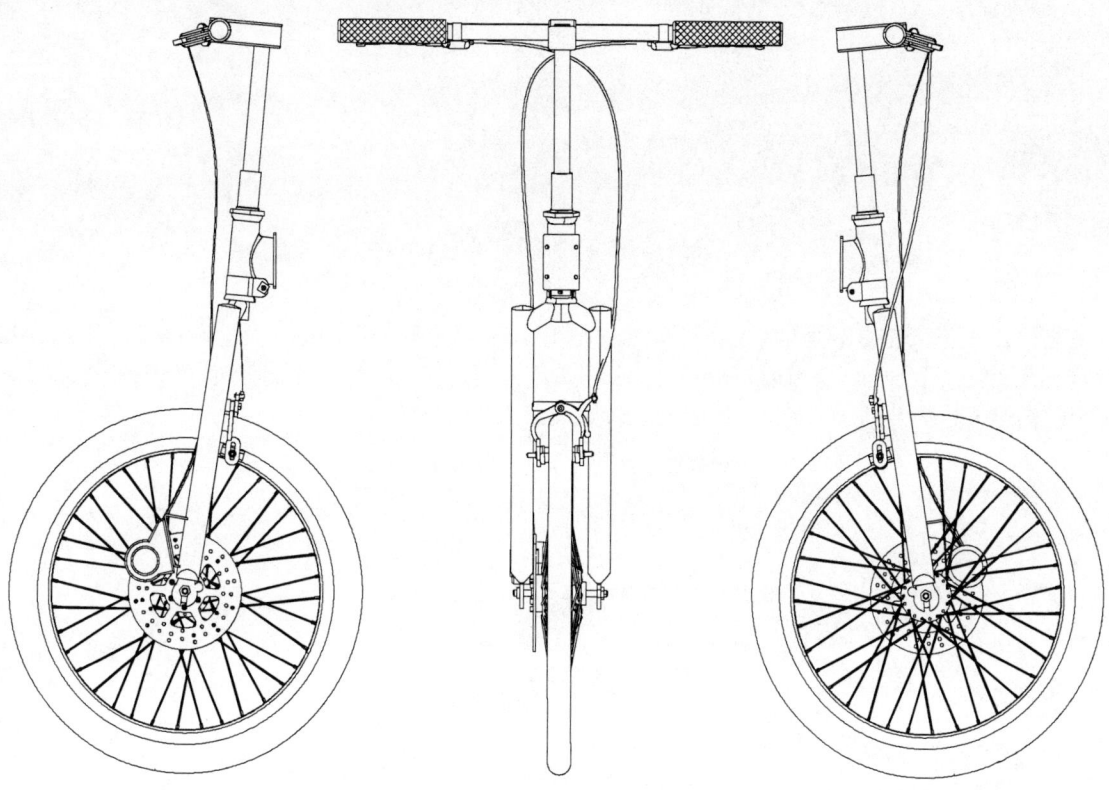

The custom front end assembly we used previously was put on the shelf in favor of more brakes. When the bike went from a single to a tandem, the lessons learned on previous bikes were rolled into the project. Brakes are in short supply on our previous efforts so we went all out. There's nothing scarier than riding a tandem down a mountain knowing that stopping is not an option. This front end has both a Sachs disk brake stolen from a EV Warrior and a caliper brake mounted backwards on an added cross piece. Both front brakes are controlled by the captain. The stoker has control of two brakes operating on the rear wheel. One is a caliper and the other a drum that comes supplied with the geared hub. The Tandem has lots of brakes and that's a good thing.

The work required to adapt the donor front end is easy. At the same time, if the process doesn't result in a perfectly square cut and weld job, then all is lost.

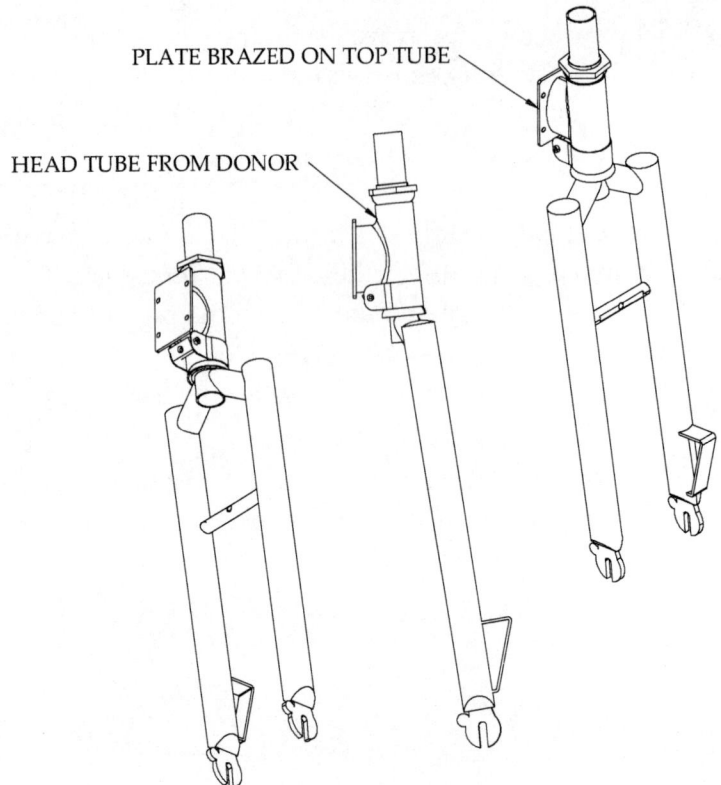

PLATE BRAZED ON TOP TUBE

HEAD TUBE FROM DONOR

Also shown in this view is the strap wrapped around the lower head tube to form a yoke. The small rectangular piece is for the turnbuckle. Since you'll be carrying this bike a lot, make it out of aluminum and insert it. You save 8 grams over steel.

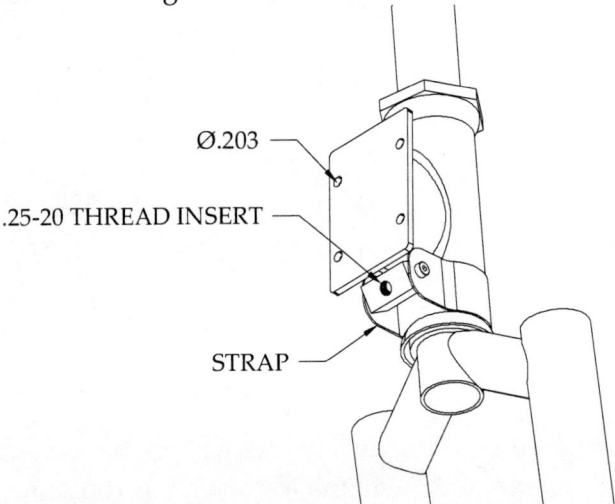

Ø.203

.25-20 THREAD INSERT

STRAP

Not everyone has access to a EV Warrior that is no longer serviceable though at the time this is written, it is nigh impossible to find one still working. There is a lesson here. A battery powered bicycle has at a minimum 25kg of batteries if lead/acid is the chemistry. The EV Warrior has something like 7kg. Lightweight was a big issue in the marketing campaign for this bike and when it was first introduced, it was quite a sensation. However, let's save the discussion of the battery powered bicycle for later.

If you want a flat land travel bike for one, a disk brake is not required. It is required for the tandem option. If you are building only the single and have no intention of going tandem at some later date, forget about the disk brake. Visiting second and third world countries with a bike having fancy smancy anything is a mistake. Stick to calipers and you won't have any trouble finding spares or a technician with the skills to help you out. This holds true for handlebars, seat posts, saddles, etc etc.

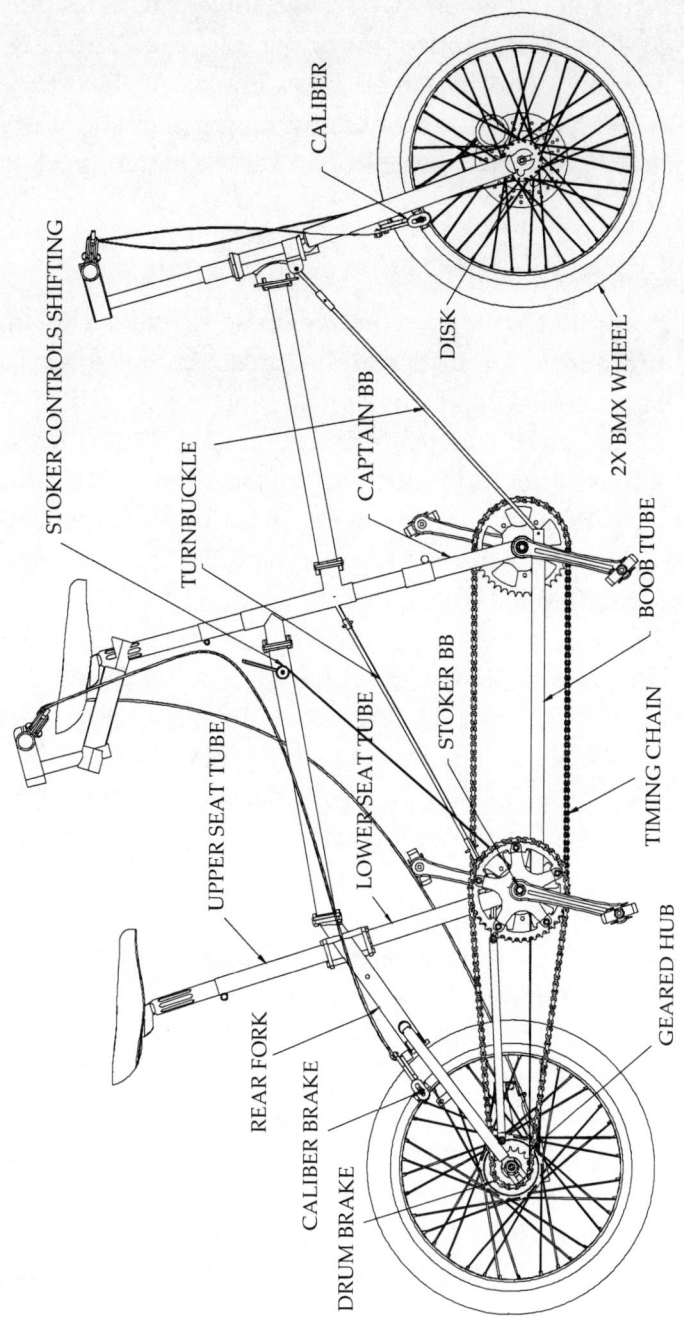

eBikes?

Bingo Sun Noon

This subject is growing in its scope daily. The information presented here is but a brief history of what Robobike did in the last decades of the 20 th century. To see what is current in the 21 st, visit Robobike.com

I once built a lightweight battery powered bike that was so efficient that I only needed to charge it every other evening. It recharged in less than an hour. After 600 charge/discharge cycles, the battery still acted as though it did when it was new. It went 20 miles per hour and I could ride it without worry for twenty-five miles. I rode it every day for years. Then I woke up.

Sadly, many vendors of battery powered bikes make unbelievable claims with a straight face. The truth is that you can have light weight, long range, high speed or long battery life. Pick one. When we build a battery powered bike at Robobike, the battery pack is item number one on the bill of materials.

Energy storage

Charging Batteries, 1911 style

"Thoroughly clean all the parts and re-amalgamate the zincs. Re-amalgamation is for the purpose of freeing the surface from impurities and is thus accomplished: Take a flat earthenware dish a little larger than the zinc plate, and put in just enough water to cover it. Then slowly add sulphuric acid, one part to the ten of water-that is, if you have 10 oz. of water, add 1 oz. of acid. Immerse the zinc in the diluted acid and pour over it a small quantity of mercury which is to be painted onto the zinc with a little brush or mop made up of tow and a few brass wires. See that the zinc is well covered. The acid may be afterward used with the charging solution and the mercury that is left may be poured back into the bottle.

After the zincs are thus re-amalgamated, charge the porous pot with a solution of 1 part of sulphuric acid to 12 of water, and the outer jar with a saturated solution of copper sulphate. On a sieve suspended in the liquid, place crystals of copper sulphate to keep the solution saturated. Do not throw a handful of sulphate into the jar to settle to the bottom. Care must be taken to keep the zinc and the zinc sediments from touching the porous pot, as this would attract particles of copper from the copper solution to form on the outer wall of the partition and cause a higher internal resistance and a short circuit."

From Electroplating : a treatise for the beginner and for the most experienced electroplater / by Henry C. Reetz, Bradley, IL : Lindsay Publications, 1989

Chemistry? Lead-acid is a good choice for the first project and if you are building to a set of specs for the race track, then battery type is probably dictated to you. If you are building a commuter and have something to prove, try one of the more volatile battery types. NiMH is another good choice but knowledge of battery management is absolutely required.

Capacity is generally given in amp-hours. Not every battery maker uses the same method to calculate capacity. Two identical batteries may have different Amp-hour ratings because one builder uses an eight hour discharge rate and the other a twelve hour rate. The battery tested at the 12 hour rate will be rated higher though it contains no more energy storage capacity than its identical cousin. Bicycles always discharge faster than the rate used to advertise capacity.

Depth of discharge refers to the final voltage to which a battery can be discharged. DoD is inversely proportional to battery life. Often, taking a battery to the lower discharge limit destroys its ability to recover fully. For bicycle use, long range usually means deep discharge and short battery life. Until recently, Robobike has always used sealed lead-acid and we always use four pounds of battery for every mile of range we design into a street bike. Other builders use closer to one pound of battery for each mile of (advertised) range. Depth of discharge is measured with a voltmeter and is described as volts/cell or as percent of total. Other chemistries do not suffer from deep discharge the same way as lead-acid cells. Ni-Cads may experience polarity reversal in a single cell which causes problems in both the charging and discharging phases.

Discharge rate has a huge effect on battery life. Taking a battery to a fully discharged state may ruin it. Taking it there quickly ruins it quickly. Race track applications, especially quarter mile drag racing, mean discharging a battery through what amounts to zero resistance. Hills are brutal for batteries. Moving up a 4% grade at ten miles per hour requires 32 amps at 12 volts. This is ½ brake horse power. Losses, both mechanical and electrical, kick this up to 50 amps. Performance like this, if included in the design specs, is why Robobike uses the four pound per mile rule. Nickel-metal hydride and Ni-Cads all have their own ratios but Robobike has no guidelines for their use. We did build a Ni-Cad powered bike once but it was ridden into a highway barrier at high speed before any data could be collected.

Just like discharge rate, the charging rate impacts battery service life. So does the first and second charge/discharge cycle. Lead-acid cells should be discharged slowly and charged slowly once or twice before entering service. This process, known as seasoning, is important. If done properly, seasoning guarantees long life unless the batteries are abused. Ignoring the seasoning is a battery killer though it may be a long slow death. Many battery suppliers deliver batteries that have been through this step already. It is a good thing to know when buying a battery pack. All chemistries have characteristics unique to that chemistry. Read the instructions that came with your cell. Do your cells have memory? I'm not talking brain cells.

Amp-hours (Amp-hr) and Watt hours are two methods of rating batteries.
A 12 Volt 20 Amp-hr battery has the same energy storage as a 24 Volt 10 Amp-hr battery.
Both are rated at 240 watt-hrs. This is true for all types of battery chemistry.

Motors   Four very different types of motors are available for bicycle use. Though different, they all perform the same task of changing chemical energy into power.

The first type of motor commonly found in traction applications has been around for a long time. A motor with a stationary field and a rotating armature all wound in series is known as a universal or series wound motor. Series wound motors pull strong from a dead stop, run on either AC or DC (universal, though some motors are optimized for AC only), are inexpensive and are easy to control. They all have brushes, usually one pair but sometimes two. They do not produce a back EMF like most motors. If run without a load they may accelerate until they fly apart. Series wound motors are found in hand power tools, kitchen appliances, vacuum cleaners and overhead heavy lift cranes. If you want to accelerate a heavy load from a dead stop, a series wound motor is hard to beat. You can expect *at least* a fifteen percent loss using a motor like this.

Shunt wound motors like those found on golf carts are similar to series wound motors but differ in several ways. The armature and the field are wired in parallel. They do not have the heavy lifting qualities that universal motors have but at the same time, they do not destroy themselves if run without a load. The armature acts as a generator to produce back EMF that balances the forward EMF when the motor reaches cruising speed. Compound motors, a type of shunt motor, possess qualities of both series and shunt types as they have a series wound and shunt wound element in the field, or stator as it is sometimes known. A good compound wound motor is expensive and is generally not used for electric vehicles. Shunt wound motors are found in golf carts, electric forklifts and similar types of equipment. Torque is constant through the speed range and that, coupled with its easy to control design, is why it is used in the applications normally associated with this type. Regen is easy with shunt wound motors.

Permanent magnet, or PM, motors are popular with the electric bike and electric car crowd. Care must be taken that they are not allowed to get too hot. If you are racing and run your motor at 600% rated capacity, then this type won't last long. Magnets don't like heat though Neodymium-Iron-Boron (NeFeB), a type of rare earth magnet, do much better than most. Avoid motors scavenged from electric lawn mowers and other kinds of cheap consumer products. Any PM motor designed to run on house current is wasteful and has ceramic magnets. Only motors designed for battery operation should be used in your ebike. A good PM motor capable of pumping out a full horsepower will be de-rated to a quarter horse to avoid the heat issue so don't be afraid to run them hard. If you are getting less than a hundred miles from a pair of brushes in a commuter bike, you need to slow down or get a bigger motor. Like series and shunt wound motors, PM motors have brushes and use variable voltage via pulse width modulation for speed control.

Brushless and induction motors are very popular with racing teams from universities and schools who have the ability to put together the sensing and transistor networks needed to control them. Brushless motors take many forms and can be some of the most efficient prime movers going. Robobike has used these types to build eBikes and have found them all to be quite acceptable. All motors have pluses and all have minuses. Ohio State University has a race car with an AC induction motor installed. It cleans up at the race track.

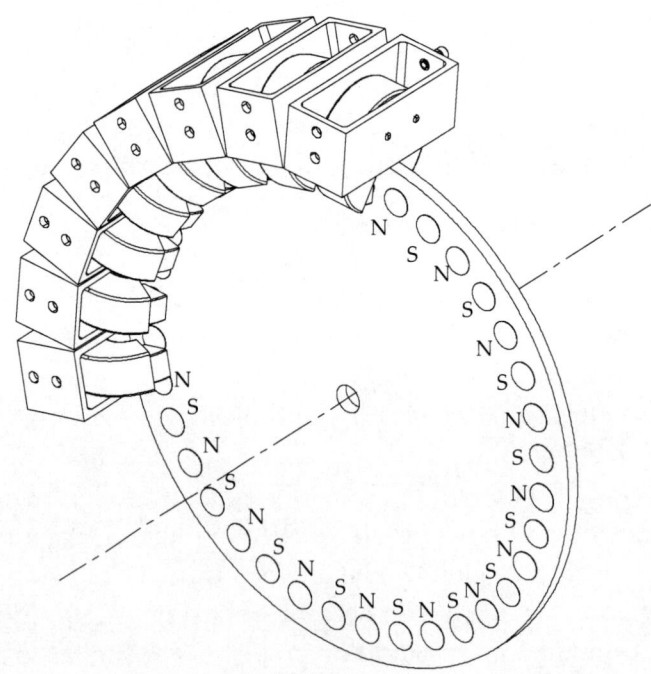

Shown here is a motor built at Robobike for a patent application demonstration.

The patent application was successful and lead to issuance of a US patent. It is a DC brushless motor that can run on batteries. The coils are wound on powdered iron toroids and are modulated using a sensor/transistor circuit. Attaching the disk to a live axle or a wheel disk is easy enough. This motor is more efficient than anything we've ever seen. An added bonus is the regen potential. When coasting, the motor becomes a generator and charges the battery pack. All that is needed is a bridge rectifier, some blocking diodes and a few other insignificant pieces.

A final word about motors. Never install one to drive the front wheel unless you want to crash. One slip and you are down.

Electric limo The Aluminum Limo with muscle

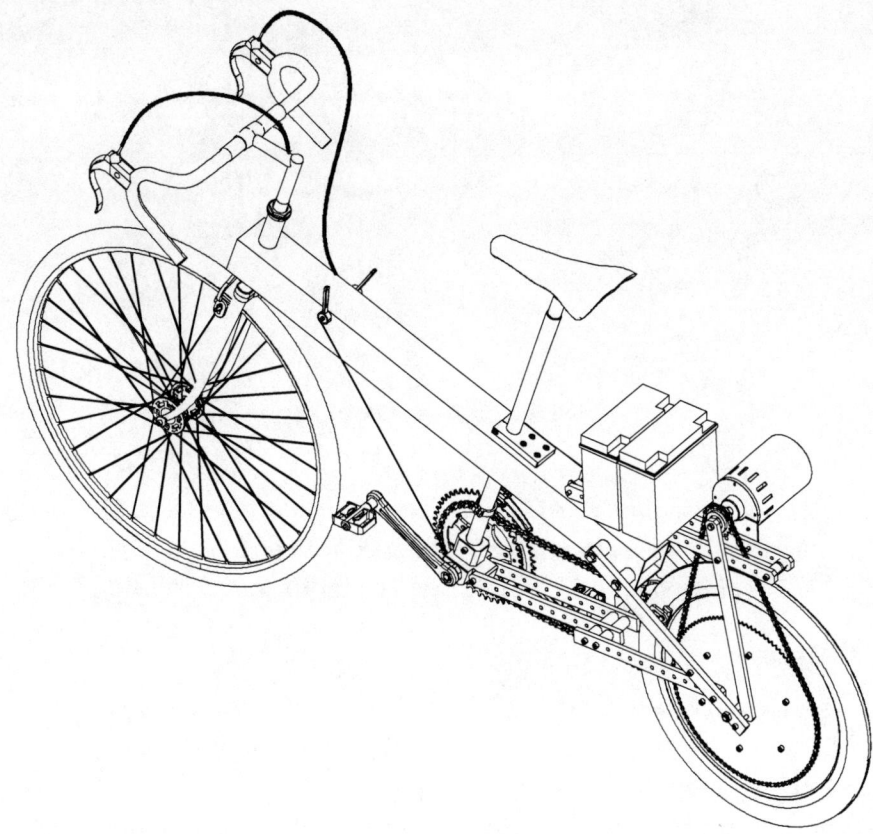

The Aluminum Limo project with the series wound motor similar to that shown here has a number of configurations. The batteries shown in this picture are used to power a 24 volt universal motor taken from the landing gear pump on a 19 passenger twin engine turbo prop airplane. The lead-acid batteries each weigh 36 pounds and are rated 600 watt-hours each. Notice the vertical strut and how it supports the end of the motor shaft.

The most successful version of this bike has a 110 vac one horsepower rated series motor driving a 104 tooth ⅜" pitch chain. Chain adjustment is done by loosening everything, rotating the motor, and tightening. The holes in the struts are ⅛" oversize so this is all that is needed. The battery pack is eight 18 Amp-hr batteries, 12 volts, each weighing about 12½ pounds. The bike has no speed control. It is intended for long straight roads. It can go from Chandler to Casa Grande, Arizona in less than an hour. This is about a 35 mile trip. At the end of this run, the cells check 1.9+ volts/cell. It is a flat run except for one small hill of about one mile length and one hundred feet altitude gain. After a round trip, the brushes need to be replaced. After two trips, we throw away the motor too unless we feel like replacing the bearings, which we do.

Since this a special purpose bike built to run between the Chandler airport and the airport at Casa Grande, very little thought was given to extra brakes, freewheeling, or lights. The road is mostly across Indian reservation and is lightly traveled. The Electric Limo has been run at the race track and always attracts a crowd. Even though it has a hundred pounds of batteries on board, someone in the crowd always asks "How much does it weigh?" What a bunch of morons.

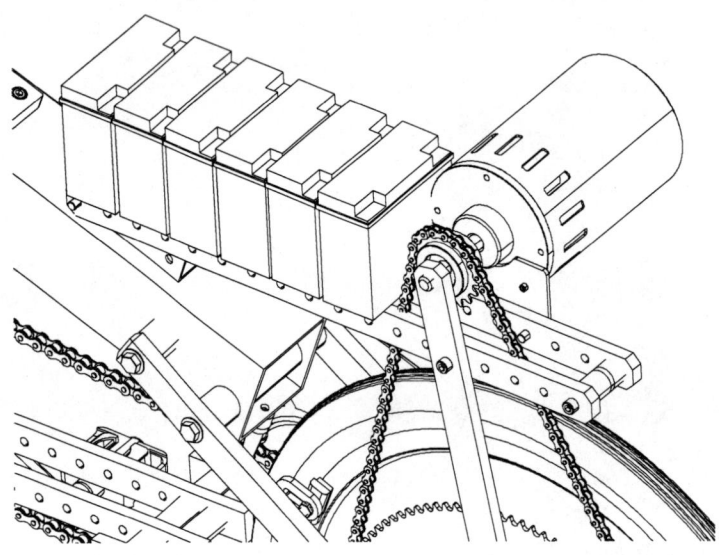

A row of 12 volt Sealed Lead Acid batteries lined up on a rack and wired in series
Battery cover removed for clarity
Shown with 110 volt universal motor rated at 1 hp
8 x 12 volts

Always use an approved, vented cover for batteries and always use an overload device such as a fuse. Batteries are held in place with hold down clamps. It is irresponsible to build a motorized vehicle without all of these safety devices.

This is a perfect example of a series wound application. The motor(s) gain efficiency when run faster and faster. That is why there is no gear reduction except for the 1:6 in the sprockets. Since the armature and field of the motor are in series it is difficult to measure the resistance of the motor as you must measure through the brushes. Our best guess is that the motor is running at close to 250% rated capacity when starting from a dead stop with a full charge. Needless to say, the motor gets hot as hell when run this hard. Remember, though, this bike is meant to go from here to there, over a known course, under known load conditions and does a great job. Just so you know, the rear wheel is a custom job and has a couple of massive angular contact bearings from a Yamaha motorcycle incorporated into the hub. The electric limo is a hot bike that goes fast and goes far considering it is not so much of a dinosaur that it can't also be pedaled home after a breakdown. It can be and it has been. A flat road in calm conditions with a well conditioned rider and it moves along pretty good when pedaled. Uphill, though, and dead batteries or a burned out motor means a long slow walk pushing a big heavy bicycle.

Building the Electric Limo is identical to the Aluminum Limo with the exception of the rear wheel. A twenty inch rim is stuffed with an aluminum disk and attached with screws through the spoke holes. A couple of aluminum cups hold double row balls against each side. The bearings share a bushing that also acts as a hollow axle. A threaded rod through the whole works holds the wheel to the bike.

The 104 tooth sprocket is ⅜" pitch. Half inch pitch works too but a sprocket with this many teeth is larger than the rim and a flat tire will wreck the sprocket. We make our own sprockets at Robobike but most go kart shops can fix you up with the stuff you need.

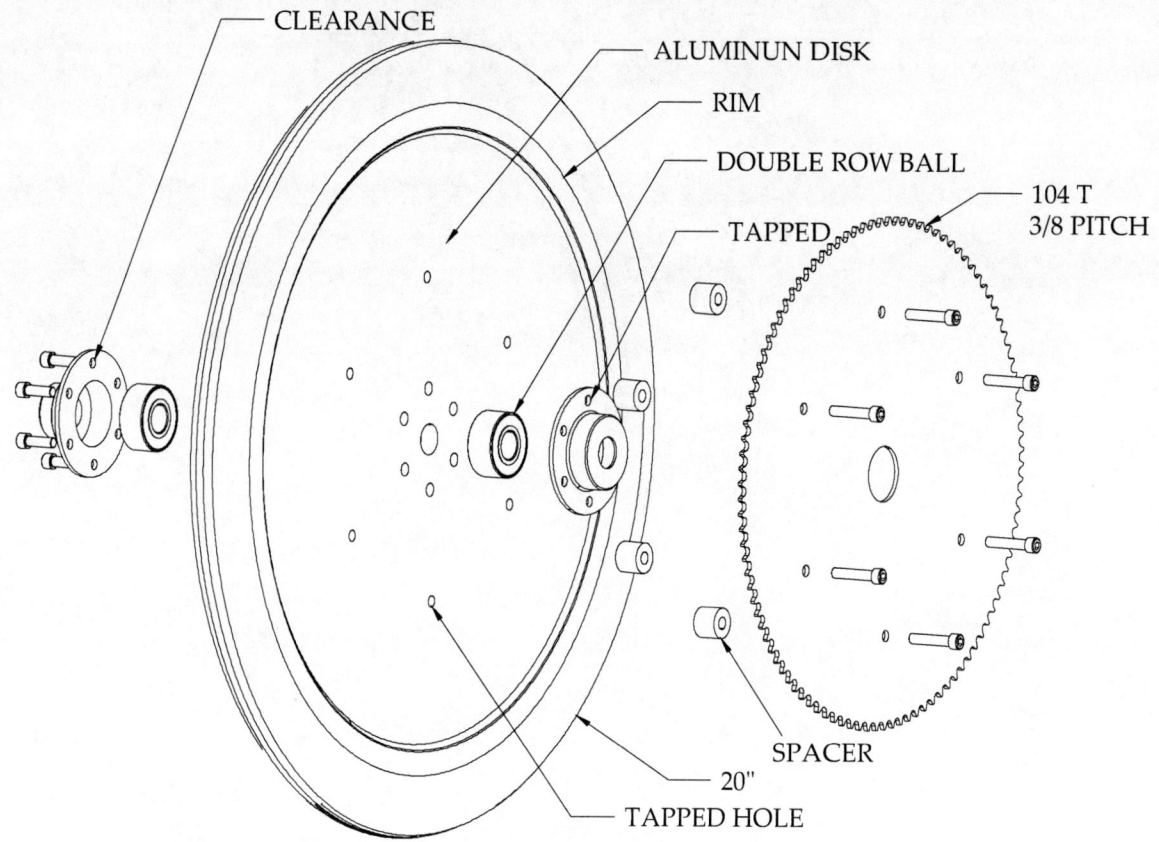

The electric bent...A demo bike for the track

Entry level ebike projects are easy to find. There are many good ones and nearly all have a modest level of performance. This is as it should be. A modest performer is the best way to describe the Robobike battery powered option for our short wheel base recumbent project. The motors are permanent magnet, 12v DC designed to power a cooling fan on a large truck. Consequently, they don't have heavy duty bearings or provision for cooling. Since they are meant to swing a fan, they do have bearings on each end of the armature. Their efficiency is low and they are cheap. Since they drive the rear wheel through a roller clutch, it is impossible to overload them. They simply slip and spin when faced with a heavy load. Nobody is going to be blown away with the performance of the electric bent, but still, it is a good solid performer. It is not meant for the street.

All ebikes have inherent risks and battery powered recumbents have even more. Recumbents are difficult to see and they handle like pigs. This is a bad combination. The electric bent is for the track only and not for the street.

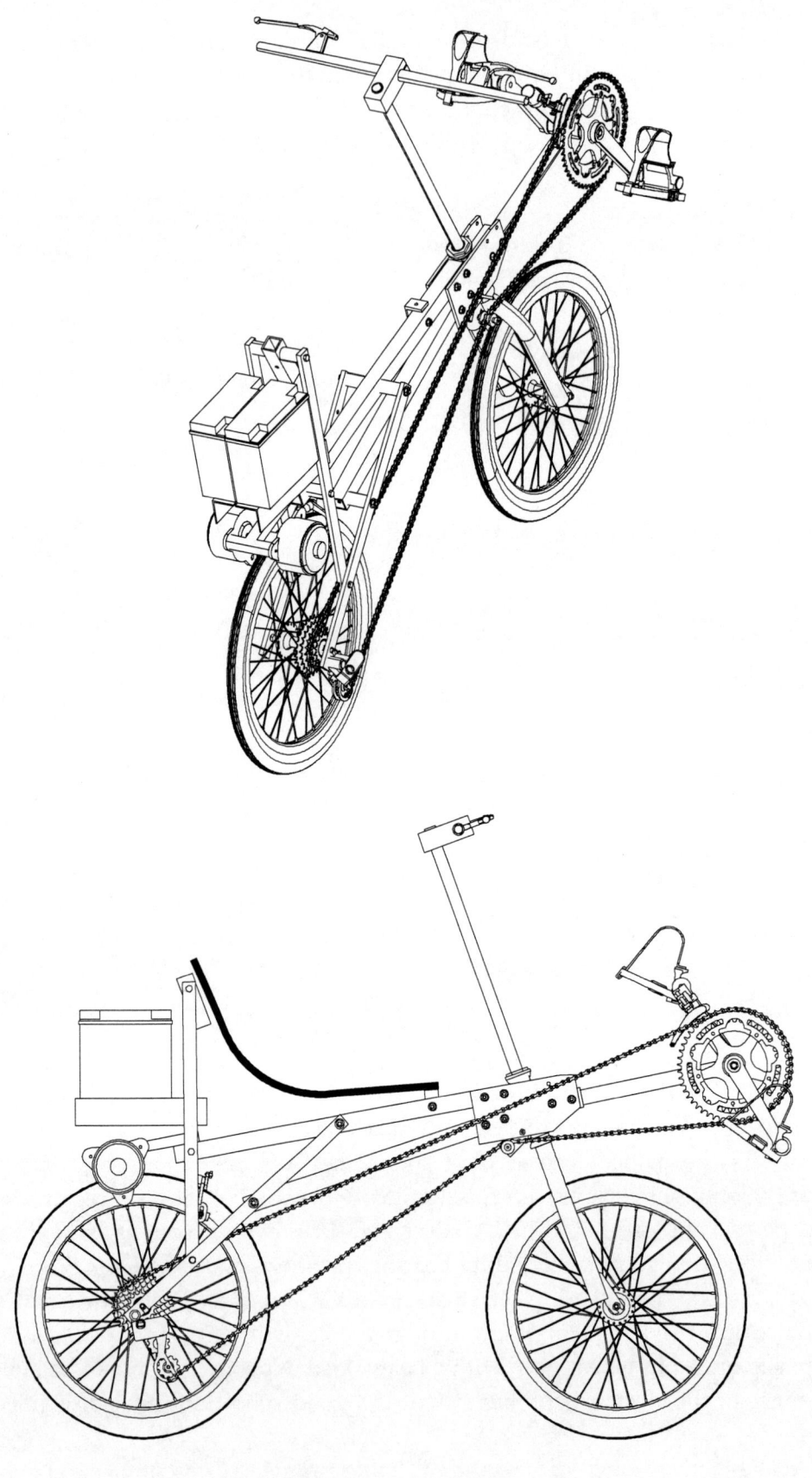

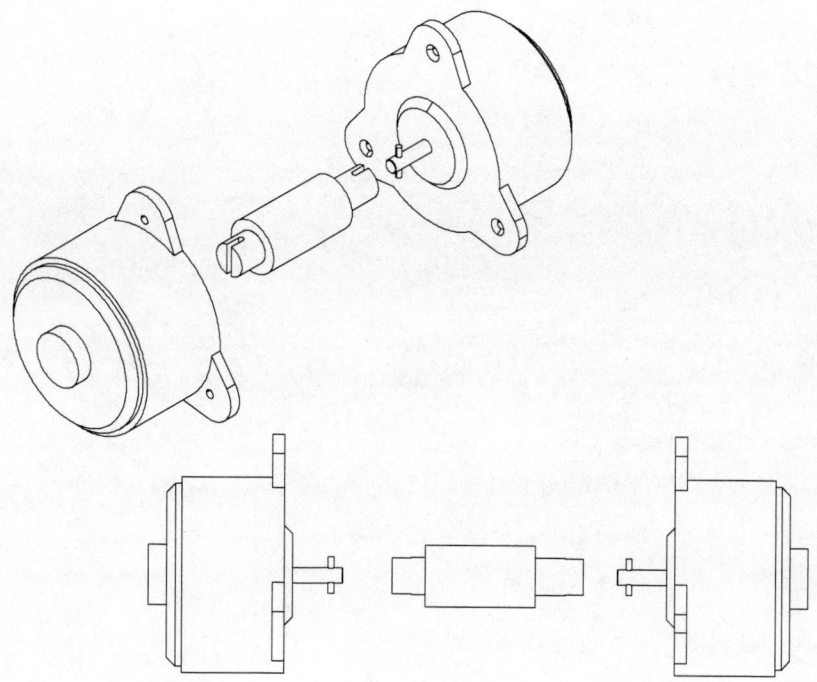

Two permanent magnet motors drive a roller clutch axle which drives the roller. The motors can run either direction. The roller bears against the wheel. The pair of motors are capable of a combined output of a hundred watts. Since this is equal to what an average rider can produce from the sitting position, a substantial boost in top speed in possible. Even more important is the hill climbing increase realized with battery power. Recumbents are awful on hills. These motors help a lot.

The electric bike project is rewarding but requires a thorough understanding of the subject. This is driven by the increased risk riding a powered cycle entails.

Motor selection can be best done by looking at what is for sale today but keep in mind; all ebike builders state performance, battery life and range in completely optimistic form. Anyone with electric vehicle experience can see this at a glance. Take these claims with a grain of salt.

Range, speed, battery life and all other performance parameters are keyed to the size of the battery. If you choose to buy your first eBike, and that is a valid option for the hobbyist, do some research into bikes such as the EV Warrior that claimed 15 mph, fifteen mile range and long battery life. The energy storage was 288 watt hours. Many riders found that you could indeed ride this bike fast for 15 miles, but only once or twice. Please notice that I use the past tense to describe this bike.

Once again, eBikes is an evolving subject. Visit Robobike.com for updates.

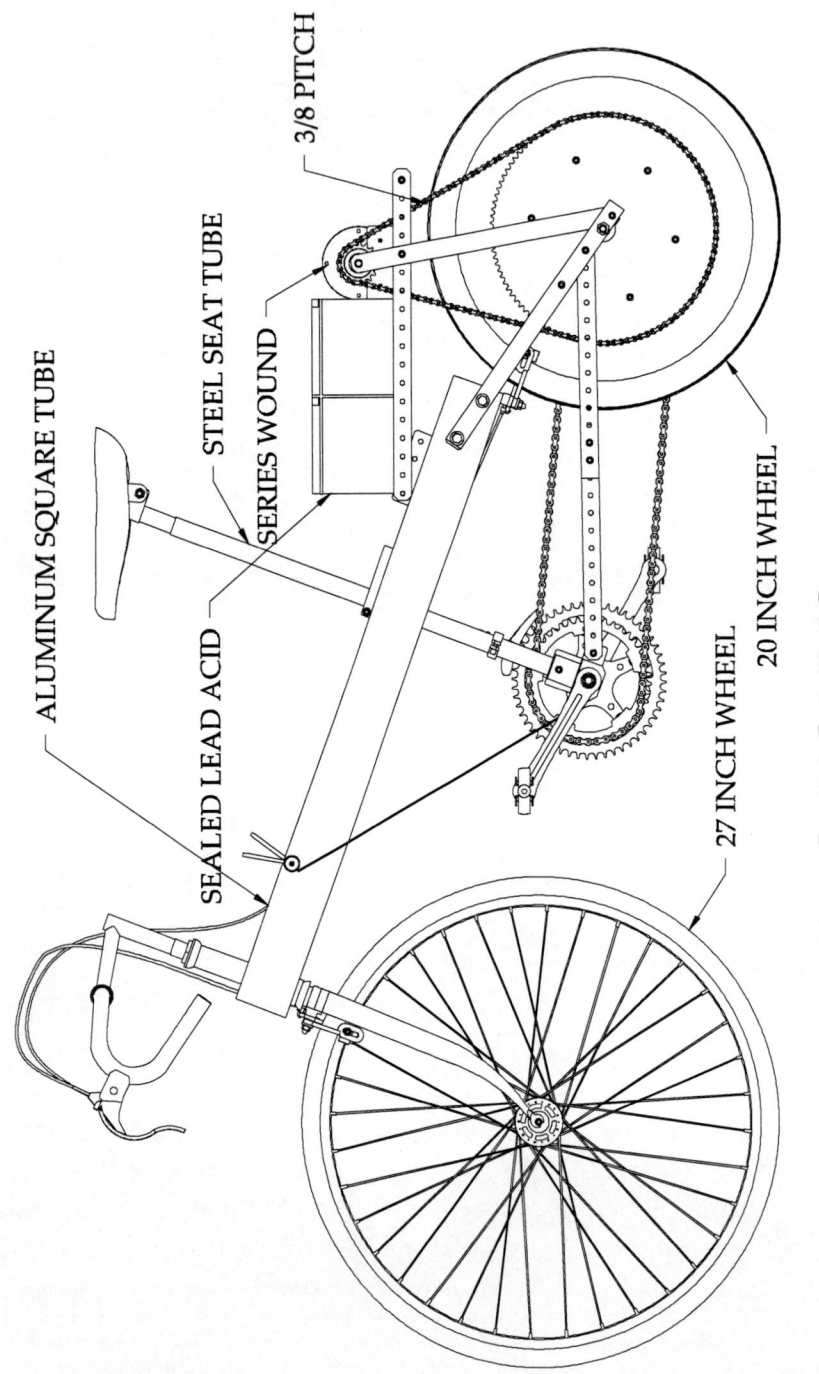

3/8 PITCH

STEEL SEAT TUBE

ALUMINUM SQUARE TUBE

SERIES WOUND

SEALED LEAD ACID

27 INCH WHEEL

20 INCH WHEEL

ELECTRIC LIMO

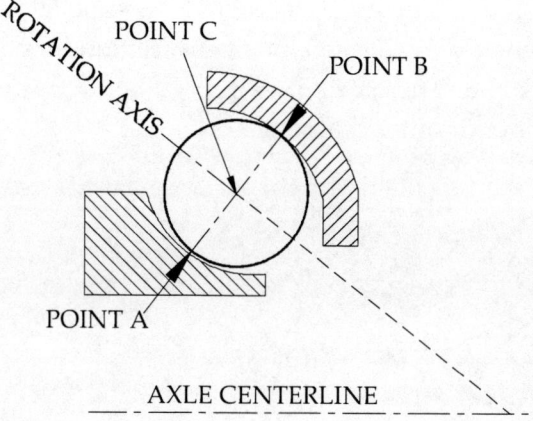

POINT C

POINT B

ROTATION AXIS

POINT A

AXLE CENTERLINE

Homemade Bearings
By Les Johnson
Custom bearings and case hardening small steel parts

Diameter over four times rpm equals surface feet per minute. Every machinist knows this equation. Knowing the speed of a work piece in a lathe or the peripheral speed of a milling cutter in feet per minute helps him match spindle speed to cutting speed. For example, if I want to cut a one inch diameter steel shaft at 200 feet per minute in a lathe, I will select 800 rpm or something close to it. This equation is actually an approximation. It should read (π / 12 inches per ft.) x (Diameter in inches) x RPM = feet per minute. This becomes .26 x (dia) x rpm = fpm. A 26" wheel traveling down the road at 528 feet per minute is turning at 78 RPM. This is 6 mph. Twelve mph is 1056 fpm and 156 RPM and twenty mph is 1760 feet per minute and nearly 260 RPM. Let's use this last combination for the following analysis.

The elements of bearing design have been worked out for a long long time. Except for advances in materials and lubricants, everything needed for controlling radial and thrust loads on a bicycle was practiced by the Wright brothers more than a century ago.

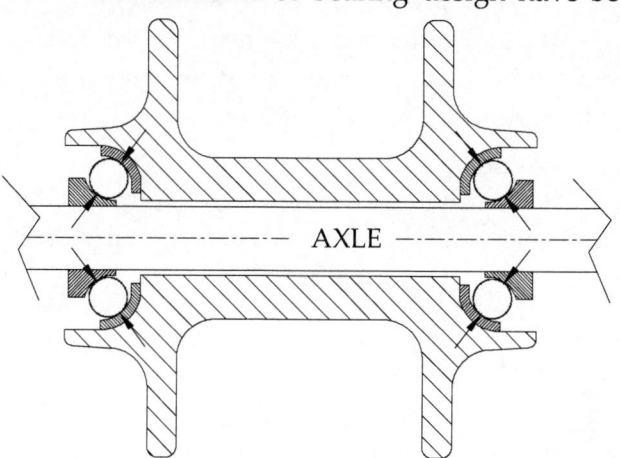

AXLE

This schematic representation of a front hub shows the relation of the bearing cups and cones. Not represented are the dust caps or seals. The arrows show the lines of force which are equal and opposite, putting each ball in equilibrium. These points being opposite, they form a diameter on the ball. The balls, like most bicycle hubs, are ¼" diameter and are grade 25 or better. The grade refers to the roundness, or more correctly, lack of. A grade 5 ball is closer to a perfect sphere than a grade 25. It is clear to see how the body of the hub is controlled radially, or around the axis of the axle, and in thrust which is represented here by displacement left and right of the hub body along the longitudinal axis of the axle. Going back to the equation that opens this article, we can calculate the rotational speed of the ball about its own center, Point C, in either RPM or feet per minute.

Assigning Point A to be the contact point of the ball on the cone and Point B to be the contact point of the ball at the cup allows the following bit of work.
The rotational speed in feet per minute at Point A is .26 (.54) x 260 = 36 ft/min.
Point B is .26(.96) x 260 = 65 ft/min.

Another way to think of it is the fact that the ball must spin at 576 rpm to roll around the cone with no slippage but spin at 1040 rpm to translate about the cup without slippage. How can the periphery of the ball travel, at the same time, around the cup at 65 ft/min while the cone rolls on the ball at 36 ft/min? It can't. Isaac Newton or some other smart fellow a long time ago proved that this is impossible. What we have is a phenomenon we call in the business friction. Friction can be good or bad. Unless you're a bearing. Then it's bad. Therefore, it is impossible to build a ball bearing that doesn't drag itself around either the inner or outer diameter.

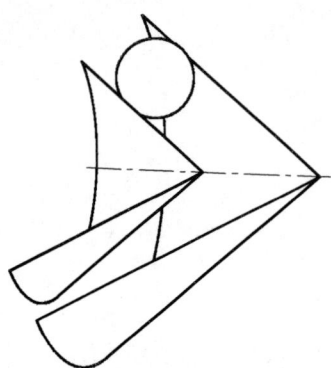

Bearings need clearance to work. Do not over tighten

Bearing design, like any design work, involves tradeoffs. It is possible to reduce friction by reducing the ball or roller diameter. This will make the contact points closer to the same size. The tradeoff is reduced rigidity and a lower load rating. These qualities are known as system stiffness by all the girls who know a lot about bearings. Other strategies and schemes are also used to improve bearing performance. The key is to decide if low friction, high rigidity, long life, low noise, low inertia, low starting torque, et cetera is the primary design goal. Bicycle bearings have evolved to such a high level that it would be foolish to think that there is room for improvement, especially by someone working in a home shop. Subsequently, it is best to copy other designs if any attempt is made to manufacture bearings. Browsing a catalog from a bearing supplier is a good first start. There are plenty of choices.

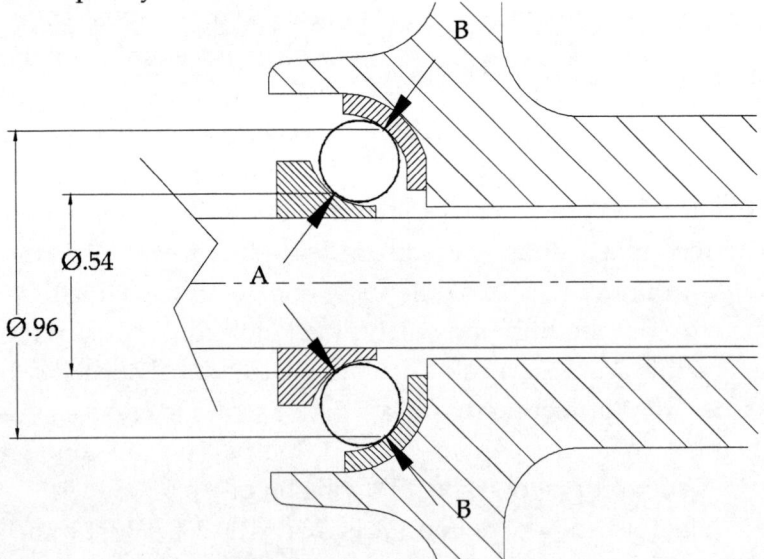

The only reason to make a bearing is so you can say you did. Unless you have to.

That's not entirely true. Robobike built a steel frame recumbent bicycle several years ago and it was found that after the welding operation, the bottom bracket cups would not install. They were too tight. We then made an undersize (thread pitch diameter) pair of bottom bracket cups from a pair of seldom used half inch drive sockets and hardened them using a case hardening compound. After years of service, they show no signs of wear. The bearing cups found on bikes are easy to make and are quite forgiving if the proper materials are chosen and the proper processes are applied. Cones are a bit more difficult. The most important process is case hardening. This is really the only process available to the home mechanic that is easy and reliable. It does not require a furnace or long soak times and the quenching medium is water. The required heat can be supplied by the kitchen stove but be sure to do everything when nobody else is home. The smell is pretty bad.

The Robotrike has a king pin bearing that is home made. It works good.

Now that we've decided that bearings are an impossibility, think about what we've done with our analysis. The balls are not fixed in spaced and simply rotating about their own axes as our model suggests. They translate about the axle. Notice that, in our example, that the difference between 65 feet per minute and 35 feet per minute is 30 fpm. Divide by two and that is the velocity that needs to be added to the inner diameter and subtracted from the outer diameter to make the whole thing work. The sweet spot is 15 fpm. A group of balls translating about the axle twice a second will make the whole thing work. If you have any doubts, pop the dust covers on your hubs and make an observation or two. Balls moving around the axle? You bet they do! In our 20 mph example, the group translates at 111 rpm and the balls spin on their own axes at 242 rpm. Grab a pencil and work it out. You'll see what I mean.

It is unlikely that you'll make bearings for wheel hubs. Not even Robobike does that, but there certainly is the possibility that what you need is far easier to make than it is to find a source for some obscure or special application bearing. Don't be intimidated into thinking this is beyond the capabilities of the average guy. That simply is not true, by controlling the stress through intelligent design, you can build a long lived bearing that does the job, no sweat.

Rules and Definitions

The only rule at Robobike is that there are no rules. Do whatever you want to do, be whatever you want to be, just don't hurt anyone. (Sound familiar?). While it may be fun to put some wheels and a steering mechanism on an old bathtub, don't get your little sister to make the test ride. However, to avoid confusion, these are the terms we use at Robobike. They are more definitions than rules. Everyone needs rules, but sorry, this is the best we can do.

123 Block (n) A hardened steel rectangular solid that measures one inch by two inches by three inches. Commonly found in machine shops for setups and inspection work.

Alloy (n) Any metal whose constituents include two or more elements from the periodic table, e.g., steel, brass, 6061 aluminum, 6Al-4V-2Sn, etc.

Aluminum (n) A light, gray metal, usually found alloyed with other elements. Sometimes referred to as alloy in the bike world. Why this is, we don't know. Ignorance would be a good guess.

Angle Plate (n) A steel or cast iron shop aid having surfaces perpendicular to one another.

Bottom bracket (n) The frame member supporting the pedaling axle.

Braze (v) to braze, to join by adhesion using heat, filler metal, and flux. Includes silver solder and torch as well as induction or furnace braze welding. Almost always used to describe a process using a torch and copper/zinc flux coated filler rod when talking about bicycles.

Caliper (n) A generic term used to describe a measuring instrument. Examples are vernier, dial, inside, outside, spring and electronic. Also, a type of brake.

Chain stay (n) part of the bike frame connecting the bottom bracket to the rear drop out.

Changer (n) Derailleur, either front or rear.

China (n) A place where things are made cheaply. See also "environmental disaster".

Damp (v) to cancel or smooth bumps, usually with shock absorbers. Not to be confused with dampen, which is to moisten.

Down Tube (n) A bike frame member usually connecting the head tube with the bottom bracket.

Flux (n) A cleaning agent used in the weld shop, becomes active with the application of heat. Common forms include paste and coated rod.

Head tube (n) That part of the frame that mounts the head set bearings through which the steering tube is guided.

High tech (adj) Anything that costs more than it should.

Jig (n) A shop aid that guides a tool used for cutting or clamps an item for assembly. Two common examples: drill jig or assembly jig.

Main triangle (n) The part of the frame comprising the top tube, seat tube, down tube and head tube.

Mic (n) abbreviation for a micrometer caliper. Pronounced mike.

Moment of inertia (n) A derived value , I, of the profile of a tube useful for comparing the mechanical properties of tubes of various shapes and sizes for the purpose of analysis.

Phugoid (n) A condition also known as porpoising in airplanes. In bicycle work, phugoids manifest themselves by wobbling out of control due to lack of rigidity.

Rear triangle (n) The frame elements that include the stays and dropouts plus any brake mounting features.

Rake (n) for bicycles, it is the bend in the forks. For motorcycles, it is head angle.

Rigid, Rigidity A property of bike frames. Rigidity can be increased by added structure or by various other means such as increasing the gauge or diameter of a tube.

Seat Stay (n) The part of a bicycle connecting the upper seat tube with the rear drop out. Is not always tubular in profile.

Seat Tube (n) That part of the frame connecting the bottom bracket to the top tube and seat stays. Usually includes a provision for accepting a seat post.

Scale (n) What a steel ruler is known as in the shop.

Shield (n) Inert gas used for welding; usually argon.

Sine Bar or **Sine Plate** (n) A tool used in conjunction with gage blocks to measure or set angles on the surface plate or milling machine.

Shifter (n) Levers used to pull cables connected to gear changers. May be mounted on downtubes, stems, incorporated into brake levers, stuck into bar ends or in special cases, amidships of tandems.

Steel (n) An alloy of iron and carbon. Alloy steel contains one per cent or more of other metals, primarily manganese, chromium and molybdenum.

Stiction (n) A made up word that is sometimes used to describe motion including that related to bicycling. Not used at Robobike except jokingly.

Stiff, Stiffness A mechanical property of materials, principally metals. Steel is stiffer than titanium, titanium is stiffer than aluminum. When comparing metals like this, decide if you are comparing by mass or volume; two entirely different things. A single tube (spring) is described by its stiffness. Multiple tubes (springs) are said to possess rigidity.

Stress (n) Force per unit area acting on an object. A one inch square bar supporting a 1000 pound weight is stressed at 1000 psi. May be compressive or tensile, bending or torsion, or a combination.

Strain (n) The result of stress. Usually expressed in inch per inch. e.g. .002"/inch.

TPI An abbreviation for threads per inch. There is no metric equivalent.

Trail Look down the barrel of the steering axis to a spot on the ground. The distance forward of the wheel contact patch is trail.

Weld, Welding (n,) A process of joining two pieces of similar metals by fusion. Common processes are oxy-acetylene, TIG or GTAW, MIG or GMAW, and stick or SMAW; (n) a fillet; (v) to weld, to make fast by a fusion process involving intense heat.

Wheel (n) An assembly comprising a tire, tube, rim, spokes, disk, brake rotor, magnet disk, hub and gear cluster if appropriate.

Robobike Today

Having designed and built special application bicycles for 25 years, teaching welding and bicycle advocacy, it was decided to share some of what we've done with anyone who has an interest in the kind of work we do and the life we live. It is true that using a bicycle for all transport needs is a challenge and requires an adjustment, but is by no means impossible. While many of our designs were done just for fun, some of the work has been groundbreaking in its nature and should be picked up by those willing to take it to the next level. The next level, naturally, is mass production or at least, availability to custom makers via plans sets and work instructions. We don't think for a minute that there is a huge demand for the recumbent unicycle, but Loveboat and the travel bikes are all candidates for serious investment of time and money. We will continue that work, to be sure, and will continue our effort to export bike building technology to other communities around the world.

Living automobile free is certainly something to crow about but for reasons that may not be apparent to most readers. Automobiles use gasoline or some other form of fuel during operation, there's no doubt, but the amount of energy consumed during the manufacturing process of the average car far exceeds the amount of energy used by the vehicle during its lifetime. Mining and the extraction industries, steel making, aluminum refining, plastic molding, etc, all the energy consumed by these industries must be included in an energy audit concerning the building of the family SUV. It's not just riding your bike to work and leaving the car at home, it's about putting the brakes on the whole industrialization craziness that is destroying all we see.

Krilson continues his work at Robobike but leaves the test rides to others. He remains our number one design engineer. John Shewmaker died, sadly, a victim of tobacco companies. Dozens of others have passed through our doors to contribute what they could to the effort. They all left us better off for it.

As for me, I have bikes on the brain. Just this morning I dreamed I rode a bicycle to heaven. It was plain to see that it was happy hour in heaven with all the fun, music and laughter coming from the waiting area. A piano quintet led by Beethoven himself was entertaining the new arrivals. It was looking good. There was, however, a bit of confusion when my name was called. Instead of being ushered into happy hour on the arm of a silicone princess, I was directed to another area. All of a sudden, the floor dropped away. The fall was long, the landing abrupt. I came to rest among a broken beer bottle on the corner of 3rd avenue and Roosevelt in Phoenix. It was hot. On all sides were Oldsmobile diesels locked in a desperate struggle for the few remaining oxygen molecules. A pack of free range dogs had spotted my arrival and were heading my way. Big dogs, little dogs. Faster and faster they came. Overtaking the whole bunch, as if shot out of a cannon, with eyes on fire, came the Schnauzer from Hell.

That's when I woke up.

Just Do The Best You Can.

Bingo

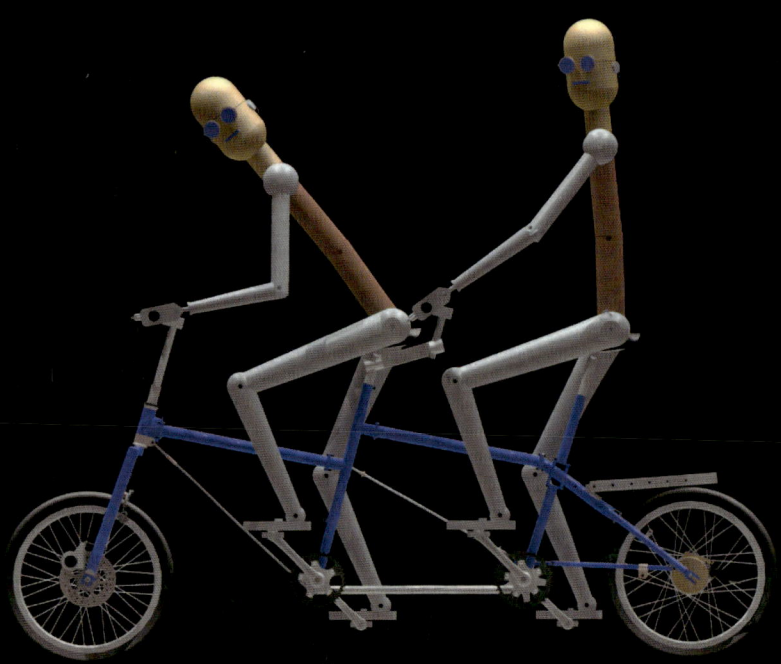

ISBN 978-0-9792754-0-1

9 780979 275401